MURDER BY GRAVITY?

JUDGE SETS A MAN FREE TO MURDER HIS WIFE! A JUROR'S STORY

CHERIE HUYETT ACHTEMEIER

Outkirts Press, Inc.
Denver, Colorado

The opinions expressed in this manuscript are solely the opinions of the author and do not represent the opinions or thoughts of the publisher. The author represents and warrants that s/he either owns or has the legal right to publish all material in this book.

Murder by Gravity?
Judge Sets A Man Free To Murder His Wife! A Juror's Story

All Rights Reserved.
Copyright © 2007 Cherie Huyett Achtemeier
v 5.0

Cover Image © 2007 JupiterImages Corporation. All rights reserved - used with permission.

This book may not be reproduced, transmitted, or stored in whole or in part by any means, including graphic, electronic, or mechanical without the express written consent of the publisher except in the case of brief quotations embodied in critical articles and reviews.

Outskirts Press, Inc.
http://www.outskirtspress.com

ISBN: 978-978-1-4327-0803-0
Library of Congress Control Number: 2007929830

Outskirts Press and the "OP" logo are trademarks belonging to Outskirts Press, Inc.

PRINTED IN THE UNITED STATES OF AMERICA

ACKNOWLEDGEMENT

I want to express my gratitude to the Clerks of the Superior Court, who were so helpful during the months I spent pouring over all of the transcripts from the trial. They literally shared their office with me! I would like to recognize:

Beverly Frame
Irene Lett
Delorez Corral
Arlene Lusk
Patti Faz
Angela Walker
Cheryl Bates
Peggy Collins
Michelle Lackey
Theresa Hernandez
Susie Quinn

I also want to thank my family for cheering me on, most especially my sister Laurie, who was always there reading my chapters by e-mail, my husband, Butch, who helped with the household chores, and fielding unwanted phone calls while I wrote this book!

I also want to dedicate this book to my mother, who passed away during the time I was writing the book and was supportive from the beginning.

DISCLAIMER

This book is based on actual events. Some of the names have been changed, and some conversations have speculatively been added for reasons of continuity and are based on the court transcriptions, interviews, and the reflections of the juror who is the author.

The title is in the form of a question indicating that the reader will be allowed to draw their own conclusion, just as the jury had to decide the cause of death in this incredible case. The findings will be given at the close of this book.

PROLOGUE

The man couldn't catch his breath as panic and meth mania converged and his plan to keep his wife from leaving him unraveled. She had just drawn her line in the sand and today was to be the showdown. The wall of lies he had built for months so he could control her and so she would pity him were about to cave in and surely she would see to it that he went to jail; or at the very least be kicked out of her life forever. What could he do? He couldn't go to jail again and she would definitely turn him in for lying. *She brought this on herself*, he rationalized.

By chance, his wife had her back to him as she sat on the edge of the bed reaching for her panties to get dressed for the day. The man grabbed the crystal clock, a wedding gift, from the shelf above the bed. Its weight felt significant and the top of it was rounded and fit the curve of his palm comfortably with its tri-leveled, squared base exposed at the bottom. In one orchestrated movement, he grasped the back of her hair with his left hand, pulled her head back and struck her solidly near the right temple with the bottom side of the timepiece. Her lithe body gracefully reclined on the bed for the last time. Did the man just assume his wife was dead or didn't he care before he tied her up and dumped her in the Gila Gravity Canal? Was she dead already or was it *Murder by Gravity?*

CHAPTER 1

Seth Sayers had been looking forward to the weekend when he and his dad, Sam, would retrieve their fishing poles from their sandy garage. They hadn't been fishing since Seth's twelfth birthday the previous September. The adobe-style house where they lived in Yuma, Arizona, was near several canals and lagoons fed by the Colorado River.

Sam, like most other residents of Yuma, didn't like to venture out more than necessary in the winter if at all possible, mainly because that was when tens of thousands of migrant retirees descended on Yuma. Arriving in their recreational vehicles, these "snowbirds," as the locals called them, stayed anywhere from two to six months. Most came from Washington, Oregon, and British Columbia in order to enjoy the temperate winter months for which Yuma is well known. The addition of these temporary visitors made maneuvering in stores, restaurants, or roads something of an endurance test and delays were inescapable.

January of 1995 had been particularly rainy for this Sonoran Desert city. The canals and lagoons were brimming full just two weeks earlier. But the water levels had begun to recede by this time and Sam felt confident that it could be worth venturing out under the circumstances.

As usual, when the pair went fishing, Sam woke Seth long before sunrise. It was a tradition that they stopped at Circle K for a breakfast sandwich and live bait. The drive down Highway 95 was as dark as only the desert night can be, accented by sparkling stars. As they drove by field after field of iceberg lettuce, cotton, and fragrant onions, a billboard sign along the way proclaimed: Every year the icebergs return to Yuma!

Seth thought the ice-cold mornings were heavenly after surviving a typical Yuma summer where the temperature routinely reached 110 and beyond. Even though most Yumans do tend to think of themselves as tougher than most folks because they endure the summer's heat, Seth still thought it was nice to wear a jacket for a change.

The turn off to the lagoons was a rutted dirt road that probably should, to Sam's way of thinking, be traveled with a four-wheel-drive vehicle to get to the best fishing areas. That part of the trip took the longest with its hilly, twisting, and turning road that skirted the meandering waterways.

When they arrived at what looked like a promising fishing site, Sam turned the ignition off. Stepping out of their brown Chevy Suburban, they were enveloped by a blanket of silence. Before daybreak, it felt as if they were on the surface of another planet. Neither of them could possibly imagine what the new day would bring.

* * *

The sky soaked up the daylight as the sun rose above the Gila Mountains. The location of the lagoon Sam and Seth chose provided a spectacular view of the rugged terrain with its domed and weathered mountain peaks. The fishing went well. They caught the limit before 10 AM and stashed them in the ice chest. The fish that they caught after that were released. It was mostly father and son bonding and that was okay with them. Sam felt it was important to set a good example for his son to obey the law-even the fishing law.

By late afternoon, the hottest time of the day in Yuma, the sun had provided enough heat that Sam got up to stretch his legs and put their jackets in the Suburban. He also took the opportunity to get rid of all the black coffee he drank earlier to wake up. He made his way through some sagebrush and salt cedar just behind where they'd been fishing and saw that the lagoon curved around behind them and had been hidden from their view. This time they'd gone further into the interior of the desert canal system than ever before. They didn't need to go this far to prospect for gold and go four-wheeling. Not for anything, actually, except privacy from the snowbirds. This was the Gila Gravity Canal near Mittry Lake and was actually quite large.

MURDER BY GRAVITY?

There seemed to be a still-pool area that looked to Sam like it might be worth investigating before they packed up for the day. Just as he began to look away, his gaze fell on something that looked out of place in the water and he did a double take. It was almost white under the water's surface and about fifteen yards from the edge. The hair on the back of his neck stood up as he hurried back to the fishing site and told Seth to stay put while he checked something out.

Sam drove around the lagoon for thirty minutes trying to find the best vantage point to prove to himself that it couldn't possibly be what his first instincts were telling him. The thing couldn't even be seen from most angles on the shore. He pulled out his binoculars from the glove compartment and could then pick out more details of the strange shape. Even with the wind rippling the water's surface, floating brown hair could be seen from this last position on a sandy knoll above the steep shore. Sam saw the bloated, nearly nude body of Joyce Handcock face down in the murky water and looking very much like a life-size kewpie doll.

That was the story that Sam told the sheriff and police until two days before the trial.

CHAPTER 2

Detective Donna Graham had been walking by dispatch when the body call was reported to the Yuma County Sheriff's Department. The report said that what looked like a human body was found around 7E, off County 5th behind the dump area, though the caller couldn't say for sure that's what it was.

The directions to the location were complicated and sketchy. Detective Graham had never been anywhere near that area in her eighteen years in the department. Although the caller said they should use a four-wheel-drive vehicle to get to the area, Donna thought she could go anywhere in her patrol car and wasn't worried, but she soon found out that her car didn't navigate the dirt road well and she scraped the bottom of it repeatedly. She could see where other cars had gotten stuck and dug holes trying to escape. She decided to pull over when she got to the bridge and waited for a ride from Captain Bender when he came through shortly after her in his Ford Bronco four-wheel-drive vehicle. By the time they found Sam, the total response time was only about twenty minutes. It had taken Sam just under that time to return to the site after he took Seth home and called 911. He knew they'd never find the body if he weren't there to point it out.

Graham and Bender could see the outline of what could be a female body. Graham remembered hearing about a lady bartender who was reported missing the previous week and wondered if this could be her.

Because every year border-crashing illegal Mexicans attempt to come to America by way of the canals, it wasn't uncommon for the local police and sheriff's department to respond to body calls at the waterways. The canals looked deceptively still, but some have stiff undercurrents and are quite deep.

MURDER BY GRAVITY?

Deputies Dylan Sopher and Robert Larson were called for their capacities as certified divers for the Yuma County Sheriff's Department. They were instructed to drive a high clearance vehicle, so they took the Ford F-150, whose standard clearance, just as with most trucks, was high enough to navigate the wash boarded dirt roads in the canal area. Deputy Larson had been certified six years, whereas Deputy Sopher had only just completed the training dives required for certification. This was to be his first body recovery. The ride was easily managed in the Ford, though it was slow going and bouncy. They noticed the dirt road was wide enough in some places for cars to pass, but they saw no people other than the recovery team and no houses along the way. Sopher had been quail hunting in the general area just the previous season and had thought about bringing his all-terrain vehicle the next time he was out.

They stretched into their stubbornly skin-tight wetsuits and prepared for the cold January water. After Detective Graham pointed to where the body was located, they could see that they would need to move to another location to find a way to get down the steep embankment. The only possible entry that they could find did not provide visual access to the body. Detective Graham coached them to the body by yelling where to turn. Deputy Sopher, at 6' 2", felt the water at mid-chest level and they began to swim in the direction of the body. Minutes later, he got tangled in some vegetation in the water so he stopped swimming for a moment to get unhooked. That's when he noticed that the water had become shallow again. Sopher suggested they walk the rest of the way out until they came to the object. Once they neared it, they could see it obviously was a female corpse. It never occurred to them at this point that it could be a homicide and didn't treat it as such. Because of the algae and knowing that wet, dead skin gets slippery and can even slide right off, they used the rope they carried with them to pull her in as they'd been trained to do. But things didn't go according to plan. Joyce seemed to be stuck in that spot somehow. They then took turns pulling the body's arms, then the legs. Then Sopher reached out and grabbed her by the hair and intended to tow her back. Through the thick gloves he was wearing, he couldn't tell that the hair was pulling right out of her scalp until a large handful came out and he felt a give. The body kept the resistance up while Larson put the rope around her arm and began to pull her as hard as he could to the shore. By the time the water was knee-deep, they decided to just carry her out to the waiting body bag. Because of the silt stirred up from their walk, they couldn't see that she was tethered to something heavy.

As they lifted her, they then saw wires and dark green strapping tape wrapped around her wrists and ankles in roughly three-foot lengths that were attached to cinder blocks, a cement pylon and a milk crate full of rocks. When they turned the body over they saw a large wound on the right side of her head and that she was clad only in a black bra. The bra was askew and one of its straps, which had been ripped in two, had been pitifully repaired with a tiny golden safety pin.

Detective Graham ordered them to lay her on the small shore area with the items used to weigh her down set above and below the body while she took several pictures of the scene. Eventually they were instructed to cut the wires and put her and the strapping and wire in the body bag before darkness quickly fell. The search of the area was done with flashlights. They tried to peer around all the chaparral and salt cedar. They found a pink "glob" that looked like fish guts by the edge of the water and a circle formed with stones that had been used as a campfire ring in a small clearing on the sandy knoll. Inside the fire ring was an 8" X 10" piece of plywood that looked like a rough picture frame as it had a square piece that had been cut out of the center and only the outer part remained. There were three other similar pieces of wood. (Most professional frames have four pieces of wood cut at a 45-degree angle and the pieces are then stapled and glued together from the back.) That was the only wood in the fire pit that hadn't been burned. The Sheriff's deputies bagged the pink glob sample and the four pieces of wood. They did what Larson would later refer to as a "small search," and they never searched the area again until one month later.

CHAPTER 3

Richard Handcock was doing life in prison on the installment plan. In 1974 he was convicted of burglary, possession of a dangerous drug, and defrauding an innkeeper. It was a conviction that kept him off the streets for a substantial period of time.

By 1989, he was well acquainted with the Arizona judicial system. At 34, he was older than most of his peers in prison. Richard was strong for his medium build and stood 5 feet, 10 inches--much taller than the mostly Hispanic population in the Arizona facility--and commanded a certain amount of respect while there. With his long blond hair in a pony-tail he was easily spotted.

Richard had been out of prison only a short time when he met Hazel Mess at the Bottoms Up Pub in the Foothills area of Yuma, where she was working as a bartender. She was cute and trim. She had hair the color that could be called dark blond or light brown, depending on the lighting. Sadly, though, Hazel's years of working behind the bar and her heavy daily consumption of alcohol etched a brittle hardness to her face. One of her loyal customers used to tell her that she gave great cleavage when she served his drinks. That would be Ted, the uncouth version of a man who lives across the street from me.

A dozen red were sent to Hazel's work where Richard knew they would garner much more attention than had he sent them to her apartment. He had learned that flowers get good mileage with women, especially when they were delivered to their work where other women might fawn over them and tell the recipient how she was lucky to have a guy who sent flowers. A few days later Richard asked Hazel out to one of the finest restaurants in town, and she happily accepted. Richard had once heard the adage, "treat a lady like a tramp, and a tramp like a lady," and took heed. He pulled out Hazel's chair and told her to order anything from the menu that she wanted. Richard lavished her with compliments; some that actually made her blush. So far everything had gone perfectly in Richard's seduction scenario.

After dinner downtown, the two decided to go dancing at Mickey B's, just off Interstate 8 and Foothills Boulevard. It was a popular place in spite of the fact that it was on the very outskirts of town at the time. This was Hazel's stomping grounds where the picturesque Gila Mountains made the Foothills area a desirable location in Yuma County. Once they arrived, Richard opened the door to the cab of his old pickup truck for Hazel, which had a large, ugly, old camper attached to its bed and was virtually a motel on wheels. That was what Richard loved about it. The truck looked sorely out of place in the parking lot where the snowbirds and locals alike had more expensive vehicles that were parked all around it. Richard seemed oblivious to it. The truck was a major turn off for Hazel and she cringed inwardly.

Hazel drank three drinks to Richard's one, and she was disappointed when he refused to dance with her. But he seemed very attentive as Hazel watched all of her friends dancing and having fun without her. Richard eventually put his arm around her and nuzzled her neck. Hazel felt an unexpected pleasant shiver at his touch. Then he withdrew suddenly and asked if she wanted to go home.

In the parking lot, Richard opened the truck door for Hazel and indiscreetly admired her long tan legs which were scarcely covered by her short skirt when she stepped up to get inside the truck's cab. It was that action that reaffirmed Richard's love for his truck.

The day Hazel met Richard, her bartender's instinct told her that Richard was very sweet and thoughtful; just painfully shy. She knew that she would have to be the one to make the first move. On the drive back to her apartment, Hazel removed her seat belt and scooted across the bench seat until she was very close to Richard to show that she liked him. She placed her hand gently on his right thigh for several minutes, then slid it to the inside and moved her hand firmly up.

Richard still wasn't used to women taking the initiative, what with all the time he'd spent away from the fairer sex, and it surprised him so much so that he jumped and inadvertently drove over the center dividing line on Frontage Road. As soon as Richard realized that he was over the line, he swiftly corrected the wheel until his truck was back in the proper lane. This happens to thousands of people everyday, but when it happened to Richard, there was a Sheriff's patrol car right behind him.

Of course! Richard thought, *one of Yuma's lousiest on my aft and Hurricane Hazel in my lap!*

Hazel was surprised by the blue-and-red flashing lights before she realized that they were being pulled over. Everything was kind of blurry and the situation struck Hazel as hilarious and she laughed too loudly, still giddy from the drinks she'd consumed. Richard shot her a punitive look as if it were all her fault.

Richard reluctantly pulled over and stepped out of the truck. The windows were all the way up so Hazel couldn't hear what the two men were talking about. She could see the officer pat Richard down, but she couldn't see that he'd also been cuffed behind his back. Hazel amused herself by playing with the radio and checking her lipstick in the rearview mirror as she waited for Richard to return to the driver's seat. After a few minutes, the officer came around to the passenger side window and shone a flashlight in her eyes. With a grim expression and a jaw set so hard it looked like stone, he opened the door and told her authoritatively to step out. Then to Hazel's total shock, he roughly clasped a pair on handcuffs on her as well.

"You two are going for a little unscheduled trip tonight," he said.

"On what charge?" Hazel demanded.

"Possession, miss. With that breath, it's a good thing you weren't driving!"

Hazel and Richard were then unceremoniously escorted to the back seat of the patrol car. After the officer locked them in, he walked back to Richard's truck and looked over the outside with his flashlight and under it. Then he gave a quick look on the inside the cab of the truck and the camper on the back and locked it all up.

The minute he left them alone, Hazel turned to Richard and said, "What's he talking about? Do you *know* what he's talking about?"

"Shhh . . . Hazel, don't worry. You'll be out in a couple of hours. I'll probably be arraigned tomorrow and then I'll be out, too."

"You'd better tell me what's going on, right now, you son of a bitch!" Hazel hissed at him.

"Okay, okay! He patted me down and I had a little meth in my pocket. Do you remember *why* he stopped us in the first place?" Richard asked accusingly.

"In your pocket? That's just brilliant! So, why am *I* being arrested, too? I don't have any drugs," Hazel whined.

"That's what I'm trying to tell you! I told him it was mine, but they have to take you in, too. That's just the way it is. After they process you, they'll let you go. I'm real sorry about this, Hazel. I hope you don't hate me for this. When we get to the Sheriff's station, I'll give you some money for cab fare, if they let me. And I'll call you when I get out," he promised.

Later, Hazel mulled it over and felt that Richard really had tried very hard to make their evening together especially nice and he had treated her with respect, which was a bit of a novelty for Hazel. The flowers were a nice touch as well. She reasoned, too, that she had been the one after all, whose actions caused them to get pulled over in the first place. Still, he didn't seem nearly as upset as she had been. He just seemed *inconvenienced.*

* * *

They were set free just as Richard predicted. Hazel received an informal three-month probation, and Richard was sentenced to one year's probation, one hundred hours of community service, and a small fine. He also was ordered to have periodic drug tests and the judge strongly suggested that Richard join a 12-step-program group. And Richard never gave Hazel the cab fare to get back home that night.

* * *

Contrary to what one might suppose, that evening somehow cemented their relationship. They eventually came to believe that they were soul mates. Richard figured any woman who went to jail for him, albeit for two hours, deserved a certain amount of respect and loyalty.

Richard, who had been living in the cramped camper on his truck when he began seeing Hazel, moved into her apartment within just a few weeks. The next two years were the most settled and peaceful of Richard's turbulent life since high school. Hazel had made it clear after their first date, that with Richard's luck, he should stay away from drugs, period; end of story, and that was the way Hazel saw it.

Raised in a family that worked in construction, Richard had learned early on how to do framing and finish carpentry. He generally managed to get a job anytime when he wanted one. Hazel had the regular job; bartending at the Bottoms Up Pub, and if Richard didn't feel like going to work everyday, that was okay with Hazel. She was an independent woman and had taken care of herself already for ten of her twenty-seven years. Whether Richard stayed or left, she knew that she would be fine. The last two months of the two years they lived together, Hazel became aware that Richard was using drugs again. She had mentioned it to him once and he became defensive, verbally abusive, then flat-out lied about it. That signaled to Hazel that their relationship would probably not make it for the long haul.

When being together had still been new, Hazel thought that there wasn't anything they couldn't talk about with each other. Richard listened to her intently and patiently. She felt that he knew the real her; the person underneath the façade she presented to the world, where she could be herself. He never complained about her drinking, as others had; which was good because she wasn't about to quit for anybody. One time when Richard wanted to buy some meth, he used the argument that if Hazel could drink, he should be able to use whatever he wanted as well. Hazel pointed out that her drug of choice was legal and his wasn't. Other than that, they used to agree on most everything and Hazel had for once in her life allowed herself to be emotionally vulnerable with a man. She had trusted him. Because of all that, Hazel had overlooked his more than occasional moodiness that he displayed in front of others, which she found embarrassing, and his unfounded rage that reared its ugly head periodically. Now with Richard's drug usage between them, Hazel felt that Richard had simply tossed their relationship away by using drugs again. The lies he told were what hurt her the most. Hazel's trust of Richard was by then on less than fragile ground. There had been a time in that last sixty days when they were together, that he lost his temper and she had been afraid that he might kill her. She could forgive, but never forget.

The night when Richard scared her had begun at the Bottoms Up Pub. One of Hazel's regulars had been flirting and kidding around with her; but nothing out of the ordinary. Both she and the regular knew it was nothing serious; he was married, anyway. But they had their heads together and were laughing. Hazel knew that Richard was watching them but she thought he trusted her after all they'd been through together. Besides, Hazel had explained to him time and again that a little flirting was good for business, which translated into good tips, and that she would always go home with Richard and only him.

Richard watched from the other end of the bar and felt his blood begin to curdle. He knew with a certainty that they were laughing about him. *Hazel wants to sleep with him or already has,* he thought miserably. He turned his glare to the pattern on the wood flooring and felt himself literally getting hot under the collar. He left without saying a word. His truck pulled out of the parking lot with a loud screech when he punched the gas pedal.

Noticing only later on that Richard was gone Hazel began looking for him around the bar. She wondered if something had happened and was getting worried because he was supposed to drive her home. When closing time finally came and there was still no sign of him, she asked her friend, that same regular she had been laughing with earlier, to give her a ride home. She was seriously concerned about Richard since it wasn't like him to leave her there stranded. The knot in her stomach tightened and she wondered if he had been in an accident.

At the curb in front of Hazel's apartment building, she stepped out of the customer's little black Corvette and said, "Thanks again for the ride. I owe you, big time, ah," his name momentarily escaped her mind. She smiled with little embarrassment." Good night!"

"No problem, Hazel. I'll just take it out of your tip money!" he joked. "I'm even going to be a good guy and watch to make sure that you get in the door okay," he called after her as she began to ascend the flight of stairs to her second-story apartment. Hazel didn't turn, but waved her hand in response.

The living room lights were on and Hazel breathed a sigh of relief that Richard was probably home already. Inside, Richard was so angry by then, he had been stabbing the palm of his hand repeatedly with a large nail to diffuse the adrenalin that pumped mercilessly through him. The crystal methamphetamine he had smoked earlier intensified his anger. Even when the blood began to flow, it did little to stop the explosive rage that filled every fiber of his mind and body. He watched through the curtain as Hazel arrived with the other man. He stabbed himself as if he were in step with her; a blow for each of her footsteps. He imagined that she might be his hand and he wished it so, though he felt almost nothing.

When Hazel opened the door she turned around to wave to her ride that she was okay. As she closed the door of her apartment, she was spun around so quickly that she was stunned. She looked into Richard's eyes and believed just then that he might kill her. She saw the blood on his hands and shirt as he shoved her back, his hands squeezing her biceps into the closed door. Her feet were inches off the ground. She wondered frantically if her ride had left already and her heart sank when she realized that he surely had.

Richard slowly let Hazel's body slide down until her feet were back on the carpet, and let his angry face make his case against her. He then pushed his forearm against her throat, easily pinning her again to the back to the door.

"Richard! What's *wrong*?" she croaked, it being difficult for her to speak.

"Who's your boyfriend, Hazel? What does he have that I don't have? A shiny, black sports car? Is that it? How long have you been sleeping with him, huh?" he spat into her face.

"What are you talking about? What 'boyfriend?' *You're* my boyfriend!"

"I'm not stupid, you bitch! The one you came home with just now. The one I saw you throwing yourself at in the bar tonight!"

"You've got it all wrong, Richard! It's nothing like that!" Hazel wailed.

Richard had her by the arms again, squeezing her biceps hard with his strong hands. She felt her muscles crunching under his thumbs. He turned her and started pushing her backwards across the room toward the bedroom. Instinctively, she sensed that things could only get worse there. She managed to wrench herself free just long enough to make a quick sidestep into the bathroom and tried to slam shut the door of the only room in the apartment that had a lock on it.

Richard caught the door before she could close it completely. Hazel tried with everything she had to push the door closed, but she never got it close enough to latch and lock. She pulled out the bathroom's vanity drawer that was next to the door and that suddenly stopped all of Richard's efforts. He made an animalistic growl sound in his throat and was angrier than ever. The door was open one-half-inch then. He could see her plastered up against the back wall of the bathroom in the vanity mirror.

He stepped back a moment and seemed to compose himself somewhat.

"Okay, Hazel. Open up! I just want to *talk*. I can't help what I did. It's just because I just love you so much. I didn't mean to hurt you, honest!"

"Go away!" she was screaming now. She knew that her next-door neighbors were home and that just a thin wall behind the large vanity mirrors where the medicine cabinets were separated their bathrooms from one another. She had often heard them talking in there. She hoped they would call the police. As loud as she yelled, she assumed they wouldn't hesitate to call the police. She opened the bathroom window and looked across the apartment building's parking lot to see if anyone beyond the alley behind it would hear her if she screamed. She saw an old man in a shop window in the backyard of a house that was backed up to the alley. Hazel screamed, "Help!" as loudly as she could. The man quickly emerged in a flood of light from the shop's open doorway, wiping his hands with a greasy rag. When she yelled again, his face turned upward and he looked right at Hazel. She knew that he had heard her cry out.

"Please help! Call the police!" she yelled as loud as she could.

Just then, Richard managed to slide his bloody hand in between the door and the jamb and was working to get the drawer closed. Hazel charged the door just when Richard had closed the drawer enough for the door to clear it, and Hazel use the door to crush Richard's hand in the door jamb. With all his rage put into one push, the door flew open, knocking Hazel backwards into the bathtub, where her head hit the side of it hard. She was dazed and suddenly queasy. Richard jerked her body up by her wrists until she was on her feet again only to push her backwards again, this time into the valance above the little window, breaking it in half with her head.

MURDER BY GRAVITY?

Her limp body slid down the wall.

"Shut your mouth, or I'll shut it for you! Nobody's going to save you, slut!" He had her by the biceps yet again and pushed her backwards into the bedroom. She was still dazed and off balance, so he dropped her and went around to her head and began pulling her by the hair to the bed where he pulled her body onto the bed. Hazel's head was swimming. Richard made her body bounce violently on the soft mattress. Richard jumped on her stomach and straddled her with his knees holding her upper arms down to her sides. She tried to kick him in the head with the only part of her that wasn't held down, but he was sitting too far forward for her to reach and her struggles only served to zap her strength.

Richard looked pleased. He was in control now. His bloody hand covered her mouth and nose until she thought she might suffocate.

"If I take my hand off, will you promise not to scream anymore?"

Hazel was quick to nod her head in agreement. She could taste coppery flavored blood in her mouth, now part of it was her own. Richard had cut her lip with her own teeth by pushing so hard on her face.

When he lifted his hand, Hazel talked fast, "Richard, honest to God, he's not my boyfriend! He's that way with all the women in the bar. I thought you knew that! He means nothing to me! He only drove me home because you didn't come to get me."

Richard seemed to calm down a bit. What she was saying had some ring of truth to it, but he said, "You were both laughing at me! I saw you!"

Hazel tried to make her shaky voice soothing. "That was when we were laughing at that song on the juke box called, *Eat It* by that guy, Weird Al. Nobody ever played it before."

"Yeah, right," Richard's heart rate was beginning to slow more. "If I ever see him in the bar again, I'll kick his ass and stuff it in his cute little car!" he promised.

"I'll tell him to leave," Hazel offered.

Richard flared again, "*You* will tell him nothing! Have that creepy looking friend of his tell him that he shouldn't come in anymore!" It was a command, not a suggestion.

"Okay! Okay! No problem. You know I love you and nobody else but you, right? Right? Can I get up now? Please?"

He said, "Do you promise that nothing was going on with you and that fool and you're not ever going to leave me?"

"Yeah, I promise! Really." Hazel said. Of course, she would have agreed to anything at that point.

Richard seemed to suddenly realize where he was and what he had done. His eyes changed and he looked like himself again, not like the monster that was just there. He was still ticked, though. "Go wash the blood off your face and change the sheets. You look disgusting and I'm not sleeping on all that blood." He lifted himself off of her and she gratefully filled her lungs with air.

"What happened to your hand?" Hazel asked. "It looks real bad."

"I cut it at work and it just opened up again. It's no big deal."

Hazel didn't let it drop. "It looks like you might need a few stitches."

Growing irritated again, Richard said, "I don't need no damn stitches! They're holes, not cuts." Hazel didn't bring it up again for fear of his wrath.

The police cars that Hazel kept expecting never did show up that night. She was disappointed by her neighbors' apathy, but she thought, maybe it was best that they didn't come. Richard would have taken it out on her for sure.

Soon their relationship resumed as it had been, at least as far as Richard was concerned. Hazel never forgot what happened that night, and she never brought it up again. After all, the incident wouldn't have happened if he didn't love her so much that it made him jealous, and she loved Richard enough to forgive him.

A few weeks after the incident, Hazel and Richard went bar hopping with another couple. The other man in their group told his wife that he'd punch her lights out after she made a derogatory remark about men. Then Richard said to Hazel's utter surprise that he would *never* hit a woman! Hazel mused to herself, *well, that's a stretch of the truth! I've been pushed, slapped and strangled, crushed, but he never did actually hit me*. She would never say that, of course. She was being careful around Richard now, so he wouldn't get violent again. It became stressful, like walking on eggshells and trying not to crack any.

After that, when Richard was arrested and convicted of methamphetamine possession and related charges, it was a relief to

Hazel. He served time in prison from 1991 to 1993. They did keep in touch during that period, he wrote Hazel once a month asking for forgiveness. She replied occasionally. Hazel was still angry with him for getting back on drugs and beating her up. But she was also miffed because he was so stupid that he got caught. She hated losers and she had her standards. It saddened her knowing what might have been if he'd only kept his word. She was also angry because she figured that Richard had wasted a great deal of her time and affections.

When Richard was released in early summer of 1993, Hazel had a new boyfriend living with her. Richard was devastated, and he was living in his truck again. His first order of business would be to find a new job.

CHAPTER 4

Joyce Martinez was cutting her time close again, but she made it a point to never be late for work. She promised herself this wouldn't be the day she broke her perfect record. She rushed through her shower and blow-dried her shoulder-length brown hair with painted red highlights. Joyce took pride in her looks and always wore her makeup flawlessly, though she was pretty without it. She loved to wear short skirts that drew attention to her long legs, thin thighs, and trim figure. To Joyce, perfume and jewelry were just a part of getting dressed.

On this particular day, Joyce felt thrown together as she jumped into her turquoise Volkswagen Bug and drove to work, arriving just minutes before her 6 p.m. shift was about to start. She worked nights at P.J.'s Tavern where she was the bartender and only employee. She held down the fort alone and by all accounts did an excellent job of it. She was always careful to have one of the customers walk her out to her car in the parking lot after work and made sure to drop her cash into the locked safe frequently so there would be nothing significant to steal. And she'd never been robbed or attacked, as her mother always feared.

Joyce was a friendly young woman and was described repeatedly as, "happy-go-lucky." She always had a beautiful smile on her face and a joke for every occasion. She had the personality and physical beauty combined that generated liberal tips. Unfortunately, it wasn't the country club set she was serving. Most of the crime in the city came from an area nearby, particularly after dark. The customers weren't rich, but they always tipped their bartender as well as could be expected. The risky part of the job was generally due to low-level local gang activity and the homeless shelter a mile or so away. In Yuma, the unofficial rule of thumb is: the further away from the

MURDER BY GRAVITY?

Foothills the higher the crime rate. That, coupled with being a pretty young woman working alone at night serving the public, Joyce knew she was statistically a target and could understand why her mother worried, but Joyce felt very at ease with the position.

After the rush of getting to work and relieving day shift, Joyce had some time to wait for customers to arrive as she prepared for business. She mused about her current love life and Jeff, the former "Mr. Perfect-in-the-Raw," who had been living with her for the last few months. Before him, she dated a guy named Bill, an ex-Marine who smashed in the windshield of her car while she was still in it.

Love had not been kind to Joyce. Lately, she always managed to fall in love with the wrong kind of man. Of course, the only men she met nowadays were at the bar. Jeff Warner had sauntered in one night about three months earlier. She had been taken by his biker-type good looks and no-nonsense sensuality. She wondered now what on earth could she have been thinking at the time. He was still jobless, although he'd supposedly been looking for work ever since she had met him that night. Joyce knew there was construction work to be had if he would just go out and look. But Jeff had no ambition. Where they lived in Yuma was and still is, booming and jobs are of all types are plentiful. Sometimes she didn't mind being the only source of income, though ideally, she thought it would be nice if working were optional on her part. Jeff was such a loser though, in a straw that broke the camel's back string of losers. He was another ex-Marine and nobody liked him except her. That should have tipped her off, but it hadn't. Yuma has a Marine Air Base, so Marines are plentiful.

Why don't they ever de-program those guys when they get out of the service? she thought. The very attributes that attracted her to him, the tough, handsome, and muscular type, also meant narcissistic with nothing left over for her. He barked orders at her instead of requesting something, and he never said he loved her. It was always *her* job to try to make *him* happy; never the other way around. She couldn't talk to him about her problems and concerns. Joyce knew it would never work out with him and it would have to be ended sooner or later. It would be nice to find someone who wanted to take care of her and treat her special, for a change.

Joyce had been married twice before in her thirty-three years, both times to the same man. The first wedding to the handsome Ed Martinez took a full year to plan and had been absolutely perfect. After the first two good years, the marriage died and couldn't be resurrected. Joyce and Ed had just been too young. It was a no-fault divorce with both parties to blame.

Ed, Sr. had asked Joyce several times to re-marry him, but Joyce was not going to let him use their two children to bully her back into a bad marriage. They had already made that mistake once when they were briefly re-married five years after their first marriage. The second had lasted less than a year. But they were still on speaking terms because the raising of their two children necessitated it. Ed, Jr., age 15, and Nichole, age 12, were Hispanic on their father's side and both very attractive.

Joyce had her tubes tied after Nickie's birth which had been unusual for a woman so young, but she insisted that having a boy and a girl was the perfect combination and she didn't want any more children. Ed had sole physical custody of both children, though he and Joyce had joint custody legally. Ed, Sr. felt that Joyce wasn't the best example for them because she was a bartender and had some unsavory friends. She also worked the hours that the children would be home from school and they needed adult supervision. The judge had agreed that both children should live with Ed, primarily due to his much higher income. Joyce was okay with Ed, Jr. living with his father, because she believed it was important for a boy to be around his dad. But Joyce longed for her daughter to live with her full-time and she was determined to make that happen.

Joyce lived in a small apartment that was in a large, eye-catching complex that had a pool just outside her front door. Joyce's sister, Lynn, who was four years younger, lived across the pool and barbeque area in the same building with her husband, David. It was important to Joyce to be close to her family. They were a rock in her sometimes unstable life. Lynn had married a year previously and had a wonderful, loving husband.

Joyce sometimes yearned to have her life like that too. She wondered what she had done in her life to deserve the unhappiness that would consume her in her most private moments. Deep in her heart she believed that eventually she'd meet the right man; at least she hoped so. Her special someone didn't have to be handsome; she wouldn't be too picky about that, as long as he treated her and her kids with respect. He had to be reasonable because she believed that you couldn't have a relationship with someone that you can't reason with, talk to, or enjoy being around. She wanted someone to love and share the joys of her life. This ideal man absolutely had to be dependable. She was tired of being the only responsible person in a relationship. And, ideally, he should be smart so she could look up to him.

With those troubling thoughts in her mind, in late summer of 1993, Richard Handcock walked in with Tammy, the owner of P.J.'s. He had just been hired to be the new bouncer. Joyce didn't think she needed one, but it would be nice to have some company when the bar was slow and she wouldn't have to share her tips with a bouncer. "You'll like him. He's a good guy," Tammy told her when Richard was out of earshot.

Richard was an unusual-looking man. Not really bad looking, though. He had long blond hair pulled back into a ponytail and a steep widow's peak. His forehead sloped back, giving him a strange profile; one might almost say Neanderthal. But from the front he looked just fine. "He doesn't have to be handsome," Joyce reminded herself. Richard had lifted weights in prison and had been working construction for a short time before he came to work at P.J.'s. She could see he was lean and muscular. Joyce very much admired that.

Richard sat at the end of the bar by the entrance. "Hey!" Joyce said with her usual smile, "Want something to drink before you have to get to work?"

Obviously intimidated by her, Richard managed a shy smile. "Do you have any orange juice?" he asked.

Joyce shot back at him rhetorically, "What kind of a place would this be without O. J. for screwdrivers?" Joyce turned just then and didn't see his face register annoyance. Sarcasm made Richard angry as a rule. Joyce went about her work after she served him his drink with a smile. It was a Monday and her shipment of liquor, beer, and munchies had just arrived and would take an hour or so to put away now that Tammy had gone.

After a little while, Richard, who'd been watching her since he walked in the door, asked, "How can I help you with that?"

Those words were music to Joyce's ears and not in Jeff's

vocabulary at all, she noted. If he had merely asked, "Can I help?" she would have said, "No." But she automatically started thinking about how she was going to move the heavy boxes when he asked, "How." He seemed to know what to say and how to say it to successfully throw her off balance. Joyce had felt his eyes on her and became strangely self-conscious. She felt a warm flush when they passed each other behind the narrow bar. Together they got everything put away by the time the earliest regulars started to arrive.

Joyce was drawn to Richard's shyness. He wasn't smooth and assuming like so many of the men she knew. Joyce could tell that Richard was attracted to her as he still watched her every move in the weeks that followed. Sometimes she would sneak a look at him, just to see if it were her imagination. But every time she looked, he really *was* staring at her with the eyes of a little puppy.

They played darts when there was little business, and she beat his pants off because she'd been playing the game for years. At least that's what she thought. It didn't occur to her that he could be losing on purpose. That was something that women did years ago to boost a man's ego. They were playing for a few dollars to make it more interesting. Richard could be very good at keeping his ego in check when he wanted. He wasn't just playing darts with Joyce; he was playing Joyce with darts.

One week, on a Tuesday, Richard asked Joyce out to dinner on their next mutual night off. That was eight days away! Men hadn't given her much more than a day's notice for a date in years. Besides, with that much notice, she couldn't think of a good excuse not to go.

On the night of their date, Richard showed up at her door with a dozen red roses in hand.

"Pretty flowers for a pretty lady," he said. Joyce thought that was totally unoriginal and cornball, but it wasn't completely without charm. Sometimes he seemed a little old fashioned, but she kind of liked it.

They went to dinner at The Hunter Restaurant, just as Richard had with Hazel on their first date.

"Order anything you want. Do you like lobster?" Richard asked. He could afford it since his lifestyle was cheap.

"I love it!" she said. This was really going to be a special treat. Joyce had been watching her pennies so she could help Ed, Sr. afford to outfit Nichole with new clothes when school started. Nichole also had her mother's love of expensive apparel. Ed, Jr. wasn't so fussy about his clothing and last year's clothes still fit him for now.

Thinking about it, Joyce realized that nobody had taken her for such a nice dinner in at least a year. Richard gave her the impression that he was not used to being around women. He seemed unsure of himself around her and a bit nervous. He certainly wasn't a womanizer, which was refreshing. He told her that she was beautiful every single night at work. Some nights she felt far from beautiful. She was beginning to feel like he'd put her on a pedestal and she was starting to be concerned that she'd fall off.

"Sometimes I'm afraid that once you get to know the real me, you'll be disappointed," Joyce said to his blue Tweety Bird eyes.

Richard had responded, "There is nothing in the world you could do that would disappoint me. You'll just have to get used to putting up with me. I plan to be your personal shadow." That statement was even scarier than falling off of a pedestal! Things seemed to be moving very fast all of a sudden to Joyce. She thought about that for a minute and decided that was okay for now. She already knew Richard well enough to know that if she told him to slow down, it might hurt his feelings, but he'd do it. Richard's feelings were tender and she found herself sometimes editing what she might normally say to him so his ego wasn't wounded. He was a sweetheart and didn't deserve to be hurt. But she'd never been around a guy that was so sensitive!

In the following weeks that passed, Richard watched as Joyce brought in painted baskets and created her own floral arrangements to help pass the time at work and to bring in extra cash on the side. He could see that she enjoyed working on the crafts. The customers bought them as fast as she finished them. He thought the most impressive part was that she got almost all of her supplies from dumpster diving late at night in the alleys behind the craft stores and she found a use for nearly everything. Nothing went to waste.

"You'd be amazed at the good stuff the stores throw away," Joyce told him. Richard watched in awe as if she were a talented artist, someone wonderfully special. And every one of those baskets was nearly 100% profit.

Richard had cut flowers delivered to Joyce every week at the beginning of her shift. Eventually, all the customers knew that

Richard had given them to Joyce and teased her continually about it. They also encouraged her to give Richard a chance.

Jeff Warren moved out of Joyce's apartment quietly about three weeks into her relationship with Richard. Neither of them talked about it. It was an understanding that they both knew it was over.

In the beginning, Joyce was slightly embarrassed when she introduced Richard to her friends in social situations. She knew that they would think that she'd lost her mind because he wasn't all that attractive and he was kind of awkward. She just hoped no one would say anything to him about it. Ruby Vasquez was Joyce's long-time girlfriend who worked the day shift at P.J.'s. They would catch up with each other's lives while Ruby counted her money in the drawer before Joyce took over the bar. Then Joyce counted it again. She knew it would be fine, but it was procedure. Ruby understood that and took no offence.

"Hey, Joyce, when are we going out to party again? It's been a long time!" Ruby said.

"You're right! We need to do that!" Joyce said and immediately afterward realized she'd hung her friends out to dry since meeting Richard. "Maybe we can go out with the guys next time."

All the flowers Richard had invested in began to do what they were intended to do; win her over. He seemed sensitive to Joyce's feelings and treated her with respect. He thought only the best of her and she wanted to live up to that; to be a better person. All at once what Richard thought became important to Joyce. Before she got too involved with him, it was time she be honest with him about herself.

Over the last three years or so, she had begun using a drug. It was methamphetamine. Usually she would just smoke a little before work to give her some extra energy and it made her feel instantly happy. If anyone didn't know that she was using, they couldn't tell it by her speech or actions unless she was out partying with her friends. Then she might allow herself to "tweak," which is what drinkers would call drunk. It was a daily routine that her family didn't know about but had suspicions. If her ex-husband ever caught wind of it, Joyce wouldn't have a prayer of getting physical custody of Nickie. But, Joyce thought, she wasn't using it to get high. She only used it because it was now a physical necessity. She wished it weren't so. But she didn't know how to stop. She was afraid if she stopped;

she'd go through a long, painful withdrawal and wouldn't be able to go to work. She couldn't afford to take time off work, nor would she expect to have a job to come back to if she did.

It began as a surprise birthday gift from another Jeff in her life; Jeff Dupre. Jeff had been a good friend of Joyce's since 1988 when they met playing darts at another neighborhood bar. They became fast friends and it never went any further than friendship. They weren't attracted to each other that way. In fact, they both appreciated their somewhat unique relationship. Jeff and her friend Ruby at that time lived together. A year after Joyce met him Jeff started dealing drugs and was always stocked with just about every drug a person could want. Joyce had put off his drug offers numerous times. But this surprise birthday gift had come at a time in her life when she was feeling low. She had been thinking that at the age of thirty, life was simply passing her by. Maybe that would change if she started saying yes to ideas once in a while instead of always saying "No." She agreed to take the little plastic bag home with her and promised to try it soon.

Jeff said, "Oh, no you don't. Not this time. I'm going to make sure you try it right now." Some other friends encouraged her to give it a try and assured her that she'd like it and it was safe. Joyce relented and took a hit. Somebody put some quarters in the juke box and played "Born to be Wild." Everybody laughed and some started to dance, although there wasn't really a dance floor. They just danced wherever they were standing. After a while, Joyce began to notice that her tongue hadn't become thick and the drug hadn't made it difficult to speak. She also noticed that she didn't get cotton mouth and bad breath like with alcohol. And she liked that she didn't get wobbly or stumble around. In fact, she felt brighter and wittier and more comfortably outgoing than ever before!

"Hey, party girl," Jeff said, "You sure are different tonight! I think I like you better this way! I need to get you home now though, because *some* of us are getting sleepy around here." He put the bicycle she had ridden to work that night in the back of his truck and drove her home.

When the truck came to a stop in front of her apartment, Joyce told him she had a great time. She retrieved the little plastic bag from her purse and handed it back to him. He pushed her hand away, "No, you keep it."

"I won't use it, so you might as well take it back."

"Just keep it," he said, "Just keep it in case. I got more than I need and I won't take it back anyway!" Knowing how stubborn Jeff could be, she shrugged, gave a little smile and put it back in her purse. In the morning she noted that she didn't even have a hangover.

Three nights later, Joyce went to a girlfriend's bridal shower at a local bar on 4th Avenue called The Showcase. Somebody made this wonderfully delicious rum and fruit punch that Joyce just couldn't seem to stay away from. Then they all started barhopping. Each bar they went to, they had to have at least one drink. Joyce knew all the bartenders, so she got complimentary mixed drinks. But she was more in the mood for boilermakers instead. She knew better than to mix drinks like that, but she was having fun with the girls and didn't care about it just then. By the time she made it home early in the morning, even the after hours clubs had shut down.

Joyce slept like the dead through the morning and into the afternoon. When she woke at 3 PM she felt like she'd been hit by a truck. It never occurred to her that she might need to set the alarm clock to make it to work on swing shift! She'd never slept *this* late before. Maybe it was more than sleep. She felt like she'd been poisoned.

Wondering if the cup of coffee she drank would stay down, Joyce thought maybe she'd feel better if she *could* throw up. She dragged herself to the shower. The hot water felt good, but it didn't make her feel much more human. She slumped into a chair at the dining room table and lit a clove cigarette, the only kind she used. She enjoyed the sweet taste of clove on her lips and tongue. Joyce had sat down to blow-dry her hair. She was too tired to stand up in the bathroom to do it. She knew she'd overdone the partying last night. She couldn't snap out of it the day after like she used to. Maybe that was because she was thirty years old now. The thought of turning thirty made her think about her party the previous week and Jeff's surprise.

Fluffy slippers clip-clopped as Joyce crossed the kitchen floor to her purse hanging on the closet doorknob and retrieved the plastic bag Jeff had given her. She remembered how the crystal meth had perked her right up at her birthday party. Maybe this would help her get through the night ahead. She wasn't allowed to drink on the job, but she could sure use something.

That night at work, Joyce had a great shift after all. She marveled at how much energy she had. Crystal meth had become her new panacea and friend.

Weeks after her birthday, Jeff stopped over to her apartment. "Hey, sexy, do you think since you're not using that meth, that I could get some of it back for a friend of mine?"

"Well, sweetie, I was just about to call you to get some more for me! I really like it." Jeff looked at her with that crooked smile of his, which then melted into a frown. "You mean it's *gone?*" he asked incredulously.

Joyce suddenly felt a little embarrassed. "Yeah, why? Is it a big deal?" she asked.

Jeff's voice went up in pitch, "Do you have any idea how much that bag was worth?" Joyce shook her head. "Three hundred or so!" He told her.

Joyce arched her eyebrows in surprise. She'd had no idea and hadn't even thought about the expense." Well, then I guess I'd better forget about getting any more of it. The last thing I need is another expensive habit." And she was going to nip it in the bud. "Damn!" she said. And she had thought clove cigarettes were expensive!

That resolve lasted all of two and a half weeks. One night Ruby came in with several of her closest customers to do some serious partying. Jeff and Ruby had been an item, but that night they were on the outs. For Ruby, that was a legitimate, good reason to get polluted. Everybody there was into meth and alcohol or something else. Since Joyce couldn't drink while she worked, she figured that nobody could smell a drug on her breath, after all. She thought, *why the hell not indulge a little?* So afterwards, Joyce decided she needed to have her own stash. She felt bad about spending the money on it, but Ruby bought her own meth and Joyce knew that her night shift tips were better than Ruby's day shift tips.

If she can afford it, so can I, she reasoned. And that was how it all started to be the daily activity that it was in 1993. In the first week, the meth also took off the ten pounds she'd been trying to lose since the kids were born. Soon she was using before work and once again during the night shift. Because the meth loosened her bowels, she was going through a bottle of Kaeopectate every two or three days. She squelched her little voice of reason that told her she was burning the candle at both ends.

Joyce felt that before she became any further involved with Richard, she should come clean about her habit. It was time to tell him before somebody else did. That night they were off work and went to an early movie. *Forest Gump* had put them both in a light mood. They pulled up to J.B.'s Restaurant for a bite, and while they sat in Richard's truck, she told him the whole story about how she got started on meth and about her regular use of it.

Richard listened intently looking down at the steering wheel as she spoke. Joyce couldn't tell what he was thinking and her stomach knotted. She watched a couple of snowbirds walk by.

Finally, Richard spoke. "I'm glad you told me. There's something I haven't told you either and I'm sorry. I don't think I ever could tell you, but since you've been so honest with me, it makes me feel like we got a serious relationship started and I wanna be as honest as you are."

"It's sort of ironic, really," he said, "Six weeks before I met you at work, I was released from prison. They said it was burglary and possession of a dangerous drug charge. The burglary I didn't have anything to do with, but I did have meth on me. The public defender said I'd be better off pleading 'no contest' as opposed to a jury trial. Tammy knew about it when she hired me, but we'd known each other before then and she did me a favor."

Joyce's eyes had fixated subconsciously on a prickly pear cactus in front of their parking space. Someone had carved one of the oval branches two eyes and a mouth so it looked like a living, green happy face. It had two flower buds on the top of it that looked like little yellow ears. She felt as if it were laughing at her. Incredibly, a tiny sparrow landed on it carefully avoiding the big needles that dotted the surface of it.

Now it was her turn to be shocked. Shocked, nothing! She *reeled!* She suddenly had an excruciating headache. She didn't want Richard to see the look on her face and how disappointed she was with him. She was already more concerned with his feelings than her own, and she was a people pleaser. So he was like other guys, after all, maybe worse. Maybe she had put *him* on a pedestal, rather than the other way around. But part of her was glad he wasn't too perfect.

MURDER BY GRAVITY?

It would be hard to live with perfect.

"How long were you in for?"

"Two years minus a week and a half."

Joyce's sense of humor suddenly got the best of her. She dead panned, "So, you wanna go smoke some now?" They both laughed so hard Richard accidentally honked the horn. Joyce had to wipe the tears of laughter from her face. Her headache suddenly vanished. They left the parking lot and went to Joyce's apartment and made love for the first time.

CHAPTER 5

Joyce knew in her heart there would be no real love connection with Richard; that the physical attraction wasn't there for her and he wasn't as intelligent as she would have preferred. But that was okay, she reasoned, because she had a goal in mind, only one that wouldn't wait any longer. The plan was to have a two-income household, become stable, and get Nickie back home with her where she belonged. She loved her daughter and missed her every day. Joyce really did have affection for Richard and usually enjoyed his company. He had a manly presence and a dependable track record with her. She thought that as long as Ed didn't know about their methamphetamine use, he would feel good about Nickie coming to live with the two of them.

Once when Joyce had the night off, Richard popped in with Chinese take-out. They hadn't made any plans together, which was rare, but it seemed like they didn't need to anymore. They had become a couple. Joyce was sitting on the floor, frustrated and working on her vacuum cleaner that hadn't been operating properly and she was disgusted that she'd have to take it to the repair shop. She'd had a busy day doing all the errands and chores one does on a day off, and hadn't even thought about dinner.

Richard said, "Oh, don't worry about that thing. That's *my* job. Eat dinner while it's still hot and I'll check that out later." They weren't just words. He actually did as promised after they enjoyed sweet-and sour-shrimp, fried rice, and egg rolls from the now closed Bamboo Garden Restaurant. They read their fortune cookies with the words, "…in bed," at the end, as the running gag goes, which so often makes the fortunes sound funny.

Not only did Richard look at the vacuum cleaner, he managed to repair it. Joyce wasn't used to men who were actually useful around the house and was impressed.

"Be careful. I could get used to this!" she warned him.

"You deserve somebody a lot better than me. I wish I could do more for you. You've worked so hard all your life," he acknowledged.

Joyce hadn't even told her family about Richard or that she and Jeff had split up. As close as Joyce was with her younger sister, Lynn, and her mom and dad, Lori and Bill Perron, she hadn't but barely said greetings to any of them since she started dating Richard. The only people who had met him were the customers at P.J.'s., and they didn't really know him. When Joyce pressed Tammy for more information about Richard, Tammy admitted to not knowing him well, only that he seemed to be a good guy and somebody told her that they thought he'd be a good bouncer. Rumor was that. ironically, Tammy and Richard may actually have been introduced by a mutual friend of Hazel's.

* * *

Two weeks before Christmas 1993, Lynn called Joyce to talk to her about their annual Christmas dinner at Lynn's apartment.

"Hey, sis! What have you been up to?" Lynn asked.

"Keeping busy. You know me. What's up for the Christmas shindig?"

Lynn replied, "We're having it Christmas Eve this year for a change and dinner is around five-ish. See, this way Dave and I can spend some time at his parents on Christmas Day. Are you bringing Jeff?"

"Oh, *heck* no! We broke up almost three months ago! I'm dating another guy and I was planning to ask him to come with me. That's okay, isn't it?" Joyce asked.

"Duh! Of course it's okay! I can't believe all this has happened since we last talked! It's not like we live far away from each other! What's his name? And what does he look like?" Lynn wanted to know.

"Well, his name is Richard Handcock and he has beautiful long blond hair that he wears in a pony tail. He works as a bouncer now at P.J.'s with me."

"I think I've seen him walking toward your apartment building. I didn't get a good look; he was across the pool at the time. But he looked like a decent enough guy. Better than these biker types you usually collect!" she observed.

Joyce ignored Lynn's reference to the losers that colored her past. "I can't wait for you and Mom to meet him! I really like him a lot! How's Dad doing?" Joyce asked.

"Mom's been taking him in for doctors' appointments and tests. They think it might be his heart."

"I feel so bad about not calling them! I'm glad we're all getting together soon," said Joyce. She hadn't realized the situation was so serious.

"What would be a good gift for Richard, since we don't know him yet? He's got to have something to unwrap while we all open our packages. I don't want him to feel left out." Lynn offered.

"Thanks, but don't worry about that. He'll be fine and I don't expect you to buy him any gifts. I'll bring the presents that I'm giving to him and he can open those while we all open ours. Okay?" said Joyce.

"Whatever!" Lynn said. "I'm looking forward to seeing you and meeting him. Love you! Bye. . . Wait! Are you going to tell Mom about him coming or do I have to?" Joyce knew her sister well enough to know that the way that sentence was worded meant, *You haven't been keeping in touch with Mom, you derelict, and it's your job to tell her about the new boyfriend. But I will tell her for you if you're not feeling guilty enough yet, because I call her everyday. Guilt, love, love, guilt; where does one end and the other begin? Or is it all mingled in a big furry ball?*

"I'll call her. Love you, too! Bye." Joyce had hung up the phone after her talk with Lynn, then hit auto dial number one for her mother.

"Hi, Mom! How are you? How's Dad?" After hearing a brief update, Joyce said, "I wanted to let you know that I'm bringing a new guy to Christmas dinner."

Lori was surprised. "What happened to Jeff?"

"We both knew it was going nowhere. He left almost three months ago."

"So, what's his name and what can we get him for a gift . . . . ?"

Joyce rolled her eyes and told her the same thing she told Lynn.

MURDER BY GRAVITY?

Are these guys alike, or what? She thought, *but in a nice way.*

Bill and Lori Perron had moved into a park model and it was too small to accommodate all the children and grandchildren for a big family meal. Her parents lived in a recreational vehicle park called Sunset RV, which was small with few amenities, but had nice shade trees and was pleasantly park-like. It was also one of the least expensive recreational vehicle parks in Yuma and one of the few that weren't strictly for people over the age of 55. Bill Perron, then age 60, received a reduction on their rent for his services as the summer manager of the park. Their park model was a darling little dollhouse of a mobile home, completely decorated and furnished when they bought it brand-new a couple of years previously. And best of all, there was no room for the children.

The Perrons loved their kids to pieces, but didn't want a few empty rooms to tempt them into allowing the kids to move back in under their roof if they hit a rough patch. The RV lifestyle is swiftly becoming popular with white-collar and the occasional upper blue-collar couples who are retiring. It offers travel and entertainment at each park. In these RV parks, which are not to be confused with the stereotypical trailer parks, residents generally are retired nurses, teachers, accountants, lawyers, engineers, and military who flock to escape the snow and enjoy friendships with winter neighbors.

Joyce's step father, Bill, was a retired master gunnery sergeant. The family had settled in Yuma in 1974 when he was stationed at The Marine Corps Air Station in Yuma, and remained after his retirement. Lori Perron was a funder at a local mortgage company that was on the grandchildren's way home from school, so Lori enjoyed seeing them every day when they stopped in to visit her. They had always been a close family.

* * *

Driving over to Joyce's on Christmas Eve, Richard was nervous. He had this habit of opening and closing his index finger and ring finger together over, then under, his middle finger when he was worried. On the walk over to Lynn's from Joyce's apartment, she noticed that he was distant and thoughtful.

"You look scared to death! You don't have to worry about my

family liking you. If I like you, they'll like you. And I love you, so they'll love you! They're real friendly people and everybody gets along with them. Just don't be scared of my dad. He's retired military and seems a little starched until you get to know him. He really is a great guy, though! I don't think I've told you before that he's my step dad. He's been my dad since I was eleven years old and I don't even remember what it was like without him anymore. He's always treated me like I was his own daughter and we've always been close, so he might try to quiz you a little before he gives you his seal of approval. He'll be impressed if you call him 'sir'," Joyce volunteered.

"Oh, thanks a lot! You're not helping by telling me this, you know," Richard commented with a tight smile. He was carrying the three-bean salad Joyce always brought to family gatherings. He wasn't used to women with close family ties and it was a source of concern. He knew they would be critical and try to come between Joyce and him. His prison buddies had told him horror stories about in-laws and family gatherings.

* * *

Richard was wooden as Joyce introduced him to her family one by one. He seemed like a fish out of water. Joyce had never seen him like that before. She knew he wouldn't win them over acting like he had something to hide, which was the way her parents would perceive his behavior. The adults collected in the kitchen getting drinks and Joyce took the opportunity to pull Richard back into the living room for a private word.

"Hey! Loosen up a little! Why are you being like this? Let them get to know the real you, like I do. They won't bite!"

That was the last thing Richard wanted them to do--get to know the real him. He took the beer Lori brought him and kept his seat on the couch, though everyone else was standing.

"How do you like working at P.J.'s so far?" Lori asked him engagingly.

"Fine," Richard replied unimaginatively.

"Joyce told me you fixed her vacuum cleaner. She's been tinkering with that thing for years trying to keep going," Lori continued.

"Oh," Richard said softly, "I'm glad I could help." His voice was flat.

"Mom's a funder at a mortgage company, Richard," Joyce said trying to work a conversation out of him.

"And I'm not planning on retiring until they take me out the office door, feet first on a stretcher!" Lori joked. Tall, blond, and still attractive at 52, she was years away from retirement. She loved Yuma. With all the senior citizens, or as Rush Limbaugh, whom she listened to on the radio every morning at work, would say, "seasoned citizens," Lori was generally the youngest person in a room. She and Bill were considered the "kids" by many of their neighbors.

Joyce's step dad entered the room and said jovially, "Richard, I wouldn't believe a word the Perron women had to say, if I were you! Joycie says you used to work as a carpenter, Richard. Why switch to barroom bouncer?" he asked.

"Oh, well, construction jobs are so undependable. I was looking for something more stable. Besides, it was the only way I could meet your beautiful daughter, sir." Richard seemed to come to life a bit.

"Dinner's ready, everyone!" Lynn announced. "It's a buffet, so everybody get a plate and help yourselves. Adults in the dining room, kids in the kitchen. David, we need a couple of folding chairs, dear." She enlisted the help of her husband, who was already busy, rather than ask Richard, who didn't seem very approachable.

"Mind if I put on some Christmas music, Lynn?" Joyce asked.

"Good idea," said Lynn, who was now surrounded by hungry children.

* * *

Lynn's Christmas dinners were always wonderful. The family talked and exchanged stories, caught up with each others' lives. Richard didn't speak unless someone asked him a question, and with his monosyllabic answers, conversations with him tapered off. Nobody thought badly of him, just that he was quiet. Joyce introduced him to her children when they arrived later. It was all very polite but with Richard, awkward at best.

After dinner, it was Nickie's turn to pass out the gifts. Richard was handed the presents from Joyce then Nickie started bringing him small gifts from everyone in Joyce's family, who hadn't listened to what she told them about not getting Richard presents.

"Thanks," Richard said without enthusiasm to no one in particular. He was quietly seething because he had asked Joyce *specifically* if he should bring presents for her family and she had said no, not to worry about it. She said that she had told her family they were not going to exchange gifts with him. He knew they had done it to make him look cheap in Joyce's eyes.

As soon as all the gifts were opened, Richard told Joyce that he needed to go home. The family gave him a warm goodbye, but thought it odd for him to leave so early. They also thought that he didn't like being with them all that much. Joyce didn't know at that time that Richard was living in his truck's camper part of the time since his release from prison. She had been curious as to why he never took her to his place. She had already asked him to move in with her, but Richard had told her that he wasn't ready, and that he had probably lived alone so long by then that nobody could stand living with him anyway.

* * *

Richard wasn't actually in his camper home much at all in those days. Shortly after he began seeing Joyce, he heard that Hazel's boyfriend had moved out of her apartment. Richard called the florist and had flowers sent to both Joyce and Hazel routinely. He had the best of both worlds. Hazel had eventually melted and given him one last chance. Richard made her feel terrible about her lack of good judgment when she allowed another man to live with her while he was in prison. Indeed, she had promised *never* to leave him once upon a time. Richard stayed in his camper when he preferred to be alone.

Richard had been vague when Hazel quizzed him about where he was working. Neither Joyce nor Hazel knew of the involvement each other had with him. Hazel and Richard worked different days and hours, so they saw little of each other anyway. She was even *glad* that he was working and had money of his own, and that he didn't have time to come into The Bottoms Up

MURDER BY GRAVITY?

Pub and bother her or her customers. He really did seem to have turned over a new leaf as far as his temper went; more settled down this time. As far as Hazel was concerned, living with Richard was better the second time around.

CHAPTER 6

With New Year's Eve just around the corner, Richard found himself in a quandary. He figured at least one of his ladies would be working that night and didn't have a contingency plan if they both were off. Joyce and Hazel each assumed that they had a date with Richard, as ladies in a relationship usually do.

Joyce had planned a quiet, elegant dinner at her apartment for just the two of them. She would set a pretty table using her mauve fabric napkins that picked up the color faintly depicted in her stoneware and use her mother's white lace tablecloth and was roasting chicken cordonbleu from a favorite recipe. She had white milk glass candlesticks and mauve tapered candles. Joyce prided herself on being a good cook and knew that Richard loved chicken. She had bought a little black dress that was sleeveless and came in off the shoulders directly to the round collar. It was very sexy and showed off her figure nicely. She didn't have new shoes, but her black pumps would look fine after she shined them. She wanted this New Year's to be extra special. If everything went as planned, Joyce visualized Richard carrying her to the bed after dinner. Then later they would go to P.J.'s for champagne and the traditional countdown to the New Year. It would be a romantic evening for both of them. In preparation for the evening, she would spend all day cleaning her house, touching up her hair color, and cooking. Richard would be impressed with her beauty and capabilities and she hoped that he might even pop the question that night.

At the other end of Yuma, Hazel had bought two very expensive tickets to a steak dinner and New Year's Eve celebration hosted by a local radio station that included (in addition to dinner) baked Alaska, drinks, music, party poppers, and confetti. She had purchased a darling slip of a red dress with spaghetti straps and red high-heeled sandals that laced up to mid-calf. Hazel was going to dazzle. Red was Richard's favorite color and it would be a nice surprise. She told him about the plans in October when it was still tentative and had reminded him twice since then.

Richard was about to fumble the ball on this game he played with his duel love life. It was time for a Hail Mary on the morning of December 31, 1993. His high school phys ed teacher once said, "The best defense is a good offense." Once Richard learned of the two dates, he had a decision to make. He had ruled out running back and forth from the dinner with Joyce to the party with Hazel. They were too smart for that and they were too far apart. No, one of his ladies would have to take it on the chin. Richard knew he would have to start an argument with one of them; and he felt that his relationship with Hazel was strong enough to survive one night of disappointment. He couldn't have been more wrong.

* * *

Late in the morning Richard and Hazel sat in her apartment reading the newspaper and drinking coffee. Hazel already knew she would have to take a nap in the afternoon. She had worked a double shift the day before so she could afford to take New Year's Eve off. Her car was acting up again and she really needed the money. Tips on New Year's Eve were always better than on any other good night during the year. It seemed like this year everybody was staying home the night before New Year's Eve. Hazel always found dead nights especially tiring. She would suffer a loss financially and have to wait another week before she could get new brake shoes. She put those thoughts aside and looked forward to partying instead. Thank goodness the party tickets were already paid for.

Richard had put off telling Hazel until the last moment. There would have been no living with her had she known ahead of time.

"Um, babe, I hate to tell you this . ." he began.

"What? You'd better not say that you're not going with me tonight!"

"I have to work tonight. Sorry. I swear I'll make it up to you," he said, trying to look disappointed.

"Are you serious? Do you know how much those tickets cost

me? I got off work tonight so I could go, and I really need the money right now! You were supposed to take tonight off too! I can't believe you're doing this to me!"

"I'm doing this to *you?*" He said incredulously. "I can't help it if I have to work! They didn't give me any choice. I just found out last night myself. Do you think I'd rather be working than out having fun with you? And haven't I helped you out financially?"

"No! And if I hadn't paid for these tickets and taken tonight off, I *could* have gotten my car fixed this week. When did you ever help me financially?"

"What about the seat covers?"

Richard had bought her new seat covers earlier in the month as part of her Christmas present, but Hazel didn't think of that as helping her out. Besides, the wild animal print made it look like she was driving a pimp mobile. She only put them on so his feelings wouldn't be hurt.

"If you had talked to me first," Hazel said, "I would have told you that I needed the brakes fixed more than I needed new seat covers! And have you ever paid for anything *else?*"

Hazel knew she was supposed to be intimidated because Richard had already beaten her down when necessary and generally she was too meek and mild in his presence. But this time she was very angry and let him know so. Richard brought his right arm up and cleared the table of the milk, sugar, and coffee cups in one fast sweep. The light-colored carpet soaked the coffee up immediately.

"You ungrateful witch, Hazel! Don't I ever take you out for dinner? And what about the shopping spree at Wal-Mart? Witch Hazel, witch Hazel!" He teased her like a child. His voice grated and she felt it vibrate the table top.

Richard stood up and spat, "That's *it!*" He began to gather everything he owned that wasn't already in his camper. He knew this fight was a possibility and figured that he might have to take off for a few days until she cooled down. He had already put a few of his belongings into the truck just in case this very thing happened.

Hazel said, "Fine. If you don't move out today, I'll move you out tonight myself!"

Richard came at her with that scary look on his face again and shoved her back to the wall. With his forearm pushed against her throat, he said, "If you so much as touch my stuff, I'll kill you!"

Then, surprisingly, he stormed into the bathroom, took a long shower and shaved. When he emerged, he was nicely dressed in a new peach-colored dress shirt with a tan tie and tan dress pants. He had thrown towels and other of Hazel's things around the bedroom.

"*That's* what you're wearing to *work?* Where are you *really* going?" Hazel insisted against her better judgment as she stood in front of the door, blocking his way out. Richard backhanded her face so fast and hard that she tripped over the low bookcase and fell to the floor. She didn't even see him walk out the door.

Hazel began to cry. She hated to cry; it made her face even more red and swollen and stuffed up her nose. It also meant that he won again. She kicked the door after he slammed it and got up slowly and shakily and went to the bathroom mirror. What she saw made her cry even harder. When he backhanded her, the silver skull-like ring Richard always wore left a one-inch cut on her cheek that was slowly oozing blood. "I'm going to have a scar!" Hazel thought. The side of her eye was swollen and already dark pink from the bruise that was forming. She winced when she touched it. Hazel had thought she would invite another guy to go with her to the party for spite. There were a few regulars at the bar that were always asking her out. But she wouldn't be going out anytime soon because of the way she looked now. A salty tear reached her cut and she wiped at it.

When Hazel's tears finally stopped, she let herself fill with rage.

How dare he? She thought. All she ever did was love him. Now she hated him to the depths of her soul.

On January 2, when Hazel went back to work, she told her curious customers that she had been in a car accident in a girlfriend's car; and that no, they didn't know her.

* * *

January 8 Richard came to The Bottoms Up Pub to test the waters. And it was far colder than he expected.

CHAPTER 7

For Joyce, New Year's Eve couldn't have been more romantic. On New Year's Day Richard brought her breakfast in bed, which is where they spent most of the day until Nickie came over in the late afternoon. Richard stayed in a good mood for the first week of 1994. He could be wonderful company when he was in a good mood. But by January 8, he changed drastically. He became picky and combative. His face was dour and his presence unpleasant.

What Joyce didn't know, was that on January 8, Richard had gone to Hazel's to make up with her and Hazel was still livid. New Year's Eve was a terrible holiday for Hazel, but not as bad as Richard taking off for eight days without even phoning to let her know he was still alive. By the sixth day, Hazel had resolved that she was finished with him, no matter what. Richard hadn't even felt the need to come up with a good excuse. After all, *he* hadn't done anything wrong.

By the next day, Richard had begun to wear Joyce down emotionally. He had become cruel. Joyce had never seen this side of him before. He tried to make her think that everything she did was wrong, but she couldn't figure out how she was so different than she was just the week before when everything was good between them.. He had accused her of flirting with her customers at P.J.'s. Then he said she wore her skirts too short and her necklines were too low. He said she dressed like a whore. Finally, before work on January 9, Joyce said, "Okay then! What do *you* think I should wear to work tonight?"

Richard started pulling clothes out of her closet and throwing them all around.

"You don't have anything I would call decent!" he said. But then he found her old clothes in the back of the closet from before she'd lost weight.

"Wear this!" Richard handed her a large crewneck pullover sweater in a color and style that was out of date, and loose-fitting jeans to go with it.

Joyce shrugged them on and slapping her palms against the outside of her thighs, said, "Well?" She knew she looked horrid and surely he could see that too.

Instead he said, "That'll work!"

Just the thought of actually wearing the outfit to work made unwanted tears cloud Joyce's eyes. She blinked rapidly so they'd go away. "You've *got* to be kidding!" she began.

Richard cut her off. "Look, Joyce, I thought you wanted to make me happy. That's what you said. If you still want to turn on other guys, maybe we should just start seeing other people."

"No, I'll wear this, if it's what you want. I really do care about you and want you to be happy with me. This just seems like, well, you might have said something about it before now. That's all." Joyce resigned herself to wearing the outfit, but she felt so ugly in it.

Richard drove them to work and when Joyce was alone at the cash register with Ruby, the tears finally tumbled down her cheeks leaving white trails in her perfect makeup.

"What's wrong, sweetie?" It was so rare to see Joyce without her usual happy smile, let alone crying. Ruby rubbed Joyce's back with the palm of her hand.

Joyce spoke softly so Richard couldn't hear. "Richard thinks I'm interested in attracting other men, so he made me wear this because he says I dress like a whore."

"He actually picked your clothes out for you?" Ruby was incredulous. Joyce nodded.

"You must love him a lot to put up with that! I wouldn't put up with that from anybody!" Ruby said adamantly.

That was the problem, Joyce thought. She was *already* dedicated to making this relationship work with Richard. But somehow she would have to fight to retain her concept of self. She wondered if it was love that she felt, or just high hopes of having her daughter back and not being alone anymore.

* * *

For the next few days, Joyce treaded lightly around Richard, sensing that he needed some "alone" time. By January 14, Richard was himself once again. His good mood returned just as suddenly, and for seemingly no rhyme or reason, just as his bad mood had come on. He went home with Joyce that night after work and reclaimed his love for her. They fell asleep in each other's arms. Joyce was so relieved. She had thought for a while that she might actually lose him. Especially after she had insisted that she was an adult and would choose her own clothing, thank you very much. He hadn't mentioned it again; not yet.

* * *

The next morning Richard asked if Joyce wanted to go to J.B.'s for the breakfast buffet. Over scrambled eggs with mushrooms and cheese sauce, Richard bared his soul to Joyce. He apologized for the way he'd been acting for the last few days and asked her to please forgive him.

"I just hate it when I feel jealous. Part of me just can't believe that somebody as beautiful as you are would really be interested in somebody like me."

"Richard," Joyce began.

"No, wait. Listen, I've been fighting my feelings for you. I've been telling myself that it's not real, because I am so afraid of getting hurt. But, if it's *not* real, why do I feel so jealous and possessive of you? I know it's because I feel love for you. I really do love you; you know that, don't you?" Joyce returned his gaze. He continued, "I know that if you ever left, I'd be lost without you." His blue eyes welled-up with tears that glistened.

Joyce was moved by his emotion. She'd never loved a man who cried, and her step-father certainly didn't. She reached around the coffee cups and put her hand on his. "I love you too, Richard."

Richard pressed onward, "I know I always want to be with you because you always make me feel so happy. You're the best time I ever had! I know I'm not saying this very well. It's hard for me to express feelings that I've never felt before. I don't suppose that I could talk you into getting married, could I?"

Joyce's fork fell to her plate with a loud clatter.

MURDER BY GRAVITY?

Richard began to chuckle, "Does that mean , 'yes'?"

"Are you serious?" Joyce just that second underwent a complete paradigm shift. It was just yesterday that doubts about the future of their relationship haunted her. Richard responded to her question with a wistful smile and a nod.

"Look, Richard, I love you. Honest I do. But this is just so sudden. Maybe we could be engaged for a while and see how it goes."

Richard halfway had expected this reaction and with as much charm as he could muster, said, "I want to make a commitment to you. I am so sure of us being together forever and it's what I really want. I was hoping that you wanted to get married, too. We could be engaged for a while, if that's the way you want it, but it's not going to change anything for me. You're already stuck with me, lady. And you really are a lady. I admire you. I respect you. I want you to be with me forever. I'd do anything for you; I'd throw myself in front of a train for you! Say 'yes' or you're going to make me cry in front of all these people in the restaurant! Say 'yes' before I go broke buying you flowers!"

Joyce laughed and remembered a few years ago being in this same situation with an old boyfriend. She had dragged her feet then and lost him shortly thereafter. With 20-20 hindsight, she had always regretted the way she'd handled that proposal.

"Where would you want us to live? Would you move into my place?" Joyce asked.

Instantly Richard answered, "No! I remembered your folks had mentioned they have a friend named Phil Seward who's into real estate. So I looked him up. Turns out he has a nice house for rent, fully furnished. We can move right in."

Richard reached for his ace in the hole. He suddenly appeared thoughtful, and said, "I have been thinking about the situation with your kids. You said that it's your income that keeps you from having custody of them. What if you could count my income onto your household income? Do you think that if we got married, it might improve your chances of getting custody of your kids?" Knowing Joyce, he was fairly sure this angle would work.

Joyce's mind raced and her face suddenly brightened. "It might! But just Nichole. My ex would never let Ed, Jr. live with us, though, which is fine. I think he should be with his father at his age. How would you feel about Nickie living with us?"

"Not only one, but *two* pretty ladies living with me, are you kidding? Nickie's such a cool kid. I think it would be great! I've never had a family of my own before."

Joyce jumped up excitedly and said, "I'm going to call Ed right away to see what he thinks about it. I know he hasn't been getting along with Nickie lately. He just might go for it!" and off she went to the pay phone. Richard hated the idea of Joyce calling her ex and talking to him even briefly, but if it got him Joyce, it would be worth it. After a couple of minutes, Richard heard Joyce's loud, excited voice when she said, "Yes? Yes!"

When she returned, Joyce had been crying. She sat back down across the table from him again and put her hand on his. "I would love to marry you! By the way, Ed said that he'd let Nickie live with us since we were getting married and getting a house. He thinks a kid's got to have a house to be raised properly, can you believe it? Anyway, now he has no excuse to keep her from me. When were you thinking of setting a wedding date?" Joyce was smiling again.

"Let's see. Today is the 15th. How about the 17th?" Joyce's eyebrows shot up then and she laughed at his joke.

"Don't laugh! I'm serious. Come on, Joycie, that house won't be available forever."

"What about the blood test and all the wedding preparations? Planning all that takes time!" Joyce asked still smiling and with her heart full of hope.

"I already checked that out. There's a place called Lutes' Wedding Chapel. Everything's all set except selecting your dress and flowers. Let's go get a blood test and marriage license right now. After breakfast!"

The waitress came by to refill their coffee cups and sensed that she had interrupted something important. Joyce had a moment to think things over. Then enthusiastically, she said, "Let's do it!"

* * *

"Hi, Mom!" Joyce said excitedly. "I'm calling from J.B.'s restaurant. Richard just asked me to marry him over breakfast! I can't believe it! I said yes before I had a chance to chicken out. But I really do love him."

"*Who* asked you to marry him?" Lori wasn't ready for this. She had enough on her mind with Bill's heart problems.

"*Richard!*"

"You mean the one that came over for Christmas?" Surely she didn't mean that guy. Joyce always was slow to arrive at a serious relationship. Lori knew that Joyce had always been popular and had her pick of men who paid attention to her.

"Yeah, Mom, it's Richard!"

"Lori said, "Is he still working at P.J.'s with you?"

Joyce replied in the affirmative.

Lori continued, "It doesn't seem like you've known him very long, but at least this one's employed!"

"I think I've known him long enough. I think that working together has been a kind of crash course, as far as getting to knowing each other goes." Joyce said. "Richard comes from a solid Yuma family that's been here forever. They're all in the construction business. That's why he knows how to build things."

"Well, honey, it's your life. Are you sure?"

"Oh, Mom, he makes me feel so special and beautiful and I feel on top of the world when we're together! I feel like I've always known him. We're planning the wedding for the day after tomorrow."

Lori felt her face slacken in shock, "Now I *know* this is just a joke! You can't possibly expect me to make arrangements that soon!" She took the phone away from her ear and looked at it incredulously.

"*We're* making the arrangements ourselves, Mom. You don't have to do a thing, but come!" Joyce added with haste.

"But, Joyce, think about it. Have you gotten your blood tests yet? Have you gotten your marriage license?"

"We're going right now."

"Then you'll probably have a waiting period after that."

"Uh-oh, I guess we forgot about that. I'll talk it over with Richard. He's on his way to the restroom, so I'll catch him when he comes out." Joyce lowered her voice a notch, "Mom, Ed said if Richard and I get married, he'll let me have custody of Nickie! Isn't that great? Oh, here's Richard already. Hang on." Joyce and Richard had a quick discussion.

"Okay, I'm back. Richard suggested January 28th."

"Sorry, sweetie. That's no good for us. Dad has that angioplasty scheduled for that day in San Diego, remember? They said it's not major, but the sooner, the better."

Joyce shook her head at Richard to indicate that the 28th wouldn't fly. With controlled anxiousness, Richard snatched the receiver out of Joyce's hand and said, "Hello! How does Wednesday night work for you? That would be the 25th."

"Well, I guess it would be okay with us. Are you going to be good to my daughter?" Lori asked. She really didn't know the man, but wanted to be the purveyor of goodwill for Joyce's sake.

"Yes, ma'am! I think she'll agree that I've been treating her good so far." *What a dumb question,* Richard thought. *Like, what was I supposed to say . . . no?*

"Well, okay if you guys are sure. Can I talk to Joyce again?" The receiver was switched back.

"Hi, again," Joyce said.

"Well, sweetie, if this is what you really want and you're happy, go ahead then. It just seems to me that you don't need to be in such a rush about it. Are you sure that you're not just doing this so you can have custody of Nickie?"

"I'm sure, Mom. Please don't rain on our parade, okay?"

"Richard does seem to be a good guy, and I can tell by the sound of your voice that you're happy and excited. Are the three of you going to live in your little apartment?"

"He's already got that covered, Mom. Richard is renting us a furnished house from Phil Seward. I can't wait to see it! He says it's really nice and has nice furniture," Joyce reported gleefully.

"Honey, as long as you're happy, I'm happy. I'll trust that you know what you're doing. Like I say, it's your life," she said with resignation. "Where are you getting married?"

"At Lutes' Wedding Chapel. I'll bet Wednesday night will be easy to book. Will you help me pick out flowers and a dress?" Joyce knew Lori would be unhappy if she were completely left out of the planning, and as predicted, she jumped at the chance.

Lori remembered that in 1932 Tom Mix, star of over 300 silent movie Westerns, married his fifth wife, aerial performer Mabel Ward, at Lutes' Gretna Green Wedding Chapel in Yuma. It's a historic building that looks like it belongs on the original Bourbon Street in New Orleans. Even still, Lori thought, it was disturbing. Particularly when Joyce said she was getting married before she could change her mind. That was precisely why Lori felt that she should wait longer, but it wasn't up to her. It was Joyce's decision alone.

* * *

Joyce spent the next week sewing lace on the two flower girls' baby blue dresses and outfitting Nickie and herself for the event. She picked out yellow and white daisies and had her hairpiece washed and re-styled. These were busy, happy days for Joyce and her family. During that week, Lori began to accept Richard and found that she liked him a lot.

* * *

The nuptials were exchanged Wednesday night, January 25, 1994, before a few of Joyce's friends and all of her family. Joyce had asked Richard beforehand as to whom he'd like to invite to the ceremony. Surprisingly, he only invited his mother, who *also* had the first name of Joyce, and his younger brother, Ben, who was also doing life in prison on the installment plan but unbeknownst to Joyce was out at that time. That night the former Joyce Martinez became the second Mrs. Joyce Handcock in addition to Richard's mother, who was the first.

Richard's mother and Ben were no-shows at the wedding. Richard did arrange for Joyce to meet his mother later on, however, once directly after the wedding.

* * *

On the following Friday morning, Bill and Lori Perron went to San Diego for his angioplasty procedure. At 5:30 P. M., they took him from his room for a test, and a half hour later brought him back.

The surgeon and cardiologist entered Bill's hospital room and told them that the angioplasty wasn't needed. What he *did* need instead was a quadruple by-pass.

Lori called her daughter, Lynn, and told her about the surgery and that Bill was doing fine, all things considered. Then she asked Lynn to call Joyce and tell her about the situation.

Later, when Lynn telephoned, it felt odd to call her sister and have a man answer the phone. Joyce's old boyfriend never answered her phone. Unfortunately, she called just after Joyce stepped out. "Richard, I need you to tell Joyce about Dad's surgery. Please try to break it to her easy. Joyce and my dad are very, very close. I thought it would be better for you to tell her in person than for me to tell her over the phone." Richard promised that he would break it to her as gently as possible.

CHAPTER 8

On the very day that Joyce's stepfather had his heart surgery a twenty-six-year-old marriage was falling apart. Forty-eight-year-old Lieutenant Dale "Red" Pollock finally understood that his beautiful wife, Sally, was leaving him for good. She had been threatening to leave him for the last few years, but Red never believed she would do it until she did.

When Red came home from his shift in the late afternoon, all of Sally's belongings were packed and most were outside in a U-Haul truck parked in front of their house. Sally had hoped to be gone by then, but the process took longer than she thought it would. She had no idea how much stuff she had accumulated during their marriage. She was afraid that Red would get ugly if he caught her in the act of moving and he'd been known to be physically forceful before. Sally knew that as a police officer, Red could cause a lot of trouble for her if he wanted to. Fortunately, her brother had taken off work two hours early to help her with the heavy articles. Red respected her brother and wouldn't pull anything in front of him at least Sally hoped not.

Red had been a lieutenant for nine years with the Yuma Police Department and was the third man from the top of the pole in the chain of command. He'd been with the department for twenty-four years. He could have retired after twenty years, like Sally wanted him to do, but they had not managed their money well and couldn't afford it. Sally had told him that the money didn't matter. He could find some other job that wouldn't expose him everyday to the hind-end of humanity. With the pension money he could afford to work for a lower wage. Sally also said that Red was changing and she didn't like what the job was doing to him one iota. He was in a black mood much of the time, drank too much, and she suspected that he'd sold out on more than one occasion, though she never saw an influx of cash in the bank statements. Red had told her from the beginning that first and foremost he was a cop. His whole world was based on that one fact. That's who he was. The truth was, he liked to be both feared and respected--in that order. He needed that to make him feel important. Which was exactly why he couldn't bear the fact that Sally was leaving him. The guys at work and all his neighbors would joke about it behind his back. It was the typical cop can't hang onto his wife scenario *Couldn't park his hostility at the door and took it out on his pretty wife,* they'd say.

Lieutenant Pollock headed straight for the refrigerator and produced a beer. At least Sally stocked it beforehand. *The neighbors knew even before I did,* he thought. He walked into the living room with his beer and the *Yuma Daily Sun* that had been delivered that morning and ignored before he arrived. His favorite chair, and the television set that had been in the den, and one floor lamp was all that now occupied the seemingly cavernous room. Red pretended to read while he was trying to get a grip on his emotions that ran the gambit from self-hate to fury at Sally for bailing out. The two kids were grown and gone, it was true, but he always thought their marriage could survive anything. Sally had always been there for him. Now who could he turn to? He wasn't the sort of man who did well alone. If there was too much time and too much quiet, his thoughts and memories could make him go insane. What was he to do?

"Sally," he said as she walked by with a box of linens, "can't we at least still be friends?"

"I don't think that's a very good idea, Red. We both need to get on with our lives separately."

"So there *is* another man! I knew there had to be!"

"No, Red. You did this yourself. You caused it and don't try to push the blame onto me. If you hadn't been so self-absorbed, you would have noticed that our marriage has been shot since the kids left for college three years ago. Now, excuse me. I have a lot of work to do yet."

"Where will you be?" Red asked while he stared at the newspaper.

"I'll be at Mom's, but please don't try to get in touch with me. We just don't want the same things anymore, so there's no point. Just get on with your life."

CHAPTER 9

When Bill Perron came back to Yuma after his bypass surgery, Lori had been told by his doctors that he would be weak and sore and that any stress would interfere with his recovery. They said she should keep him away from day-to-day problems. Lori took off work for a week to care for him.

Down the street from the Perrons park model lived a retired nurse named Rachel Hammer. Rachel would walk over every day to check Bill's vital signs and protect him from potential visitors. Bill's friends had been told to stay away and even his adult children were only allowed five-minute visits.

Though worried about her stepfather's health, Joyce was a happy newlywed during this time. Lori was grateful that Joyce had Richard to lean on and she didn't need to wonder if Joyce was doing okay anymore. Lori had her hands full with Bill's recovery problems. The whole experience had been a glimpse at his mortality, and all too real. If they hadn't gotten Bill to the hospital when they did, she might have lost him. It was frightening seeing the once robust ex-Marine so frail.

Joyce and Richard moved into their newly rented house. Phil Seward, the old family friend of the Perrons and one of Yuma's most influential businessmen, had personally given them a proper welcome to their new home. His real estate office had rented the property to the Handcocks in late January 1994. It was all furnished and ready to walk right in with toothbrushes and suitcases in hand. Phil met them at the door to give them each a key and take a walk-through. Anything that wasn't as it should be would be noted by them in black in white. It was good business, even though he considered Joyce, and now Richard, as friends.

Phil was attractive for a man in his early fifties, and usually wore a suit in any one of a number of shades of gray, to set off his salt-and-pepper hair. He wore it stylishly long in the back in an effort to look more youthful. It was his best feature. He had blue ice chips for eyes and a nose that had been broken playing football in college. Tall and tan, he was still a decent figure of a man and he knew it.

Seward brought a fresh apple pie from the bakery in Albertson's as a welcome present. As he set it on the kitchen table, he said, I almost bought some vanilla ice cream so you could have pie a la mode, then I remembered that the refrigerator was still unplugged!" I hope you two will be very happy here. I know you'll be comfortable. The neighbors are great here and they have a neighborhood watch program on this street and the street behind this house. I don't know why. It's a very safe neighborhood. I understand that your daughter, ahh. . . Nickie, isn't it? Richard said she was going to be living with you again. I think that's just wonderful! A young lady *should* be raised by her mother."

Joyce answered smiling, "She's moving in on Saturday. She's going to love her new bedroom! We're very excited about it." And changing the subject, added, "I can't believe all the brick work that was put into the family room! It's so beautiful! I can't wait to sit in front of a cozy fire tonight! How about it, Richard?"

"Sounds great to me!" he said. "I'm glad you like it, too. I was a little worried that since I had already rented it for us and all. . . . "

"I'm really glad you did, too!"

"Well, I'll leave you two lovebirds alone. With Nickie gone, I'm sure you'll want to 'initiate' the house right away," Phil said with a devilish grin and a wink. It was the first time Joyce felt like he treated her as an adult. That comment made her blush and feel a little awkward, but Richard took her hand on cue.

"You're reading my mind!" Richard said.

"If you guys need anything more, just give me a call at the office or at home even. Here's my card. It has both of my phone numbers on it."

"You know, Joyce is like a member of my own family," Phil told Richard. "I've known her since she was just a teenager and she was as pretty then as she is now." Richard smiled and thanked him for personally coming to the house. Joyce always worried and stiffened slightly when a man said she was attractive in front of Richard. It would usually make him pout for a while. But in this case Phil was so much older; she didn't think Richard seemed to be too upset about the comment. Richard tended to be insecure about Joyce belonging to him and she felt that in time those jealousies would vanish. She would just love the insecurity right out of him.

* * *

As predicted, Nickie loved the house. She arrived on Saturday in Lynn's car. Lynn was usually the go-between for Joyce and Ed. She provided the buffer zone. Nickie thought her mom's house was even nicer than her dad's. As far as Nickie knew, the only problem connected to her living with her mother was that Joyce was always so broke and her dad's family had a stigma about children being raised in apartments, no matter how nice, as opposed to living in a house. Her dad felt that kids need a house to grow up in and the stability of not moving around.

Joyce's parents felt that this was why she had waited so long to re-marry; she finally found a man who treated her well. It was so good to see her happy. It was hard not to be happy too when you were around her. The Perrons felt that Joyce had chosen well and that Richard would take good care of their daughter.

Joyce enjoyed her new house. After cleaning it and making a few minor changes, she would walk outside and come back in, pretending she was seeing it for the first time as her friends would. They would be impressed and maybe a little jealous. She was hoping that they could get an option to buy it. Phil had told them that he thought the owners might eventually go for an option. He failed to mention that he *was* the owner. Maybe he could even use their rent money as a down payment! At 32 years old, Joyce felt like she finally was having the normal life she always wanted.

* * *

By late March of 1994, Bill Perron's health was much better. He and Lori both noticed that when Joyce and Richard visited, Richard was not as friendly as he had been previously. They told themselves that he was probably just having a bad day.

On one occasion, Lori visited Joyce at her new house and found that her daughter spent all of her time in her craft room, doing what she loved. She also noted that Richard would be in another part of the house doing his own thing and that they didn't seem to do anything together anymore. Not like when they were first married. There was something else. She noticed when Richard and Joyce did speak to each other, which was rare, and that their tone of voice was noticeably different. There was no "smile" in their voices. She could feel the strain between them and heard the sarcasm when they spoke to each other. It was like they would rather be somewhere else rather than with the other.

Shortly thereafter, Lori began to notice large bruises on Joyce's legs in varying degrees of freshness. Some of them were blue, purple, raspberry, or green and yellow. Joyce had said that she'd tripped at work behind the bar, but the marks looked like they couldn't all be from the same fall. Lori never knew her daughter to be anything less than graceful, but she let it go for the time being.

Joyce's mother had been physically abused by her first husband and knew the signs. She had always emphatically told both of her girls as they were growing up never to let any man get away with laying a hand on them in anger. She knew absolutely that she had impressed that upon them. This was exactly why Joyce *wouldn't* tell her mother and suffered in silence. Richard never hit her when Nickie was home, but the girl heard arguing almost every day after the end of March. It was impossible not to hear it, so usually Nickie would leave the house and walk over to her Grandma Perron's work to visit. The young girl didn't realize that she was putting her mother in physical jeopardy by her absence.

CHAPTER 10

By the end of March 1994, Richard had become disillusioned with his new bride. He had been confident that in time, Joyce would come around to his point of view in critical areas. But there was still that issue of the clothes she wore and the way she flirted at work. The men in P.J.'s gawked at her. Joyce was his wife, not theirs, and wives weren't supposed to dress sexy in public.

"It ain't right," his mother would say. "Married women ain't supposed do that way."

Richard visited his mother every week, as she lived just a couple of miles away from their newly rented house, and he *never* brought Joyce with him. The elder Mrs. Handcock lived in the same house that she and her husband had purchased in the 1940's before their two sons were born. It now needed fresh paint badly. Where it once stood stately on its high foundation, the house was now shrouded with junk strewn about the untended yard which was mostly left by Richard and his younger brother, Ben, over the years for storage.

The one time Joyce saw her mother-in-law was when they met once after the wedding. Mrs. Handcock, Richard's mother (the other Joyce in Richard's life), had told him to be patient with his new bride. She said that Joyce was just used to being single and probably would dress more appropriately in time. She hated to see Richard so unhappy. Even though he hadn't told her many details, she knew the marriage wasn't going well. She had been totally shocked when Richard hadn't married Hazel. Mrs. Handcock liked Hazel and they had a friendly relationship. Hazel sometimes came over to visit without Richard, and Mrs. Handcock thought she was such a lovely young woman.

"You know that Hazel has always been the love of your life. What on earth possessed you to marry another woman? You must'a had a fight with Hazel is all I can figure. But you know the two of you always kiss and make up eventually. What were you thinkin', for goodness' sake? You even found another bartendin' gal! Can't you see you were just tryin' to replace Hazel?" Richard shrugged.

Mrs. Handcock continued, "Maybe it would help if you got Joyce to quit workin'. Then you wouldn't have to worry so much if she was stayin' home workin' on her crafts that you been tellin' me 'bout." Just then Mrs. Handcock's little, black teacup Chihuahua jumped up to be cradled on her lap. The dog was still wearing a red Christmas tee shirt saying, *Ho! Ho! Ho! Y'all* on the back of it. Mrs. Handcock petted the dog's head with two fingers. Richard and his mother seemed oblivious to the thread bare furniture that surrounded them that had been there for as long as Richard could remember.

"I've already asked her to quit work, but she won't. She won't even look for another kind of job! I never had this much problem with Hazel working as a bartender. Hazel never flirted around like Joyce does," said Richard, selectively forgetting that he and Hazel had had several arguments about just the same thing.

His mother said, "Well, you didn't ask me first what I thought about you marrying that gal, but you made your bed, now ya just sleep in it. But if I was you, Mister, I'd put my foot down on 'er and be done with it." Mrs. Handcock knew how difficult Richard could be to live with, and secretly hoped he'd go back to Hazel. Hazel knew how to handle her son.

Richard started wistfully thinking of Hazel and missing her. He resented Joyce for coming between him and the "love of his life," like his mother said. He called the florist and again began sending flowers to Hazel at The Bottoms Up Pub twice a week. Most of the accompanying cards said, "I still love you."

He hadn't told Hazel about the marriage, but she had heard about it from reliable bar room gossip. She knew that he'd only married Joyce on the rebound and to get even with her. Richard didn't know that Hazel already knew who his wife was because Joyce had been in The Bottoms Up Pub a few times in the past. They had a conversation once about the pros and cons of bartending and some of the experiences they each had at work. They could never imagine how their two lives would become so intimately linked to each other. It was Joyce who didn't know about Richard's past or present with Hazel.

MURDER BY GRAVITY?

* * *

In late March, as Richard began to resent Joyce so much, she seemed to become even more defiant. She was tired of Richard telling her how to dress. She'd thought they were finished with that issue before they got married. He seemed to enjoy pointing out every little thing she did wrong. If she dropped something, he'd jump up and say, "What did you break now?" drawing everybody's attention to it and embarrassing her. Now Joyce was even more determined to maintain her own identity and she resented Richard for picking on her all the time. After all, it's not like he was such a prize.

One morning after Joyce got ready to go out Richard asked her where she was going. With the laundry basket under her arm, she thought it was rather obvious. "I'm going over to Ruby's to do the laundry."

"I don't want you to hang out with her. She's a slut!" He stood in her way and put his hands on his hips.

"I don't give a damn what you want!" Joyce said, her chin held up. "You can't tell me not to see my friends! Get out of my way!"

"So you finally admit it! *That* is the whole problem!" he hissed in her face. "You don't give a damn what *I* want! You smell like you took a bath in perfume. Is that for Ruby's benefit?"

"Get out of my way!" Joyce began to walk around him and as she did, Richard stuck his foot out and tripped her. It seemed to Joyce that from the time she began to fall until the time she hit the floor, everything moved in slow motion. She tried to grab onto the coffee table to break her fall, but it just ended up breaking her fingernails and scrapping her elbows and forearms. The air was forced out of her when she hit the floor with a thud. She was stunned and incredulous. The laundry had been flung across the entry.

This can't be happening! Joyce thought. But then Richard grabbed her by the calves and started pulling her down the long hallway toward the bedroom. In seconds, her backside started to burn from the carpet and she felt his hands bruising her legs.

"I *told* you . . . you're not visiting that slut and that's final! I been hearing about you and a guy named Mike Deere. Is *he* going to be there too?" He had seen the look of alarm on her face when he said Mike's name. Was it possible that Richard had heard about Mike

Deere and didn't realize that he was one of the regulars whom Richard had seen many times? She had been prepared for a talk about Mike when she and Richard were dating, but Mike just acted like any other customer when he came into the bar, and therefore the subject hadn't seemed necessary to bring up. Richard continued, "Ha! Didn't think I knew about that, did ya? Don't forget you're married to me and as long as you are, you'll see who I say!"

Then the seemingly impossible happened. Richard stopped suddenly and let her go. "You ain't worth it." And then he stepped over her and walked away. She heard the truck peel off as he backed out of the driveway and down the street leaving quite distinctive rubber marks on the driveway. Joyce's immediate reaction was relief from the fear of what she imagined he was about to do to her. Then, realizing that she was failing again at marriage, the tears came on and off for the rest of the day.

"I can't lose custody of Nickie! I've got to make this one work!" she sobbed. She washed a few of the clothes by hand in the sink and hung them to dry in the back yard.

* * *

As luck would have it, it was one of the customers at work who had mentioned to Richard that Joyce had history with a guy named Mike Deere before she began dating him. Joyce had been involved on and off with Deere in the past, but Richard had the misconception that something was still going on between them.

It was shortly thereafter that Richard devised a plan to alleviate his problems. He went to work early one night to have a heart to heart talk with the owner of P.J.'s. Tammy listened with grave interest while Richard told her about Joyce's illegal distribution of drugs from behind the bar at work and occasionally not ringing up bar tabs and pocketing the money. Tammy shook her head. It was all so hard to believe. She thought she knew Joyce better than that. But Richard had told her out of concern for his wife and had seemingly nothing to gain by telling her, as far as she could tell. He feigned being on the verge of tears by the end of his story. Tammy put a hand on his shoulder.

"It'll be okay. You did the right thing by telling me. We'll get her the help she needs, Richard. Try not to worry. I appreciate you being so candid with me about this. We will both keep an eye out to see that it doesn't happen again, but you should have a talk with her and convince her to stop immediately. Will you promise to let me know the next time it happens? I'm sure you realize how devastating this could be for me and the bar."

"Of course," Richard said, but was disappointed that Tammy didn't decide to fire Joyce immediately. He'd have to think of way to make that happen . . . and soon.

* * *

Joyce remembered when she was a little girl and crying for too long, her mother would give her shoulders a gentle shake and say, "Now stop that! Go wash your face and happy up!" Joyce did just that. At least she tried to. This wasn't a scraped knee or a broken toy. This was a marriage disaster. Joyce resolved that a divorce wasn't going to happen to her again in this lifetime. Not if she had anything to say about it. She managed to stop crying long enough to put her makeup on and get ready for work. But on the way to the bar, she started thinking about it again. She'd worn her designer jeans to cover her bruised legs. She dreaded seeing Richard at work, if he even showed up at all, which he didn't. Tammy said Richard had been in earlier to pick up his paycheck and that she couldn't imagine why he didn't return. Tammy also seemed angry to Joyce, but Joyce thought it was because Richard was a no-show.

That night at work, Joyce held herself together well until she saw Mike Deere. Though their on-and-off affair had ended well before Joyce met Richard, he still came to the bar often and they had remained friendly. She almost lost control of her emotions again in the telling of the day's events and other occurrences between her and Richard, but would reel her emotions back in with only the occasional tear. She had always been able to talk with Mike. They had been friends above all else. They called themselves "sex buddies" once upon a time. They always had fun in bed and liked role-playing sex games. It wasn't like "real life" but it had been a lot of fun. Joyce was missing fun in her life at the moment. Sex with Richard was unsatisfying and infrequent. The only time she smiled was at work anymore and not so often because Richard would accuse her of flirting. She was enjoying very much talking again with Mike, especially since Richard wasn't there to give her the evil eye. But as the night wore on, Joyce became more curious about what Richard might be doing. She couldn't have imagined that at the same time she was talking to Mike, Richard was having a similar discussion with Hazel.

* * *

Richard's recounting of the events portrayed Joyce as violent and unfaithful. That *he* was the one always getting hurt by Joyce throwing objects at him and punching and scratching him if everything wasn't to her liking. He was just a miserable, unloved victim stuck in a joyless marriage that should have never happened. He said that Joyce hadn't been like that before they got married. He said he'd only known her two or three weeks before the wedding. Marrying had been a sudden decision based on the devastating loss of Hazel on New Year's Eve. Joyce tricked him into marriage while he was on the rebound.

Hazel felt satisfaction from Richard's unhappiness, but part of her had softened after the flowers began arriving. These weren't just cut flowers this time; they were beautiful elaborate arrangements in reusable baskets, bowls, and vases. Hazel could physically feel the resolve to keep him out of her life begin to cave. She still loved him.

* * *

Joyce felt herself begin to relax again with Mike. She wondered why they had broken up in the first place. He sure turned her on more than Richard ever had! The old feelings began to stir for both of them. Mike hadn't had any serious relationships since the breakup with Joyce. It excited him to be coming on to a married woman. Could he break her resolve to be faithful to Richard? *Oh, yeah!* He thought. He held her when she cried. He knew she'd come back around.

"Will you let me buy you lunch tomorrow?" he suggested later. "You could tell Richard that you're doing laundry over at your

MURDER BY GRAVITY?

sister's and I'll bet she'll cover for you! He knows you didn't get the laundry done today."

Joyce thought about it for a minute and said, "Thanks, but I'd better not. I don't want to lose custody of Nickie, as much as I'd like to see you."

CHAPTER 11

Lori Perron looked at her watch and saw that she would have the afternoon free. She had taken the day off to take her husband to the cardiologist and there had been no waiting. The doctor had been optimistic about Bill's recovery because he had taken an active part in his own recovery. The concept of lifting and pushing no more than five to ten pounds with his arms for weeks during the recovery period had been a tough pill to swallow at first, but Bill finally made peace with it somehow. At first he had been invigorated with his increased blood flow, and understandably wanted to do more rather than less, but he still required a lot of sleep and rest.

Since Lori hadn't heard from Joyce during the weeks that followed, she knew that usually was a bad sign. Generally she called or stopped by when things were going well. Joyce didn't want her parents to know when she was going through a rough time; especially with her dad's health problems. She didn't want to upset either of them. Lori decided to stop by her daughter's house before Joyce had to leave for work.

* * *

When Lori arrived, she found Joyce busily working in the bedroom which had been designated as a craft room, where she was putting the finishing touches on a beautiful centerpiece. It was the only messy room in the house, but it was an organized mess of sorts. Joyce took pride in her new home and hoped to stay there forever. She was still optimistic about her marriage; at least to her mother she to appeared to be. Richard was at the other end of the house doing a project by himself; he was crudely cutting square frames for Joyce to paint and decorate. Even still, Lori thought she discerned an air of tension between the two of them. At one point Lori started down the hall to the bathroom and passed Richard then in the kitchen on her way. She stopped to say hello and chat a bit. After they exchanged greetings, Richard seemed reticent. She thought that perhaps he was just having another bad day, or that she had interrupted an argument. Joyce suddenly appeared in the doorway to steer her mother away from Richard.

"Mom, did you see how I fixed up the bathroom?" Joyce asked.

"No, I haven't been there yet," Lori said.

"Come with me. You've *got* to see the cute little hand towels I appliquéd. They look great with the floral arrangement I put in there. This is *my* bathroom."

Lori noted that Joyce didn't acknowledge that Richard was in the room. Quite a difference from the loving newlyweds they appeared to be so very recently. Later on they heard Richard yell, "Joyce, you left your damn craft crap in here!"

Joyce hollered back, "Leave it alone! I'll get it later." Lori thought that they sounded more like a couple who had been married five years instead of just three months. Their voice tones were strained and sarcastic.

"Is everything okay with you and Richard?" Lori asked softly when they were alone.

"Oh, yeah, everything's okay. Richard's not feeling so well today, that's all."

"I noticed he wasn't as friendly as he used to be. What's wrong with him?" Lori asked.

"He just feels a little punky. He doesn't have much energy. Probably just fighting off a bug of some kind." Lori let it drop.

* * *

The next time Lori saw Joyce a week later, she noticed more terrible bruises on her daughter's legs the size of grapefruit. Joyce told her she'd crashed into a wooden crate at work. Again, Lori knew her daughter was far from clumsy. A suspicion formed faintly in the back of her mind. She had seen these signs before firsthand when she was married to her ex-husband. She tried to toss the idea aside by telling herself that she was just being paranoid.

Joyce had witnessed some of what Lori had gone through years before when Joyce had been a little girl. Knowing that, she felt that Joyce would never stay with a man who abused her. Lori made sure that her daughters knew that if they found themselves in an abusive relationship, the only thing to do was leave. She told them that abusers almost always only get worse, very seldom better. Even counseling rarely helped these pathetic individuals. The violence was too deeply rooted in their personality. Lori's ex-husband never thought he was responsible for her black eyes and bruises. He said that she *made* him do it. Even so, he always apologized profusely after an episode of violence.

Lori felt assured that Joyce knew that if anything was happening at home of that nature, she should leave immediately and have someone else with her when she did decide to move out. Lori made sure her daughters knew that a large percentage of women are aggressively attacked while they are in the process of moving out of a marriage or relationship. They don't realize that they're putting themselves in danger by packing up alone after the spouse is notified of their intent to leave. When Joyce left Ed, there had been no problems, but mother and daughter discussed the possible scenarios beforehand. Ed wasn't violent, but he was macho.

The horror Lori experienced years ago flashed into her mind vividly. The first time her ex-husband attacked her was after they had been married for just two weeks. She had left the ceiling light on and was severely punished. These violent punishments over nothing became a common occurrence during their brief marriage during which time Joyce and her sister were born. Lori realized this behavior of her ex-husband's was all wrong, but no one had ever heard of "battered wife syndrome" back then. Her then-husband, Marc, assured her that all couples were like this behind closed doors. Lori knew her parents never fought physically and didn't believe him. Marc had told her that he'd witnessed his father, step-father, and grandfather beating their wives. He felt that it was only natural and Lori couldn't reason with him. She learned to be agreeable eventually, because she could never win an argument with him, and had to walk on eggshells around him or he would be punitive. Her nerves were shot. Her doctor told her she needed to change her life drastically soon as she was on the brink of a nervous exhaustion. He reminded her that if something happened to her, her husband would be left to raise the children.

Lori informed her ex-husband when he returned from work that same night that she had decided to move out. She told him that her doctor had told her to do it. To her surprise, her husband was calm; almost pleasant.

He said, "So when are you going to do this?"

She said she was taking the children and staying at her mother's house immediately and would be back in the morning while he was at work to get all of her things.

He said, "You don't have to stay there tonight. I'll sleep on the couch and I promise I won't bother you."

Lori was confused. This wasn't like him. He was actually being nice to her.

"If you leave now, you'll have to wake the girls. Why don't you just wait and leave in the morning?"

Lori said, "Well, I am tired. . ." She decided to take their bed and he slept on the couch as promised. At 5:00 A.M., when Marc's alarm went off, Lori went to the couch to wake him so he could get ready for work and went back to the bed to get a little more sleep before the girls awoke.

As sleep approached, she heard a noise that alerted her subconscious that something was nearby. She turned over and opened her eyes and saw Marc in the doorway.

"I think you should perform your wifely duties before you leave." His smile was grotesque.

"Forget it!" Before Lori could get up, he was all over her and ripping her night gown. "Please, noooooo!" He tried to beat her into submission, but Lori was determined that he was not going to have his way. She fought hard, but tired quickly. She was viciously raped. Marc was skilled in judo and had once shown her several possible ways to attack if she ever needed to protect herself. That's how she knew what was coming. He was sitting on her chest with his knees holding her biceps down to her sides, which efficiently eliminated the use of her arms for self-defense and caused serious bruising. He drew his right hand back with only his index finger and his ring finger extended. He had told her before that was how you could blind somebody; by poking them in the eyes. Just before the blow made contact with Lori's eyes, she turned her head quickly and sharply to the side. His fingers only caught her in the corners of her eyes. He was angry at her for moving and hit her in the face, breaking her nose. There was blood all over her and the bedding which enabled her to realistically pretend that she was dead.

As Lori had hoped, her ex-husband began to panic and ran to the bathroom down the hall to apparently fetch a cold washcloth or wash the blood off himself. He kept muttering, "Oh, no!" over and over to himself. It was then Lori seized the chance to dash out of the apartment and to the apartment managers who lived next door while trying to hold her tattered nightgown together. Lori sobbed as she told the management couple what happened and they were sympathetic and let her inside. Marc came to their door and they wouldn't let him inside. He stated that Lori was his wife and they were interfering. The manager was an elderly man but big in size and he just closed his door in Marc's face and called the police and let Lori call her mother.

When the police arrived, Marc was still there getting ready for work like nothing had happened. Thank goodness the children had slept through the entire assault. The police saw the state Lori was in when they arrived and the blood, but it was the year 1970 and they said that in the state of California this was considered a domestic problem and they couldn't get involved or make a report. Legally a man could do what ever he wanted to his wife short of killing her.

The police did let her get her children and Marc left for work at the same time. The whites of Lori's eyes were blood-red and stayed that way for a month. Lori didn't discover until later after the police left, Marc had taken a knife to all of her clothes hanging in her closet and shredded them. Lori wore clothing with several areas of zigzag hand stitches where the items had been slashed. It was two years before they all were eventually replaced with new ones. To this day, and after two surgeries, Lori still suffers from severe headaches caused by sinus problems complicated by the broken nose she received that day.

Lori and her daughters briefly moved in with Lori's mother until she could afford to move out into her own place. During that time, Lori's mother received a phone call from Marc saying that he was going to burn down her house.

MURDER BY GRAVITY?

After that, Lori knew it was better to live alone than to wish that you were alone. There are worse things than loneliness. Experiences of that nature tend to follow a person throughout life. In this case, it was manifested in Lori's inability to trust men. Bill had to break the fear and anger Lori had during the first two years of their marriage. It was only then she abandoned her *fight-or-flight* approach to relationships and life in general. But Bill loved her deeply and reassured her daily. Lori still locked her doors and windows when she was alone even in the daytime.

One day when Lori was working in the kitchen, Bill came into the room to make a sandwich. He hadn't realized that he'd inadvertently blocked her exit from the room. Lori began to perspire profusely and felt like she was going to vomit. She had begun to hyperventilate and would have eventually passed out. That was from just being blocked in a room! He also learned early on not to come up behind her quietly; no surprises for Lori. He occasionally forgot to watch out for these situations and felt badly when he saw her reactions. He would have beaten the tar out of her ex-husband if he had a chance, but the ex was long gone. Bill would have loved to have just ten minutes alone in a room with him. As a Marine, he had some slick moves himself. It galled him to think of a man laying his hands on a woman like that.

CHAPTER 12

In April of 1994, Richard had the occasion to drive Joyce's sister to the garage where her car had been repaired. It was awkward for Lynn, but Joyce volunteered Richard to drive her in his rusty, old and noisy pickup truck. Joyce had been insistent, and Lynn finally relented. Once on the main highway, Richard finally broke the silence that had fallen between them.

"I guess you know by now me and Joyce been having problems in our marriage," he blurted out. Lynn feigned ignorance and uncomfortably wondered what to expect. She had been against Joyce marrying Richard from the beginning and had told Joyce so. Quite simply, it was impossible to know a man well enough in the short period of time they'd been dating. It wasn't like Joyce to be so impulsive about a thing like marriage. When Joyce first announced the wedding was to be in the next couple of weeks, Lynn asked her privately if she could be pregnant and Joyce had denied it. When she found out that Joyce would be getting custody of Nickie because Richard's income could be counted in, it became crystal clear to Lynn why Joyce was getting married.

It seemed like a little thing, but Lynn had noticed from what Joyce had said that Richard didn't have any friends since high school; male or female. That made Lynn suspicious, especially because Joyce had mentioned that Richard came from a local family. Lynn was uncomfortable being alone with him.

Richard continued talking like he had found a comrade, "Joyce doesn't understand how a marriage is supposed to be. She always wants to take off with her friends like a school girl and I think she just needs to grow up!" Richard seemed to gain momentum and definitely volume as he spoke, "She needs to get away from all of 'em! I keep seeing Mike Deere drive by our house. Do you know if

MURDER BY GRAVITY?

Joyce is having an affair with him?" Lynn was dumb-struck by the suggestion. When he didn't get a response, he said, "I'm going to move us out to Phoenix pretty soon." He was silent for a moment then, "How come you don't dress the way she does? She does everything she can think of to look sexier. You grew up in the same house. Why aren't you like that?"

Lynn was incensed and tried to contain her rage. "First of all, Joyce and I are two *very different* people. And no, I don't think she's having an affair with anybody. I would know if she was. Also, I think Joyce always looks terrific, and you must have thought so too, or you wouldn't have looked twice at her! Furthermore, Joyce has always taken care of her responsibilities and that tells me that she's mature enough! I think that you should talk to Joyce about moving to Phoenix *first* before making a decision for all three of you."

Richard paused mulling over her words, but he was still whining about the clothing Joyce wore. "I think I'd be okay about her clothes if she'd quit working at the bar. The men are always looking at her and I've seen her flirting with the customers lots of times." Lynn loathed hearing a man whine. "I'm thinking about going back to carpentry. Then Joyce could stay home, work on her crafts and cook me and Nickie a good dinner."

After that last remark, Lynn realized that Richard was a hopeless chauvinist and reasoning with him was out of the question. It just seemed all the more peculiar that Joyce would choose him to marry. Still, there was a grain of truth in some of what he said. Joyce was different from the rest of her family. She had always been the "goodtime Charlie," as her dad would call her. Lynn and her parents were solid, middle class, and hard-working

Joyce loved people, but she loved to be alone at times too. She was comfortable in her own skin. Lynn was too self-conscious about her own body to dress the way Joyce did, not that her lifestyle and innate modesty would allow her to do so. Joyce loved attention, while Lynn liked to blend. She sometimes envied her sister's frankness and openness and secretly wished that she could "let go" like Joyce. Joyce was the most fun-to-be-around person Lynn had ever known. It was that same openness that caused Joyce to get hurt so many times in her life and Lynn hurt when her sister hurt.

***

Joyce and Richard argued persistently on a daily basis, often in front of Nickie, who came to dread going home from school and many times went to Grandma Perron's office instead. Sometimes Joyce came to pick her up from the office and her mother noticed still more of the large bruises on her legs. Joyce would always say she walked into furniture or fell over something behind the bar at work. Joyce knew her mother's facial expressions well; she knew what Lori was thinking. But Lori was holding her tongue, for now, and Joyce pretended not to notice.

The argument was usually the same. Richard wanted Joyce to quit working at P. J.'s, quit flirting and stop wearing sexy clothes. Joyce could never understand his position. She honestly didn't believe that she *was* flirting. She was just being a friendly bartender, which was part of her job. She knew her clothing was a little sexy, but that was just *her* personality and style. In high school, she'd once cut her hair very short and was mistaken for a boy a few times and she had been mortified. She never, *ever* wanted to be mistaken for a man from any angle again.

***

In mid-April, Joyce found Nickie in her room crying. She had worked hard to save the money she earned babysitting. She had temporarily left fifty dollars in cash on the coffee table while she put her books away in her room. When she came back, the money was gone. Nickie knew that Richard was the only other person in the house, so it had to be Richard that had taken it.

Nickie asked him for her money and she expected him to get after her for leaving cash lying around, but instead said, "What money?" Richard had always been nice to Nickie, even if he and Joyce were arguing. This was the first time he'd actually done something dirty to *her*. Nickie started to yell at Richard and he yelled back louder. Nickie stomped into her bedroom and slammed the door.

When Nickie told Joyce the story she was sobbing and angry. Joyce became livid. She went to Richard in the garage and spat at him, "You've done a lot of really rotten things before, but this is too much even for you! Stealing from a kid. . . . ." Richard didn't seem to care, he just laughed.

Within weeks of the incident, Joyce began missing pieces of jewelry. Believing she misplaced them, she asked Richard if he had seen them.

"Nope!" he answered, not missing a beat, "A lot of my things been missin' lately, too. We musta had a break in or maybe even two! Better call the cops and report it."

Joyce did as she was told; completely believing that someone had burglarized their house. Still, it seemed odd to Joyce that the television and some other electronics had been left and just jewelry and tools stolen.

Near the end of April, Joyce came home from work to find that Richard had left her. The previous day, Richard had a big, blowout fight with Tammy at work and he'd quit his job on the spot. Joyce couldn't believe how hotheaded he had acted and how he'd embarrassed her at work. They had not spoken a word to each other the following day. Richard then waited until Joyce went to work that evening then loaded his truck and disappeared into the night.

Joyce called everybody she could think of, hoping they would know his whereabouts. After two days, she started to worry seriously. She realized that now she could lose custody of Nickie and became frantic. She asked Tammy at work if she could take some time off to look for Richard. She was disappointed when Tammy said she couldn't.

Joyce said, "You've put me in the position of choosing between my job and my husband."

"Joyce, think about it. You can still look for him in the daytime and I can't imagine your savings would be enough to live on for long. Working would probably do you good!"

Joyce knew she wouldn't be able to concentrate on anything else and she'd be totally useless until she found Richard. And she just couldn't lose custody of her daughter again. This was her first priority.

"I just can't! I hope you can understand." And so it was that Joyce and Richard both had walked off from their jobs at P.J.'s within seventy-two hours of each other.

* * *

By June of 1994 Joyce was without a husband or a job. She realized by then that she'd made a terrible mistake and Tammy had been right. Shortly after Joyce quit, Nickie and Joyce's son, Ed Jr., made a three-hour journey to Phoenix to stay with their aunt from the Martinez side of the family for the whole summer. Her ex-husband, Ed, had unilaterally made an executive decision and informed Nickie that she was going and Joyce was in no position to stop him. He now had the upper hand legally.

Joyce felt that she had lost everything important to her, including the house they had rented. She didn't have the money to pay June's rent but hoped that she wouldn't have to move out before the first of July. She had once planned to spend the rest of her life in that house and had spent hours in customizing it. She was heartbroken and at her lowest point. She hadn't been this depressed when her first marriage ended. This time it was different. She had *appreciated* everything she had, even though it hadn't been perfect, it was better than being alone.

* * *

Monday, June 13, 1994, Joyce watched television with the rest of America as news unfolded in the Nicole Simpson and Ron Goldman dual murder case. A knock at the door led her to Phil Seward's kindly face saying that he was embarrassed to ask why they hadn't paid the rent for June yet. Joyce invited him in and they sat at the kitchen table drinking coffee while Joyce sobbed and told him the story about Richard leaving and Nickie being sent to Phoenix and her being out of a job. Phil had been sympathetic.

Joyce excused herself to clean up her smeared mascara and walked into the bathroom, but left the door open. Within seconds Seward was all over her like a cheap suit; groping and trying to fondle her. Joyce was utterly stunned.

"What the hell are you doing? Stop that! Get you hands off me!" she started slapping him, but it only seemed to excite him further. He laughed.

"Come on now, Joyce! You know you want it as much as I do!" He had a sickening leer on his face and his after-shave was overpowering.

MURDER BY GRAVITY?

"No, I *don't want it!*"

He wrestled her down to the carpet in the hall. It became almost comical in a bizarre way. Phil would unbutton and unzip her blue jeans then he'd discover that she had her ankles crossed and legs locked together. Next, he'd manage to pry her legs apart and found that Joyce had been re-zipped and re-buttoned her pants while he'd been occupied by her legs and ankles. When he undid the pants again, her legs would be locked together again. During the whole process, Joyce kept trying to push him away so she could get up, but each time, she just managed to push herself back further up the hall. She could feel the rug burning her shoulders blades and buttocks as she pushed herself backwards and away under his weight.

Finally, in desperation, she said, "Phil, if you don't stop this right now, I'm going to sue you for everything you have! You know I will, too! Haven't you heard that sexual harassment is against the law?"

Phil had been about to unlocking her ankles again, but he suddenly stopped and rocked back on his heels and spat, "Fine! I want you out of this house immediately! And the furnishings *stay*, or it'll come out of your deposit. In fact, forget about getting your deposit back at all, you bitch!" He then got up and stomped toward the door while adjusting his clothes. Joyce thought he was acting like a two-year-old having a tantrum.

She called after him, "I'm leaving the end of the month and you'd better not try to move me out any sooner! Do you hear me?"

"You're a bitch just like your ol' lady!"

At that moment they both noticed Ruby had arrived and let herself in the unlocked door. She had been standing in the entry quietly and heard enough to get the gist of what had happened between Joyce and Phil.

As Joyce pulled herself upright, she said, "Yeah, well, *this* bitch has a *witness!*"

* * *

Just before the end of June, Richard swung by the house to pick up some tools he'd forgotten to take with him. Joyce had been so happy to see his truck in the driveway. She assumed that he'd returned for good.

Richard was not happy to be there and he wouldn't talk to her when she asked questions about where he'd been and why he left. She followed him through the house trying to get his attention. Richard found whatever it was he needed and headed back out to his truck. Joyce was crying hard by then and tried to physically get him to stay with her. She begged him and pleaded. She figured that if he stayed, they could work things out. He knocked her down onto the cement driveway and she grabbed his ankles trying to prevent him from getting into the truck. Her fingernails sunk into his calves and drew blood. Richard had made the cuts worse by pulling away from her. He physically dragged her body with his leg to get back to his truck and was seemingly unmoved by her tears and pleas. In his mind, this was just another incident of Joyce being violent towards him.

CHAPTER 13

The sweet scent of jasmine lingered in the living room from the large bush outside the sliding doors of Lynn's apartment where Joyce went to stay. Lynn had never seen her sister look so beaten by stress and had insisted that Joyce remain with her for a while so she could keep an eye on her. Joyce had no idea what to do with herself for the first time in her life. She had put off thinking about her situation and she realized that she was unprepared to make any life-altering decisions.

Joyce was unable to focus her mind on anything other than Nickie and Richard and the Phil Seward episode. From what Lynn saw, it seemed almost like Joyce was suffering from post-traumatic stress disorder. She tried to draw Joyce out of her private thoughts and into conversation. For the first three days, Joyce sat on the sofa staring out the window. She noticed after a couple of days that her sister had made pets out of several roadrunners, by giving them small balls of raw hamburger in the afternoon. Joyce watched them gather around the back door, their posture straight, and movements rapid. Every little while, from seemingly out of the blue, she would begin to cry again. The only time she looked alive was that she was eating more food than she ever ate in her life. She was voracious. Lynn was unsure when this behavior had begun. Joyce had been like this when Lynn came by the house for a visit sometime around the end of June. Joyce told her then that she had to move out of the house by the first of July because she couldn't pay the rent.

Lynn had taken Joyce over to You Store It, and had her rent a storage locker about the size of a good walk-in closet. Joyce's friend, Mike Deere, had stopped by Joyce's when he saw Richard's truck was gone and Lynn's car there in its place and volunteered to pay for the first few of months rent on the locker until Joyce was on her feet again. He took the cash from his wallet and said he was glad to do it for her. He had been driving by Joyce's house in his beige Jeep nearly every day; hoping that Richard and Joyce would split up. He was certain that it would happen eventually. All he had to do was wait it out. His routine drive-bys did not go unnoticed by Richard, who had finally put it together by then that Mike Deere was Joyce's old boyfriend and each time Mike passed their house it was a catalyst for Richard's anger and arguments ensued. Richard no longer believed Joyce's claims of fidelity, which infuriated her.

Lynn and her husband did most of the packing and moving for Joyce, being careful to take only the items they knew were Joyce's and not part of the home furnishings. They brought some of her clothing, makeup, and sundry items to their house along with some unfinished craft supplies for Joyce to work on when she felt better. Joyce seemed trance-like, moving slowly, eyes dull and staring. When Joyce wasn't eating, she was sleeping for ten to twelve hours at a time and longer if Lynn let her. Lynn got their mother on the telephone at one point and both she and their mother tried to get Joyce to tell them what had happened, but she would just shake her head when they asked.

Lynn said into the phone, "Mom, she just keeps shaking her head!"

On the morning of the fourth day at Lynn's house, Lori came to visit Joyce in person. She always had a way of bringing her sometimes flighty daughters back down to earth when they got carried away as youngsters. Joyce broke down when her mother walked in the door and Lori took her in her arms. Joyce's whole body was wracked by the force of her sobs. When she finally was able to get herself under some control, Joyce told Lori and Lynn about Richard's disappearance, and how they both had quit their jobs at P. J.'s. When she got to the part about her ex-husband sending both of her children away from her for the entire summer, she started to cry again.

Lori wasn't really surprised; secretly she had been hoping she was wrong about the feelings she had about the sudden marriage. After she got Joyce calmed, the pragmatic Lori started making regrouping plans.

MURDER BY GRAVITY?

"It seems like the first order of business is for you to get yourself a job," Lori said as Joyce rested her head on her mother's shoulder. "I ran into Roy, you know, the guy that works at our RV park? He said they're looking for a bartender at the 8th Street Tavern. I guess it's not such a great location, but at least you could start right away and look for something better during the daytime."

Lynn was enthusiastic, "That sounds like a good idea, Mom. Joyce, how about we go over there tomorrow morning around eleven? I'll wait in the car while you're doing your interview and we can go out for lunch afterwards, my treat. What do you think?"

Joyce sat up straight and for several seconds looked seriously at the two of them. Finally, sounding tired she said, "I guess I have to do something . . . I mean, I can't stay here with you and David forever."

"You know you're always welcome here," Lynn responded automatically, but sincerely.

Joyce smiled, "And that's the way I want to keep it! What the hell? Okay, let's do that." Lynn and Lori grinned at each other and at Joyce. With the family's love, she would get through this.

* * *

Richard waited impatiently for Ron Gene to get off the phone which had interrupted his sales pitch. He hoped to talk Ron into letting him live in a twenty-four-foot trailer Ron owned in exchange for fixing it up. Richard also offered to help out at his construction materials supply lot.

Richard had met Ron, a down-to-earth gritty businessman in his late fifties, while purchasing items for different jobs he had worked on over the years. If Ron didn't have it on his lot, you didn't need it. While Ron had initially not been interested in his spiel, Richard felt he was softening up just before the phone rang. The trailer Ron owned was already parked in a nicely kept RV park in the Foothills area. There were no frills, but that was just fine with Richard. His truck camper was so full of his stuff there was nowhere to sleep in it.

"Where were we?" Ron said as he hung up the phone. "Oh, yeah . . . the trailer on Araby Road. Yeah, needs some siding work done on the inside, steps built, paint, shelves built and what not. A little tender loving care would make a big difference."

"I already peeked in the window and that's no problem. You know I'm a carpenter."

"Yeah; industrial. There's a difference!" Ron said.

"I've worked on every house or apartment I've ever lived in. Besides, I cut my teeth on carpentry in residential when I was a kid."

"How long do you think it'll take?"

"A few weeks, maybe."

"Okay, then," Ron said as he extended his hand to shake with Richard. "I think I have plenty of little jobs to keep you busy for a while. You can go ahead and move into that trailer. You don't need no key. Lock's been busted for a coon's age."

"Great," Richard said as he shook Ron's hand.

* * *

Though she felt like death warmed over, Joyce forced herself to go through with the interview. She didn't tell her family that on top of everything else, she had been suffering from the lingering effects of methamphetamine withdrawal ever since she ran out of funds. She let the others attribute her tremors, nausea, and flushing to her timely nervous upset. Mike had slipped her a small amount of meth in an empty film container, enough to get her through a few days of work. Joyce started the job at 8th Street Tavern the next day. The day she found out that she got the job, she called her mother to tell her the good news, knowing it would make Lori happy.

Lori said, "I'm so glad! You know, I think you're probably better off without Richard around," she said with a mixture of sympathy and relief. I noticed your bruises from your 'accidents' are going away." Joyce became stoical and silent, which is always awkward on the telephone.

"Mom, there's something more I didn't tell you yet. A week or so after Richard moved out, Phil Seward came over and almost raped me!"

"What? Oh, come off it, Joyce! Phil isn't that kind of man. He has a beautiful wife and family. Why would he try to attack *you?*"

"*I* don't know, but he did."

There was a pregnant pause then and Lori sighed. "We've known him for so long, honey. I just don't believe it."

"Oh, good! Insult added to injury! Thanks for the vote of confidence, Mom! You could believe my husband was beating me, but not Phil Seward trying to rape me! Well, I've already sworn out a complaint of sexual harassment against Phil, and we're going to court over this. I can't believe that you're taking his side! At least Lynn believes me. This is just great!" Joyce said sarcastically.

"I'm sorry, but I just can't see Phil as a would-be rapist! I know for a fact he's in love with his wife. Please don't do this. You'll ruin your reputation, his reputation, and hurt his whole family! What good do you expect will come from this? Can't you give a good friend a little slack? He's been there for us many times. I'm sure it must have been a misunderstanding."

"Such a good friend, huh? He called you a bitch, Mother!" Then Joyce hung up the phone on her.

That day Joyce moved out of Lynn's place to avoid seeing her mother and into her friends Ruby and Jeff's apartment. In fact, for the next two months, Joyce uncharacteristically didn't speak to her mother. Even Lynn, who received the occasional phone call from Joyce during that period, couldn't get her sister to say where she was staying. She knew better than to press too hard. Lori tried to telephone Joyce at work and Joyce hung up the phone immediately. Knowing Joyce's state of mind, it was a particularly worrisome time for Joyce's mother and sister.

* * *

Soon after starting work at 8th Street Tavern, Joyce fell back into her daily use of methamphetamine. She began to snort it instead of smoking it, particularly at work. The drug wasn't as potent that way, nor as quick-acting, but at her present job, she didn't have anybody to watch over the bar while she stepped outside or into the restroom to smoke the drug. This way, she could conveniently snort the chemical from behind the bar discreetly while she pretended to retrieve some item from a bottom shelf. Normally, the use of meth progressed from snorting to smoking, not the other way around, the next step being to shoot it directly into the veins. Her habit, which had begun as twenty dollars a day, grew quickly to between thirty and fifty dollars. That was not a problem for her as she usually received enough tip money to cover the cost of it. Still, she was not just a recreational drug user; she was addicted. More importantly, Joyce quit caring about her life and any goals or hopes she may have had at one time. She lived one day at a time in an altered state, usually a combination of meth and alcohol, which has the effects of being high or inebriated from the alcohol, but wide awake, energetic, and euphoric. Fortunately, Joyce was young and in otherwise good health and had no residual health problems from her drug and alcohol use.

Joyce began to date Mike Deere to help forget about her failed marriage. He was a lot more fun than Richard ever could be. He liked for them to dress as characters and act out their sexual fantasies. They were both always trying to surprise and delight each other; the more outrageous the fantasy, the better. Drugs and alcohol were always part of the mix. Whether it be meeting in bars and pretending that they were strangers picking each other up, or thumbing through the Kama Sutra, fetishes or voyeurism and exhibitionism. They were into all of it. Sex was a sensual celebration. Richard didn't have a clue.

Sometimes their fantasies included other people joining them. One night, Mike asked a friend of his, Danny Brooks, to join them in a threesome. Danny worked with Mike at the United States Mining Company on day shift. Danny was lanky and tall, well-built, good-looking with sandy blond hair and an easy, relaxed smile. Nothing against Mike, but Joyce's relationship with him had never been a serious one. Danny was something else. Joyce could really fall for him. When he flashed his dimpled smile at her, she felt like a school girl with her first crush.

After that first night with Danny, Joyce began seeing him exclusively for the next three weeks. Danny kept company with Joyce in the evenings while she worked at 8th Street Tavern. In July the patronage was slow enough that they usually played darts together. Joyce never won playing against Danny, but she didn't mind. The two of them had become inseparable. Though Joyce was immensely happy with Danny, he wasn't enough to fill the void of losing her daughter. In Joyce's mind, the only way she could get custody of Nickie again was to find Richard and convince him to

MURDER BY GRAVITY?

come back to her as her husband. But she had no idea where he was. She did wish, however, that she had met Danny before she met Richard. They agreed on nearly everything and he was gentle. To Joyce, that was incredible. Danny was also much better-looking than Richard and there was no comparison in bed. Danny was an ardent and giving lover. Not at all like Richard's two-minute teasers, as she had come to think of it. Joyce had realized too late that she couldn't teach him sensuality. People either had it innately, or they didn't have it at all.

* * *

On July 30, 1994, Richard appeared at the 8th Street Tavern. He sat at the end of the bar and waited quietly for his turn to be served. Joyce saw him almost immediately. Other than trembling hands, she kept her cool. She approached him with a cautious smile. He smiled back and asked if he could have a beer. As Joyce fetched his favorite, she tried to gain control of her nerves, but seemed powerless. Her heart felt like it would burst through her ribs and she almost dropped the bottle before she got back, which drew attention from some of the regulars. Her mind raced as she tried to find the words to make him come back to her. Danny was playing darts and unaware of what was transpiring at the bar.

"I forgot how beautiful you are," Richard began. Joyce was quite taken aback. She thought he might say something about her flirting with customers when he came in, but he didn't. She suddenly remembered Danny and glanced discreetly in his direction. To her relief, she saw the back of his head. He very easily could cause a problem, though, and she silently sent up a little prayer.

Richard lowered his voice, "Can we talk here?"

"Sure, for a while. . . "Joyce replied. "It's good to see you, Richard."

"I want to talk about us getting back together, baby. I can't even remember why I left now."

"I think it was over a dumb job," Joyce offered, eyes tearing up slightly. "Not exactly a good reason to break up a marriage over."

Richard quickly agreed with her. "Where are you living now? I drove by the house first. Looks like it's empty now . . .?"

"I'm staying with Ruby and Jeff right now. What about you? Where are you living?" she asked.

"Winterhaven RV Park, in a trailer. I get to live in it in exchange for some repairs the owner wants on it and I also help out at Swift Sales for a little cash. Remember I introduced you to Ron Gene at Swift Sales when we went there once for some wire?" Joyce nodded. "He also owns the trailer, which is nice, but it doesn't have any air conditioning in it. I'll probably have to get a motel for the month of August." Richard paused then said, "Look, I've got to go right now. I didn't see your car in the parking lot. What if I come over at quitting time to take you home? Maybe we could swing over to my place on the way. I'd like to show it to you. Maybe you can give me some ideas on how to decorate it."

"Jeff Dupree gave me a ride this afternoon. I don't have a ride home yet." It was a lie, but she figured that she could make it true soon enough. "So, I guess I'll see you around one o'clock then." It's the law that all bars close at 1:00 AM in Arizona.

Richard chug-a-lugged the last of his beer, handed her the empty bottle and left a $5 on the bar for her as he belched. "I almost forgot. . ." and handed Joyce a red rose from behind his back. "I'll see ya later."

Joyce knew that night there would be no decorating going on later. She needed to have a "bump" of meth and talk right away with Danny. But at least she had been honest with him from the beginning that getting back together with Richard might happen down the road. "I'm sure going to miss him," she thought.

"Our timing was just wrong." Joyce was surprised that Danny was so crushed when she told him. That was when he chose to tell her that he loved her. Joyce wanted to be with him too, very much, but she wanted Nickie back even more. "Let's just see how it goes for now, okay?" Joyce said to him.

Defeated and reluctant, he would do whatever she wanted. "I can still see you at work, at least, can't I?"

"Sure you can. I hope you know that I'm only doing this to get custody of my daughter. I have to do this."

* * *

MURDER BY GRAVITY?

The next day Joyce moved in with Richard. Two days later at work, Joyce heard that Danny had been arrested for possession of meth and would do some time in jail; most likely, six months. To Joyce it was a sign that this was meant to be.

Four days later, Joyce and Richard unloaded the junk from Richard's camper and stored it in the trailer and the two of them took off for Mittry Lake near the Gila Gravity Canal. They reasoned that since they were going to be hot anyway, at least they could take a dip in the lake when they wanted and go fishing together, which they both enjoyed. And they'd have all the privacy they wanted. They made love under the stars and, while Richard wouldn't talk about it, Joyce got him to write down his sexual fantasies, which included a threesome with them and Ruby. Joyce was delighted and couldn't wait to tell Ruby about it.

CHAPTER 14

The August temperatures in Yuma average between 106° and 116° in the shade. Some rare years it's as high as 126°. Locals call it the monsoon season because clouds move in and cause some palpable humidity, not generally rain, but it is a contrast to the usual arid climate. Even with the Mittry Lake nearby, Joyce and Richard found living in the camper unbearable. Overnight temperatures didn't drop below 92°, so there was never any relief from the heat in which to sleep. Being hot and uncomfortable did little to improve their temperaments. They decided to move temporarily to The Palm Terrace Motel. It wasn't fancy like the dozens of upscale chains in Yuma, but it did have air conditioning.

Richard stopped by to see Ron Gene at Swift Sales to tell him that he had put off working on the trailer on Araby because of the heat and that he'd left a few of his things in it. Richard had the lock on the trailer repaired and gave Ron one of the keys.

"So, where are you staying, then?" Ron asked.

"My wife and I are staying in a motel right now."

"Wife? You never told me you were married! A motel, huh . . . well, that's too bad," Ron paused looking thoughtfully at the manufacturer's pamphlets stacked on the front counter. "I just had an idea. If you guys agree to fix it up, I have another trailer out back. It needs a lot of sprucing and repairs, but the air works good. Why don't you go out there and see what you think?" Ron said, handing Richard another set of keys.

* * *

Later the same day, Richard and Joyce moved into the trailer on the Swift Sales Supply lot, which covered several acres. They were glad to be in a bigger rig: a thirty-two footer, but it needed far more work than the trailer on Araby. They spent several days just cleaning in their free time before they could really call it home. The first night they had to sleep outside, or more romantically speaking, al fresco as Joyce preferred to call it, in their two well-worn chaise lounges. They were surrounded by Joyce's craft debris, Richard's tools and Swift Sales' large bric-a-brac and heavy equipment that were gathered there in the back of the lot where the trailer was located. Huge spools of wire, strapping, cement pylons and machinery partially blocked the view of the trailer from the office in the front of the lot and from the street, but it could be seen if one put a little effort into looking. Joyce and Richard were by now accustomed to living by the lake and sleeping outdoors. But they were also *unaccustomed* to having company around them.

The next night, they put away their belongings that had been stacked on the bed, nearly up to the ceiling, so they could walk more easily through the trailer to the bathroom. The trailer was built with a multitude of storage areas to fill, tuck, or load.

It wasn't long before Joyce was known and noticed by all who worked and bought at Swift Sales. She would come out of her trailer late in the morning in a bikini to sun herself on the chaise lounge. After a few days of this, Joyce came out as was her custom, anointed herself with tanning oil, then remembered that she needed to do some grocery shopping. Since Richard was out on an odd job, Joyce walked up to the Swift Sales office, still clad in the bikini, and asked if she could use Ron's office phone to make a call.

Ron Gene was rather shocked, but managed to compose himself, and said that she could use the office phone occasionally if she kept her conversations short and local. Two contractors who had been talking with Ron before Joyce's entrance stopped and stared at her. Ron noticed that his lot employees, who had been deployed to other various areas on the lot, were gathered outside the glass door of the office on the pretense of getting water and were also taking in the view. Ron knew for a fact that this happened frequently since Joyce's arrival. Whenever she was outside they would gather nearby and talk amongst themselves and joke. Those within earshot listened to Joyce's phone conversation that morning as she turned her back to them, providing the opportunity to gaze at their leisure.

"Hi, Mike. I need to go to the store today. Are you using your car for the next couple of hours? Richard's gone and my car's battery is dead. Can I borrow the Jeep?" Joyce stopped to listen to Mike then said, "No, that's okay. I'll ride my bicycle over and pick it up. Thanks, Mike." She turned around in time to find that her backside had been intensely scrutinized as she saw their embarrassed faces search for something else on which to focus their eyes. She smiled with enjoyment, proud of her figure.

After that incident, the men at Swift Sales saw Joyce riding her bike and driving Mike Deere's beige Jeep. It got so bad with the employees gawking at Joyce that Ron felt that he needed to have a word with her about it. The brief discussion took place in his office the next time Joyce came up to use his phone dressed in tight biker spandex shorts and a tube top.

"Hello, Ms. Joyce," Ron said. "I've got to ask a little favor if you don't mind. I need you to dress a little more conservatively around here. My employees ain't getting a lick of work done!" he chuckled, but his looked told Joyce that he meant it.

"Can I still sunbathe right next to the trailer?" she persisted.

"They can still see you back there, dear. Sorry."

"That's okay."

Ron was relieved that part of the conversation was over, but then he remembered that he hadn't heard any sounds of repair work going on back there yet and felt he might get a more truthful answer from Joyce than he would from the fast-talking Richard, so he asked her, "How are the repairs going on the trailer back there? Any progress yet?"

"Richard's workin' on it! The air conditioning is wonderful! We're both very grateful. Would you mind if I use your phone again now?"

"Not at all," Ron replied.

Joyce picked up the phone and dialed. "Hi, Mike! I thought I'd come over, if you're going to be home for a while." Then she laughed. "I'm going to call Lynn and see if she'll cover for me if Richard calls looking for me. I'll see ya later, then."

Ron was a little surprised that Joyce would make a call like that in front of him. He was uncomfortable, so he prepared to go outside on the pretense of checking for some inventory. Before he left, he heard Joyce make another call.

"Lynn, can I get you to do me a favor?" Lynn must have agreed. Ron rifled through some invoices on his desk to take outside with him. Joyce continued, "Could you tell Richard, if he calls, that I came over to your house to do laundry and I just stepped out to run some errands in your car today?" Joyce listened for a moment then said, "No, everything's fine right now, I just want some time to myself, that's all. I might go over to see Mike today, too." She listened again. "I know, I know. But will you please just do it?" Then, "Thanks, hon, I owe you one."

Ron ventured a look up at Joyce before he walked out the door and she winked and smiled at him and walked out the door before he could. Joyce hopped on her bicycle and rode off. Ron just stared after her in disbelief. Once again, seeing Joyce on her bike riding back and forth and driving the beige Jeep was a common sight. He couldn't get over the fact that she would be that obvious about sneaking around in front of him. He didn't like that she was making him feel like he was part of her deception.

* * *

Late one afternoon, Richard came into the supply lot office from one of his construction job locations where he worked during the day and used the phone to call Joyce at the bar where she worked. The conversation had been brief and heated and Richard hung up the phone abruptly.

"Damn woman!" he said to Ron's distracted face. He had been working. "Have you seen a guy who drives a beige Jeep around here during the day?"

Ron answered honestly, "Nope, I sure haven't." He only noticed when Joyce was driving it.

Richard was standing near the front picture window in the office and shouted, "Look! There's the son of a bitch driving by right now!" as he pointed his finger at the street. Richard got back in his truck and peeled boisterously out of the lot leaving behind a cloud of dust.

* * *

The next morning, Ron was opening up the office for the day when Bryce, his right-hand man and supervisor, walked in and asked him if he'd seen Joyce sleeping in front of the trailer.

Ron wasn't terribly surprised, but he walked to the window at the far end of his office to see for himself. The old floorboards creaked in complaint of his weight as he moved across the room. Sure enough, Joyce appeared to be sound asleep in one of the loungers, fully dressed in the same clothes she had on the day before. The lot crew employees saw her still there whenever they walked by that area all morning.

Just before noon they heard Joyce pounding on the trailer door, insisting that Richard open up. Richard's truck was there, but he didn't answer her as far as anybody could tell. Joyce came up to the office to use the phone to call her sister. Ron heard Joyce tell Lynn that Richard had kicked her out of the trailer and wanted to know if Lynn could come pick her up.

While Joyce waited for Lynn, she went back to the trailer and pounded loudly on the door again. "Could you at least give me some clothes so I can go to work?" She pleaded with Richard, but he didn't budge or comment. Finally, Joyce left.

During the month of September 1994, Joyce Handcock spent nearly a half-dozen nights sleeping outside the trailer because she had been locked out by Richard time and again. During that month, people at the lot and next door at the Jordan Seed Company, which is more than 100 feet away from the lot line, heard Joyce and Richard yelling at each other and arguing almost daily. Ron felt sorry for Joyce. A number of times she came to the office to use the phone and would be crying. Joyce admitted to Ron that she and Richard were having problems and she cried on his shoulder.

Ron did express his concerns to Joyce about her sleeping outside that time of year when the nights were warm and the occasional snake or scorpion might make an appearance. Every year they found a rattlesnake, tarantula, or a sidewinder sleeping under the equipment around the lot. Joyce said that she was aware that could be a problem and always watched where she walked at night and used a flashlight. But she felt that she didn't have any choice but to sleep outside. It did make her nervous, she said.

One time Joyce came to the trailer in a car and loaded it up with her things while Richard was gone. A few days later she was back again. Ron saw Joyce outside one afternoon hanging onto the chain-link fence that divided his property from The Seed Company's property. She was sobbing hard as she clung to it.

Shortly thereafter, Joyce began to dress more conservatively. She bought a battery and started to drive her own car again. By then, everyone around the lot knew that the guy who drove the beige Jeep by the lot nearly everyday was Joyce's old boyfriend.

Joyce finally got in touch with her mother again and they had several heart-to-hearts. Lori kept advising Joyce to leave Richard and move out of that "junkyard," but her words fell on deaf ears. So did her pleas to drop the Phil Seward sexual harassment case.

Joyce drove over to P.J.'s to visit Ruby, who greeted her with a hug. Joyce brought in a huge cardboard box in her arms.

Ruby said, "Okay. I'll bite. What's in the box?"

"I brought you some of my clothes," Joyce said.

"Why on *earth* would you wanna do that?" Ruby was incredulous.

"Richard says I'm being greedy because I have so many and wanted me to donate some of them to the Salvation Army. But I thought these might look real cute on you."

Ruby sorted through the contents and made an observation. "These are some of your nicest outfits!" she exclaimed.

"They're also my sexiest outfits, and you know how Richard feels about that."

"So what? Are you giving in to him now? There's absolutely nothing wrong with the way you dress! He should have his head examined. You're only going to encourage him by doing whatever he wants you to do. *He's* got a problem. Not *you!*"

Joyce was resigned to it. She looked away somberly and said simply, "Do you want them or not? If not, they're going to the Salvation Army."

Ruby said, "Okay, already! I'll take them, but with the understanding that you can wear them whenever you want. In fact, I'll just *save* them for you."

Perceptibly relieved, Joyce smiled and said, "Thanks, kiddo."

Just then, Red Pollock and his new girlfriend, Leigh Gerard, burst into laughter at the other end of the bar. Red was definitely feeling better than when he'd walked in the door an hour earlier. He had become a regular since January, and he had been obviously brooding over something when he first came in and ordered a double bourbon, neat, instead of his usual draft beer.

Ruby had tired of hearing him talk constantly about his soon-to-be ex-wife walking out on him, just because he was a cop and spent long hours working. Ruby didn't buy it, anyway.

Ten minutes after Red entered that early evening, Ruby's friend Leigh came in for a drink and to talk. She was in the middle of a nasty divorce and she didn't look particularly happy either.

Ruby prepared Leigh's drink and said, "Come with me, I have somebody I want you to meet over here." And for the last hour, Red and Leigh had become as thick as thieves, so to speak.

Ruby asked Joyce if she had met Leigh and Red before. Joyce said, "Um, I've seen her in here before but I'm not sure about the guy. Why?"

"Come on, you've got to meet them! Joyce usually enjoyed meeting new people, so she followed Ruby's lead. She didn't have the energy to argue about it with her anyway. After the introductions, Red started telling jokes and soon they were all laughing.

A little later, when Joyce was preparing to leave, Ruby said softly to her, "Red's a cop." Ruby enjoyed the shocked look on Joyce's face. Red always had that effect on people.

"Really? He doesn't seem like that, you know what I mean? Besides, I happen to know Leigh does drugs. I've seen her smoking ice in the restroom before. Does she know he's a cop?" Joyce asked.

"Probably so. He doesn't keep it a secret, or anything. He's a pretty cool guy, though. He's got a lot of friends who do drugs. He *has* to know about it. I don't see how he *couldn't* know. He told me once that he was third in command in the Yuma Police Department! Hard to believe, huh? He hangs out here rather than the cop bar because he lives in this neighborhood."

"You should warn people before you introduce them to him. I could have said something to incriminate myself!" Joyce said. She then retrieved her car keys from her purse and headed for home, sweet home with dread.

* * *

MURDER BY GRAVITY?

Red kept the details of his bad day to himself. Earlier, the chief had asked him to join him in his office. He said, "Red, I know what you've been going through this year. We've talked about the divorce and all the women you've been, ah, dating and so forth since Sally left you. Unfortunately, you seem to be distracted from your job. You're not dependable like you used to be. Hell, we can't even *find* you half the time! And when you're here, you're mentally shot or hung over. You've got to get control of yourself, at least here at work. If you don't, I'll have to insist you take your retirement. Now, I'm sorry, but I had to give you a poor work review."

Red took the report from the chief's hand and saw the box checked that read, "employee did not meet expectations." Red had been friends with the chief for more than twenty years and he was livid to think the chief was doing this to him. He crumpled the paper in his hand, left the office without a word and headed straight to P.J.'s for a drink.

Leigh had been a godsend for Red. They hit it off immediately. Leigh's husband had walked out on her two weeks earlier and she was about to be bounced into the street by her landlord. Leigh told Red that she came in to see if Ruby knew of anyone who needed a roommate or had a room to rent.

"I just need a place where I can regroup and get my life back together," Leigh told Red. I don't have any money yet, but I'm going to find a job. I was going to crash on my girlfriend's couch, but her brother-in-law's already on it."

"You look pretty young. What about going back to live with your folks?" Red suggested.

"Thanks, but I'm twenty-four years old and moving back in with my mother and stepfather would be like taking a giant step backwards," Leigh said indignantly.

At the age of forty-eight, exactly twice her age, Red knew he would be robbing the cradle, but he couldn't resist. "How soon do you have to be out?" Red asked.

"Yesterday," Leigh said. Red leaned over and lit her cigarette, ever the gentleman.

"I have a guest room in my house that you can stay in, if you don't mind living with an old man . . ."

Leigh smiled demurely and said, "Oh, you're not so old! I've always felt that men are at their sexiest in their late thirties and forties. They're a lot smarter and more sure of themselves than men in their twenties are. I've never been attracted to men my age. Older men are better lovers, too." Leigh looked deeply into Red's blue eyes and knew instinctively that she had him in the palm of her hand. She felt safe with him and right now, that was just what Leigh needed; that and the methamphetamine she smoked daily.

* * *

Joyce hoped that once she was rid of the offending clothing articles, there would be peace in her marriage at last. And for the first five days since he'd locked her out last, there was a sort of cease-fire. Richard had been somewhat impressed when she put the clothes in the box and told him that she was going to take them down to the Salvation Army like he'd wanted. However, after the middle of September, Richard happened to see Ruby wearing some of the clothing that Joyce claimed went to the Salvation Army and a terrible argument ensued between Richard and Joyce. This time, he packed some things and left their trailer at Swift Sales.

At first Richard didn't know where to go. Hazel wasn't happy with him at that point in time, because he had not recently been attentive toward her and he didn't feel up to more fighting.

Aware that he couldn't concentrate on driving after he nearly hit a pedestrian in a crosswalk, Richard pulled into the parking lot of 84 Lumber and smoked a cigarette. The last thing he needed right now was a ticket. He knew that he hated Joyce and that she couldn't be trusted ever again. He thought that maybe Hazel would take him back if he could wait out enough time to send her flowers first to soften her up. Richard could stay in his camper, but the temperature outdoors was still too hot.

Richard decided to go to P.J.'s to cool off with a drink and to talk to Ruby about Joyce and the clothes. But when he arrived, Ruby was gone. The owner's daughter, Ellie, was tending the bar while Ruby went to a doctor's appointment. Richard had met Ellie a year previously when he worked at P.J.'s with Joyce. She was quite a bit younger than he, and always treated Richard with respect. She hadn't been around the night Richard got angry at her mother and quit his job.

The bar wasn't busy that day in the mid-afternoon, and it wasn't long before Richard told Ellie of all of Joyce's misdeeds and that he needed to get away from her for a while. He admitted to being consumed with jealousy and he loathed feeling that way.

Being single, young, and trusting, Ellie felt sorry for Richard and told him he could sleep on her couch for as long as he needed. Richard had been hesitant, but in the end he didn't have much of an alternative.

Ellie worked on honing her culinary skills and treated Richard to some good home cooking, which he thoroughly enjoyed. It had been a nice change for Ellie, doing for somebody else. Their friendship grew stronger while he was there. They had long talks and did drugs together.

Because Ellie had worked with and actually knew Joyce better than she did Richard, she decided to give Joyce a call at the 8th Street Tavern and let her know that Richard was at her place before somebody else did. Joyce started crying with relief when Ellie told her.

"Thank God!" she said, "I've been going crazy worrying about him! I still love him so much, Ellie. Is he alright?"

"Yeah, he said he just needed to get away for a while. Joyce? You didn't hear this from me, okay? I don't like what you did, but I thought you should know he was at my place and he's been working on that trailer on Araby Road.

"What did he say, Ellie? Is he coming back?" Joyce implored.

"Maybe eventually. He just needs time, I think," Ellie replied.

Ellie left for her regular day job the next morning and she hadn't been there but an hour when she received a frantic phone call from her neighbor Marion. She said that Joyce had been pounding on Ellie's front door for more than fifteen minutes, and yelling for Richard to come out. Her neighbor knew Joyce from when she worked at P.J.'s.

Eventually Joyce gave up after she'd worn herself out on the door, fists and ego bruised as well. Richard never answered her or let her in, but after a full week with Ellie, he did return to Joyce.

* * *

On October 1, Ron Gene returned from a short vacation and no sooner had he opened his office when he saw two Yuma police officers waltzing Richard past his door.

This was the last straw. Ron stepped outside and said, "I want to talk to you, Handcock!"

Richard kept walking and just said, "No!"

By now, Ron was very angry and he shouted after Richard and the two police officers, "I want you out today, Handcock! Do you hear me?" Richard showed no sign of acknowledgment.

Ron stepped back into the office. "Bryce!" Ron yelled into the walkie-talkie, "Come to the office *now!*" Bryce came running inside two minutes later out of breath from running. Ron said, "What the hell is going on around here? The cops just escorted Richard to my trailer!"

"Uh, I hate to be the bearer of bad news. . . ," he began, "I wasn't here when it happened last night. The guys at the seed company said they heard Joyce and Richard fighting and yelling inside the trailer, even worse than usual. Then they heard the door slammed shut, and a few minutes later they saw the fire." Bryce was afraid Ron would have a heart attack on the spot. His face went from red with anger to white with fear.

Bryce hastened to add, "Don't worry, not that much of your stuff burned. Most of it was Joyce's."

"Show me!" Ron demanded.

When they got to the back of the lot, Ron could see a circle of black scorched into the asphalt, the circumference of about six-and-a-half-feet. Inside were the remains of wicker baskets, silk flowers, and clothing. There was an unfamiliar blanket, blackened and laying near the circle. Unfortunately, it was near a huge spool of plastic-coated electrical wire. It looked like the outer wire had been destroyed on one side, but with luck, they could cut the burned part off and salvage the wire underneath. Considering all the acreage of materials, it was only a minor loss for Swift Sales. The two police officers came up to Ron and Bryce to find out what they knew about the incident.

Ron said, "I'm just now trying to find out what happened myself! I'm the owner here and I'd like to know what's going on with Handcock."

MURDER BY GRAVITY?

According to the officers, Richard had smacked Joyce around the night before and, according to them, she telephoned the police department from her sister's house and Richard had been arrested. It turned out that Richard had some methamphetamine in a plastic bag inside his sock. They had to turn him loose in the morning, so they brought him back and were investigating the scene. They also wanted to make sure that there would be no more violence. After talking to Joyce who had returned to the trailer, they felt assured that she would be okay, so they were just taking another look outside.

"Everything seems okay now," the tall officer said, "So we're going to be on our way."

Ron was still trying to digest this information when all of a sudden, everybody except the police who had just left, heard loud crashing noises coming from inside the trailer. Ron thought it sounded like a wrecking crew was in there.

"What *now*?" Ron shouted. He and Bryce jogged over to the other side of the trailer where the doors of the trailer were located and Richard's truck was parked. There they saw Joyce and Richard moving everything they owned out of the trailer. Joyce came out of the front door and laid kitchen articles on the lounge chairs, while Richard came out of the back door carrying larger items and tossed them into the back door of the truck camper carelessly. Jim approached Richard and politely asked what the hell was going on now. Richard turned his back to him to throw more stuff in the camper and ignored Ron's question. Ron tried again when Richard came back to the truck with more of what appeared to be junk to Ron.

He said, "Look, guy, I think you owe me an explanation to say the least!"

"I don't owe you jack, Ron! But since you asked, I'm moving out now just like you said to. Why don't you get the hell out of here while I do it?"

Then Ron and his crew witnessed the full strength and range of Richard's wrath. He tossed a thirteen-inch black-and-white television into the back door of the camper. But by then, the camper was already fully loaded and the television fell out onto the ground, bringing several other items with it. Richard withdrew a hammer from the tool belt he was wearing. Ron and the others watched in astonishment as Richard proceeded to beat to smithereens everything that had fallen out of the camper with the hammer. Richard was quite obviously hysterical as he pulled the dining nook's upholstered bench seats out of the camper and pulled out a switchblade that was hidden in a leather strap inside his sock. He proceeded to stab the seat covers until all that remained were ribbons of white Naugahyde.

It was then that Ron ordered his crew to back away from the area and he moved back with them. They all continued to watch in horror from a position twenty-five feet away. They were amazed as Richard continued to hammer to bits and slash everything the couple owned that wouldn't fit in the camper. Then he kicked the truck a few times for good measure. All the crew agreed that as many times in their lives that they've seen people upset for one reason or another, none of them had ever seen anything to compare with the way Richard was behaving. His frenzy was *scary!*

* * *

A police officer telephoned Ron the next day and asked him to have a look to see if any of his property was missing. He said someone called in a tip the previous night saying that they thought Richard was in possession of materials stolen from Ron's supply yard, and that Richard was trafficking them as well.

Could that have been Mike Deere?

CHAPTER 15

Richard stepped inside the loaded truck and camper and exited the Swift Sales lot. Joyce jumped in her car following him. She watched as Richard drove in such a way as to shift everything stuffed inside the camper and she winced. Joyce was visibly shaken by Richard's actions, plus the loss of some of her personal property. She instinctively knew that discussing his actions that day would have dire consequences. She had a pretty good idea too that Richard didn't even want her company. Once he signaled for the turn off on Highway 95, Joyce knew that they were headed for Mittry Lake, by way of the Gila Gravity Canal once again.

Over the next few days, Joyce gave Richard plenty of space but it was she who grew depressed. She tried to shake it off, but it seemed impossible. When Richard wasn't around her, she'd give in to the impulse to cry, but kept her tears hidden from him. She grew very lonely.

Eventually, Joyce worked up the courage to talk to Richard about it. "I need to ask you a question and I want you to promise not to get mad at me."

Richard just looked at her without emotion as he had been doing since leaving Swift Sales. The look was intended to silence her. But instead Joyce felt that she couldn't turn back once started.

"I really miss being close to my family. Dad's still not in the best of health, and my mom could use a little help. But the main thing is I just would rather be living closer to them."

Richard seemed to be weighing the pros and cons in his mind. "Where did you have in mind?"

Joyce imperceptibly breathed a sigh of relief. Richard was sounding rational for the moment. "I was thinking of checking with Dad to see if we could get a space in their RV park and how much it would cost us. It would be nice to be able to use the park showers and laundry facilities, don't you think?"

Without batting an eye, Richard said, "Fine, see how much they want." Joyce fleetingly wondered if he gave in so quickly because he was planning to leave her again once they got settled near her parents.

* * *

Lori and Bill Perron were thrilled that their daughter was moving into their RV park. Bill told them that in the summer, the rates were only $10 a night, and as summer manager, he was able to extend the summer rates through October since it was still pre-snowbird season. Joyce gave them $20 for two nights only. Then Lori and Bill learned that Joyce and Richard hadn't been working since they moved out to Mittry Lake from Swift Sales. It was never made clear to them just why Joyce quit working at the 8th Street Tavern, but they suspected it had something to do with Richard. Until he entered Joyce's life, she had only quit a couple of jobs in her whole life. The Perrons paid the balance for the rest of the month to help the kids out.

Though Joyce's parents were excited by her re-emergence, the Perrons knew they didn't want to have Joyce and Richard living next door where they would be able to hear them arguing, so they put them in a space on the other side of the park where they could see them across the empty lots in the summer months and partially in the winter, yet not be tempted to get involved with their marital problems.

Richard's eight-foot camper looked ridiculously inadequate after they moved it into the park. Most of the recreational vehicles that were in the park were either nice park models like the Perrons had, or fifth-wheel trailers, generally thirty- to forty-feet-long with several slide-outs. Bill Perron had pushed the limit as to what kind of rigs they allowed in the park. This was not what the owners had in mind, and he knew it. Richard removed the camper shell that contained their step-up, over-the-cab bed, tiny kitchen, dining nook (sans the bench seats) and toilet cabinet off the truck and set it on the ground so they could travel around town unfettered.

Joyce began to look for work again. She stopped at P.J.'s to see if Ruby had heard of any openings for bartenders. As luck would have

MURDER BY GRAVITY?

it, Joyce arrived at just the opportune moment to check there. Tammy, the owner, was having lunch with her old friend Stephanie Lynd, who owned a bar on the main drag of Yuma called The Show Place. Stephanie, or Stevie, as her friends called her, also owned a sister bar called The Dark Place that was further downtown on 24th Street. Stevie was a lovely, elegant woman of the world somewhere in her forties. She was dressed more east coast than the usual Yuma apparel that consisted of a polo shirt and walking shorts. People went everywhere except church dressed like that, and in some cases church too.

Joyce spotted Tammy and walked over to her table, throwing a wave at Ruby behind the bar. Tammy was pleased to see Joyce again.

"Hi, stranger!" Tammy stood up to give Joyce a hug. "I heard through the grapevine that Richard came back."

Joyce glanced again at Ruby, smiled and said, "It sounds like the grapevine is as reliable as ever," Joyce laughed.

"How are you guys doing now?" Tammy seemed genuinely concerned.

Joyce sighed, "Still on and off again, I'm afraid. We're together today, but I couldn't swear about tomorrow."

"Well, that's too bad," Tammy said. "I feel bad because I'm the one that introduced you two." Tammy shook her head, "Oh, where are my manners? Stevie, this is Joyce Handcock. She worked here earlier this year." Stevie smiled at Joyce. "Have you two met before?" The two women shook their heads. She motioned then for Joyce to sit down and join them at her table. "Stevie owns The Show Place and The Dark Place. Do you know them?"

"Of course," Joyce said enthusiastically. "Maybe one of you can help me. Do either of you have, or know of any bartending jobs available? I'm ready to go back to work and I won't be side-tracked again."

"Well, I don't have any openings right now, but Stevie's looking for an experienced bartender." Tammy looked at Stevie, "I can recommend Joyce very highly. She's a good worker, friendly and popular. You can count on her to show up, too. And, as you can tell, she's easy on the eyes." Tammy had reconsidered the facts that Richard told her about Joyce and decided that she did not believe that

Joyce sold drugs at work or dipped into the cash register.

Stevie reached over and shook Joyce's hand. "I'm glad to meet you! Since Tammy recommends you, that's good enough for me. The job's six nights a week, 5:00 P.M. to closing and it's over at The Dark Place on 24th Street and the wages are just the same as Tammy pays. Think you can handle that?"

"I can start today, if you like," Joyce said smiling.

Stevie discussed the differences in the bars she owned with Joyce. The Dark Place was surrounded by residential and it's not as glitzy as The Show Place. "So if you don't mind a little neighborhood bar where 'everyone knows your name,' I need you to bring your driver's license and Social Security card in with you this afternoon. Well, then, as they said on the *Titanic*, 'Welcome aboard!'" They all had a good laugh.

"Just don't steal all of my customers away, Joyce," Tammy tried to look stern. "You'll be working for the competition this time!" And they all giggled again.

* * *

Joyce enjoyed her first week of work at The Dark Place, getting to know its regulars from the area. Bob DeVore was one such regular. Three years prior to meeting Joyce, Bob had broken his back while working at the Yuma Proving Ground, where various tests are conducted, mostly by the government. Bob had some kind of classified position there, working for a subcontractor. He would walk into The Dark Place every night at 10:00 PM, after prime time television ended, and stay until closing. Working six nights a week, Joyce got to know Bob quite well. He was friendly and jovial. Joyce felt like she could discuss anything with Bob because he was one man who knew how to keep his mouth shut. He was also the one who watched out for her when she closed the bar at 1:00 AM and volunteered to walk her out to her car without trying to hit on her.

* * *

Exactly one week after the Handcocks moved into the Perrons RV park, the Yuma police knocked on their camper door. It was only

MURDER BY GRAVITY?

8 o'clock in the morning and Joyce and Richard were still sleeping. Richard had been out of work since the Swift Sales incident and wasn't actively looking for work either.

Joyce was asked to step outside with her husband because the police had a search warrant for the camper and Richard's truck cab. They also had a warrant for Richard's personal storage unit which Joyce knew nothing about prior to the search warrant. The officers kindly let them put their sweats on first, with the door open, of course, before stepping outside.

"What's this all about, Richard, or do you know?" Joyce whispered when they were alone outside standing under a paloverde tree; she smoking the clove cigarettes that Joyce found in her pocket.

Richard replied, "I'm not sure, but I'll bet it has something to do with Ron Gene at Swift Sales."

Joyce felt humiliated as a few of the early snowbirds peeked out of their curtains to see what was going on. Even if her parents weren't watching this, they would definitely hear about it from the neighbors. Joyce was terrified they would find the meth that they had in her stash box. Richard had one somewhere else. She never knew where he kept it.

Joyce studied the search warrant in her hands. "It says that they're searching for property stolen from Swift Sales and evidence of trafficking it." Joyce suddenly recalled seeing a few questionable items after the move that Richard had taken to his mother's house. She began to realize this could be serious.

Then the police officers exited the camper and said, "Richard Leon Handcock, we are placing you under arrest for possession of stolen property, damages to property belonging to Swift Sales, and trafficking in stolen property."

They cuffed him and gave him the Miranda. Richard said, "*What* property? You didn't find a damn thing in there! You couldn't have, because there was nothing to find!" Joyce was grateful they hadn't found the drug stash box's hiding place either.

"Do you understand these rights as I have explained them to you?" the short officer asked tersely.

Richard looked at Joyce and rolled his eyes and said, "I'll see you later." Then the squad car pulled out onto the park's main road and left with Richard in it.

* * *

True to his word, Richard was driven back home that afternoon. He looked tired and cranky.

"I'm surprised you're back already! I was wondering how I was supposed to post your bail," Joyce said to him.

"They didn't have anything concrete on me. They found some stuff I left in the trailer at Araby, but it was Ron's stuff and his trailer."

"What about damages?" Joyce asked.

"It was just a couple of feet of wire is all. Ron's probably going to drop charges now. They're supposed to let me know."

"It seems odd to me that Ron would do this to you without any evidence."

"Are you sayin' I'm *lying?*" Richard said in that tone of voice that scared Joyce.

"No, of course not! It just seems weird, that's all."

As one might expect, the charges were not dropped. The police department found stolen items in Richard's storage locker and they had a witness from the Winterhaven RV park on Araby who reported that Richard tried to sell him some materials from Swift Sales.

* * *

When Richard was arrested he called his mother for help, but this time, unlike the other times, she turned him down flat. Mrs. Handcock was sick and tired of his criminal activities. Being bailed out twice in less then three weeks time was too much to ask of any mother. She needed to worry about her own bills first. It hurt so much to see Richard out of control. She just couldn't understand him. She had always been there for her son, maybe too much. Perhaps that was why he was always finding trouble, because she enabled him. Perhaps a little "tough love" was in order. Richard's brother, Ben, seemed doomed to repeat the same misbehaviors. Mrs. Handcock almost couldn't make herself say the words, but she was determined. She would watch the sons she loved flounder from an emotionally safer distance, where it wouldn't hurt too much. Hearing about his problems and being in the middle of them were two

MURDER BY GRAVITY?

different things. Mrs. Handcock put her house up for sale and was planning to buy a new park model in Prescott. She was ready for a fresh start away from her two wayward sons.

* * *

Richard used his head this time and managed to talk his way out of being jailed. Years earlier, a guy in prison with him said he had heard about a television show in which a perpetrator was not put in jail because he was dying of cancer and that the court felt that it would be better to let the man go, rather than pay for all of his medical bills. He said it was a true story. Richard didn't have any proof that he had a fictitious cancer, but he decided to throw it out there on the table to see what the police would do. He was pretty sure he could convince them, so long as they didn't ask for medical records.

While Richard waited to be interrogated, he began to act like he was in pain. In pain, but trying to *hide* the pain. He would suddenly grab his stomach until he got someone's attention. When they looked directly at him, he would attempt at a brave smile. Some of the people around him seemed to grow concerned. One of the desk workers asked if he wanted a glass of water, which Richard gratefully accepted to help complete the picture.

Everyone seemed to know he was sick before he was even called into interrogation. The short police officer was doubtful as he got in Richard's face and said, "You didn't *look* sick when we drove you here in the patrol car!"

Richard said politely and tiredly, "You couldn't see me all the time. But I'm actually doing much better today. I have to go back to Tucson for chemotherapy the day after tomorrow. I go every two weeks for a couple of days. Look, my hair's starting to fall out." He then pulled several long, blond hairs off of his shoulders that he had casually pulled out and planted there while waiting for interrogation. "It's stomach cancer."

And the rest, as they say, is history. The police bought the cancer story hook, line, and decree. They *never* once asked for medical records, receipts, or a letter from his oncologist. He was released on his own recognizance, though he would have to return to court in two-and-a-half months. The Swift Sales problem was far from over, but he was out of jail for now. Richard wouldn't tell Joyce the truth unless he absolutely had no other alternative. In fact, it might be helpful down the road if she bought the story too.

* * *

Three days after the arrest, Richard told Joyce that he had to go to Somerton, a small city approximately twenty-five miles outside of Yuma, for a job and that he had to be there by 9:00 AM. Joyce said she didn't want to be home alone on her day off, and that her car was running a little "iffy" and she didn't trust it. Richard offered to take her to Ruby's apartment on his way out of town.

Joyce helped Ruby paint a large basket country blue with gold gilding on the edges and showed her how to gild and arrange the flowers inside. It was to be a fun girls' day off together. They snorted some methamphetamine, or crank as it is sometimes called, and went shopping. They loved to browse at Michael's and Old America, two of the major craft stores in Yuma at the time. They would look for ideas and items they could later copy, depending on the results of their dumpster diving, which they only did at night under the cover of darkness. The shops would complain to the police if they did it during the day.

They were back at Ruby's early, by two o'clock, since Joyce was unsure when Richard would be returning. At 2:30 PM, Richard telephoned Joyce to say that his truck had broken down, something to do with the U-joints, he said, and that he had to walk better than three miles one way to get to an auto supply store. Considering the desolate area he had to drive through, it was actually pretty lucky to only have to walk three miles, Joyce thought. Richard told her that he loved her and not to hold her breath until he got back. He would be there as soon as possible.

At 7:00 PM that night, Joyce telephoned her mother. "Hi, Mom. Have you or Dad seen Richard at all this evening?"

"No . . . why?" Lori asked. "Are you two fighting again?"

"No, everything's fine." She explained that she was still over at Ruby's apartment. "He called at 2:30 and said he was having trouble with his truck, and he told me that he loved me."

MURDER BY GRAVITY?

Lori conferred with Bill while Joyce waited on the phone. She said, "Just hang tight for a while, honey. Daddy's going to drive out toward Somerton and see if he can spot Richard or the truck."

Joyce said, "Okay. Tell Dad I said thanks!"

* * *

Richard returned to the park before Bill did an hour later. Lori knew Richard had arrived when she heard the unique noise of his truck all the way across the park. It had the distinctive sound of having a hole in the muffler.

When Bill arrived home, Lori told him Richard was back. Bill said, "Maybe we should make sure he picked up Joyce."

The Perrons walked over to their son-in-law and observed him putting boxes that had been scattered outside around the camper into the bed of his pickup. He had a tiny, black Chihuahua in the cab of the truck that was barking its head off.

"Hi, Richard," Lori and Bill said in unison. Bill said, "How's the truck running? Do you need any help?"

"Nah," Richard replied, "Everything's okay right now."

Lori chimed in, "Joyce is still waiting for you to pick her up at Ruby's, I gather? Shall I call her and say that you're on your way?"

"Yeah, sure," Richard said.

After Bill and Lori walked several yards back towards home, Bill said, "I wonder where the *camper* is!"

Lori said, "And where did the dog come from? I was so worried about the truck and the stuff he was putting into it, I didn't even notice the camper not being there. But I knew *something* wasn't right. Fishy, huh?" When they reached home, she called Joyce and told her everything.

Joyce said, "Uh-oh. There's got to be a good explanation. I can't wait to hear it." But Joyce would wait a long time until she heard one.

By morning, Joyce called her dad and asked if he could pick her up, since her car was still at "home." But when Joyce got "home," she found nothing there, except most of her things stuffed into her car. Richard and his truck and camper were gone. He had left Joyce homeless this time.

CHERIE HUYETT ACHTEMEIER

* * *

Joyce was relieved that her car started the next morning, and was going to drive over to Ruby's, but decided to make a stop first. She headed out to Araby Road on the off chance, the *very* off chance that Richard might be there, which he wasn't. But on the way home, she drove by David's 25-Hour Towing and something shiny caught her eye. She had to get a better look. She pulled in and saw that it was an Avion, old and about 26 feet long. Joyce asked the manager if it was for sale and if it was, could she have a look on the inside.

When Joyce and the manager entered the shiny metal structure with its rounded roof, he told Joyce, "Avions were built originally by the same people who engineered airplanes. The front, rear, and ceiling were rounded for aerodynamic purposes. In other words, it cuts through the air easier and therefore the pull vehicle uses less fuel. The structure is still sound as a dollar. A lot of people buy the older Avion trailers and re-do the interiors. These things never go out of style because the new ones don't look much different from this one here. This trailer was last used on a construction site and was neglected and later used for storage. The appliances all work. That's the important thing. It just needs a little tender, loving care, that's all."

Joyce didn't need to be told to use her imagination. She already knew exactly how she wanted to fix it. "What about all this junk that's still in it?" Joyce asked.

"You can keep anything useful you find in there. It's mostly trash, though, and we sure don't want it."

Joyce was excited. "Would you take my car in trade for it?"

The manager scrutinized her car and said, "Well, yeah. But I'll need an extra $400 on top of the car."

Joyce went for the deal after bartering her way down to $300. She had been taken for a ride financially, but she didn't care. Right now she needed a place to live more than she needed a car. She signed the back of her paycheck over to the dealer. She could easily ride her trusty bicycle the four blocks to work.

Jeff Dupre borrowed a truck with a trailer hitch and sway bar on it. After the Avion was hooked up and ready to tow to the RV park, Joyce stayed outside near the back of the trailer to watch as Jeff pulled it free from overgrown weeds and dirt that covered the bottom half of the tires, which were low. She could see where the plants had wedged their way in through the floor and frame of the trailer. She had a lot of work ahead of her, but she was looking forward to it immensely.

Mike Deere came over to help Joyce set the trailer more permanently with cement pylons under each corner and two in the middle area. He also rigged a tarp that was held up with PVC pipe and used as a side awning. Joyce was tickled to death with her new home.

Mike was thrilled to be back in Joyce's life again, although he was beginning to feel a bit like a puppet. He couldn't understand how Joyce could waste her time on that maggot she called her husband. Mike was the one who was always there for her. He was going to do everything he could to prevent Joyce from letting Richard back in her life, now that he was gone.

Lori walked over to see her daughter's latest project. The first several days of ownership, Joyce was spending all of her free time hauling out trash. Lori was amazed at the pile that was 6-feet-high of useless, filthy junk that Joyce set out by the side of the trailer to be taken to the trash later. Lori's eyes fell on the remains of a mummified house cat and was horrified.

"Joyce, aren't you about finished hauling trash out of there?" She said as she peeked inside the door. "You can't seriously consider moving into that!"

"But Mother, you don't understand. It's all *mine*. I even have the pink slip!" Joyce came outside and threw her arms around her mother. "You'll see. I'm going to make it so beautiful! I found a pretty Southwestern printed fabric that I'm going to glue to the front of the cupboard doors in the kitchen and paint everything else in there a coordinating color. I also bought enough of the fabric to make myself a matching bedspread, and some beige quilted fabric to recover the little benches in the dining room. That also makes into a single bed, by the way. I'll need to borrow Dad's staple gun when I get to that part. I got a solid pastel to cover the valances and make curtains." Joyce pulled the edges of the fabric out of a Walmart bag to show to her. "Can't you just picture it in here?" Joyce said, dreamy faced.

"As the Sundance Kid said to Butch Cassidy in the movie, 'You've got vision; the rest of the world wears bifocals!'" Lori and Joyce laughed. "If anybody can make it beautiful, I'm sure it would be you, sweetie. Do you have the propane and water hooked up?"

"I did that first thing, Mom," Joyce said.

"Is there air conditioning in this thing?" Lori asked.

Joyce said, "Somebody took it out, but there is an evaporative cooler in there that works great. I just need to buy a new filter for it."

"Well, it sounds like you know what you're doing," Lori said, "I wish you luck! Make sure you don't leave that pile of junk there too long, they don't allow untidiness here and you might get your dad in trouble."

"I won't. Thanks, Mom," Joyce said grinning from ear to ear.

"And, Joyce," Lori said, "I hope you wash your hands after touching that dead cat!"

* * *

For the next three weeks, Joyce kept busy working at The Dark Place and fixing up her little trailer. She got to know her neighbors in the process of working on the Avion. Somebody would always stop by to ask what she was doing, or to check the various stages of her progress. Lori always called the residents in the park her "sidewalk supervisors." The neighbors grew to admire Joyce's tenacity and good taste. Several told her that Joyce reminded them of her mother.

At The Dark Place, Joyce did indeed do what Tammy feared. Many of the customers of P.J.'s switched watering holes to where Joyce was working. She had many loyal patrons.

For the first time in a long time, everything was going well for Joyce. Her depression had evaporated almost completely. She lowered the amount of meth she was using and hoped to get custody of Nichole, who had returned from Phoenix at the end of the summer, and went to live temporarily with Joyce's sister, Lynn. That way, she was still able to continue going to the same school, as she would if she came to live with Joyce again. Joyce still needed to show more income in order for that to happen, but she wasn't giving up yet.

On Joyce's one day off the first week of November, she was

visiting at her parents' home when the phone rang. Bill answered it then handed the phone to Joyce. "Honey, it's Richard."

Lori's smile melted as she and Bill exchanged looks of concern. But Joyce was instantly elated. She took the cordless phone out on the deck where she spoke to Richard for almost an hour.

When Joyce came back inside, Bill and Lori were waiting for her. "What's up?" Lori asked.

"Well," Joyce said sitting down on the sofa so she could speak to both of them. "Richard's coming back!" A single tear rolled down Joyce's face from her bloodshot eyes.

"What's wrong?" Lori asked, her voice alarmed.

"It turns out that a couple of months ago Richard was diagnosed with stomach cancer."

The Perrons were stunned. "Oh, we're sorry to hear that, sweetie," Bill said. Because of his heart problems, Lori hadn't told Bill much about the problems Richard had caused Joyce since just after the wedding. Lori didn't like Richard very much by this time, but she was saddened for her daughter's sake.

Bill asked, "What's the prognosis?"

"It depends on how the chemotherapy goes, which he's already started. If it doesn't help, they don't give him more than a few months to live." Joyce began to sob and put her hands over her face. Lori put her arm around Joyce and patted her back.

"Don't you see?" said Joyce, "That's why he wouldn't talk to me before. He was trying to push me away so I wouldn't get hurt. That's why he kept locking me outside at Swift Sales. So I'd get mad and go away. But he said he just couldn't stay away anymore. He says his hair has all fallen out already and he's lost a lot of weight. He's on his way back here from his treatments in Tucson and should be here in a few hours. Oh! I've got to get the trailer ready for him! I can't wait to show it to him. I'm so proud of it. I'll bring Richard over to visit later on today."

"I thought you were done with him, Joyce. You've been doing so well for yourself since he left. . . ," Lori began.

"Mom," Joyce interrupted her. "He's my husband and he has cancer. I can't desert him now! Besides, Ed, Sr., said if Richard ever came back, I could get custody of Nickie again. She loves being with her aunt and uncle, but she still needs her mother."

The Perrons were still trying to digest this new development. Then they watched Joyce take off and jog over to her trailer. After a little while Bill saw Joyce outside her trailer doing something. He thought maybe she was washing it.

"What on earth?" Bill said to himself. "Lori, take a look at this!" It now appeared that Joyce was writing on the shiny silver exterior of her trailer with blue spray paint. When she backed off, Bill read aloud, "I love you, Richard!" Bill mused, "I'm going to get complaints about this."

CHAPTER 16

For the weeks Richard was out of Joyce's life, he had been living with Hazel again. He brought her flowers and begged her to take him back. He tested his stomach cancer story on her next after getting away from the police with it. Richard had collected several brochures which he bestowed on Hazel containing information about cancer, chemotherapy, and radiation therapy. He had collected the brochures from the Yuma Regional Medical Center where they were available to the public at no cost, so he made sure he had plenty. Richard told her that his specialist in Tucson had given him the brochures before he started his chemotherapy. He wanted Hazel to understand "just what he had to go through" and, of course, invoke sympathy and maybe a little kindness. Hazel once more took Richard into her apartment to live.

Richard worked to improve his sickness hoax. He shaved his head daily and rarely ate, thereby dropping several pounds quickly, because meth bingeing causes loss of appetite. After eating anything at all, Richard would go to the bathroom and make loud, retching noises. At the same time, he poured a glass of water sporadically into the toilet to convince Hazel that he was throwing up in there. Sometimes he really was sick and didn't have to pretend.

For some unknown reason, Richard suddenly took to wearing camouflage jumpsuits that he purchased at The Surplus Store. It could have been part of the psychosis that meth bingeing can bring on; part of a paranoia episode playing out. With his bald head and fatigues, Richard looked like a radical white supremacist. On his bald head he wore a black stocking cap. Hazel found the image unsettling. When he came into The Bottoms Up Pub, he actually scared some of her customers away. At that time, Richard was wrapped so tight mentally, his temperament was explosive. Hazel wanted to ask him to drop the militia look, but was too afraid of him by then.

Hazel began to stay away from Richard, even though that included staying away from her own home, which she formerly thought of as a refuge. It seemed to Hazel that there was something dark about Richard now. He spooked her. Fortunately, Richard didn't seem concerned about her being gone so much. He seemed preoccupied. Hazel attributed it to his illness. But Richard didn't seem fearful. More like he was planning something. Could it be his own death he was planning? Hazel didn't know, but it unnerved her. She had never seen Richard like that before.

Richard stopped in to see his old friend from P.J.'s, Ellie, who was understandably taken aback by Richard's new appearance. Richard explained that he had been very sick lately. He told Ellie that he and Joyce were on the outs again and asked her please not to tell Joyce that she had seen him. Ellie promised not to tell. He told her then that he had cancer of the stomach and he only had eight weeks to live.

* * *

Yuma Police Department's Lieutenant Red Pollock decided to call it quits. It looked to him like the chief was getting ready to can him, so Red beat him to the punch by putting in for his retirement after twenty-five years on the force. He had started to get flack at work about his young, "druggie" girlfriend that he had living with him and he felt that it was none of their damn business, as long as *he* wasn't doing anything illegal himself.

Red and his girlfriend, Leigh, went out every night for what they called "last call," though it could last for hours. They left home and either went to P.J.'s or The Dark Place around 11:30 PM and stayed until closing at 1:00 AM, or "hopped" from one place to the other. They became part of a group of friends and regulars that partied and hung out together at the bars. Joyce's friend Ruby and her live-in boyfriend Jeff Dupre usually came in for a while and Jeff sold crank, be it powder or ice, at the bar. And, of course, Bob DeVore and Mike Deere were usually there while Joyce worked. DeVore and Pollock abstained.

* * *

MURDER BY GRAVITY?

During the three weeks after Richard left Joyce, Mike Deere once again became intimate with Joyce. Their relationship just resumed almost like Richard never existed. At least, that's what Joyce said. To Mike it seemed like their separations were agonizingly long. Mike let Joyce drive the Jeep whenever she needed it. He tried to help her with her drug problem, by monitoring her doses. Mike simply would do anything for her.

Joyce told Mike several times that her sexual relationship with Richard was frustrating for her and that Richard didn't know how to satisfy a woman. She also said to Mike that she fantasized about being with him while making love to Richard. Mike despised Richard for the rough way in which he had treated Joyce and his lack of respect. In his opinion, Richard had no idea what a lucky man he was. Mike once offered to teach Richard a lesson after he saw Joyce with all of her bruises, but Joyce refused. It hadn't been a big deal at the time when Joyce hooked up with Danny last summer. It was his own idiotic fault for asking Danny to join them in a threesome. It wasn't until Danny put that special, glowing, happy face on Joyce that Mike felt like he wanted to be the guy Joyce looked at in that way. For the first time, Mike gave some serious consideration to his feelings for her. Last summer, he had been afraid that Joyce was in love with Danny, but then Danny went to jail and Joyce took Richard back. It confused him. But one thing he was sure of was that he was unlikely to ever meet another woman like her twice in his lifetime.

This last time when Richard left Joyce, there was no Danny waiting in the wings to sweep her away. That gave Mike a clear field to Joyce. As far as Mike was concerned, everything had been going great between Joyce and him. They spent dozens of hours together the three weeks that Richard was gone. But Joyce wasn't glowing like Mike wanted. She must care about him a little, anyway, Mike reasoned, because she seemed to enjoy being with him. He would not accept the thought that Joyce might be using him. Then he wondered if he wanted her *because* getting her to love him was a challenge.

Then the unthinkable happened. Joyce informed Mike when he came into The Dark Place one night in late November that Richard had returned. Mike tried to talk her out of taking him back, but he discovered it was too late. Richard was already living in her trailer. Joyce also told Mike that Richard had cancer and that he needed her to take care of him for the last few weeks of his life.

"Can I still see you?" Mike asked her.

"I don't see why not," Joyce said. "It's not like chemotherapy is an aphrodisiac. I'll call you when I can set something up for us to get together."

To Richard's chagrin, Mike resumed his daily drive-bys, hoping to find Richard's ugly truck gone forever.

* * *

Joyce kept her word to Mike and asked her sister to lie to Richard saying that Joyce was at her place when she was really going to see Mike. When Richard did call her to check up on Joyce, Lynn would say,

"Joyce is here, but she's not available to come to the phone right now."

Richard knew she was lying and she knew that he knew. It was awful and Lynn didn't feel good about it. But she knew how cruel Richard could be and that sometimes Joyce needed a break. Lynn also knew that the only reason Richard was living with Joyce was because he had cancer. The family was unhappy about Joyce taking him back for any reason, but they understood.

* * *

Joyce was stunned when she saw Richard for the first time after he "returned from Tucson where he went for his chemo." He was wearing a black stocking cap to cover his bald head and a camouflage jumpsuit. It also appeared that he'd lost a good twenty pounds. Richard had the look of a gangster. Nevertheless, she ran to his outstretched arms and kissed and hugged him.

Given the way Richard looked, Joyce figured he couldn't possibly have very long to live. He was pale and had dark circles under his eyes, but it was because of his excess use of methamphetamine, not cancer.

Richard oohed and ahhed as Joyce showed him the trailer. He tried to imagine how bad it looked before Joyce changed it. While a couple of her makeover projects were yet unfinished, he could see what she was doing and it looked cute. He praised her for it and did indeed truly admire her talent and skill. He offered to put up shelves for her in the bedroom. Since he "couldn't work," it would give him something to do. Joyce had the bedspread all finished. It had been time-consuming because she hand stitched the hems. She only recently finished it and it felt right that Richard would be the first to sleep under it with her, though it certainly wasn't the picture she had in mind while she was sewing.

Joyce planned on making whatever time Richard had left on earth as pleasant for him as possible. She would work while he stayed home and rested or puttered. Whenever she stood up to do something around the house, she asked Richard if she could get him something while she was up. She became a typical caregiver. That first night, and for several nights thereafter, Joyce and Richard just held each other until they fell asleep.

Nickie came back to live with her mother once again and slept on the futon sofa that Joyce had purchased and centered on the wall of the living room. Thankfully, when she visited her father he didn't ask Nickie about her sleeping accommodations. He wouldn't have approved if he knew.

Quietly, the next ten days passed. By the second Saturday afternoon in early December of 1994, Richard told Joyce as she was about to leave on her bicycle to go to work, that he would come get her at 1:00 AM as usual, but during her shift, he said he was, ". . . going to try to talk to Ron Gene over at Swift Sales, and see if I can buy him a drink. Maybe I can talk him into dropping the charges against me. Just in case you were gonna call home or anything."

"Okay. Good luck!" Joyce said off handedly as she peddled away.

* * *

Saturday night was always the busiest at The Dark Place. Everyone was happily singing along with Bonnie Raitt's rendition of "Let's Give Them Something to Talk About" on the jukebox. Joyce was busily washing down the bar countertop and putting dirty glasses in the sink to soak in soapy water. The phone behind her rang and she quickly dried her hands on a towel before answering it.

With a smile in her voice, Joyce answered, as usual, "The Dark Place. Can I help you?"

A unfamiliar woman's voice answered, "Yes, well, I hope so. A friend of mine said that Richard Handcock was hanging out at The Dark now. Do you see him anywhere?"

"Uh, no. He had some other place to go tonight. Wanna leave a message?"

Joyce's curiosity was piqued and wondered if there were a need to concern herself.

"Yeah. He was supposed to be here an hour and a half ago."

Joyce replied, "And where is that?" She was getting confused.

"At *my* place. Just tell him Hazel called. He knows the number."

Joyce hung up the phone as she mentally ran that call through her mind again. What Hazel could Richard know? She'd never heard him mention that name. It's an usual name and she would have remembered. Like Witch Hazel. It was too late for an odd repair job call. "And he *knows* the number!" kept ringing in Joyce's ears over and over again.

CHAPTER 17

Nickie woke up when Richard threw open the back door, which made a loud "thunk" as the back of it hit one of the thin walls that a previous owner had installed, knocking things off a couple of the makeshift shelves that Richard hung after the redecorating. Nickie had been asleep less than an hour after she returned home from babysitting Ruby and Jeff's children.

"I know you've got something going on, Richard!" Joyce started.

Richard was quite obviously angry, and resorted to his old football coach's rule of, *"The best defense is a good offense,"* and countered with, "Yeah? What about you and Mike Deere?"

Joyce spoke more quietly, but Nickie could tell that her mother was very upset.

Nickie curled up in her bed looking at the back of the door that separated the living room from Joyce and Richard's tiny bedroom. Every once in a while she could see their shadows move underneath the door as they walked past it. She didn't need to hold her breath to hear every word they were saying to each other. Nickie sometimes secretly wished she were someplace else when the stress got to her. She had heard them argue time after time in the last year about Mike Deere. It didn't bother her that much because it took their attention off whatever trouble *she* might be flirting with. It was just *lucky for them that she was a good kid,* that's what she always thought, anyway. Then suddenly she noticed that their conversation was starting to get *interesting* this time.

"Don't try to turn this around, Richard. This isn't about Mike!"

"I told you already, Joyce," Richard said in an elevated voice, "She's just an old friend! I don't even know her that well."

"But you told me that you were going to Swift Sales. So why

was this Hazel person expecting you?" Joyce said accusingly. Nickie knew well and good that her mother was capable of holding up her end of an argument.

Richard explained, "I told you the truth! I went over to Swift Sales but Ron was already gone for the day. So then I went to the Bottoms Up Pub to see if a guy I know, Bud, was there. He usually has a bunch of used tires at his place that I could buy off him for my damn truck. I had a beer and waited around for a while."

"Then the phone rang and the bartender said to me, since he knows I used to hang out there a while back, says, 'Hey, Richard. Hazel's on the phone. Want to say hi?' Cause he knew that I knew Hazel from way back, because her and her boyfriend go there all the time. So I said, 'Yeah,' and we talked for a couple of minutes. I told her I was looking for the guy that usually has used tires for sale. So Hazel says, 'If you don't see him, come on over because my boyfriend has some tires that he might just *give* to you for nothing.' So, I left the Pub then I was trying to follow the directions she gave me to her house, but I got lost and couldn't call her because I never got her phone number. She must've *thought* she gave me the phone number when she gave me the address, but she didn't." Richard thought of this lie rather quickly and hadn't had time to iron out the bumps in it yet. He thought that by saying that Hazel already had a boyfriend would negate any feelings of jealousy Joyce might have.

Joyce said eloquently, "Oh, bull!"

After a little while, they settled down and went to bed, but Joyce couldn't sleep. She wished she believed Richard, but she had seen him lie with a straight face more than enough and knew better than to trust him. Unfortunately for Joyce, she generally believed Richard far too much.

* * *

That was the beginning of what was to be a continuing argument for roughly 10 days. Richard accused Joyce of sleeping with Mike, and Joyce would say that he was probably sleeping with Hazel.

Joyce planned to look into this Hazel issue. She remembered the lady bartender at Bottoms Up Pub that she once spoke with a year or so ago while barhopping with the girls, and wondered if Hazel was

MURDER BY GRAVITY?

her name. If that were true, Richard didn't know that Joyce had any idea who Hazel was. She suspected that Hazel was the bartender and not just a customer like Richard wanted her to believe, and that Hazel was young and cute. Joyce was just barely beginning to scratch the surface of Richard's façade when things really began to take a turn.

***

Over those days when Richard and Joyce argued so much, Richard again increased the amount of methamphetamine he was using. He was bingeing, which can last for days. Joyce began missing jewelry and among other items, including a small handgun that Jeff Dupre had given to her years earlier to protect herself.

Richard told her again that he also was missing tools and that there must have been another robbery and pointed to a window screen that had been removed, bent, and was laying on the ground next to the trailer. It was Richard that did it, of course, to make his story more believable.

He said, "Somebody told me that a couple of other rigs were broken into besides ours, and they took off with a bicycle, too. They said it was a pair of young boys that did it."

Richard pawned the items at a shop near the Big Curve Shopping area of Yuma. Some of Joyce's earrings turned out to be only costume jewelry and they wouldn't give him anything for them. Then he found out that there would be paperwork involved if he hocked the gun, so he kept those items and hid them at his mother's house.

Richard managed to get enough money together to feed his growing drug habit. He became even more agitated and paranoid. He convinced himself that Joyce was sleeping around, but *in* the bed of their trailer whenever he left home without her. He began going to The Dark around ten o'clock every night Joyce worked and would sit by himself in the shadows near the door and just stare at Joyce.

At the moment when Richard entered, Joyce would perceptibly change enough that nearly all in the bar noticed. Her friendly, happy nature became one of all business, and she spoke almost curtly. Her smile evaporated and she grew tense under Richard's glare. Non-regulars would turn around to see who had affected Joyce this way. While most never met Richard directly, everyone knew who he was. The men in the bar sensed Richard's hatred of them, and they couldn't understand what they had done to be on the receiving end of his vengeful stare.

Richard had seen Joyce playfully flirting with the customers before she saw that he had entered. He knew the "Little Goodie Joycie Two-Shoes" routine, as he thought of it, was all an act for his benefit. Because of that, he changed his habit of walking into the bar when Joyce would be expecting him. He would drive into The Dark's parking lot that consisted of a couple of handicapped spaces in front of the bar, ample parking on the side, and on the rear of the building that was usually empty. Richard would park his truck in a shadowy position in the back parking lot where he could see all of the customers before they entered the bar from the side lot. He couldn't see the handicapped spaces, but the only person who ever parked there was Bob DeVore, the regular who'd hurt his back on the job. The parking spaces in the back of the lot didn't get used often because there was no lighting there. Instead, customers parked in the lot at the convenience store next door which was well lit by florescent street lamps. Richard was readily able to see those customers as well when they walked across the parking lot on the side to get to the entrance that was on the front leftside corner. Most of the customers never even noticed Richard parked stealthily in the back. Without a good look at the truck, one might assume it was abandoned there or waiting to be towed away.

The Dark Place was an unassuming structure with wormwood siding on two of the sides. The other two sides were cement blocks. Its' brown roof was low in the front in an effort to make it feel more cozy and intimate. It could almost be a large garage, except for the simple neon sign in front.

From the shadows, Richard monitored the arrivals and exits. He saw Mike Deere often and Ruby and Jeff when Nickie babysat their children--his two, her two from former marriages, but no "theirs" together. Red and Leigh were there usually and a lot of regulars who were mostly men, as Richard noted.

It was during those hours he spent parked in the shadows that he conceived of a plan to catch Joyce in her adulterous acts. He planted a small tape recorder underneath the bed in Joyce's trailer where she and Richard slept together. Each time before he left home during the day, he would switch on the recorder. Within a couple of days, he felt that he had proof which he was anxious to confront Joyce about.

The next day, Richard volunteered to take Nickie to babysit at Jeff and Ruby's home. When the children all left the living room to play with their toys and games in the bedroom, Richard produced his evidence to Jeff and Ruby. Excitedly, he began waving a tape recorder at them.

"You've got to listen to this! I caught Joyce on tape with another guy in our bed having sex! I hid this thing under our bed!" The three of them went into the dining room and sat down at the table to listen. They all leaned their heads together over the recorder, straining to hear.

When the noise finally started, Joyce could be heard saying, "Where is it?" Then they heard drawers opening and closing, then coat hangers being pushed around on the closet rod, television on in the distance.

Richard nearly shouted, "Do you hear *that*? Right there! That's Mike Deere's voice!" Richard saw Ruby and Jeff exchange looks, which Richard interpreted to mean that they thought he was just a head case; that they pretended not to hear anything. Richard thought that was odd until he realized that Jeff might just be trying to save himself from being found out. "It sounds a lot like you too, Jeff!"

"That's just the television, Richard. We don't hear nothing else! Nobody's making love," Ruby explained. She could see that Richard was absolutely convinced that there was a lover on the tape. Richard broke down and cried then.

He said, "Right there! Why can't you hear it?"

Ruby replied, "I can hear Joyce or somebody breathing while she seems to be opening drawers looking for something. That's *all*, Richard."

Richard laid his head down on the table and cried hard. Ruby could see the guy was coming apart before their eyes and lightly touched his back and tried to console him. Jeff thought the whole tape thing Richard did was very weird, but he did feel sorry for him. Ruby and Jeff both knew a little about Joyce's indiscretions with

Mike, but knew that Joyce would *never* do anything with him at her own place. Joyce and Mike always got together at Mike's house. She had no reason to risk being caught at home either by Richard or by her daughter. Jeff knew it was not in Joyce's character to do this. She had her own rules about things like that around Nickie. Jeff remembered that firsthand. It would be out of the question for Joyce to do that.

Jeff and Ruby could see it from both sides. They knew Joyce would no longer be with Richard if he didn't have terminal cancer. Richard had, indeed, treated Joyce very badly during the last year. That much was obvious. Jeff thought that Richard must be going through serious physical pain by now and he sure didn't need the additional mental anguish of Joyce cheating on him. He also didn't like for him and Ruby to be stuck in the middle of the Handcock's marital battles. Ruby and Jeff weren't getting along very well themselves these days, and this was not helping their already stressed relationship. Jeff was unsure if he and Ruby would even make it through the winter together. Both had two children each living with them, and the four kids seemed to understand that it was time to rally around their own parent and draw away from the other's children and begin to find fault with the other clan. Without realizing it, they did this to protect themselves emotionally in case Jeff and Ruby were going to split up. The constant arguing between the children added to the unrest that they were all feeling. Jeff tried to cheer up Richard and before the gut-wrenched guy left their house, Jeff slipped him some meth at no charge.

Ruby watched Richard hang his head as he walked outside to his truck. Jeff was standing next to her when she made the observation that Jeff was a bleeding heart and an easy touch.

When Richard pulled away Ruby said to Jeff, "It's almost Christmas, and we have four kids to get presents for! Then here you are, Mr. Genius Businessman, and you're just giving it away. Wow, what a great guy you are!" she said sarcastically. "It's not like he's your good buddy or anything. It's not right to cheat the kids like that. . ."

"Ruby," Jeff said softly, "shut up."

CHAPTER 18

Bob DeVore waited patiently as Joyce locked up The Dark Place for the night.

"Are you riding your bike home tonight, Joyce?"

"Guess so. No sign of Richard yet," Joyce replied.

"We can put your bike in my hatchback and I'll drive you home. My back's acting up real bad tonight, so I'll need you to help me get the bike in there,"

"Thanks, Bob, but if you'll just walk me out to my bike, that'll be fine. I'm leaving my craft stuff behind the bar tonight," Joyce said.

The minute they stepped outside, Richard appeared. "I'll take over now, *pal*," Richard said to Bob with an edge in his voice. There was something strange about the way he'd said that, but Joyce couldn't see his face well enough to read it.

Bob studied Joyce and she seemed okay with that arrangement. "Okay, fine," Bob said affably. It was the first time Bob had heard Richard's voice and it made him feel uneasy. "See ya tomorrow, Joyce."

Richard picked up Joyce's bike with one arm and tossed it roughly into the camper shell on the back of his truck after Bob took off. Joyce bit her lip as she knew for a certainty by then that Richard was angry about something again. She hoped that whatever it was, it would keep until morning. She had a splitting headache.

Richard walked around to get in the driver's side of the truck and didn't open Joyce's door for her as had formerly been his custom.

Once they were both seated and Joyce belted in, Richard backhanded her face with lightning speed. Joyce cried out with surprise and too late put her hands to her face for protection. She felt wet by the side of her mouth, but couldn't tell if it was from her mouth or nose. Her eyes began to water from the sting. The parking lot was empty but for them, and Richard picked up the tape recorder off the dash and pushed the play button.

Joyce could hear a television first, then drawers opening and closing, then breathing.

"What's that supposed to be?" she asked.

Richard couldn't conceal his pure hatred of her. "You *know* what it is, and don't play Little Miss Innocent with me!" he roared. "That's you and one of your boyfriends foolin' around in our bed!"

When Joyce realized that his allegations were groundless, she felt relief and laughed. It was her reaction to the stress and pain she was experiencing, and the realization that this also meant Richard didn't know about her interludes at Mike's house and that he was dead wrong.

Enraged by her laughter, Richard reached over and grabbed her by the hair. With his other hand, he released her seat belt and pushed her head down hard on the truck's dirty, old dashboard. Joyce's arms flailed as she tried to get his hands off of her. He pushed her head down one more time in the same way before he released her.

Joyce quickly opened the passenger-side door and just as she was about to jump out, Richard pushed her from behind; hard enough that she landed cockeyed on one shoulder and her hands and knees, scraping them on the parking lot's rough asphalt surface. Joyce stayed in that position for a moment, stunned. She winced when she tried to get up. She had twisted her wrist and ankle when she landed and her hip and shoulder hurt. Suddenly, Richard was there beside her, pulling her up by her hair. Joyce was disoriented and stared at her husband's distorted face as he kept ranting and raving at her about his bogus "proof." Her neck and head throbbed from the dashboard. Joyce brushed off her palms as she stood up.

"I want my bike *now*," Joyce said indignantly as she walked difficultly around to the back of the camper until she came to its small door. Richard easily caught up to her and shoved her head against the side of the truck's camper.

Doggedly, Joyce kept reaching for her bike until she managed to extricate it. Richard watched her sadistically. She managed to get several feet away from Richard until she felt it was safe enough to crawl on her bike and ride away.

Over her shoulder, Joyce shouted, "Don't come back to the

MURDER BY GRAVITY?

trailer, Richard. If you do, the police will be waiting for you."

* * *

Early that morning, Joyce filed charges against Richard and there was a bench warrant issued for his arrest. Joyce took Nickie and moved into Mike Deere's house for a week in case Richard came back to the trailer. Mike spent his evenings in The Dark Place with Joyce and drove her to his house at the end of her shift. He never complained when his alarm went off at 6:00 AM to go to work at the mine. Joyce's safety was more important at the moment than his sleep. Joyce's bruises were hidden behind her hairline, but tender when she moved her forehead or eyebrows from the dashboard incident and her other wounds were scabbing over.

That week, Nickie had homework every night and went to bed around ten o'clock. She was going to have tests at school before Christmas vacation in three of her classes. Mike was thrilled to have them both there with him.

After a week, Joyce received a phone call at work from the Yuma Police Department. It seemed that Richard had been stopped on a routine traffic violation. He also was found to have an illegal substance on his person at the time and was being held over pending his bail hearing the following Monday. The charges were speeding, possession, and her charge of spousal abuse.

Joyce felt that it was safe for Nickie and her to move back into the trailer again the next day. When they arrived, there was a sternly worded note from the RV park manager stating that they had until the end of the month to clean up the debris under their trailer and on their space or they would have to move out.

"Oh, great," Joyce thought, "It's mostly all Richard's junk. What am I supposed to do with it now?"

Just then Rachel Hammer walked across the street from her park model to welcome Joyce and Nickie back home. They had become chummy when Rachel cared for Joyce's father voluntarily every day after his heart surgery. Rachel walked a mile on a daily basis for exercise and as a preventative cardiovascular measure, as many seniors do in Yuma. Rachel used to stop by when Joyce was remodeling her trailer and admired her daily progress. Joyce felt like she could discuss almost anything with Rachel and knew she could be trusted not to tell her parents about any confidences. Rachel was a very compassionate woman, a quality that made her a fine nurse before her retirement.

"Hi! I haven't seen you two for a while. How are Richard's cancer treatments going?" Rachel asked.

Joyce's annoyance at the mention of Richard's name was obvious. "I don't know. He says the cancer has spread to his stomach, from where I don't know, but he still looks the same and I know for a *fact* that he's still plenty strong physically," Joyce replied.

Rachel said, "Yes, I heard that you had a problem with him last week. Are you still hurt?" Rachel was just concerned, not nosey.

"Mostly just my pride," Joyce said.

Joyce had given Nickie the key to the padlock on the trailer. When she opened the door Nickie said, "Mom, look at this mess Richard left!" Nickie was tired and on the verge of tears as she began picking up items that had been thrown around the trailer's interior, many of which were hers, since her bedroom was the living room. She was tired of being stuck in the middle of grown-ups' fights.

"I'll be there in a sec, hon," Joyce said. Then to Rachel she asked in a quieter tone of voice, "I'm beginning to wonder if he really *does* have cancer. What do you think, Rachel?"

"I think he's pulling your leg, dear, since you asked me. His symptoms and the shaved head . . . the whole thing makes no sense at all. The progression is all wrong. When does he say he's supposed to go for chemotherapy again?"

"He said this week, last I heard, but today he's in jail, so who knows?" Joyce replied.

"What does his doctor say about Richard's condition?" Rachel asked.

"I don't even know his name, only that his practice is in Tucson," Joyce said thoughtfully.

"It might not be a bad idea to get the whole story, dear. I'd start by talking to his oncologist."

"Thanks," Joyce said and squeezed Rachel's hand, "I'll do that."

* * *

MURDER BY GRAVITY?

That night a man phoned The Show Place and said, "Joyce has AIDS" and hung up. Stevie Lynd, the club's owner and Joyce's boss at The Dark Place, had been the one to pick up the telephone. Stevie was upset and called her friend, Tammy, at P.J.'s, saying that she didn't recognize the voice and she was angry that she'd let it rattle her so. "It's so creepy!" she said, "Do you suppose there's any truth to it?"

Tammy said, "Probably not, but I think you'd better tell Joyce about it."

* * *

Earlier that evening, Richard had called Joyce at the trailer. Joyce was just about to hang up on him when he said, "Listen! Don't hang up . . . please! I only get *one* call! Look, I know you're pretty pissed at me and you got a right to be."

"No kidding. What do you want now?" Joyce said sarcastically.

"I need you to come to court on Monday when I get my bail hearing."

"And just why would I want to do that?"

"In case they need to ask you about my cancer. I heard that I can get out with only house arrest and one of those electronic monitors on my ankle."

"I have a good reason for not wanting you out, remember? I know I'll never forget that you left a big impression on my mind."

"Please, Joyce. You know I don't have a long time left to live. Don't make me die in jail. I'll do whatever you want. I'll leave you and Nickie alone. I promise I will."

"And how do I know for sure that you even have cancer?"

Richard said, "I can't believe you're asking me that! How could you *not* know? Okay, wait a sec. Next week, if I get out of here, I have to go to Tucson for my chemotherapy treatment. How about if I bring you a letter from my cancer doctor? You already seen the brochures he gave me, but I'll ask him to write down the diagnosis and how long they expect me to live. I'll be in Tucson for a week or more depending on what all they have to do this time. So what do you say? Will you help a dying man out?" Joyce didn't respond. "They probably won't even ask you nothing when you go on

Monday, but I need you there just in case."

"If they put you under house arrest, you'll have to stay someplace else. No way are you staying here!" Joyce said emphatically.

"No problem. I'll stay at my mother's house," Richard responded.

Joyce faltered, "You promise to leave Nickie and I alone and not come over to the trailer?"

"I promise," Richard agreed.

"I'll think about it. I need to sleep on it, Richard. What time is the hearing?" Joyce asked, hedging.

"10:00 AM. I'm beggin' you, Joyce."

"I'll think about it, I said," and hung up noisily.

An hour later, Joyce's phone rang again. It was Stevie calling to tell her about the weird phone call she'd received at The Show Place.

"Did you recognize the voice?" Joyce was puzzled.

"No, he kind of whispered it. Joyce, I hate to ask, and you can tell me to mind my own business or go to hell, but is there any truth to what he said? Do you have AIDS?"

"No, of course not!" Joyce said with alarm, "Why would anybody call The Show Place and say that about me? I'm hardly ever there! It doesn't make sense!"

"Could it be Richard?" Stevie asked.

"No, way. He's in jail tonight and he already used his one and only phone call on me."

"Bet I can guess why. Okay, if I hear anything more, I'll let you know. You take care now, honey," Stevie said, "Bye."

* * *

The next morning, Joyce was trying to sort out the junk that was stored on her lot. It was hopeless and a lot more of it was her craft materials than she had realized. She remembered seeing a card on the laundry room bulletin board, advertising a storage shed for sale by somebody in the park for $35. Mike Deere volunteered to come over to help her move it. With Roy's help, Mike put one end of the shed up on the back of Roy's maintenance golf cart and a dolly under the other end. Joyce drove the cart as the two men guided the shed while it was towed across the park to Joyce's lot. Mike had to leave right

MURDER BY GRAVITY?

after, so Joyce chatted with Roy a little bit before he took off. It was her first real conversation with the man. Her bartender's instincts told her that he was one brew short of a six-pack, even if he did give her mother the tip about the job at 8th Street last summer.

When Joyce was alone again, she began to sort and load up the shed with the things she felt that she couldn't do without. She decided to wait before doing anything with Richard's stuff, depending on available space. Maybe his things could go to his mother's house or the trash, in her opinion.

Joyce was shaking several spray-paint cans to see if any were empty enough to toss away and wondered if they would be okay in the shed during the heat of the summer, when she heard a car pull up behind her. Joyce turned and saw that behind the wheel of a patrol car was a young YPD officer in uniform. Joyce knew that whatever he was selling had to do with Richard and she felt wary, but then as he approached her, she could tell that the officer seemed uneasy and she became curious.

"Mrs. Handcock?"

"Yeah?" Joyce kept shaking the paint cans to keep her hands busy.

He cleared his throat then said, "I was the arresting officer on the warrant you swore out against your husband last week."

"Oh?" Joyce wished he would get to the point.

"Uh, yeah. We caught him in a routine moving vehicle violation. He had some pictures on him when he was arrested. We didn't know if they were evidence at first, so we hung on to them. Today it was decided that these weren't pertinent to this case, so I was instructed to bring them to you." He then opened his own personal wallet and retrieved several photos. Joyce was dumbfounded when she saw that the contents were nude photos that Richard had taken of her one night when she was trying to spark up their marriage several months ago. As she thumbed through the stack, she was sickened and embarrassed as she was reminded how explicit they were. She had been high. Joyce nodded her thanks as he returned to his squad car. Joyce took the photos inside and burned them in the kitchen sink immediately. Tears streamed down her hot cheeks. She began to wonder how the police might think her nude photographs could be important to any case whatsoever. In her anger and confusion, she wondered if the pain Richard brought into her life would ever end.

* * *

 Monday morning as Richard was waiting to be transported to the courthouse from the detention facility, he stood somberly looking out of the narrow floor-to-ceiling window in his cell. The building had hundreds of such windows, so he could do so without easily being detected from the outside. He could see the entire main entrance of the courthouse. Hopefully, he would be able to see if Joyce showed up, unless she used the side entrance hidden from his view on the far side of the old building. Richard always thought it was funny that they let the criminals view the daily comings and goings of the people in the courthouse, especially the witnesses. He already recognized some of the women by sight who worked at the Clerk of the Superior Court's Office inside. Bailiffs were more difficult to spot, as they didn't wear uniforms for some reason and most were women. They appeared to be hostesses in the courtroom and served to make everyone in the court feel more comfortable, like a Tupperware party, but not.

 The uniformed guards marched the prisoners into the courthouse for bail hearings in shackles, chained to one another. The guards shouted at everyone down the hall from the doorway, "Clear the halls, prisoners coming through," and continued to do so as they moved throughout the building. They closed all the interior office doors before the prisoners were paraded by in their neon orange Department of Corrections jumpsuits, chains clanging noisily on their wrists and ankles. Several of the prisoners used this opportunity to gawk at the some of the more attractive women along the way through the glass walls of the offices. Many of those women avoided their looks and turned away from them, though some of the visitors in the courthouse seemed transfixed by the display.

 When Richard arrived at the bail hearing, Joyce was not there. He kept looking back at the doors hoping to see her. Travis Jordan, Richard's former parole officer, and the people from the Electronic Monitoring Service were there. There was a soft buzz as they seemed intent whispering to each other before court was called to order.

 They took Richard's case first, since he had the largest group of

MURDER BY GRAVITY?

people gathered there on his behalf. Richard was concerned about going first because Joyce wouldn't have spare time to get to Judge Mancini's courtroom.

A *suit* was a general name Richard attached to the men that wore them, making them nameless. One came up and introduced himself as Russ Kosta, and said that he was Richard's court-appointed attorney and that Richard was going to plead not guilty, which suited Richard just fine. Richard had the distinct impression that Kosta was not happy about the situation.

Richard's ankle chains were removed just before the bailiff said, "All rise. The Honorable Judge Mancini presiding."

The judge spoke first saying, "Mr. Handcock, I have been informed of your medical condition and have spoken with the people at Electronic Monitoring Services about your case. The city of Yuma's budget is ill-prepared to take on the expenses your deteriorating condition would undoubtedly amass, and I see no reason to interrupt the care you are receiving now through State assistance. The city of Yuma has no public defender at this time, so Mr. Kosta will be representing you in this case filed against you regarding spousal abuse, possession of an illegal substance and a moving traffic violation. The court needs to know if you have a telephone in your residence."

"Yes, I do, Your Honor," Richard now realized that because Joyce hadn't bothered to show up in court, he had the opportunity to control where he lived by getting the judge to enter her address and phone number into the official court record. They *were* married, after all, therefore the trailer was half his since Joyce purchased it while they were legally married. He had a legal right to be there, since there was no restraining order against him.

"Excuse me, Your Honor. My name is Christy Shannon, and I'm employed by Electronic Monitoring Services." She was an attractive, petite brunette in her late twenties. Richard could tell that she had bad news written all over her face.

Ms. Shannon continued, "I've reviewed Mr. Handcock's criminal record and I've concluded that he is not a good candidate for the monitor because of his spousal abuse and repetitive return to criminal activities once out on his own."

"Normally, I'd say you're right, Ms. Shannon," Judge Mancini began, "but Mr. Handcock is in the advanced stages of colon cancer, and I think that negates the normal conditions."

"Your Honor! Mr. Handcock had enough strength to attack his wife violently just a few nights ago, and if you let him return home, you may be endangering Mrs. Handcock's safety."

"Ms. Shannon, Mr. Handcock simply requires too much medical attention to expect the system to adequately care for him. I'm ordering that Mr. Handcock have the monitor attached following this hearing until his court date early next year. As you well know, Electronic Monitoring Services provides 24-hour, around the clock, unannounced visits by his worker who will also know where Mr. Handcock is at all times. This is considered a level 4 release. There will be serious accounting for all of his actions. If Mrs. Handcock feels that she is in danger, she can certainly exercise her right to leave."

Richard tried to conceal a smile as the judge spoke. He wished he could see Joyce's face when she learned of the judge's decision. As it happened, it took a few hours for the paperwork to be concluded before he was released. During that time, he caught a glimpse of Joyce through the window of his cell. Joyce had been physically escorted out of the courthouse. Richard could see that she was hopping mad and hurling insults loud enough for all around to hear. It was quite a scene and Richard was pleased with himself.

Early that evening, Richard's EMS (Electronic Monitoring Services) worker, Ike Groves, drove Richard to where his truck was parked and followed him home. Ike was a small-built, wiry man, who looked much older than he actually was, and had a definite Texas accent. Joyce and Nickie were both present at the trailer when the two men arrived and Richard introduced Ike to them. Nickie understood immediately that this was a grown-up situation and she preferred to leave. Since she couldn't go to her room, she said she was going to walk over to her Grandma and Grandpas. Joyce was calmed down by then, but still very cool toward Richard.

Ike explained that the monitor worked through their private telephone line. He picked up their telephone and opened his briefcase to retrieve some equipment. As he set up the phone, he spoke to them.

"Let me explain this program to both of you. Basically, my job is to gather information for the judges to help them make release determinations and to supervise people under my care. There are four levels of determination: level one is the least restrictive, and level four

MURDER BY GRAVITY?

is the most restrictive and that's the one where we use this electronic monitoring unit. Richard already has one attached to his ankle which has its own little transmitter. The receiver is a unit that I'm attaching to your telephone now." He held up a small electronic device and said, "This will always be looking for the transmitter on Richard's leg."

"When the unit cannot find the transmitter, it will send out a signal over the phone line to our monitoring center, indicating that you are away from the phone, or basically away from where you're supposed to be. We then will receive what we call an alarm away."

"Basically, Richard, you are under house arrest. If you are out at any time other than what has been authorized, we will be notified. We've done this successfully more than five hundred times, so we already know any trick you might think of to fool the system. I'll keep notes regularly and report any aberrations from your release conditions to the judge."

Richard asked, "How far away from the phone can I be before the alarm sounds off?"

"Good question. It depends on what this trailer has in its walls," Ike said, looking around.

Richard then asked, "Can I go outside? I have a lot of clean-up work I need to do just outside here on our lot."

"If you leave your front door open, you shouldn't have any problems. Consider yourself lucky," Ike said laughing, "I have some people who can't even walk to either end of their own house, because maybe there's some rebar or something in the way."

"It helps, too, if you keep your microwave, if you have one, the television and any radio equipment out of the path between you and this device on your telephone. Make sure when you return home to get close enough to the device so it will register that you're back or it will register as continually away."

"Okay, now, let's go over your schedule so you can get your time allotment away from home. What time do you leave for work and when do you get back?"

Richard, who didn't have a job at the time said, "11:00 AM to 7:00 PM. That's Monday through Saturday."

Ike asked pleasantly, "What kind of work do you do, Richard?"

"Oh I work in construction as a framer. I also have to pick up my wife from work at night, because she don't have a car right now. . ."

"No problem," Ike said. "What kind of time do you need for that?"

Richard replied, "Well, her hours vary so much. I think 11:00 PM to 2:00 AM ought to cover it for us."

Ike repeated it as he wrote in his notebook, "11:00 PM to 2:00 AM. Do you go to church on Sunday?"

Richard said, "Yeah, that would be 8:00 AM to 2:00 PM. We have really long prayer meetings. Joyce, who had been gritting her teeth through the whole session, rolled her eyes at him, while Ike wrote the hours down in his notebook.

"Okay, now that we have your schedule all set up, it will go into effect tomorrow morning when I fax it to the office. If for some reason you're not at work when you're supposed to be, you must call in to report it to me first. Here is my card. I can, and will, be popping in here anytime for field visits periodically. You will be remanded to lockup again if I catch you shopping at Wal-Mart while you're supposed to be at work."

"Moving on, Richard, the ankle bracelet has been sized with room for two fingers under it. It can't be slipped over the heel. You can dunk it in water. If it's cut off, we will be notified that the device has been compromised in three or four minutes."

"This contract explains all the rules that we just went over. Take a minute to familiarize yourself with them, then I'll need your signature and the date at the bottom. You do get to keep a copy of this, but if you have any questions, just call me or wait until I'm here doing a field visit, which will be about three times a week or more if I think it necessary. Needless to say, I will *not* be calling before I stop by, but it will only take a few minutes of your time. Richard, in your case, I'd better not see any signs of drugs or bruises on your wife. One more thing," Ike said with a grin. *"There will be no call forwarding."*

Richard thanked Ike, and he left into the night with his briefcase in hand. After they heard his car leave, Richard said as he laughed, "Is this a great system, or what?"

Joyce was miserable about this turn of events. Now she would have to put up with Richard again under her own roof. She knew that Richard was basically getting all the hours away that he could want. She also knew not to say otherwise to Ike Groves. For the life of her, she couldn't understand why the guy would believe that construction crews worked from 11 o'clock to 7 o'clock. They all usually start at 8:00 AM at the latest and quit just before dark. He didn't even question those three hours needed to pick her up from work. Ike never asked what kind of work she did, Joyce mused. Now Richard could freely bug her at work again. Sunday, she thought, Sunday was the most ridiculous of all. Six hours for church and she knew he hadn't been to church since they were married in Lute's Wedding Chapel. Richard was agnostic at best!

Joyce firmly resolved then that if Richard ever laid a hand on her again in anger, he must leave, regardless of whether he had cancer or not. She would find a way to get him out of her home, even if that meant petitioning the court to do it. It never occurred to her, that since she purchased the trailer while they were married, it was half his.

CHAPTER 19

Two nights a week, on Joyce's nights off, The Dark Place was Marcy Montgomery's work turf. The two nights before that, she worked as the relief bartender at The Show Place.

Marcy was in the process of cleaning nooks and crannies around the beer equipment while she sang along with Patti La Belle's hit song, "A New Attitude," on the jukebox. Its fast beat seemed to feed her energy. Her husband was a Marine and she was glad to be stateside after living in Japan for nearly two years. She had originally met Joyce as Joyce Martinez, when she still went by her ex-husband's last name in 1992. The two worked at P.J.'s together and occasionally barhopped back then, but only once since Marcy's recent return to Yuma for what used to be their traditional girl's night out.

Marcy noticed a vast difference in Joyce's personality in December of 1994. It seemed to her that Joyce was unhappy and distant with people now. Her tip money must be way down, Marcy had observed, knowing how a bartender's personality can make all the difference in the amount of tip money they made.

A half hour before the regulars were expected to arrive, Marcy was lost in thought as she worked behind the bar doing her menial duties. The ring of the telephone startled her from her intensive cleaning.

"The Dark Place," Marcy answered, drying her hands off on a cloth towel.

A male voice said without preamble, "Joyce has AIDS. She's a dead bitch." Then the phone went dead while she held the receiver in her hand trying to process the information.

Suddenly, it made crystal-clear sense as to why Joyce had changed so much. It must be true, she thought. Marcy automatically began trying to remember all of the surfaces she had touched during

MURDER BY GRAVITY?

her cleaning spree and examined the small cut on her finger that she'd inflicted on herself earlier that afternoon while picking up a broken glass that had fumbled from her wet hands onto the floor. She asked herself why she hadn't bothered to bandage it before going back to work. Such a stupid, little thing like that could . . . fear struck her hard in the pit of her stomach. Her hands shook as she flipped through the papers and messages attached to the bulleting board behind the bar to find Stevie Lynd's phone number. She knew that, as the owner of The Dark, she would want to know about an employee who had AIDS working behind the counter of her bar.

Marcy had so convinced herself that it was true, that she was incredulous when Stevie told her over the phone that it was just nonsense that some kind of crank had made up.

Stevie said, "Whoever that was, also called The Show Place a few days ago, so I checked it out with Joyce, and she says there's no truth to it."

"Well, that's a relief," Marcy said with a sign. "Still, how do we know for sure?"

"Because I believe Joyce, that's how. You know Tammy? The lady who owns P.J.'s? She says it's probably Joyce's husband. They're not getting along and he doesn't want her to work in a bar."

"I guess that explains why Joyce seems so sad lately," Marcy replied.

* * *

Richard squared it with Ike, his electronic monitoring worker, to be gone for a full week. He had told him that he had to go to Tucson for his chemotherapy treatments.

"Why don't you go to Phoenix? It's sixty miles closer," Ike asked him.

"My insurance only covers me in Tucson. You know, part of my insurance is through the Veterans Administration," he improvised. "That's where the V.A. hospital is. I wish it was in Phoenix, since my truck's in such crappy shape." The truth was, Richard had no insurance at all and he really didn't need any at the moment; except possibly for a rehab facility, which he would never consider had it been offered for free.

"Well, that's too bad you have to drive that far," Ike said, as he wrote in his notebook releasing Richard for seven time-away days. *Poor bastard,* he thought to himself. "Okay, you're all set for the trip. Stay out of trouble, Richard."

* * *

Joyce felt the dark clouds lift and she felt free again in Richard's absence. Joyce and Nickie celebrated by going shopping and out to lunch. They looked more like girlfriends, rather than mother and daughter, as they chatted about everything under the sun *except* Richard.

By early that evening, Joyce was still in a happy mood as she peddled her bicycle over to The Dark to begin her shift. She admired one of Yuma's beautiful sunsets during the trip over. When she arrived, she locked her bike in front of the bar, as was her custom.

Marcy worked the early shift that day and always made sure that everything in the bar was spotless, which Joyce appreciated as she turned on the lights behind the bar. Joyce marveled at Marcy's attention to details and wondered how she ever found the time to make everything so clean and perfect. It was Saturday night and she knew that it wouldn't be clean for very long.

Soon the regulars and their friends arrived and the jukebox played Gloria Esteban's song "Turn the Beat Around," defying anyone to be anything but cheerful. There was a party atmosphere. Later, Joyce suspected that a few people in the crowd were looking at her in an odd way. She locked the cash register for a quick break to the restroom so she could check herself out in the mirror and take a "bump" of meth. Her hair and makeup seemed okay, though she did add a touch of lipstick. She checked out her skirt and blouse to see if she'd spilled anything on herself or sat in something that she didn't know about. Looking at her image in the mirror, she lamented again over her stolen jewelry and had to make do with the only decent earrings she had left, which were three gold hoops. Two earrings on the right ear, the top hoop was smaller than the hoops she wore on bottom of both earlobes. At least they were real gold, she thought to herself. Her parents had given them to her for her birthday two years previously. Thank goodness she had been wearing them

MURDER BY GRAVITY?

and her wedding band on the day of the most recent burglary. She smoked some crystal ice and gathered her thoughts. Joyce felt that she looked fine and there was no reason that she could think of for anybody to be looking at her so peculiarly. It must have been her imagination.

By the time Joyce returned to her place behind the bar, Bob DeVore had arrived and was motioning for her to come over to him. She took it as a gesture that she should bring him his usual brew and brought a glass of it over to him with a smile. When she got a closer look at him though, he looked stricken.

"Joyce, do you have any paint around this place?" he asked.

Curiously, Joyce replied, "I think so. But why? What's going on?"

"When I got here a few minutes ago, somebody had already taken my handicapped space in front, so I had to park on the side of the building," Bob began.

"Oh, I'm sorry. . . ," Joyce assumed that was the reason why he looked upset.

Bob stopped her and said, "No! No, that's not important. Somebody painted graffiti on that exterior side wall of the bar."

"Stevie keeps some brown paint in back that might match pretty well. Don't worry about it. I'll paint over it before work tomorrow while it's still daylight. I don't think they've had any graffiti around here in a long time from what I've been told," Joyce said.

"Joyce, I'll stay by the cash register . . . *you* need to go outside and look at it for yourself," Bob said.

Joyce cocked her head to the side, looking at him in puzzlement. Finally, she shrugged her shoulders and acquiesced. She stepped outside and turned to her right to go to the side of the building. She saw that something was written further away on the wall as Bob said, but she couldn't read it from there. She walked behind the row of cars parked up near the wall and walked away from the building towards the convenience store next door and down, almost to the rear of the building.

The graffiti was written in white paint, which stood out very well on the dark brown siding. It read plainly, "JOYCE HAS AIDS." She was stunned and mortified. It was in large block letters and it was impossible to recognize the handwriting.

"Who would do this?" she said out loud to herself. Richard was always talking about the guys from Swift Sales who kept trying to get even with him. Who else would do something like this, she wondered. Joyce thought the phone calls were probably from them too. This all had to do with them, Joyce believed. She became angry and involuntarily trembled. She knew that she had never done anything to them to warrant this. She had even thought of Ron Gene as a friend before this. Yet Richard still had Joyce completely believing his conspiracy theory against them.

Joyce's jaw was set and tilted upward and she quickly walked back into the bar nearly on the verge of tears by then. Some heads turned her way. She ignored them and went straight to the storeroom where she found the brown paint quickly. Joyce stopped for a minute to collect herself again, then emerged with a brave smile. In truth, she resented them all for not telling her about the graffiti before Bob did. It had to have been there before the cars were parked in front of it, so they must have seen it. She discreetly gave the paint and a brush to Bob behind the bar.

"It's not true, Bob," she whispered to him.

"I never thought for a second that it was!" he whispered back as he put his arm around her and gave her a hug.

"Don't worry," he said, "I'm a good painter," he winked and smiled at her for encouragement. He saw her eyes searching the faces in the room.

"To hell with them," Bob said to her before he went outside.

* * *

Instead of going to Tucson for his non-existent chemotherapy treatment, Richard went to Hazel's home after spending a couple of days at his mother's house. Richard had generally kept in touch with Hazel while he was living with Joyce by going to The Bottoms Up Pub during Hazel's bartending shift two or three times a week. Going to Hazel's home was a different thing entirely. She pretended to be angry at him when he arrived unannounced, but the truth was that she had been going through a period of being lonely and pitied herself. She didn't fight when Richard took her into his arms.

It wasn't until later, when they were together in bed, that Hazel felt Richard's ankle monitor as it scraped her shin roughly.

"Ouch! What the heck is that?" Hazel said, surprised.

Richard lay on his back and brought his leg out from under the covers and held it up for her to see the device.

"I'm going steady with the State of Arizona," he joked. "This is the only reason I'm still with Joyce. The police are keeping me there by *force!* I have this week away from the monitor for my cancer treatments and I only needed two days for it, but they gave me the whole week off with no questions asked. It's really just a little slap on the hand, that's all."

"Why do you have that in the first place?"

"I got pulled over for not stopping at a four-way stop sign that was blocked by an over-grown tree. They spotted a joint in my truck. I don't even know where it came from, 'cause I haven't touched that stuff in a long time," he said with his best *"I'm-being-honest-with-you"* face.

Hazel looked deeply into his eyes and knew without a doubt that he was most certainly lying, but it didn't matter to her anymore. This was only for a few days' enjoyment. She had known it within minutes after his arrival. Hazel knew better than to pin hopes and dreams on Richard this time. Hazel would be happy with just the now. In fact, that suited her just fine.

* * *

Joyce forced herself to call Stevie and give her the rundown on the graffiti on the bar wall before somebody else did.

Stevie said, "You know, ever since the City of Yuma hired that guy to paint over graffiti full-time, you never see any of it around town anymore. The gangs don't bother to tag a territory if it's just going to be covered up the next morning. I read all about it in the newspaper. You call to report graffiti, and he'll come out and paint over it. He's got a whole truckful of colors of paint. We did have something similar happen here about four years ago. I guess bartenders must be good targets."

"One of the regulars already painted over it for me with the brown paint you keep in back. Anyway, I don't think picking me out was an arbitrary thing. I think this was done by a few people who are trying to get even with Richard. They've been after him ever since we moved out of Swift Sales the beginning of October. Richard's not even in town this week to see this. Pretty stupid of them," Joyce said, blindly, still believing in Richard.

Later that week, there were two more phone calls to the bar saying, "Joyce is a dead bitch." Joyce was becoming frightened by the written and verbal attacks and threats. The caller never phoned during Joyce's shift more than likely because she might recognize his voice. She wondered sometimes if Phil Seward could be behind all of it. She had recently received a notice from the Clerk of the Superior Court stating that her complaint of sexual harassment against him would be heard by a judge on January 13, a Friday. Joyce hoped that wasn't a bad omen.

* * *

Richard and Hazel began to fuss and feud again the last day he was at her place. He could tell that Hazel was beginning to pick at him purposely so it would be easier for her to say goodbye to him that afternoon. It was the same old issues with her about his drug usage and she kept asking how that worked out with his chemotherapy treatments and if his doctor knew, as she did, that he was heavily into meth again. He kept insisting that he was clean, but he couldn't fool her so he became angry and abusive instead.

"This time when I leave, it's for good," he told her.

"Good riddance," she said simply. Hazel turned her back to him and he got in his truck and drove away. They never would sleep together again.

CHAPTER 20

Lori knew that Richard was out of town for the week, so she decided to pay Joyce a visit at her place for a change; the mountain was going to Mohammed, so to speak. As Lori walked over, she purposely walked on the shady side of the street. Even in December, it wasn't unusual for temperatures of 80° or more in Yuma. Lori studied Joyce's tiny trailer and felt a little twinge of sadness. She knew Joyce could do a lot better than the way she was reduced to living then. She wondered how the prissy little girl that Joyce had been could grow up to live in such a ramshackle trailer. "I love you, Richard" still greeted her where Joyce had painted it on the trailer's exterior, not so long ago. Lori wondered if it were still true.

Joyce had been doing better by herself before she met Richard. If only Ed had let Joyce have custody of Nickie in the first place, Joyce wouldn't have married Richard and Lori's granddaughter wouldn't be sleeping in the living room with no dresser space to call her own. Joyce and Nickie didn't seem to mind, so Lori felt sorry for the both of them. She came over that day determined to come clean with Joyce in the matter of Richard.

Once inside, Lori settled down at the little dinette while Joyce poured them each a glass of diet soda. The dinette cushions were so flat that Lori had to sit up straight in order to sip her drink like a child.

"Have you heard anything from Richard yet?" Lori asked.

"No, but I didn't expect to. He says that his insurance company doesn't cover any long-distance phone calls and we can't afford it. I hope he's not too sick to drive himself home. They're supposed to be giving him radiation therapy in addition to chemotherapy this time," Joyce said. "He should be real sick when he comes home."

The more Joyce expressed her concern for her husband's life-threatening disease, the more outraged Lori felt. She would force herself not to mince words about what was happening before her eyes.

"Honey, you know I love you and Nickie very much," Lori said trying to keep her voice steady.

"But . . .," Joyce said, knowing that something bad was coming and hoping she would just spill it.

"But I have to tell you right now that man, Richard, has been lying to your face. He doesn't have cancer!" Her heart ached when she saw the affect her words had on Joyce. "I know that you say you love him and *want* to believe him, but *he's a liar and we are not going to have any sympathy for him because there's nothing wrong with him."*

Joyce's face became red, her eyes shiny with tears and she looked away from her mother.

"I just want you to know that Dad and I love you and want only good things for you." Lori reached for her daughter's hand under the table and Joyce flinched away.

Lori got up to leave and said one more time for emphasis, "He is *lying* to you." She left quietly knowing that Joyce would need some time to think it over and to redirect her anger to Richard instead of at her mother.

* * *

A few days later, Lori saw Richard's truck was back in Joyce's driveway and Richard capably unloading some of his boxes out of his truck. He didn't even *try* to appear looking sick. Surely, she thought, Joyce could see this too.

Joyce came over to visit her parents the next day.

"How's Richard doing, dear?" Lori asked casually.

Joyce's smile was wry when she said, "He said the doctor told him that his cancer is still spreading, but he looks pretty healthy, doesn't he?" Joyce said sarcastically as she glanced out her mother's window at Richard working outside on his truck.

In that moment, Lori's heart warmed knowing that Joyce was beginning to understand where her mother was coming from.

"Sorry it took so long to sink in, Mom," Joyce said as she gave her mother a warm hug. "What do you think I should do about it?"

"Well, tell him you want to know who his doctor is, so you'll know how to care for him and if Richard has any special needs such as diet. Then ask the doctor, if in fact Richard produces the name of one, what symptoms to look for and about his treatments. Find out who's paying for all of it."

"Good point. I don't even know the name of the hospital where he supposedly goes. He's very evasive about everything in connection with those details. I think we're going to have a little talk today," Joyce said with a smile that held no delight.

* * *

Richard had been too preoccupied and angry with Hazel to remember to act sick when he first returned home. Joyce soon began sticking her nose where it didn't belong. He realized for the first time that she doubted whether or not he was really sick. Her timing couldn't have been worse as far as he was concerned. Joyce had to work that night, so Richard was alone with Nickie. Nickie was the only female who wasn't angry with him at the moment. She seemed to have forgotten about the $50 he had stolen from her six months ago. Richard had grown to like Nickie a lot in the last year. He thought that it might be in his best interest to get Nickie on his side.

At six o'clock that evening, Richard had one hour left before the electronic monitor sounded an away signal. He asked Nickie if she would like to go with him to pick out a couple of videos to watch that evening. Nickie agreed to go by saying, "What*ever*."

In the truck alone with Nickie, Richard said, "How's school going?"

"Fine," Nickie responded.

Richard wondered why it was always so difficult to have a conversation with a teenager. He tried again.

"What kind of movies do you like?"

"Comedies, mostly."

When they arrived at the video store, Nickie went directly to the comedy rack and took out "The Distinguished Gentleman" with Eddie Murphy and "Out on a Limb," which is based on the chronicle written by Shirley MacLaine. Richard preferred good suspense or action movies, but he wanted to please Nickie so they checked out the comedies.

They made it back home with time to spare. Richard ordered them a large pepperoni pizza to share while they watched the videos. Nickie was spending time in the tiny bathroom, doing "girl things" Richard figured. He opened the kitchen cupboard and retrieved a couple of paper plates and napkins for them and poured two glasses of milk which he placed on the coffee table so they could see the television while they ate. Richard went into the bedroom and smoked some more meth while he was waiting for the pizza delivery.

Just then Nickie came out of the bathroom and headed to the front door.

Richard put the meth down and came out of the bedroom.

"Where are you goin'?" Richard said with alarm.

"I've got a baby-sitting job tonight," Nickie said as she opened the front door and said over her shoulder to Richard, "I hope you enjoy the movies. Your pizza is here."

Richard was incensed. His jaw twitched as he tossed money at the poor delivery boy. He grabbed the pizza and pulled the door closed. Then he threw it down on the floor, stepped in the middle of the box, and kicked it under the coffee table.

Richard began to pace back and forth in the small trailer from the kitchen to the bedroom and back like a caged animal. He felt that the bump of meth he had taken wasn't working like it should have. The meth had been indeed working when he took more and waited impatiently for eleven o'clock when he could get away from his electronic monitor. He tried to watch a video, but doing that only made him angrier at Nickie and all women in general. He was stuck with two movies that he had no interest in and a pizza he couldn't eat now. It would have been nice, Richard thought, if she had mentioned earlier that she had to baby-sit and wouldn't be there to watch the movies with him.

Damned women! Richard thought. *It's like they're all on a personal crusade to make me crazy!* His rage grew stronger with each passing hour. The methamphetamine, which is a child to the mother drug, crack cocaine, had suppressed his appetite and his central nervous system was running on fumes, so to speak. Methamphetamine produces very high levels of the neurotransmitter dopamine, which plays an important role in the regulation of pleasure. Richard thought that his hatred and paranoia were blocking the pleasure, so he smoked more.

The meth he had taken earlier was still in his system and would be for several more hours or possibly days. This is aptly called a "binge" that caused his body temperature to rise very high and made his mind manic. Some people imagine bugs on their skin at this point. With prolonged high-dose use or long binges, stimulant psychosis may develop. The psychotic user may feel intensely paranoid or hear voices or experience bizarre delusions; believing, for example, that other people are talking about him or following him.

Meth-induced panic and psychosis can be dangerous and may result in incidents of extreme violence. It would not be unusual for the psychosis to persist for days after the last dose. There have been reports of users remaining paranoid, delusional, apathic, and socially withdrawn for weeks after ceasing their usage according to The American Council for Drug Education, which is an affiliate of Phoenix House.

Waiting two minutes for good measure, Richard left the house just after eleven o'clock and drove his truck to his personal storage unit, the one Joyce didn't have access to, where he killed the truck's engine and snapped off the headlights. The storage yard was stone quiet. No one was there except him. The stars twinkled above him as if everything were normal; but not normal for Richard. Everything was far from normal.

* * *

Richard unlocked the roll-up storage door with his key. Next, he reached into his truck and brought his battery-operated lantern inside with him and rolled the door back down to the ground behind him. He looked at the messy piles of his belongings and sat down heavily on one of the boxes where he began to cry like a baby. His shoulders heaved as he cried and his high body temperature went higher still. Richard began clawing at his shirt to get it off as quickly as possible, ripping a sleeve in the process and scratching himself. The scratch felt good as it gave his overworked mind something other than his problems to focus on. Richard thought the bloodletting helped him to reassert his rational self through the pain.

Richard knew what he had to do as he picked up a number sixteen penny nail, which is very large, and began scratching his body just below his sternum and above his stomach. He hesitated with the first few scratches because the pain was great. Then he thought about Joyce and Hazel and Nickie as he proceeded to dig the nail into his flesh over a hundred times on his arms, sides, back, and stomach. He removed his camouflage pants and dug the nail deeply into his legs dozens of times. Richard had reached a state of frenzy with his self-punishment. His body was covered in blood. The blood washed all the bugs away.

When the frenzy subsided after he ran out of unmarred skin, except his head and where his boxers were. He sat waiting for his pulse to slow down and enjoyed the feeling of his heart pumping blood through the open gashes.

Richard soon realized that he would have to get himself together to pick up Joyce from work. He looked at his watch and he was bewildered that so much time had passed. How would he explain the blood and scratches to her? Then an idea formed in his mind of how to explain the scratches and manipulate Joyce to feel sorry for him at the same time.

He arrived at The Dark with twenty-five minutes to spare. He pulled into the parking lot of the convenience store next door to the bar and yelled at a man returning to his car with a six-pack of beer.

"Hey, man, can you help me out?"

Even with Richard in his truck, the man could see some of the blood on Richard's shoulders and chest. "What the hell happened to you? Was there an accident?" The man looked in both directions on 24th Street and saw no flashing emergency lights. He put the six-pack on top of his car and walked up to Richard's truck window.

Richard said, "Something like that. My wife works in the bar there. She's the bartender. Could you go in and ask her to come out here? All I've got on is boxers." When Richard motioned toward the direction of the bar, the man saw even more blood. Richard said, "Her name is Joyce."

"No problem. You just sit there and take it easy and I'll go get her. Don't let anybody run off with my beer."

Joyce was in the process of cleaning up the bar and her only customer, Bob DeVore, was waiting patiently to walk her out. They were chitchatting when the man from the convenience store came in, Joyce said, "Hi! What can I get for you?"

The man said, "Are you Joyce?" Joyce nodded her head. "Your husband's outside in a truck and it looks like he's been hurt pretty bad. I don't know what happened to him."

Joyce said, "Thanks." She had just been talking to Bob about Richard's tricks when the man came in the door and the two of them exchanged looks after the man spoke.

Bob said quietly to Joyce, "Another trick?"

"Probably." Joyce reached over and locked the cash register and said to Bob, "Will you go outside with me?" Joyce couldn't help but feel irritated by Richard's constant dramas. Bob and Joyce both saw the blood when Richard opened the driver's door. There was blood from his neck to his feet. He was dressed only in boxers and had a bloody towel wrapped around his bald head. Richard acted woozy.

"What happened?" Joyce asked. Her voice had an edge to it, from annoyance more than concern.

Richard said, "I stopped over at my storage locker to clean it up for a while before I had to pick you up from work. I thought I had some stuff in there that I could sell at a yard sale."

Joyce crossed her arms in front of her and said, "Well, go on!" Her body language was blatantly guarded

"I heard a voice behind me, but I didn't think he was talking to me, so I just ignored it and began loading some stuff into the camper. Then I heard another voice and I turned around and somebody hit me in the head with something and knocked me out."

"When I came to, I had been kidnapped, stripped of my clothes and my arms were tied behind my back. They had me inside my camper and whoever was driving slammed on the brakes and I went flying around back there. Then two Mexicans came to the back door and dragged me out, threw me down to the ground and started whipping me with some kind of wire rope. I asked them why they were whipping me and they never gave me an answer."

"Then, when I was able to get one of my hands free, I grabbed a stick that was laying there on the ground next to me and I came after them with it. There was another truck parked next to mine and they both got in it and drove away."

"I sat in the driver's seat and I could see the Cocopah Casino in the distance, so I knew they had taken me out to the Indian reservation and I started to drive back here. On the way, I caught up with their truck and they started chasing me again. They had a gun and shot at me three times before I lost them in Old Town. I think they were a couple of guys that work at Swift Sales."

To Bob DeVore's surprise, Richard then produced a marijuana joint from behind his ear, lit it, and took a long drag from it. After he blew the smoke out of his lungs, he said casually to Bob, "It's okay. It's legal for me. The doctor gave me a prescription for this, to make me feel better."

Joyce believed every word about the kidnapping, but she was still angry at him for lying about the cancer and forcing himself into her home.

"I think you'd better go back to the trailer and get some clothes on and call the police."

"I don't know why we need to get the cops involved in this," Richard protested.

"Look, you were kidnapped. That's what people do when they get kidnapped. They make a police report! Maybe they can get the guys from Swift Sales off your back."

* * *

Officer Rolland De La Bree had been in the Yuma Police Department since January of that year. He had been without a partner for four months. He received a call to respond to a "delayed kidnapping," which indicated to him that whoever was kidnapped had been released. They wouldn't have sent him if it were otherwise. He drove to the RV park and saw Richard sitting in his truck with his door open in the parking lot in front of the management office.

Richard's head was down to the side and he had a towel wrapped around it. As Officer De La Bree approached, Richard fell out of the truck fully clothed, but managed to stay on his feet.

"Are you Mr. Handcock?" De La Bree asked.

"Yeah."

"Looks like you need some medical attention for your head," De La Bree suggested.

MURDER BY GRAVITY?

"No, I don't need any medical attention," Richard said. Then without any warning, Richard pulled up his shirt and dropped his pants.

Officer De La Bree was surprised but saw the linear gouges and lacerations all over Richard's body even in the poor lighting. The blood had been wiped off and most of the wounds were dry. He went to his patrol car and requested assistance in a possible kidnapping after which Richard proceeded to tell him the story, much as the story he'd told to Joyce and Bob. Except in this version, he had more information about the perpetrators. He described two of the Swift Sales employees and one of their trucks. Richard hoped that by involving Ron Gene's employees, he could barter with Ron to drop the stolen merchandise and trafficking charges against him. In exchange, Richard would drop the kidnapping and conspiracy to commit kidnapping charges.

De La Bree interpreted Richard's behavior to be possible intoxication by alcohol, not realizing it was a meth binge combined with marijuana intoxication.

Richard finished the story by telling the officer about his cancer and chemotherapy. That was when De La Bree's supervisor and another patrolman arrived at the scene.

At the sight of the other uniforms, Richard rolled up his body into a standing fetal position. De La Bree had never seen anything like it before and went over to steady him so he wouldn't fall.

When Richard felt his touch, he jumped up and screamed, "Don't touch me! Stay away!" Richard's paranoia took over.

The two officers backed off, but the supervisor walked up to him and said, "Hey, guy, it's okay." He put up his hands. "Look . . . nobody's touching you. I'm the officer in charge. How about telling me what happened to you tonight."

While Richard repeated his story to the supervisor, De La Bree filled in the other officer about what Richard had said. Then the supervisor left Richard standing by his truck and came over to speak with the other patrolmen.

De La Bree asked, "Should we take him over to the hospital and get him a physical and mental exam?"

The supervisor said, "No. He's lying, but you better take him to Behavioral Health Services to get checked out."

An hour later, the officers caught up with their supervisor again on the phone and told him that Behavioral Health Services wouldn't take him because he wasn't considered dangerous."

"That's par for the course. Bring him down to the station."

After arriving, the supervisor had Richard sit in the chair across from his desk. The office was quiet due to the late hour. He said, "Mr. Handcock, we haven't received any reports of gunshots or speeding tonight. There were no bullet holes in your truck. What do you think about that?"

He leaned back in his chair and studied Richard.

"There're some people at Swift Sales, where I used to work. I think it was them. I think it was a vendetta because I had an argument with the owner and a couple of the employees."

Persistently, yet politely, the supervisor, Jack Moer, said, "But there were no shots reported. People almost always report shots. Would you remove your shirt please?" The supervisor noticed that three or four of the scratches on Richard's chest showed hesitation marks. They started real light, kind of skipped a little bit, then got deeper. The way Richard was cut was not consistent with marks from being whipped.

The supervisor asked Richard to turn around. The cuts in his back went up a few inches from his waist and were slightly diagonal and went in different directions on each side. The marks at the top were straighter up and down and started from his neck and the top of his shoulders to his shoulder blades, leaving the center of Richard's back unscathed. The marks were consistent with Richard inflicting the wounds on himself. He saw that the marks on Richard's arms went straight up and down and were parallel to each other with maybe a half an inch between them, two to three inches long.

The supervisor said, "Would you please reach your hands behind your back as far up as you can?" Richard obliged. As he suspected, the cuts ended near where Richard could no longer reach. "Thanks, now I need you to remove your pants. I have to take a few photos of your injuries." Then he noticed that the cuts on Richard's thighs were straight up and down and were by far the deepest of the wounds next to the cuts on his arms. By that time Richard no longer seemed so intoxicated.

After taking pictures of Richard from all directions, he said, "I'm

MURDER BY GRAVITY?

afraid that I don't believe that you're being quite truthful with me. It looks as though you did this to yourself. People quite often make false reports to the police department for one reason or another. Are you having any problems at home?"

Richard dropped his gaze to his feet. He surprised the supervisor with a forthright answer. "You're right. I did it. My wife and I haven't been getting along lately. The reason my head is bald is because I have cancer and I'm getting chemotherapy treatments. I'm afraid my wife is going to leave me . . . "

"And the cuts were a play to make her feel sorry for you and stay around?"

"Yeah."

"What about the story that you got hit in the head?" said the supervisor.

Richard said, "No, I wasn't hit . . . I slipped in the blood when I was getting into my truck and I hit my head on the ground."

The supervisor had tried not to offend Richard in order to get a complete and true story from him. He'd used this technique successfully many times before, "What about the people involved from Swift Sales?" he asked.

"That was a lie," Richard admitted. The supervisor wrote down several notes in his pad as they talked. At this point he entered the phrase: "Doesn't show remorse *at all*. Seems to feel like this behavior is normal."

The supervisor said, "I'll bet you could find a better way to keep your wife's attention. One that isn't so painful. . ."

Richard interrupted, "Oh, this doesn't hurt at all!"

"Really? Well, it would sure hurt me! Anyway, you know what I mean about finding a better way. Now go home and make up with your wife."

"Thanks," Richard said with what seemed like sincerity. The supervisor had treated him with respect and he appreciated it.

When Richard returned home to Joyce, he never told her the truth as she cleaned his cuts with hydrogen peroxide. She and everyone else, including her family and friends, always believed that Richard had been kidnapped and whipped by the people of Swift Sales.

CHAPTER 21

The Dark Place was ablaze with Christmas lights and other festive holiday decorations, including a small tree. Three different regulars brought in mistletoe and hung it strategically around the bar.

Marcy enjoyed the atmosphere in the bar by herself before the regulars arrived. She reflected on the large box of her belongings that contained, among other possessions, all of her cherished Christmas decorations. She vividly remembered packing them securely in Japan before their departure but the box got lost and the military had yet to track it down. Marcy and her husband couldn't afford to buy new decorations this year because they had gone crazy buying gifts before they left Japan and were short of cash. The time Marcy spent at The Dark was pretty much going to be the extent of her Christmas environment that year, and she was glad to have it. She fussed with a piece of tinsel on the little tree.

"Ho-Ho-Ho!" Marcy heard a female voice say before she looked up and saw Joyce enter the bar carrying a large cardboard box that had "X-mas Decorations" written with a black felt marker on the front of it.

"Hey!" Marcy said. "There ain't no 'Ho's' here! Not yet anyway. What's that . . . more decorations for the bar?

Joyce laughed at Marcy's joke as she set the box on top of the bar and sat down on a stool next to it.

"Well, no, not exactly. Stevie mentioned to me the other day that your Christmas decorations didn't make it back here from Japan. Since I have so many decorations and so little space anymore, I thought maybe you could use these."

Marcy was very moved by Joyce's unselfish gesture. Except for the occasional bar-hopping together with Joyce, she didn't feel like

MURDER BY GRAVITY?

she knew Joyce all that well--mostly just in passing at work. Marcy accepted graciously and Joyce felt good when she left.

Two years earlier, Joyce took Nickie on the four hour drive to Disneyland in Anaheim, California. Joyce had exited the I-5 Freeway onto Harbor Boulevard, which seemed to have a signal every twenty yards. While waiting for traffic to move, Joyce and Nickie noticed a young homeless woman cross the street in bare feet. She had no shopping cart and no obvious belongings. Joyce remembered the black stretch sandals that she had pushed under her car seat several months previously in case of emergency and on impulse, pulled into an IHOP restaurant's parking lot. Joyce told Nickie that she would be right back as she quickly grabbed the sandals and ran after the poor woman for a half a block. Joyce was surprised when the woman saw Joyce approach; she backed away and looked scared. The woman looked around to see if others were coming with her. Joyce had never seen another person so afraid of her before. It was strange.

"Excuse me," she said giving the woman plenty of space, "I happened to notice that you haven't got any shoes and I have an extra pair here that I have never worn that you can have."

"For free?" The woman asked skeptically.

"Yes, of course."

The woman took the sandals and looked critically at them then said, "No. I don't want them."

Joyce pointed out that they were stretchy and that they would surely fit her.

"I don't like them," the woman replied and walked away.

When Joyce returned to the car, slightly winded from the run, Nickie saw a peculiar look on her mother's face and that she still had the sandals in her hand.

"What happened, Mom?" she asked.

Still puzzled, Joyce said, "She said she didn't like them or want them!" Joyce removed her baseball cap and wiped at the perspiration on her forehead with the back of her wrist. "Well, hon, we tried."

Ever since that incident, Joyce understood that some people clung to the only thing they had left, the right to their pride. She was glad that Marcy hadn't been insulted by her offer.

When Joyce returned home afterwards, she hurried to unlock the trailer door to catch a ringing phone.

"Merry Christmas!" Joyce answered, her good mood about to vaporize by the manager of their RV park. Joyce was told in no uncertain terms that despite her father being the summer manager, she would have to pick up all the junk around her trailer or the property management company would not accept her rent check next month and they would have to move out of the park.

* * *

Joyce spent the holiday at the Perrons with both of her children present. Richard didn't bother to show up even though he had been invited. Joyce was relieved.

On December 30 Ike Groves, Richard's electronic monitor worker, dropped by to see Richard for the eleventh time while Joyce was there. When he was seated in their tiny living room on a folding chair, he dropped his bomb.

"The probation department called me today. Somebody told them that you don't have cancer but that, in fact, you probably have AIDS." His statement drew gasps from both Joyce and Richard.

"I was also informed that Joyce has been beating you up. I can see evidence of that by the scratches on your arms that are healing." Of course that was what Richard had told several people who asked about the scratches on his arm. There were probably many who believed it even if the police officer responding to the kidnapping didn't. The comment of Richard having AIDS instead of cancer must have come from somebody who had seen his graffiti on the bar wall a couple of weeks previously. They would have just connected the dots. If Joyce had AIDS, then so did he. Both an AIDS victim and a long-time meth abuser can have similar outward symptoms. Richard had dark circles under his eyes and skin ulcerations and infection from picking at imaginary bugs on his face, coupled with his gross loss of weight. All due to his increased and continued meth abuse.

Richard verbally jumped all over Ike. "*Who* said that?"

Joyce was shocked and her eyes began to tear up.

Ike said, "Are you saying that this is not true?"

Richard shouted, "No way! The marks on my arms are because I was kidnapped and whipped a couple of weeks ago. Joyce has never hurt me physically." Richard continued, "I don't think AIDS makes all your hair fall out like chemo does. Whoever said that doesn't have a clue! No, sir, there's not a word of truth to any of that."

Ike said he would report Richard's objection to his supervisor and left the trailer still looking doubtful. Ike knew that eventually Richard might need to be tested in order to be sure what disease he had. AIDS carriers that didn't cop to it really ticked him off, he thought shaking his head as he walked to his car.

After Ike drove away, Joyce and Richard were left alone. Nickie had walked over to her grandparents' home to watch television with them when Ike arrived. She did that often when they had visitors or when she felt tension at home, which was a lot at that time. Everyone in the proximity of the Handcocks' trailer heard a lot of yelling on a daily basis. December 30 was no exception.

Ike had planted the seed of doubt in Joyce. Richard *was* starting to look like he could have AIDS (Acquired Immune Deficiency Syndrome). He was thin and sickly looking with a couple of sores on his face that didn't seem to be healing very quickly. Joyce needed to know once and for all. She gathered her courage and asked him if he could possibly have AIDS. In the blink of an eye, Richard's hand rose up and he slapped Joyce's face hard. Her head reeled to the side.

Joyce persisted, "I *need* to know if you have AIDS or not!" Richard lifted Joyce by the arms into a standing position, turned her around and intended to back her against the wall, but had forgotten that the folding chair that they had brought in for Ike was in the way and Joyce fell over it. Her legs would be badly bruised once again, she thought.

"Yeah, Joyce, I have AIDS. Either way, I'm going to die soon. What difference does it make?"

"If you have AIDS and not cancer, *I* might die too!" Joyce explained, trying to be assertive from a disadvantaged position on the floor.

"Oh, yeah, Joyce . . . you're going to die all right. In fact, you might die even before I do!"

Joyce's blood ran cold as she saw in Richard's eyes a deep hatred for her. He wasn't kidding. Richard stepped over Joyce's body kicking her in the leg as he did so. Then he said, "oops," like he had done it accidentally. Then he smiled at her, "I'd be more careful if I was you."

CHERIE HUYETT ACHTEMEIER

* * *

In the late morning of December 31, Lynn came by to pick up her sister in her mini van. They headed west about three miles and over the Colorado River, which is the unofficial state line dividing Arizona from California. The I-8 Freeway took them three more miles to the Quechan Indian Tribe parking lot in Andrade, California, where they walked 100 feet over the border to Algodones, Mexico.

Lynn was in the market for a leather handbag, while Joyce would only be helping her look. Money was scant this time of the year for the Handcocks.

Joyce and Lynn enjoyed walking by all of the street vendors vying for their attention and attempting to make deals with them. The two women took pride in their bartering skills. They refused to pay full price for anything; to pay full price would be like the tourists and snowbirds, not for locals like them.

A shiny silver herringbone necklace caught Lynn's eye and she asked the vendor, "How much?" in her limited Spanish. She was only mildly interested in buying it because she was there, after all, to buy a purse. This attitude gave her more control over the bartering process. One must be willing to walk away from the vendor's shop and not buy unless the price is acceptable.

The vendor replied in broken English, "For *you*, pretty lady, only ten dollar."

Lynn said in Spanish, "I'm not a tourist. I am a Yuman. You want too much money for it!" Joyce wasn't sure what was going on, so she let her sister lead them. Lynn turned to walk away and the vendor said as he walked after her, "Okay, lady, nine dollar."

Lynn replied, "That's still too much!"

In his heavy accent, the vendor said, "Okay. How much you wanna pay?"

Lynn said without batting an eye, "Five dollars," knowing it was worth well over ten dollars in Yuma.

"Okay, lady, you pay eight-fifty."

"Five dollars," Lynn insisted as she let her eyes begin to search the wares of the next vendor down the street.

The vendor spoke loudly, "Eight dollar!"

MURDER BY GRAVITY?

"Five!" Lynn shouted back at him without bothering to turn around.

After Lynn and Joyce had walked three vendors past his shop, they heard him shout at them again, "Four!"

"Four?" Lynn spun around on her heels with the thrill of victory and began to walk back to his shop, but just before they got there, the vendor said,

"Yeah, lady four! Four-get-it!"

Joyce started laughing at Lynn and gave her a bad time, until both of them were laughing. Lynn said, "Well, now that I have you smiling again, how about I buy you a couple of margaritas when we get to the restaurant at the corner?"

Joyce said, "Sounds great!"

Once they were settled into a booth, they ordered nachos and drinks. It felt good to get out of the warm sun (even in December) and sit down. Joyce gathered her shining hair back into a ponytail and twisted it upwards, securing it with a fabric-covered plastic clip. There were a few locks of hair that didn't get into the clip, but on Joyce, it looked cute, Lynn observed with admiration of her older sister.

Lynn said, "How are things going in the front lines of the love war?"

"I'm pretty sure now that Mom is right about Richard. She says that he's lying and that he doesn't have cancer at all. The house-arrest worker said he received a report that Richard didn't have cancer, but that he does have AIDS! Somebody also said that I was the one who made all those cuts on him when he was kidnapped!"

"You've got to be kidding! So what did Richard have to say about that?" Lynn asked.

"He denied it when the guy was there, but I asked him again after the worker left last night, and he slapped my face and kicked me. He got real pissy about it."

Lynn said, "You shouldn't let him get away with that. So, did he ever give you an answer?"

"Actually, he said that he *does* have AIDS, but he was being sarcastic. I don't think we're going to make it to our first-year anniversary on the 25th of next month. Either he'll be dead, or I'll be dead, or we'll both be dead."

Joyce's good mood dissipated and she looked sad. Lynn extended her hand across the table to try to comfort her.

"Honey, you've got to leave him. Kick him out of the trailer!" Lynn said with anger and squeezed Joyce's hand for emphasis. Joyce sighed and tried to stretch her shoulders down and moved her neck around to ease the tension that seemed to have settled into her body.

"That's no good," Joyce told her, "Since I bought it while we were married, it's legally half his. I can't afford to put a deposit on an apartment right now. He's supposed to clean up his junk from under our trailer, or they're going to kick us out tomorrow. I keep thinking that he's got that stuff out there so he can grab it and leave at a moment's notice. I wish he would. I really do."

"You and Nickie are welcome to stay with us until you can get money ahead. You know that, don't you?" Lynn responded.

"Yeah . . . thanks. I might take you up on that. Richard scares me now. He's really changed since we were married. I guess in a way, I have too."

"I hope you don't wait too long to leave," Lynn admonished, "Richard sounds like he could be dangerous. You know Mom would tell you to leave right away because of what she went through with our father years ago. She always says that guys that beat up on women only get worse, not better. Where exactly are you going to draw the line? When he *kills* you?"

* * *

The Handcocks and a few others in their circle of friends had plans to go barhopping on New Year's Eve. Joyce took her time getting madeup and dressed. She wore a black strapless unitard in spandex under a black velvet blazer and had a black velvet ribbon tied neatly around her throat. She looked like she could be a model in those billboard ads for Black Velvet liquor that reads, "Feel the Velvet." The Halston cologne that Nickie had given her for Christmas trailed after her. She told Richard as he was about to leave the trailer for the park showers that she was going to run over real quick to show her outfit to Lynn.

Richard looked at her disapprovingly and said, "Whatever." Nickie always used that word a lot and he found it to be contagious.

MURDER BY GRAVITY?

Joyce was sick of the word, but ignored it.

In reality, Joyce went to P.J.'s to wish her old boss and friends a Happy New Year. She looked fabulous when she walked into P.J.'s. The last few weeks had taken their toll on Joyce, but tonight she looked like her old self--stunning.

Ruby, Leigh, and Tammy greeted her warmly with hugs and told her that she looked fabulous. Ruby had soon turned their girl talk into a women's bitch session with her complaints that Jeff was getting on her nerves more and more. Tammy asked Joyce how things were going with Richard.

Joyce surprised everyone when she said suddenly, teary-eyed, "If I don't get out of this marriage, he'll kill me."

* * *

Nichole was baby-sitting later that night for Ruby and Jeff's children. Nickie would have liked to go out too, but Joyce wouldn't let her daughter date until she was older.

Jeff and Ruby met the Handcocks at The Dark Place. Bob DeVore was already there. Marcy and Stevie were working the bar. Red, the former Yuma Police officer and his live-in girlfriend, Leigh, joined their friends to barhop in separate cars. Most, except Red and Bob, started the evening smoking meth in the restroom, then began serious alcohol consumption.

When the women gathered in the restroom later to check their lipstick and get another bump of meth, the conversation that they started in P.J.'s earlier continued.

Ruby said, "I'm about ready to leave Jeff." All looked at her with some surprise. She answered their unspoken question by saying, "He constantly bitches about every little thing I do. I'm not married to him and I don't have to put up with that crap. I was talking to Red and Leigh a little while ago and Red said that I can move into his house whenever I want to get away permanently or whatever. I'm seriously thinking about doing it."

"Your kids too?" Joyce asked.

"No. I'm going to leave them at my mom's place for a while. They love it there because she has a swimming pool and baby kittens. Mike Deere also told me I could crash on his couch if I want.

At any rate, I think next year will be better than this one."

Leigh said, "That would be great if you moved in with us. Red's such a sweet guy. But I predict that Red and I won't be together very long in the New Year. He's just too *old* and boring!" Leigh complained, wrinkling up her nose with distaste.

Ruby replied, "I'll take a sweet man over a critical one at any age. It don't matter to me. Is he cool? Would he mind if we do a little crank or grass?"

Leigh said, "I do it in my room and he pretends he don't know, 'cause he was a cop. Don't get me wrong . . . he wants me to quit and I keep telling him that I'm trying to quit, but I don't think it's that big of a deal to him compared to some of the scum bags he's had to arrest."

Ruby was visibly relieved and said, "That's good, because I don't plan to quit anytime soon. I'm going to be free to *par-tay*!"

The others laughed. Ruby said, "What about you, Joyce? What do you predict for 1995?"

Joyce replied, "That's easy. I'll either be a widow, divorced, or he'll kill me."

* * *

Later that night at The Dark, Stevie Lynn observed Joyce crying. After that, Joyce seemed to grow distant from her. Stevie figured that her unfamiliar behavior had to do with her husband somehow.

CHAPTER 22

An overcast sky greeted Joyce early the morning of January 6 as she broke the sound of silence in the recreational vehicle park by opening her squeaky trailer door. Joyce was so used to sunny days, one after the other, that the clouds made her feel even more oppressed and depressed than she was already. She carried her one-load laundry basket filled with two loads of laundry with a box of off-brand soap balanced on top to the park laundry facility.

Once inside the concrete block building, Joyce was relieved when she saw that no one else was ahead of her. Joyce dropped the basket on the floor in front of the washers and reached into the front pocket of her tight jeans for the quarters she had squirreled away from her tip money.

"Psst!" She heard from behind her. When she whirled around, she saw Mike Deere smiling at her in the doorway.

"Hey, Mike! If I were more awake, you might really have scared the crap out of me," she said dryly.

"Uh-oh. What's the matter?" Mike asked instantly assessing her mood as usual.

Joyce answered, "You should be asking me what's *not* the matter. It would take less time to tell you." She walked over to give him a brief hug. She rested her forehead against his chest for a few seconds, looking utterly defeated to Mike.

"That bad?" Mike asked.

"My life is so screwed up. I hate being in my own home," Joyce complained. "Do you think you could help me load the washers then take me for a ride? I've got to get out of here," Joyce complained.

"Sure, no problem," Mike was pleased to do it. In fact, it was lucky Joyce came out when she did, because he wouldn't have knocked on the door.

Soon they hopped into his Jeep together. Joyce held on to the roll bar as they drove to Mike's house without uttering a word to each other. Nickie was at school and Richard was still sleeping.

Mike opened his never-locked front door for Joyce and she strode over to her usual stool at his breakfast bar. The radio was already on as two recorded male voices debated the evidence challenging Fuhrman's credibility, and if it would be admitted into the O. J. Simpson trial.

"If they could punch holes into Fuhrman's testimony, the bloody glove at the mansion would be questionable--compromised at best. The assumption could be made that Fuhrman could have planted it at the mansion from the crime scene," the recorded broadcaster reasoned. A live, local broadcaster's voice added, "F. Lee Bailey and Robert Shapiro are reportedly not speaking to one another just days before the Simpson murder trial is set to begin." This same broadcaster, who would soon report a murder in Yuma, would be later called to jury duty in another local murder case.

Mike changed the station to classic rock then walked into the kitchen. "Coffee Royale or Bloody Mary?" he asked Joyce.

"Mary, thanks," Joyce said and spaced out while she watched the wind blow the paloverde tree outside kitchen window. Its green bark always struck her as a fresh splash of color in the desert. A storm was headed their way.

Mike poured Joyce's tall drink and set it in front of her, then stood strategically between Joyce and the window.

When Joyce focused on Mike's handsome face, tanned deeply despite his job underground at the mine, ice-chip blue eyes, she smiled at him halfheartedly. "What? No celery?" she joked referring to the drink's usual garnishment.

"Sorry, fresh out," Mike said then raised a sun-bleached eyebrow at her and smiled warmly, "I know just what you need right now and it's not celery! Hold tight and I'll break out the leather," he said playfully. In no time at all, he fetched a spiky dog collar from a dresser and twirled it around his index finger. His other hand held his drug stash box and a fetish whip with feathers on the ends.

"Who gets to be slave this time?" he asked seductively, bringing the collar up to his neck. "Sticks and stones my break my bones, but whips and chains excite me!"

MURDER BY GRAVITY?

* * *

Over the first eight days of 1995, Joyce and Richard argued nearly non-stop. They didn't trust each other and for good reason. Neither could be trusted. Nickie spent her spare time at her Grandma and Grandpa Perrons or baby sitting away from their trailer. She was worried that her father would find out how bad things were going at her mother's home and he'd force her to come back to live at his house. He was very restrictive compared to her mother.

After a big blow-up fight with Richard on Sunday morning, January 8, Joyce walked over to Bob DeVore's apartment. He was surprised to see her at his door because he had never seen Joyce any place other than The Dark.

He felt a little awkward in the bright daylight seeing her, but soon came to his senses and invited her inside.

"How did you know where I live?" Bob asked.

"You told me which intersection your apartment was at, remember?"

Bob said, "Vaguely."

"Yours is the only apartment building on this intersection. All I had to do was find your name on one of the mailboxes out front. Pretty simple, actually," Joyce replied. "Wow! Nice place." Bob's apartment was furnished with thick throw rugs on oak parquet flooring and high-tech equipment of one kind or another and modern, black-enameled furniture with leather cushions. The apartment didn't fit Joyce's image of Bob. She was pleasantly surprised.

Bob smiled in response. "Let me guess. You and Richard are at each other's throats again." He motioned for Joyce to sit down.

"Yeah. Before I left my place a while ago, I said a great exit line to Richard, so I had to leave and stay away for a while. I knew you lived close by. I hope I'm not intruding?" Joyce asked.

"Not at all. What was the exit line?" Bob asked.

"See if you can jump up high enough to kiss my ass!" Joyce said with a laugh. Bob cracked up laughing too, imagining Richard's face. "Anyway," she continued, "You're the most reasonable and unbiased friend I have and I wanted to run some ideas by you to get your take on my situation if you have the time."

"I don't know about being unbiased, but my afternoon is free, so lay it on me. You want a glass of wine?" he offered.

"Sure, if you'll have one with me." Joyce said, "It feels weird; *you* getting *me* a drink for a change. You've never seen me anything but sober, have you?"

"New Year's Eve, but we didn't talk much. If you include meth, I've never seen you *straight!*"

"Ha, ha. I need to talk, Bob. My mother told me that she thought Richard was lying about having cancer."

"If that's true," Bob replied, "He is one crazy son of a bitch! Think about it. . . . he'd have to be shaving his head every day and not eat! If that's the case, where do you think he goes when he says that he's going to Tucson for treatment?"

"That's a good question. He's supposed to go again this Wednesday. I'm thinking of telling him that I want to go with him. That's a natural thing for a wife to want to speak with her dying husband's doctor, right?"

"Absolutely," Bob said. "I'd like to be a fly on the wall when you tell him!"

"I hope he admits the truth before I have to be with him in the car four hours each way to and from Tucson," Joyce said plaintively.

"You know, if this is a hoax, what was he going to do for a grand finale?" Bob and Joyce just looked at each other, thinking.

* * *

Joyce spent a few more hours tossing ideas back and forth with Bob. She finally decided that, no matter how many reasons Richard had for her not to come along, she would insist on going with him to Tucson on Wednesday. She wouldn't give him any advance warning, though. Joyce would spring it on him Wednesday morning before he had a chance to make up an excuse.

Joyce walked two blocks from Bob's apartment to The Dark Place just before dusk. She knew there was a good chance that she could catch Stevie there.

When she walked in, Stevie Lynd said, "What a nice surprise, Joyce. What are you doing here on your day off?" She noticed a serious look on Joyce's face and asked her if anything were wrong.

"No, everything is okay. I just wondered if I could get an

advance on my paycheck today. I still have to pay my rent for this month. Also, I need Wednesday off. I'm going to Tucson with Richard to meet his doctor and find out what's happening with the cancer."

Stevie teased, "Well, you just want everything, now, don't you?"

"Yeah, that's me. I like to push your buttons," Joyce said smiling.

Stevie asked, "Does Richard know you're planning to go with him?"

"Nope!" Joyce replied succinctly.

"Oooh! You're going to surprise him. You got guts, Joyce, I'll give you that. And since you've never asked for a day off before, I think that Marcy or I can cover for you."

Marcy had overheard their conversation and said, "I'll be glad to do it for you, Joyce. After you brought me all the Christmas decorations last month, it's the least I could do. They looked so pretty!"

Joyce took the paycheck from Stevie's hand and said, "Well, great! Guess I'm all set. Thanks a lot, you guys!"

* * *

Later that evening, Mike Deere suddenly remembered the reason he had originally gone to Joyce's house two days earlier. It was a case of selective memory, perhaps. The plan was that Mike would be a stand-up guy and tell her that his friend, Danny Brooks, the one man Joyce loved more than him at the moment, was getting out of jail on Wednesday morning. His drug possession conviction put him away for six months. The news would be better coming from him. That way, he would be able to control the damage.

Mike felt a little guilty knowing that the events of that morning they spent together might have been different had he told her about Danny's upcoming release first. He felt guilty, but not *that* guilty. He called The Dark and had Marcy take a message for Joyce to call him whenever she showed up there.

* * *

Joyce was, among other things, a good daughter. Most afternoons before she went to the showers in the RV park to get ready to go to work, she would stop over at her parents' home to visit.

That Monday, January 9, Joyce popped in as usual. "Hi, Dad!" She said as she walked into the den. "I think I just got my shower today walking over here in the rain! Some storm, huh? So, how are you feeling today?"

"If I'd known I was going to live this long, I would have taken better care of myself!" Bill Perron responded with humor. It was an old joke, but Joyce laughed anyway.

Joyce responded in kind, "Well, you should have known you would live this long!"

"Why is that?" Bill asked.

"Because they say that the *good* die young!," she said, laughing. "Hey, Dad, here's $100 to give to the office for rent, if you could ask Mom to do it for me."

"Sure, but why?"

"Well, we don't have all the rent money yet and I'm afraid that with Richard's junk outside, they won't take a partial payment from me. But I think they will from Mom."

"Okay, honey. I was just thinking, you know, I think that you're wasting a lot of make-up when you get ready for work. You always cover up those cute freckles!"

"I love you, Dad," Joyce said and gave him a hug. "Wednesday I'm going to Tucson to meet Richard's oncologist. He doesn't know it yet, so don't tell him, okay? I don't know how his truck is going to make it all that distance. It's been acting up again."

Bill said, "I asked him yesterday when I saw him out there working on the engine again, if he needed a ride to Tucson this month. His truck sounds bad, so I told him that I'd be glad to drive him out there. He said, 'No, I think it'll make 'er.'"

Joyce said, "Hmmm!" She was thinking that Richard probably was not planning on going to Tucson at all.

* * *

Joyce's good mood was precarious Monday night at work. She had a lot on her mind, but was trying to appear pleasant. Bob DeVore

MURDER BY GRAVITY?

came in at his usual time and sat down at the bar.

Joyce said, "The usual?"

"I don't drink anymore," Bob said very seriously.

Joyce replied automatically, "Yeah, you don't drink any less, either!" The corners of her mouth lifted slightly in a smile..

"That's right! So how are you holding up?" Bob asked her.

Joyce answered, "I'm kind of scared, but my mind is made up. Richard is going to talk with the electronic monitor guy tomorrow to get permission to leave early Wednesday morning. I plan on going with him, but I won't tell him ahead of time so he can't think of an excuse that's better than, 'I just don't want you to see me get sick afterwards.' I'll just spring it on him and I'm not taking 'no' for an answer."

"Good girl. I thought you might want to know that Richard's already in the back of the parking lot," Bob said.

"Tell me something I don't already know," Joyce said disgustedly.

"Something you don't already know? Okay, I'll tell you that we've already had our entire year's worth of rain this week. Last I heard, we've had three and a half inches so far," Bob said. That comment sparked a lively discussion involving everyone present. All were in agreement that they had never seen it rain so much in Yuma before. Somebody said the Gila Wash and the canals were flooding over.

Joyce didn't see the message for her on the bulletin board behind the bar from Mike Deere. She had been about to check messages when she heard Bob say "Marcy!" from behind her. Joyce turned around to see Marcy Montgomery in the doorway, closing her umbrella.

"It's raining cats and dogs out there!" Marcy exclaimed.

"Joyce smiled when she asked, "What's up with you being here on your night off? Just slumming?"

Marcy laughed, "Nah, my husband pulled the night shift and I didn't feel like watching television. Okay, the truth is, my electricity went off and I *couldn't* watch it. The whole grid is down. At any rate, I thought I'd come over here and harass you just for the heck of it. That's got to be more fun than sitting alone by a candle."

Marcy's entrance did not escape Richard's attention as he

watched people come and go from his usual place, hidden in the back of the parking lot. His short fuse was getting the better of him again and he'd been obsessing about Joyce for the last couple of days. Somehow he figured that Joyce had gone off with Mike on Sunday and that on this day she had been over at Bob's apartment. There was no doubt in his mind that she was cheating on him. He had been stewing about it for a couple of days.

The pouring rain, so unusual for this desert city, made Richard's viewing difficult. When he saw Bob DeVore exit the bar, Richard smoked some crystal meth before making a sprint in the rain to the covered doorway of the bar. It was his habit to sit outside in the dark truck cab and just watch for a couple of hours. Of late he usually came inside around midnight and stayed until Joyce closed at 1:00 AM. Once inside the bar, he either sat at one corner of the bar or next to the door, and always by himself. He almost never spoke to anyone, but his scowling presence was definitely felt by most of the patrons and noticeably by Joyce.

Sometimes Richard would also telephone Joyce at work just for the sake of arguing and she would hang up on him and begin to cry. She tried to hide it, but Bob witnessed this happen repeatedly.

This time Richard entered The Dark Place soaking wet. He looked like a concentration camp survivor. He hated rain and never could understand why people lived in other areas of the country where there was so much wet and snow. He had a chill then and his joints ached. The methamphetamine made him more paranoid than ever and elevated his body temperature.

Richard walked in quickly and went directly to the bar where he whispered a couple of sentences in Joyce's ear. She became clearly irritated and asked Marcy to watch the bar while she stepped outside to have a discussion. Joyce grabbed a windbreaker and hurried after her husband as he walked back out the door.

Five minutes later, Joyce walked back in alone. She had her windbreaker off and held it up to cover one side of her face. She said nothing as she went behind the bar to get her denim purse and took it to the ladies' room.

"Joyce?" Marcy tried to see Joyce's face more clearly, but Joyce kept her head bent down. Marcy looked around the bar and assessed that it wasn't very busy, so she locked the cash register and followed

MURDER BY GRAVITY?

Joyce into the restroom.

Joyce was trying not to cry, but her nose wouldn't stop running and was pink. Her hands shook as she took a concealer stick out of her makeup bag and began to dab it on raised red blotches on her cheek.

"Joyce, are you all right?" Marcy asked when she entered the restroom. She gently touched Joyce's shoulder. The red blotches began to blend with the rest of her face only when Joyce let the tears come and then her whole face became red.

"Honey, what did he do to you? Please talk to me!"

"He's gone now," Joyce said. "I'll be okay this time, Marcy, but I just can't take much more of this crap from him."

"What exactly did he do?" Marcy prompted.

"He's been like this for a while lately. I think he's following me. Last week I went to Mike's place and on Sunday I went to Bob DeVore's . . . just to *talk*." The Bob part of that sentence was accurate enough. "Anyway, he thinks that I'm sleeping around on him. He grabbed my face with one hand, then hit me with the other. Right here . . . see this? It's already starting to turn black-and-blue. I think he stopped only because traffic was coming."

"You have to call the police on him! If you don't call, I will," Marcy said matter-of-factly. She dragged Joyce out of the restroom by the arm to the phone behind the bar. Marcy dialed while Joyce stood with her back to the patrons who were there at the time. Joyce took the receiver and reported the incident.

The police officer who responded to the call listened to Joyce's story in the poolroom, where they had a modicum of privacy. As it happened, they could have talked anywhere because most of the customers suddenly remembered that they had to get home after the police car arrived.

The officer said, "We're going to pick him up now and he'll spend the night in jail, so he'll have some time to cool his heels before he gets back home. You'll have to come into the police station in the morning to make a statement."

"What happens if I don't?" Joyce asked.

"Well, we'll have to release him, but I strongly recommend that you do it. He sounds like a loose cannon from what you've told me."

***

Tuesday morning Joyce rode her bike over to her mother's office for a cup of coffee. Lori became livid when Joyce related to her the events of the night before and then Joyce was in the position of trying to calm Lori down.

"Mom, it'll be okay. I plan to go with him to Tucson tomorrow to talk with his doctor about the cancer. If he really is dying, I feel like I have to stay and take care of him. His strength can't last much longer if that's the case. If it turns out that he doesn't have cancer, I'll make him move out of the trailer immediately. I'll change the lock. How's that sound?"

"More than fair to him, I'd say, but okay. By the way, the management wouldn't take your partial payment for rent. They also insist that you to get the junk out from under the trailer first before they'll accept the entire month's rent."

Joyce said, "I got most of my stuff in the storage shed out back. The other stuff is Richard's. He just bought another shed for his stuff too. It's used and he has to reassemble it first. We'll get it done even if I have to do it myself, Mom. I don't want to move away from you guys."

"Dad and I talked about it and decided that we'll help you out on the rent this month, so it will be paid in full."

"Thanks, but no thanks. We'll figure something out so we don't have to do that, okay?"

"Just know it's there if you need it."

"I love you, Mom, thanks."

***

It began to rain again early Tuesday afternoon, so Joyce asked Richard if he'd give her a ride to work later. She was still so angry at him when he came home from his night in jail that it chagrined her to have to ask him. He nodded his head in the affirmative, but scarcely spoke.

Between the periods of rain, Richard busied himself with the shed assembly and managed to get three walls up. Compared to other sheds in the park, his was rather pathetic looking.

MURDER BY GRAVITY?

Joyce stopped by her parents' house that afternoon. Lori said that Phil Seward had come over to their house to plead with them to get Joyce to drop the sexual harassment charges. The court date was on the docket for that Friday, the 13th, she reminded Joyce.

"Mother, I have a witness. He was out of line," Joyce responded.

"Every woman has had to put up with a little grab-ass at one time or another. That's all it was," Lori said.

"He was trying to rape me! Why are you on his side?" Joyce felt tears well up in her eyes. Wasn't she already going through enough without this in addition?

"We've known him for so many years, honey. We know he could never do a thing like that," Lori said.

"So you think I'm lying? Is that it?"

"I don't think that you're lying. Just think about letting it go. No harm, no foul. It's not going to do a bit of good to take him to court," Lori tried again.

"And what if I could stop him from maybe doing it again to somebody else? I still feel it's something I have to do, Mom. I wish you could try to understand that. I have to go get ready for work now," Joyce said without giving her mother her customary peck on the cheek.

* * *

"I'm ready," Joyce said to Richard. It was raining again, so they made a dash for the truck. Once inside, they didn't speak. Joyce felt really awkward with her own husband; awkward and scared.

The Dark's parking lot was void, save for Stevie Lynd's vintage white Mercedes parked near the door. Richard stopped the truck next to it and Joyce gathered up her purse and umbrella. She stopped what she was doing to put on her windbreaker first. She remembered how chilly it had been the night before. She had one arm already inside the jacket and the other arm started when Richard suddenly grabbed the center piece of Joyce's bra which was just below the V-neck of her blouse and pulled her towards his face. She felt her bra rip somewhere and her shirt twist up.

"What the *hell*?" Joyce had been completely caught off guard. She held her breath.

"You behave yourself tonight, you slut. Don't make me come after your boyfriends. I'll be watching you," Richard warned.

When his hold eased up, Joyce quickly gathered her things and ran into the bar. Stevie was startled when Joyce whizzed in the door with her clothing in such a state. Joyce headed straight to the restroom and Stevie followed her inside.

"Damn it! Could you help me with this bra strap?" Joyce said, visibly shaken and teary-eyed in spite of her best efforts. Her light-skinned chest was red and welted and her hair was a mess. Joyce's green silky blouse was pushed down and she exposed her shoulder and a delicate black bra to Stevie so she could check it for her.

"Your bra strap is completely ripped off in the back! I don't suppose you have a safety pin in that huge purse of yours, do you?"

"A Girl Scout is always prepared," Joyce sniffed as she went fishing in her purse. Joyce kept everything important in her purse and she was never without it. She gave the little safety pin to Stevie who reattached the right strap back together.

"Did you know he followed you into the bar?" Stevie asked softly. "I'm staying with you until he leaves."

"Can I get fired for being married to an asshole?"

"If I did that, I wouldn't have any employees," Stevie said, half serious. "Don't worry about that."

Richard stood, obviously angry still, in the doorway. When he saw the defiant look that Stevie was giving him and that she wasn't going to leave, he finally left the bar in a huff. Stevie was perceived by Richard to be a strong woman, and he usually steered clear of her.

* * *

Soon, Joyce was calm and Stevie went on home. A little later, Mike Deere came in for a visit.

"Hey, don't you ever check you phone messages?" Mike asked. "I see on the board that Marcy wrote it down that I called yesterday."

Joyce said she was sorry and told him what Richard said and did earlier and he was angry enough for the both of them.

"Got any crank on you?" Joyce asked.

"Sure," Mike said giving her a little plastic bag.

"Is that all you've got?"

Mike said, "Yeah . . . you want me to go scare up some more?"

"No, this is fine," Joyce said after debating. "I'll pay you for it later. Is that okay?"

"No problem," Mike said. "The reason I called yesterday was to tell you that Danny Brooks is getting out of jail tomorrow morning. Do you want to get together, the three of us, for old time's sake?"

Joyce said, "Maybe, yeah! But I can't tomorrow. I'm going to Tucson with Richard, remember?"

The two of them made tentative plans to get together with Danny the following Saturday. Joyce was excited that she was going to see Danny soon. She needed something to look forward to in the worst way. She wrote Danny a message and left it on the bulletin board in case he came in while she was gone. She had a strong feeling that Danny would be coming in tomorrow night. She dialed Stevie's home phone number.

"Hey," Joyce said, "I was just thinking. I should be back tomorrow evening in time to go to work. Would you let Marcy know I'll be working Wednesday, after all?"

"If that's what you want, but won't you be too tired?" Stevie asked.

Joyce said, "No, I'll be fine, honest."

"All right, then. Has everything been okay since I left? Has he come back?"

"No, I don't think he'll be in until it's time to pick me up later on."

"I hope everything goes well for you tomorrow, honey. I'll say a prayer for you." Stevie said.

After a while, Joyce started to think more about not having enough meth for the next day in case she had to leave. She began to wish that she had taken Mike up on his offer, but he had already left.

Then Ruby, Leigh, and Red walked into the bar together. *The Three Musketeers*, Joyce thought. Ruby gave Joyce a hug. While she was close to Ruby's ear, Joyce quietly asked, "Do you have any crank that I can buy off you? I don't have enough to last me tomorrow."

Ruby said, "No, not with me, but I've got some at Red's house that I can bring over to your place later on, if you're going to be awake for a while after you get off here."

"Sounds good," Joyce said. "Did you move in with Red and Leigh?"

"Yeah, but Leigh's going to move out soon. Mike Deere told Leigh that you're going to Tucson with Richard tomorrow."

"Good news travels fast," Joyce observed.

"No kidding."

"Do you have your own room at Red's house?" Joyce asked teasingly.

"Hell, no! I started sleeping with Red the first night I moved in! Then both of them, but Leigh can't handle it. That's why she's moving out." Ruby said.

"Ruby, you shock me!" Joyce joked.

Before Joyce left The Dark that night, she scribbled down a note to Danny Brooks and tacked it up on the bulleting board just in case she missed seeing him. It read, "Hope to see you soon. I love you, Joyce."

* * *

Later that night after Joyce closed the bar and went home; Red drove Ruby and Leigh over to her trailer to drop off the drugs. Richard and Nickie were asleep, so Joyce stepped outside in her robe so as not to disturb them.

The threesome was very jubilant and high. Ruby was the only one to get out of the car and she was having a difficult time keeping her voice down. Joyce took her arm and walked her back toward the sheds.

"Shhh!" Joyce reminded her that Nickie had school the next day and she and Richard had a long trip to make in the morning.

Ruby said, "I'm sorry, I don't want to get you in trouble with Richard."

"That's okay," Joyce replied, "I'm *always* in trouble with Richard. Thanks for bringing this over," Joyce said, handing Ruby some money. "By the way, are you still planning to testify against Phil Seward this Friday for my sexual harassment case?"

Ruby said, "Of course. I didn't forget. We're going to nail Seward to the cross!"

"I owe you big time," Joyce said.

MURDER BY GRAVITY?

That was the last time Ruby ever saw her friend. The following morning, Joyce disappeared. While the world waited to find out if O. J. Simpson actually murdered Nicole Simpson and Ronald Goldman, Joyce's body was found nine days after she disappeared. On January 20, 1995, Sam Sayers discovered Joyce's body on which the deputies grizzly noted that her arms and legs were tethered to weights and she was floating facedown in the Gila Gravity Canal, near Mittry Lake, dressed only in her black bra that was held together by a little golden safety pin.

CHAPTER 23

Detective David St. Jons had been in the Yuma Police Department for nearly thirteen years. He was assigned to investigate cases that dealt with major felonies. In January, 1995, he had a huge caseload and was in the process of prioritizing them. It seemed that Yuma was having growing pains.

On January 16, five days after Joyce's disappearance, Detective St. Jons came across a missing person's report that someone had left on his desk, apparently while he was out finishing other follow-ups.

The report was called in by the spouse and contained Joyce's general description. There was nothing to be done at the moment.

The next day, Detective St. Jons received a phone call from Joyce's worried mother. Lori told him that she hadn't heard from Joyce in six days and that this was totally out of character for her daughter. She said that she knew something was wrong when Joyce didn't show up for the work the night of January 11. In fact, Joyce hadn't telephoned her employer that night or at anytime since she vanished. More importantly, Lori said that Joyce had not made any arrangements to provide for her young teenage daughter, which is something she would normally do without fail if she were planning to go somewhere without her. St. Jons asked her to tell him more.

* * *

Armed with a few general details of Joyce's life, St. Jons went to The Dark Place that night. It was his plan to take his time talking to customers as they arrived. Not having any idea how late some of the regulars generally came in, St. Jons arrived early in the evening and found Marcy Montgomery alone, readying the bar for business.

Marcy looked up and saw an attractive man in his mid-thirties

MURDER BY GRAVITY?

approach her. He had a more wholesome look than her usual customers. Marcy greeted him and asked what she could get for him. St. Jons returned her smile and ordered a cup of coffee. When Marcy returned to serve him, St. Jons pulled out his badge and identified himself and asked her if she had any idea where Joyce Handcock could be.

"I wish I knew!" she said. "Between working here and at the sister bar, which is The Show Place on 4th Avenue, I've had to work every night since last Wednesday when Joyce disappeared." Marcy told him what a sweet person she thought Joyce was and that she hoped that Joyce was okay.

"The owner of the bars, Stevie Lynd, and I have been really worried. Two days ago, Stevie called Richard, you know, Joyce's husband. She had already called a few times to find out if he had heard anything from Joyce. The last time she called and he said that he hadn't heard from her, Stevie told him that he should call the police to report her missing. She told me that she didn't trust Richard to report it and said that I should call the police later just to make sure that he actually had reported it. When I did, they said that he had called and reported Joyce missing just a few minutes before I called. If you ask me, I think that he sure took his sweet time about it. I think that he should have called the police right away because we all knew that Joyce wouldn't just take off without calling her work. Richard said to Stevie that Joyce hadn't told her kid that she was leaving either. That was a red flag to us, and it was obvious that something was wrong."

Detective St. Jons noticed the bulletin board hanging behind the bar and asked Marcy to remove it from the wall and lay it on the bar for him to read all of the messages, of which there were several. He came across the note from Joyce to Danny Brooks saying that she was looking forward to seeing him again and that she loved him.

He asked Marcy, "Do you know who Danny Brooks is?"

"Sorry," Marcy said, shaking her head.

"Did you see this?" he asked, passing the message to her.

"No. I usually check the messages only if someone asks me to or if I've taken the message and I know them when they come in," Marcy explained.

"So, more than likely, if this Danny came in, he would know to check for his messages?" St. Jons asked.

"More than likely," Marcy said.

A short time later, Tammy, Joyce's former boss at P. J.'s, came in with The Dark's owner, Stevie, who looked curiously toward the new face and smiled.

Marcy introduced Detective St. Jons to the two middle-aged women. He was pleasant-mannered, yet professional as he let them inspect his credentials.

"Do either of you have any idea where Joyce Handcock might be?" he asked.

Stevie spoke first, "Well, she was going with her husband to Tucson on that Wednesday when she went missing, and come to work after the trip that evening. I could understand if the trip took longer than she figured. I even planned that day to be ready to come in early to take her place, just in case she didn't make it back early enough. That's a long drive . . . well, what is it? Four hundred and seventy miles round-trip?" The question was rhetorical, but St. Jons nodded in agreement. "They were going to see his doctor there, but I thought, how could Joyce know how long it would take? I know *my* doctor keeps me waiting in his office forever and a day."

Tammy took over when Stevie paused. "You know, the poor guy has cancer and he must be in pretty bad shape from what Joyce told me."

"Poor guy, my ass!" Stevie interjected. "Joyce said she was going to the doctor with him to find out if he really *does* have cancer. Plus, when he dropped her off for work the night before she disappeared, they had a fight in the parking lot. He roughed her up and busted her bra, so I had to pin it for her," Stevie said, and pausing to catch her breath. Her emotions began to take over and her eyes filled suddenly with tears, but she continued, "She had these red welts on her chest . . . Joyce has sensitive, fair skin, so you couldn't miss seeing them. She had to button her blouse all the way to the top to cover the marks." Detective St. Jons was taking notes on a pad.

"Oh, Lord!" Tammy burst out, interrupting Stevie's story, which was difficult to do. Tammy's voice trembled, "I just remembered something she said on New Year's Eve. Joyce was crying and said, 'If I don't get out of this marriage, he'll kill me!' I thought she was just exaggerating at the time. She told that to several people, not just me."

"Meaning her husband?" St. Jon asked, very interested that Joyce may have predicted her own death so soon before her disappearance. That never happened before in any of his investigations, but he knew it wasn't unheard of.

Stevie asked St. Jons about Joyce's daughter. She was concerned for her welfare and it occurred to her that Nickie shouldn't be left alone with Richard in the trailer.

St. Jons told her that the girl's grandmother had brought Nichole over to her house the night after Joyce was gone and she was currently staying with her aunt. "I'm fairly certain that she won't be going back there to live with Mr. Handcock if Joyce doesn't return."

"Well, that's a relief," Stevie said.

"This bar reminds me of one on television 'where everybody knows your name.' Have either of you heard Joyce ever mention a guy named Danny Brooks?" St. Jons asked.

"No," Stevie and Tammy said in unison. "Who's he?" Stevie asked.

St. Jons' answer was candid, "I don't know yet. Has Richard Handcock ever called here looking for his wife since she disappeared?"

Stevie held up her index finger to St. Jons, indicating for him to wait a minute while she walked behind the bar to consult with Marcy, who had been checking the stock behind the bar. When Stevie returned, she said, "I was the one that called *him*. He *never* called either one of us, and Marcy and I are the only ones that have been working here since Joyce left."

St. Jons said, "That's interesting, isn't it? By the way, can I verify the spelling of Joyce's last name with you?"

"Of course," Stevie said.

"The missing person report had it written H A N D C O C K. Shouldn't that be H A N C O C K, without the D?" St. Jons asked.

"Yeah, normally, but that's how Richard's family spells it. Almost vulgar, huh?" Stevie's hearty laugh was a delight. Her sense of humor helped cut the stress they were all feeling. "I do hope that you can locate Joyce," she said. "She's one of the best workers I ever had except for Marcy here."

* * *

Detective St. Jons sat at the end of the bar smoking cigarettes and waiting for regulars to show up. His practiced eye searched the bar trying to find possible clues that might lead him to Joyce. He noted her name written in blue felt-tip pen on a white dartboard tally on the wall. A game had apparently been stopped in progress with somebody named Bob. He read and re-read the notes he had taken, trying to figure out and write down some of the words he had abbreviated in his rush to get the information on paper. He knew from experience that if he didn't translate the strange shorthand he'd developed over the years soon afterward, he'd have a heck of a time later trying to figure it all out.

A husky man somewhere in his late thirties walked into The Dark Place with an obvious limp. Upon closer observation in the darkened room, St. Jons discerned that the man was wearing a black back brace with suspender straps. The two men acknowledged each other with a nod. Bob sat a couple of stools down from St. Jons.

After Bob ordered, he felt the detective's eyes fixated on him, so he turned toward him and said affably, "How's it going?"

"Great. How are you?" St. Jons replied.

"Okay . . . the name's Bob DeVore," Bob said, leaning forward with care so as not to hurt his back, and extending his right hand. "And you are. . . ?"

"Detective David St. Jons," he said shaking Bob's hand then showing him his badge.

"Are you the Bob whose name is over there on the dart tally?"

"One and the same," Bob said, looking over to the tally board where his eyes fell on Joyce's name with his. "Are you here because of Joyce?"

"Yes, I take it that you know her?" Bob nodded in answer, slowly realizing that his worry about Joyce might be valid. "Do you have any idea where she might be?" St. Jons asked.

Bob said, "I was hoping that Joyce might be here tonight."

"Her family is very worried about her. Is there anybody that Joyce might have been afraid of?" St. Jons asked.

Bob began to lay out for the detective everything about Joyce that he could remember from their conversations and his observations. He went into some of detail of how Richard always tried to control Joyce and the worry Joyce had about insisting that she meet his doctor and that she had planned to do it that Wednesday when she disappeared.

"Joyce and I became good friends ever since she started working here."

"Just friends?" St. Jons asked non-judgmentally.

"Yeah, just friends, which is not to say that I'm not attracted to her, but she is married and I don't fool around with married women; never have. But I was the one who encouraged her to confront Richard and insist she meet his doctor. Now I'm afraid that something bad happened to her because I interfered."

St. Jons asked if he knew who Danny Brooks was.

"I've never heard Joyce mention that name before, why?" Bob asked.

"Just curious, she had left a message for him here. Hey, what happened to interrupt the dart game that you and Joyce were playing?"

"Richard came in."

* * *

The following morning, Detective St. Jons called the *Yuma Daily Sun* and asked them to run an article about Joyce's disappearance and gave them the brief description of Joyce that Richard had supplied in the report to find anyone who might know of her whereabouts.

Detective St. Jons ran a check on Danny Brooks, and found that Brooks had been released from prison to the Inmates' Work Program on the same day that Joyce disappeared. In the work program, the inmates are allowed out during the day to work and the rest of the day and night they are incarcerated. If an inmate failed to show up for work, he would lose his work privilege and would be put back behind bars for the rest of his sentence. In Brook's case, he had served six months inside a cell and he was to be in the work program for six additional months. St. Jons called Brook's parole officer and was assured that Brooks was at work that day and at no time was he out of his supervisor's sight for more than a few minutes.

Mike Deere had been mistaken when he told Joyce that Danny would be freed on January 11. The earliest he could have partied with Mike and Joyce wouldn't have been until the following July, unless he were willing to risk a bench warrant for his immediate arrest.

St. Jons had an old, heavy wood door that lead to his well-seasoned office, which he often closed when he needed time to think. The ornate antique brass doorknob clanked when touched because it was always loose, and gave the detective a heads' up before someone entered his office. The wood grain and knots in the dark wood, when stared at, seemed to make pictures to Detective St. Jons; pieces of his current puzzle. So far, his main pieces were Joyce, Richard and Danny. He wondered why no one knew who Danny was. St. Jons reasoned that if Danny were indeed Joyce's lover, she might have thought to run off with him or, worst-case scenario, that Richard might have harmed her because of it. Unless a body turned up, there could be no case against Richard, even though he was certainly, at this point, the person most likely to have harmed her, as the spouse is the killer, more often than not.

* * *

Richard had put off reporting Joyce missing to the police department, and it wasn't until Lori's and Stevie's unrelenting badgering of him that he finally admitted to himself that he could no longer avoid reporting Joyce as a missing person. Initially, Richard thought that everyone would naturally just assume that Joyce had gotten herself drugged-up and taken off with one of her customers.

* * *

By this time, St. Jons decided it was time to have an impromptu visit with Richard Handcock to get a feel of the man and see what he had to say in more detail about his wife's disappearance. He arrived in the afternoon to find Richard outside picking up tools, scraps of wood, spray-paint cans and other debris from around his trailer and tossing it all into the back of his pickup. St. Jons parked behind the truck and saw that the camper had been removed from the truck and placed on the ground next to it. Though St. Jons had arrived in an unmarked police car, Richard knew intuitively that he was a cop and was resigned that from this time forward the law would be nosing around in his life for a while.

MURDER BY GRAVITY?

Detective St. Jons walked up to Richard to introduce himself and the men shook hands while sizing each other up. Unknown to St. Jons at the time, Richard was cognizant that if the detective were to take a good look in the back of his truck or inside his trailer, Handcock would have a lot of explaining to do. Therefore, Richard redirected St. Jons attention and motioned to a couple of resin lawn chairs outside under an olive tree for them to sit in while they discussed the disappearance of his wife.

"Mr. Handcock, do you have any idea where your wife might be at this time?" St. Jons began.

"I wish I did," said Richard, sounding more concerned than he outwardly looked.

"Were you and your wife having any marital problems before her disappearance?" The detective hoped to catch Richard off guard.

Richard acted wounded and said, "Absolutely not! In fact, we were planning to renew our wedding vows on our anniversary later this month," Richard stated, for he had been prepared for that question. "I hope she makes it back in time."

"You reported your wife missing since noon on the 11th. Was that the last time you saw her?" St. Jons asked.

"No, it was earlier that day."

"Can you tell me what, if anything, happened that morning?"

Richard took a deep breath and sighed audibly. "Nothing much at all *happened*," he said. "Joyce and I woke up when her daughter, Nichole, knocked on our bedroom door to ask if she could borrow Joyce's hairbrush. My wife wasn't wearing anything, so she held the covers up around herself while she leaned forward to hand the brush to her. Then Nickie left the trailer and walked over to the park showers to get ready for school. While she was gone, my wife and I made love." St. Jons listened intently, never changing his facial expression, although he was surprised that Richard would bring up something so personal that was unnecessary for him to mention at the time, unless purposely trying to paint the scene of a loving marriage.

Richard continued what seemed like an impartial narration, "When Nickie came back, she ate breakfast, then she said goodbye to us, and walked to school at about 7:15. That's the time she usually leaves for school," Richard looked at the detective for approval, but found none.

"What happened after that?" St. Jons prodded.

"I called the electronic monitoring company to see if I could get permission to look for a job," Richard said as he lifted the bottom of his fatigues to show St. Jons the ankle monitor that was affixed to it. "After they said I could go, I got dressed and left at eight o'clock."

"What's that all about?" St. Jons asked.

Richard looked a little embarrassed. He said, "About a month or so ago, I got stopped in my truck by a patrol officer and he spotted some methamphetamine that Joyce had left in it."

"Really," St. Jons said, grimly. He'd be sure to check that out later, but said, "We had a report that January 11 Joyce was planning to go to Tucson with you to talk to your doctor about your cancer treatments. Are you saying that report is incorrect?"

"That's completely untrue. First of all, I don't have cancer so why would we go to the doctor? That's absolutely ridiculous. I told you that I went to look for a job. You can verify that with my parole officer," Richard insisted.

"Can you tell me what Joyce was wearing, if anything, when you left her that morning?"

"Yeah, she had a gray sweatshirt and off-gray sweatpants."

St. Jons discreetly lifted his notepad to the original missing person's report. Just as he remembered, Richard had previously reported that Joyce had been wearing a black shirt and Levis.

"Okay now, was Joyce going to stay here while you went out to look for work?"

"No, I think she was going to catch a ride with her friend, Ruby Vasquez, and they were going shopping. Joyce and I were planning to meet back here at noon to go to Wal-Mart together."

"So, you're saying that you believe that Joyce's friend, Ruby, was the last person to see your wife alive?"

"I honestly don't know that," Richard replied.

"Where did you go that morning to look for work, Mr. Handcock?" the detective asked.

Richard said, "I'm a carpenter, by trade. I drove out to the Foothills to see a guy named Dick Kidd. I went to the new construction site behind The Grocery Store, that's actually the name of the store by the way, at nine o'clock, or maybe I went to the Mesa

Del Sol construction site first . . . anyway, I waited about forty-five minutes for Dick, who's the boss there, and he never showed up." Richard sighed again, "Then I went to Mesa Del Sol, which is also in the Foothills, and looked for a guy named Hernandez, who is the construction superintendent there, but he wasn't at the site either." Richard smiled a little with embarrassment when he realized how lame his story sounded, but he figured it was so bad, it had to be believed. After all, Richard thought, it was obvious that if he'd been involved in any foul play, he would have had a better alibi. Surely a detective would be aware of that.

"Where did you go after that, Mr. Handcock?" St. Jons was clearly not amused by Richard's pathetic accounting of events and St. Jons serious tone of voice stopped Richard from smiling.

"I went to visit a friend, who is actually an old girlfriend. She's a bartender at The Bottoms Up Pub on Fortuna Road." Richard felt that by giving this bone to St. Jons, at least Hazel could verify that he was in the Foothills that morning. Richard knew also that the Foothills area was in the Yuma County Sheriff's Department area, rather the Yuma City Police. He figured correctly that St. Jons wasn't familiar with that area. "I had a V-8 and stayed about forty-five minutes."

"So you sat and drank juice for forty-five minutes?" St. Jons asked, incredulous.

"Well, actually, I was looking for a guy who goes there a lot. He sells used tires and I needed some for my truck."

St. Jons said sarcastically, "He wasn't there either, I assume."

"Yes, he *was*," Richard said, trying to make his story sound more believable.

"What's his name?" St. Jons asked.

Richard replied, "I don't know his name, but he's a regular at the bar and everybody knows him there. Then I came back home sometime before eleven o'clock, to wait for Joyce so we could go to Wal-Mart."

"Ah, your wife's boss said that you and Joyce had a fight the night before your wife's disappearance in the parking lot where she works. Did you have a fight that night, Mr. Handcock?"

Richard said emphatically, "There was no fight! That night, when we got back home from the bar, I saw a man with two of Joyce's friends come to our trailer about 1:30 or 2:00 o'clock in the morning. Joyce's friend, Ruby, got out of the car and I think they were selling her some illegal drugs. I saw them when I looked out of the bedroom window. Joyce's friend, Ruby, handed something to her and I think Joyce gave her some money."

"What kind of drugs does your wife use, Mr. Handcock?"

"Crystal meth and herb," Richard said using the slang for marijuana. "All of her friends do, too."

"You've seen this yourself?" St. Jons asked.

"Yeah."

"Do you use drugs?"

"No, I don't need them."

"Mr. Handcock, why did you wait for five days before reporting your wife missing?"

"It's not unheard of for Joyce to take off for a few days to be with her friends. She's sort of a free-spirit type of person," Richard replied. "Sometimes the drug parties lasted two or three days and Joyce loved to party."

"So, are you saying it was okay with you that your wife left for days at a time to party with her friends?"

"We had an understanding. It wasn't a big deal."

"Really? Okay, I have just a couple more things to ask you before I leave . . . were you ever violent towards your wife and did you ever assault her?"

"No way, man! I told you I love my wife. When she comes back, you can ask her yourself. I was married twice before Joyce, and you can ask my former wives if I was ever violent."

St. Jons continued, "Can you think of anybody who might want to harm your wife?"

"Yeah," Richard replied with obvious distaste, "Mike Deere. He's one of her former bar buddies."

"Why would he want to harm Joyce?"

"Because he used to date her and she married me instead of him."

"I see. Do you know who Danny Brooks is?"

"Yeah, he's a friend of Mike's."

Richard then complied with St. Jons request to obtain the phone numbers of Mike and Ruby and any other of Joyce's friends who might know where she went.

CHAPTER 24

Richard was relieved when Detective St. Jons finally left his RV space. He still had the task of eliminating all the junk that was scattered around their trailer in order to keep on living in the same park. The manager had told Richard in no uncertain terms that she wanted the area cleaned up and all of January's rent money. The used shed that he had purchased just before Joyce's disappearance was far from being assembled due to the heavy rain and there was no way he could put all of the bent pieces together with assembly parts and bolts missing in the next couple of days. Even if he could, there wouldn't be enough space for all of it. Richard was a pack rat.

The manager had been receiving complaints from some of the other neighboring RV'ers ever since Joyce and Richard moved in with only the older truck and its camper on top, but soon after the time she was made aware of it, Richard moved out and Joyce bought a trailer. She was relieved until she started getting complaints again about the mess and writing on the side of it, saying, "I love you, Richard!" She had made concessions due to the fact that Joyce was the summer manager's daughter, but that only let them go so far.

The manager had driven her familiar pink golf cart over to the Handcocks' space to check it out. It was indeed, looking worse than the last time she had seen it, and it had been a mess then. The neighbors were right when they said that the Handcocks' trailer was in danger of making the whole RV park look like "trailer trash." Joyce had signed an agreement to keep their property neat and free of debris as stated in the park rules when they moved into the park. This untidy mess would not be tolerated under any circumstances and the Handcocks' had been given all of the legal requisite warnings and notices. Richard's time had run out. He drove his loaded truck over to his mother's house where he unloaded several of his tools and stray building materials that he had collected from Swift Sales. Much of these materials he had not paid Ron Gene for before he and Joyce moved off his lot the previous October. Richard hitched up a small, wooden utility trailer that had been sitting in the rear of his mother's property ever since he could remember to the back of his truck. Mrs. Handcock wasn't home at the time, which was probably just as well, Richard thought, because his mother wouldn't be thrilled about him bringing any more of his stuff to store at her house in addition to what was already there. As a matter of fact, she'd been complaining to him for years about getting some of his things out of her house and off of her property.

Richard went back home with the trailer and was loading it up when Lori Perron walked across the park, carefully avoiding deep-water puddles that still lingered after the last few weeks of mostly rainy days.

"Richard," she began, "we've been looking all over town; in the grocery stores, laundries, restaurants, and everywhere we see a bulletin board, and we haven't seen *any* of the missing person fliers that we gave you money to print up."

"I got the flyers made up by my friend over at Quick Copy and she gave me a discount so I got fifty instead of just twenty-five, but I had to wait around for the police to call me back. They took a long time too, but I didn't want to miss their call. We don't have a telephone answering machine, you know. Today they finally sent a detective over here to ask me a bunch of questions about Joyce. I just haven't had time to get out yet, but I did take some flyers to The Dark Place and asked around there if anybody had seen her. Some older woman told me that she saw Joyce over at a biker bar on 16th Street. She said that Joyce was on the back of some guy's Harley. Look, I know you're scared, I am too, but I'm sure she'll turn up eventually. Joyce can take care of herself, you know that. Joyce left me with no rent money and all of this mess to clean up around our trailer and if I don't do it now, the office lady said they're going to kick us out of here. As soon as I get this done, I promise to post up the rest of the flyers. Excuse me," Richard said as he picked up a scrap of wood at Lori's feet. She looked down at the cement pad next to the trailer's front door and saw a fresh spot of black oil that would not warm the manager's heart. Then Lori turned and walked back home, exasperated with him. She didn't believe Richard's story about the biker for an instant.

When Richard arrived at his mother's house with another truckload of junk and the trailer full too, she came rushing out of the house to catch up with him and started shouting. "You can't leave that stuff here! I got the house up for sale and it doesn't look good. Besides, you got your own storage space. Why can't you put that crap in there?" Mrs. Handcock insisted.

"Mom, I can't put it there because it's full already. I just need the space for a couple of days until I can get another storage locker. Okay? Joyce left me with no money for rent and the park won't let me keep my stuff there anymore. I don't know what I'm going to do, Ma. I've had to wait at home for the cops to call me back and move this junk before I can really go looking for a job. Heck, even if I *did have* a job, I would've been rained-out anyway! I did go to a few places who might hire me the day *before* Joyce took off. I don't know what I'm going to do for rent. It's $250 that I don't have now. I might need to live in my camper again."

"No, you know I don't want you to do that. You got to have a shower if you're going to find work. I maybe could come up with a loan for your rent, but you got to get your junk out of here!"

"That would be great, Ma. I promise I'll get this stuff out of here in two days. Would that be okay?"

"Forty-eight hours, *for sure*?" his mother was weakening.

"I promise."

"Okay, but no longer than that."

* * *

Richard worked hard all afternoon and managed to bring everything that wasn't already ruined by the rain that wouldn't fit in Joyce's shed, his old storage, or their trailer over to his mother's house. He unhitched and left his mother's utility trailer loaded with boxes of junk. Richard's mother had a check for $250 made out to the park waiting for him to take back home. She knew better than to make it out to her son. He wouldn't pay the rent if she had made it payable to him.

CHERIE HUYETT ACHTEMEIER

* * *

That night, instead of parking his truck where he usually did next to the trailer Joyce shared with him, Richard parked his truck in a parking lot across the street from the RV park. Unfortunately, there was a terrible fire of mysterious origin in the bed of his truck that night in the wee hours of the morning. Fortunately, Richard saw the flames in time to put the fire out with an extinguisher just before the fire department arrived and he managed to save the cab from being damaged. It was a good thing he didn't have his camper on his truck at the time. It was impossible to tell what, if anything, had been burned inside of the bed of his truck that night.

"You're darn lucky, dude!" one of the five firefighters that arrived after the blaze was extinguished said just before they went back to the station. "You can still sand that bed down and have one of those spray-on bedliners applied to it. In fact, there's a place just around the corner that does it. You can't miss their big sign."

"Oh, yeah, I think I seen that before," Richard replied. "Thanks!"

* * *

When David St. Jons returned to his office at police headquarters, he was anxious to check out Handcock's background. His experience told him that Richard seemed disingenuous about his relationship with his wife and generally speaking, if St. Jons caught somebody in a lie, he tended to be skeptical about everything else they had to say.

He wasn't surprised much that Richard had a list of prior arrests, primarily involving drugs and that, in all fairness to Richard, possibly that was why he quit using drugs, *if* he actually did quit. The fact that Joyce had Richard arrested for assault on two previous occasions, once just before she disappeared, made Richard a blatant liar. St. Jons marveled how stupid it was of any suspect to lie about his arrest history, because they always checked that first. He looked over his growing list of Joyce's friends and acquaintances that he planned to question sometime during the week.

St. Jons was startled when his phone rang, since his usual workday ended two hours earlier. He still wasn't used to the long hours of late. The feminine voice on the other end identified herself as Lori Perron, and said that she was calling about her daughter again. She was very upset after reading the description of Joyce that was in the newspaper and stated, "I've already asked Joyce's husband about this and he told me that somebody else, either at the police or on the newspaper staff, had made the mistakes. Richard said that wasn't the description he gave to the police."

"I checked out the paper already myself, and that most certainly *is* the description Handcock gave us when he called in the original missing person's report," St. Jons replied.

"That's what I was afraid you'd say. I should tell you that there are serious discrepancies in my daughter's description than what was given to you. I think that her husband may have purposely tried to mislead you." She said that Joyce's name and age were correct, but everything else was wrong. The article described Joyce's medium-to-light brown hair, which currently had red highlights added, as dark brown. It also said her eyes were dark brown instead of the strikingly pretty eyes she had that were green with gold flecks.

St. Jons sounded dubious when he said, "I don't think that's a real big difference there."

"The article also said that she was four inches taller than she actually is. Can't you see a pattern here?" Lori asked with growing irritation.

"I'm very sorry that happened, Mrs. Perron," St. Jons said, trying to calm Lori down. "We'll have the corrected description of Joyce in tomorrow's newspaper. It appears that Mr. Handcock has been deceptive about other things so far. Thanks for your help. If you think of anything else, or if you get any new information, please call me. Otherwise, I'll contact you if we have anything new that develops on our end of things. Please don't call the police department every day to find out if we have any new information. The phones are already busier than the staff can handle."

Lori, who was trying to remain polite because she needed his help, uttered her thanks, but was annoyed by St. Jons,' last comment and decided afterward that she would call him whenever *she* felt it was necessary. Staying by the phone and waiting for a call was unthinkable for her.

* * *

On the next day, January 20, St. Jons worked on his other cases that he'd been neglecting while he had been working on Joyce's disappearance. By day's end, he had made tentative plans for further interviews of Joyce's friends for the following day. When his phone rang, St. Jons thought about not answering it because he was suffering from a splitting headache and was anxious to go home. He forced himself to pick up the receiver in case it was important.

"Detective St. Jons? My name is Donna Graham and I'm a detective for the County Sheriff's Department. I'm out at the Gila Gravity Canal, where a female body was just discovered. The body has similar physical characteristics as the description in today's newspaper. I think it might be your lady bartender. Do you want to come over and have a look?"

"Yes, of course! Just give me directions," St. Jons said as he pulled out his top desk drawer and retrieved an ibuprophen tablet from a bottle that he had purchased in Mexico. The large tablet was 800 milligrams and couldn't be purchased in the United States without a prescription. St. Jons washed it down with bottled water and was getting a fresh burst of adrenalin as he wrote down the complicated directions to an area near Mittry Lake to the Gila Gravity Canal. Detective Graham told him the terrain was rough, so he borrowed the keys to a departmental four-wheel-drive vehicle from another officer and headed to the site where the body was discovered.

As St. Jons approached the scene, he saw that a vehicle from a mortuary was already there. How it maneuvered the dirt roads was a mystery to him. He would have thought it impossible. The rest of the vehicles were four-wheel-drive County Sheriff's cars and trucks. There was a dark body bag near the edge of the water and he could tell by its bulge that the victim was already inside it.

Detective Donna Graham had been squatting near the body when she saw St. Jons's police vehicle pull up. She brushed some dirt off her hands and walked over to him. "I'm agent in charge, Detective Donna Graham," she said while shaking his hand solidly. "I'm the one who called you. Thanks for coming all the way out here."

She continued, "The divers had a tough time pulling this one out of the water. Someone tied weights to her arms and legs."

MURDER BY GRAVITY?

Detective Graham walked St. Jons over to the body bag and opened it for his inspection. St. Jons saw that the body met the description of Joyce, though she was so bloated and dirty from the days and nights in the murky water. He noted that she had three pierced-earring holes in one ear and two in the other. Detective Graham continued, "See, at the corners of the bag, are the articles that were used to weigh her body down. We had to cut them off so we could get her in the bag. I took two rolls of pictures of the scene, including the contents of a campfire pit up there on the hill made out of rocks. There are some plywood pieces with blue paint and purple drops on top of the ashes that haven't been burned. They look like picture frames. We were just about to bag the wood and this pink goo that looks like fish guts that's there on the water's edge."

"That's good. I saw some paint and plywood pieces outside the victim's own home yesterday. The victim was into crafts and her husband was in the process of loading his truck with similar items like those that were used to weigh the body down when I was there to talk to him. I sure hope that he hasn't moved everything somewhere so we'll never find it."

"Small world," Detective Graham observed. "Look, how do you want to work this case? The victim lived in the Yuma City limits, but was found in the county, which is under our jurisdiction. It's okay with me if you want to work in concert with us, but I'd like both of us to question the husband."

"I don't have a problem with that at all. Are you done with your search of the area?" St. Jons asked.

"Yeah, it's getting dark. I'm going to have them wrap it up soon," Graham said, nodding toward a spread-out group of deputies.

"Do you want to follow me over to inform and question the victim's husband now?" St. Jons didn't want to have to wait on Detective Graham before he got to Handcock.

"Let's go," replied Graham.

CHAPTER 25

Detectives Graham and St. Jons parked their vehicles on the main road in front of the RV park where Richard lived and walked several yards to his space. Detective Graham looked around and braced herself for meeting the inhabitant, after she observed the condition of the Handcock trailer and the general appearance of the space where it was standing. It stood out like a sore thumb in what was otherwise a pleasant recreational vehicle park.

"Didn't you say that you saw similar wood pieces and paint cans outside here?" Detective Graham asked, looking at nothing more than several pieces of trash that Richard hadn't picked up yet and the wind was threatening to blow into the oleander bushes on the far side of the trailer. There was blue spray paint on the cement pad similar to that on one of the wood frames that was found in the campfire pit at the crime scene. Similar paint was used to write the words, "I love you, Richard" on the front of the trailer, an apparent silent testament from a woman now on her way to the medical pathology department in Tucson.

"Yeah, looks like he moved all of it yesterday. We'll have to call the self-storage places nearby and ask if any of his friends or neighbors know where he took the stuff when we interview them. I'm betting he dumped it somewhere out in the desert," St. Jons replied. Then he noticed that Richard's truck was backed into the driveway. This struck him as odd, considering Richard didn't have it backed in the previous day when he was loading it. As he looked over the truck from a distance, he noticed that the top lip of the bed had something black smudged on it. St. Jons had been leading Graham to the front door, but he changed course and walked over to the back of the truck. "Damn it!" he exclaimed, when he saw that the interior of the truck's bed had been incinerated. "Looks like the son of a bitch decided to go another way with it."

"We're a day late and a dollar short. You must have spooked him yesterday," Graham said, exhibiting a firm grasp of the obvious as she stepped up to the door of the trailer. St. Jons felt physically ill. By the time he knocked on the front door, he was angry, but controlled. They could hear the television inside through the thin walls. The drapes had been closed to keep out the blinding late afternoon sun, and Richard hadn't seen or heard them approach.

Richard opened the door, which swung to the outside. Graham, who was standing on the blind side of the door, had to jump down from the step to avoid getting knocked off by it. Richard recognized St. Jons immediately and was annoyed.

"Good evening, Mr. Handcock, this is Detective Graham from the Yuma County Sheriff's office." She stepped up once again to the door. "May we come inside?" St. Jons asked.

"Sure," Richard said as he opened the screen door, which is customarily located inside of the exterior door of a trailer and also opened outward. Graham moved off the step for a second time with embarrassment, nearly losing her footing. St. Jons didn't seem to notice her awkwardness. "What's this about?" Richard did not offer them a seat, so the three stood in the small living room.

Graham's eyes took in the shaved head and military fatigues with surprise. She had expected him to be a long-haired hippy type, for what reason she couldn't be sure. She said softly, "A fisherman spotted a body in the Gila Gravity Canal today that appears to be your wife."

Richard was obviously surprised, but he didn't act grief stricken. "What do you mean *appears?*" Richard asked, his words laced lightly with sarcasm.

"The body fits the description *your mother-in-law* gave us, Mr. Handcock," St. Jons responded with equal sarcasm. "She also has three earrings holes in her left ear, and two in the other."

"How do you know for sure that it's her?" Richard demanded.

St. Jons firmly restrained himself from getting in Richard's face when he spoke evenly, "We won't know positively until the lab does the DNA tests or until we match dental records, but the victim had a scar from a broken clavicle, the same as your wife did. In addition, the body was clothed only in a black bra that matches the description given by her employer. She said Joyce was wearing one the night before she disappeared and that one strap was broken and she had reattached it with a small safety pin. The same bra that you ripped apart when you had a fight with her the night before she vanished."

"I told you yesterday, that never happened. Are you saying that I'm a suspect or something?" Richard asked acting wounded. He backed up to the futon sofa and collapsed. "I might have had a disagreement with her, but I could never *kill* her!" He rubbed his eyes until he produced a muddy tear with his dirty hands.

"May we sit down, please?" St. Jons asked rhetorically, as he sat in the only chair in the room across from Richard, leaving Graham to sit next to Richard on the tiny futon sofa. Graham glared at the other detective, feeling annoyed and out maneuvered. Oblivious to Graham's seating problems, St. Jons continued, "We'd like you to go over again what your activities were on Wednesday, the 11th of January. You don't have to talk to us now, but it would be better for you if you cooperated with our investigation, Mr. Handcock."

Richard looked at Graham for sympathy and understanding, but found none on the petite blonde's face. He noticed that she was attractively dressed in a blue denim pantsuit with an extra button undone at the top of the red blouse she wore underneath. Even given Richard's current situation, he could picture her in something low-cut, black, and slinky. He could feel the warmth of her knee next to him as his eyes darted from her face downward to the small bulge of pale skin inside her curiously unbuttoned blouse. In a flash, his eyes switched suddenly to look forward at the floor while he went over his mental list, "Like I said, I made love to my wife after my stepdaughter left for school." Graham calmly leaned forward and held her knees with her hands as far away from Richard as possible. "Then I left here at 8 o'clock in the morning and went to look for work. First, I stopped at a gas station on Pacific to fill up the tank." St. Jons jotted down these deviations from his original story: Richard had said previously that he and his wife had made love while Joyce's daughter was in the shower, not after she left for school, and had he just added the gas station pit stop perhaps to fill in the time? "Then I went to the construction site behind The Grocery Store in the Foothills."

"When did you arrive there?" Graham asked casually.

"At about 9 o'clock," Richard answered.

"That drive would take ten to fifteen minutes, tops," Graham commented.

"There's more traffic this time of year . . . more people waiting to buy gas!" Richard protested.

"Even still, no more than thirty-five minutes . . . but go ahead with your story," Graham said, irritated and rolling her eyes at St. Jons after Richard looked back to the floor.

"Okay, then I went the Jack in the Box they're building on Fortuna. I heard they were hiring rough-in carpenters there."

St. Jons interrupted finally, "My notes say you went to Mesa Del Sol."

"Yeah, I did. I went there, too."

"In what order did you go to these places?" St. Jons asked.

"I can't remember."

"Who did you talk to while you were at those places?" St. Jons continued to pump him for more information.

"Like I told you yesterday, I waited for two different supervisors, but neither of them showed up. I did talk to a couple of the construction workers that I know, though. You can ask around yourself."

"We will," St. Jons said. "I want their names."

"I don't know their names, only their faces," Richard was beginning to sound whiny. Graham hated whiny men with a passion.

"Who did you speak to, if anyone?" Graham asked.

"I talked to my ex-girlfriend, Hazel, who is a bartender at The Bottoms Up Pub on Fortuna, the other side of the freeway. I know she remembers me being there, you can even ask her. I stopped in there to look for a guy who sells used tires. I stayed forty-five minutes and talked to him, but I don't know his name either, but I'm sure Hazel does."

Graham said, "So, your only witness is your ex-girlfriend? That's kind of convenient, isn't it?"

"We're still friends, but it's not like she'd lie for me or anything." Richard explained.

"And you drank V-8 juice for forty-five minutes, I remember. That's it? Then you came home?" St. Jons asked, knowing that's what Richard had said before, but this time Richard said, "No, I stopped at a mini-market and bought a Thirsty-Two-Ouncer drink to take home."

St. Jons sighed in frustration. He calmed himself again and said, "So you were still real thirsty. Uh-huh. Which store did you stop at?"

"I don't recall," Richard answered.

"Why am I not surprised?" St. Jons commented. "Then what?"

"When I got home and Joyce wasn't here, I waited for her because we had plans to go to Wal-Mart around noon, and when she didn't come back, I went over to a neighbor's trailer. Her name is Cricket and she lives a couple of spaces down the street, to ask her if she'd seen Joyce around and she said she didn't. We talked for a while and then I came back home and waited some more. About an hour later, I went over to Joyce's parents to see if they knew where she went and they didn't either."

"So you were worried?" Graham prompted.

"No, I just kind of thought it strange at that point," Richard replied.

Graham changed the subject, "It sure looks like a tornado went through this place!"

"Yeah, I need to pick up stuff. Joyce always done that, and I guess I'm out of practice." Graham looked at a huge assortment of men's clothing strewn around the room, over chairs and on the floor. Food was on the table and dirty dishes in the sink were piled high. Richard's tools were tossed in a corner.

It was hard for Graham to understand how a person could live like that. She stood, as if just to stretch her legs, and wandered to the doorway of the bedroom. "Have you noticed any of Joyce's clothing missing?" She didn't see any feminine clothing when she walked toward the bedroom doorway. The closet doors were open.

"Yeah, her black shoes. That's all I noticed missing," Richard answered.

"Really. What happened to the bedding?" Graham asked, noting a bare mattress with a few dirty clothes on top.

"See that shelf over the bed? I had a Thirst Buster set on one end of it and it spilled all over the bed. The board just sits on the shelf brackets and I had all the weight at one end . . . it tipped over," Richard explained.

MURDER BY GRAVITY?

Graham nodded and looked at St. Jons for a moment before she started for the door.

"You're a carpenter by trade and that's the best shelf you could put up above your own bed . . . ?" St. Jons commented, not waiting for Richard to reply. "What happened to the back of your truck, incidentally?"

"I suspect that someone tossed a cigarette in there while I was parked across the street last night," Richard said, straight-faced.

"Gosh, that's too bad. You sure have been having a bad run of luck lately," St. Jons commented mockingly. He rose to his feet said, "Okay, that's it for now, Mr. Handcock. Don't leave Yuma for a while. I'm sure we'll have more questions to ask you."

"My truck isn't running too well right now, so I can't go far. Am I a suspect?" He looked up sheepishly from his seated position on the futon.

St. Jons gave Richard a long, serious look before he spoke. He said, "You bet your boots you are."

* * *

Handcock may be our killer," Donna Graham commented to Detective St. Jons as they walked across the RV park to Mr. and Mrs. Perron's home and rang the bell. Mrs. Perron turned on the porch light and opened the door. Lori had seen the police cars roll up to the park entrance earlier and she watched out of the curtains to see which space they walked to, and was not surprised that it was her son-in-law's. When she saw the same two people at her door, she said, "Is this about Joyce? Did you find her?" She opened the sliding-glass door that served as a front entry and motioned for them to come in and sit down anywhere in the living room. Mr. Perron moved his recliner to an up-right position and stood up as they entered. Lori protectively placed her hand on her chest, just below her collar, the other hand held it there. Her bloodshot, questioning eyes were full of fear.

St. Jons ignored her questions momentarily while he introduced the other detective and himself to Joyce's parents, his tone solemn. Graham remarked that they had a lovely home and admired Joyce's picture in a silver frame on their upright piano. When they were all seated, St. Jons told them the bad news of their gruesome discovery in the canal. Lori's body seemed to cave in on itself and her husband rushed to her side and held her while she cried.

"Are you absolutely sure?" she asked, looking up through tears and hoping that there was some mistake.

"She had the scar you told me about and the earring holes, just as you said. Do you know where she had her dental work done? We'd like to be able to confirm her identity with X-rays."

Bill Perron spoke for the first time, "I took Joyce to Mexico when she had a toothache six months ago. They took X-rays, but I don't know if they kept them in their records because they ended up just pulling it out. I'll call in the morning to find out. Other than that, she never had any trouble with her teeth. She was still so young . . ." he choked up.

"If necessary, we can take a blood sample from your wife and Joyce's sister to confirm if it's Joyce's DNA. After seeing her picture, I can tell you that we are quite sure, at this point, but we want to be positive."

"What happens now?" Mr. Perron asked, through tears.

"Her body has been taken to Tucson for an autopsy. Both of us will be present for the procedure tomorrow and I'll be in touch with you afterwards. Mr. Perron, I would very much appreciate it if you can locate those X-rays tomorrow, if possible," St. Jons said. "We would both like to extend our condolences to you. I think we'll let you two be alone for now."

"I forgot to tell you earlier, when you go to the autopsy, please check this. Joyce had her tubes tied. When do you think that we will be able to put her body to rest?" Mrs. Perron asked.

"That will depend upon how long they need to do tests and examine the body. I will let you know on that and if the body had the tubes tied. Thank you for that information," St. Jons answered. "If you'll excuse us, we have an early morning coming up."

Bill Perron continued to hold his wife, who had buried her face in his sweater. He nodded to the detectives as they left and muttered his thanks to them.

* * *

MURDER BY GRAVITY?

"Good evening, Electronic Monitoring Services, this is Christy Shannon."

"Hello, this is Detective David St. Jons from the Yuma Police Department. I need to speak with Richard Handcock's worker," he said.

"That would be Ike Groves and he's already left for the night. Maybe I can help you. I personally reviewed the case and made the recommendations to the court . . . or should I say, I made the *lack* of a recommendation," Christy said.

"Why is that?" St. Jons asked.

"It was my opinion that Mr. Handcock was not a good candidate for our program because of his continuing criminal conduct and, most importantly, his spousal abuse, but I was outgunned by Judge Mancini and Russ Kosta, Handcock's attorney."

"Looks like you can tell them, 'I told you so' now. Richard's wife was murdered and he's our prime suspect," St. Jons told her.

"Damn. Sometimes I hate being right," Christy said somberly.

"I wonder if you can look up Richard's 'time aways' for January 11th? That's the day his wife come up missing," St. Jons asked, hoping that he wouldn't have to wait too long for the worker to get that information.

To his relief, Christy said, "Sure, hold on while I pull up his file. Here we are. Ike dropped by the Handcock home for a field visit the night of the 10th. It looks like Richard changed his schedule then because he had to leave for a new job at 0730," Christy said.

St. Jons interjected, "You mean to *look* for a job."

"No, he told Ike that he already had a job. Write this down," Christy dictated, "On the 11th, Richard left at 0008."

"Eight o'clock in the morning?" St. Jons asked.

"Uh-uh. We start each day at midnight, so he left at eight minutes after 12:00 AM, probably to pick up his wife from work. He was okayed for that. He returned home at 0124, which is . . . "

"1:24 AM," St. Jons said to indicate that he got the idea now.

"Correct. There was an automatic alarm away at 0741 when he left that morning because Ike hadn't faxed in the new schedule yet, but he did give his permission verbally the night before. The next entry was his return at 12:44 PM," Christy said.

"Are you sure?" St. Jon was honestly surprised. "That would

make him gone that morning for a total of five hours and three minutes. The first time I talked to him, he told me he left home at 8:00 AM and returned before 11:00 AM. That's an extra two hours he lied about being gone. That's really interesting . . . a person could do a lot in five hours," David commented.

"Exactly right. I could fly to Hawaii in five hours!" Christy said wistfully.

"I've never had a suspect who was on electronic monitor before. He had to *know* that we would find out when he was gone. Why lie about it?"

"You'd be surprised how many law enforcement officers don't think to ask about it. Okay, here we go again. Handcock left again at 1423 and returned at 1501," Christy said as she read the computer screen.

"That's 2:23 PM to 3:01 PM So, he was out a total of thirty-eight minutes. Then what?" Jons asked.

"Then nothing. He stayed home the rest of the day and night."

"Really? He didn't go out to look for his wife?"

"Apparently not," Christy replied, "There's no note saying he asked for time off to look for his wife, because I'm sure Ike would have okayed it."

"Can you tell me his hours for say, the next seven days?"

"No problem," Christy said, eyeing the stack of paperwork on her desk. St. Jons heard her punching keys on a computer. "Thursday, January 12th, he was gone from 12:57 PM until 1:36 PM."

"So, roughly, forty minutes all day," David said to himself.

Ms. Shannon continued reading, "On Friday, the 13th, he left at 3:12 PM and was back by 3:57 PM.

Saturday, the 14th, he left home at 1:18 PM and returned at 2:06 PM. He left later that day at 4:43 PM and returned at 11:53 PM, but with his new hours, he wasn't supposed to be gone at that time of night and he hadn't asked for permission beforehand, so an alarm away was sounded."

"You mean that he told Ike Groves on Tuesday night that he wouldn't be needing time off late at night to pick up his wife from work?" St. Jons asked, incredulous.

"It doesn't say anything specifically about that. Maybe Ike remembers something that will help you. I'll leave him a message to call you. I can't understand why *he* didn't notice that Richard hadn't gone to work on Wednesday, Thursday, or Friday. Ike should have caught that."

"You'd think so. That brings us to Sunday. . ."

Christy picked up the cue, "On Sunday, the 15th, Handcock left at 10:52 AM and returned at 11:40 AM. Are you getting this down?"

"Yeah, could you give me Monday and Tuesday too?" he asked.

"Of course, Monday the 16th, he left at 11:05 A M and returned at 12:18 PM. Then he left again at 12:20 PM and came back at 1:35 A M. Tuesday, the 17th, he left at 10:57 AM and returned at 2:08 PM and that's all for that day," Christy said. "But there is a note on Wednesday, the 18th of January, that Handcock asked for some additional time away to look for his wife for the first time."

"Wow, this is great! You have been an enormous help and I really appreciate your time. Tell Groves that I'll be gone all day tomorrow . . . no, wait, I'd better call him myself instead. Thanks again and have a nice evening," St. Jons hung up the phone, his mind racing in overdrive, but he had a 6:00 AM date with Graham to go to an autopsy in the morning, so he finally gathered his notes and headed for home.

* * *

Donna Graham had been to Tucson once before to watch Dr. Rolland Andrews, who was a qualified pathology expert in the Yuma courts, perform an autopsy and, oddly enough, she looked forward to it during the four-hour drive to Tucson. Detective St. Jons insisted that he do all the driving and Graham relented, sensing it would be futile to question his archaic notion of the male role. Both of them made several attempts at small talk, but they just didn't click together. Graham felt St. Jons's unspoken disapproval of a woman performing a man's job, but she had toughened up over her years on the job. They ended up talking about the case most of the time on the road. St. Jons filled her in on the conversation he had the previous night with Ms. Shannon at Electronic Monitoring Services.

Graham said, "Handcock had plenty of time to kill his wife, dispose of her body, and look for work!"

"Yeah, but we've only just touched the surface of this case. Joyce

Handcock knew a lot of weird customers and drug dealers, we can't rule them out yet," St. Jons reminded her.

"But he had motive, opportunity, and he was the last person to see his wife alive," Graham said.

"The last one that *we know of,*" St. Jons reminded her.

The two detectives arrived at The Forensic Science Center in Tucson with enough time to get into lab coats and put blue paper booties on to protect their shoes from possible biohazards just before the staff wheeled Joyce Handcock's body in on a transportable steel table from the X-ray department. As they positioned the table by the dissecting sinks and the doctor's instrument trays, the odor became overwhelming. Graham pulled a bottle of peppermint oil out of her pocket and dabbed some under her nostrils, then handed it to St. Jons, who gratefully accepted.

St. Jons said, "I've heard Dr. Andrews is very good at what he does."

Graham replied, "Yeah, he's one of the best. He's also the assistant clinical pathology professor at University of Arizona Medical School."

"Do you know him?" St. Jons asked.

"I've attended one of his autopsies before," she gushed, "I'm kind of a fan. There he is now . . ." St. Jons was not surprised when he looked at the door to see a good-looking, well-built man in his mid-thirties walk into the autopsy room with a "take-charge" air about him. If ever there were a pathologist that could have his own "groupies," it would be Dr. Andrews. St. Jons smiled with amusement.

"Good morning, Detective Graham. How nice to see you again," Andrews said. Graham flushed pink against her platinum blond hair and introduced her temporary partner from the Yuma Police Department to him. "Welcome," the doctor said. "We have the whole autopsy room to ourselves this morning. While we were waiting for you to arrive, we went ahead and drew blood for our toxicology screening, HIV tests and so forth." He pulled on his latex gloves and commented that Agent Mulder on the "X-Files" television show calls these gloves "misspent latex." Graham giggled and St. Jons felt nauseous, but was determined not to show it.

MURDER BY GRAVITY?

Dr. Andrews spoke into the overhead microphone of the tape recorder, "We have a moderately decomposing body of a young woman who was bound by her wrists and ankles to two types of wraps and ligature materials." He looked up at Donna Graham and said, "So, tell me, what were the circumstances in which you found this body, Detective?"

Graham explained where she was found and how long she had been missing beforehand.

"Interesting." Dr. Andrews then parted Joyce's hair with his hand and stated that there were three significant wounds to the right side of the head. He asked one of his assistants to shave the injured area of the scalp and asked the other to take photos of everything as they went along.

"The body is covered with slimy, greenish, plant-like material, which is more than likely due to her time in the canal. The skin is starting to slip off, which is common due to decomposition, but the coloration is not normal."

"The ligatures on her wrists and ankles, one is a ribbon-like fabric, tight enough to cause injury and quite complex in the way it was tied, not just simply wrapped around. The other ligature is wire about the thickness of a wire coat hanger which is rusty from the water, and wrapped multiple times around the limbs. The wire goes in and out, around and between the hands multiple times. The flesh is indented due to the tightness of it. The wire was first, followed by the ribbon-like material. The victim obviously did not do this to herself. The fingers have a froggy-type appearance, as if one were to soak in a pool for a long time."

Dr. Andrews continued, "There is no clothing, except for a black brassiere which is pushed up over her left breast. Let's cut the ligatures off now. We'll never be able to untie them, wouldn't want to; might be evidence." Then Andrews and his assistants attempted to gather any trace evidence from the surface of the skin with cellophane tape. There wasn't any. The doctor said again into the microphone, "There is a greenish marbling of veins seen on the surface of the skin. The whole body is bloated and filled with gas produced by bacteria. There are no injuries to the victim's back or legs. Let's clean up the body now." The assistants were careful not to slip the skin off during the washing. "You can easily see wire indentations and fabric lines which match the ligature materials."

As the assistant finished shaving the side of Joyce's head to better view the injuries, Dr. Andrews said, "There are three lacerations to the left side of her scalp, all in a three-to four-inch area which are significant. They are each an inch to an inch-and-a-half long, probably an eighth to a sixteenth-inch-wide and one-inch to one-fourth-inch deep. They produced a significant amount of hemorrhage, but not a fracture. The two cuts that are visible on the victim's face are slightly curved and of the same orientation, both going horizontally and are close to each other. The third gash is behind the hairline in the same area, but slightly higher and towards the back of her head above the right ear. This is more superficial, but of the same orientation and curved in a semicircular appearance. These were not caused by being lifted in water or by rocks or debris or random post-mortem injuries. The wounds were caused by three *separate impacts* to the right side of her head. It's unlikely that she fell to receive these clustered wounds. These are classic injuries from a linear object, which most likely was intentionally done to the right side of her head. The possible objects are too numerous. . . maybe a piece of wood, a brick, tire iron, a long piece of metal . . . anything that can cause linear, slightly curved lacerations. It would have to be fairly heavy and have velocity behind it. Basically, it was a severe blunt-force trauma."

Dr. Andrews spoke to one of his assistants, "Will you reflect the scalp back as I cut it? Here we see considerable hemorrhage but the skull is not fractured. This was a homicide. Let's do a rape kit right away."

Later Andrews continued, "Rigor has come and gone, so she's been dead at least one to two days. She's also had a significant amount of decomposition. Canals waters act as a cooler, so decomposition occurs more slowly," he said to Graham, ignoring St. Jons.

This was the part St. Jons hated, the Y-incision and removal of bodily organs and fluids for further toxicology tests. He looked away from the body until he heard Andrews say, "This woman has had her tubes tied and was *alive* when she was put in the canal! To get this amount of hemorrhage from the wounds on the face and scalp certainly implies that there was blood actively pumping into this area of the scalp. There is a 50-50 chance that she became semi-conscious or was unconscious with the head wounds, but she was still breathing when she was drowned. She may have been completely alert and aware or anywhere in the spectrum of consciousness when she entered the Gila Gravity Canal. *One might say it was <u>murder by gravity</u>,"* he quipped.

St. Jons asked, "Wouldn't there be signs of a struggle, if she were alert?"

"Yes, she was most likely for that reason unconscious when she was put in the canal. Well, that's about all I have for you at the moment. I'll be in touch when I get the results of the toxicology from the blood, fluids, and the organs," Dr. Andrews said as he removed his gloves and flipped open the biohazard trash can with his foot.

CHAPTER 26

The following day, Detective St. Jons obtained search warrants for Richard Handcock's trailer and truck. He and Detective Graham had made arrangements during their ride back from Tucson to meet at the trailer as soon as St. Jons had the warrants in hand. They each brought a partner with them to help with the search procedures and the cataloging of possible evidence.

St. Jons knew that, according to Ike Groves, Richard's EMS worker, it was an hour designated for Richard to be home, according to his monitoring schedule. When Richard opened the door, Detective St. Jons said, "Mr. Handcock, we have search warrants for your truck and trailer. You'll have to wait outside while we search the trailer's contents." Outside, another officer brought over one of the resin lawn chairs and placed it by the front door near the truck that was parked in its usual location next to the trailer, so he could keep an eye on Richard while they conducted the search of his truck. As St. Jons and Graham entered the trailer, the other officer took Richard by the arm to lead him to the chair. Richard sat down quietly and read the warrants without comprehension.

The search of the trailer netted them little more evidence than they had seen visually the first night they both came to interview Richard. They could find none of Joyce's clothing, but did find her purse. The bed was still stripped and Graham assumed that Richard had probably been sleeping on it the way it was, most likely in his clothes, because they looked slept-in. Outside the trailer on the ground, they found two paint can lids with blue paint dried on them, which they bagged and the officer from the Sheriff's Department scraped a sample of purple paint from the cement pad next to the trailer.

Under the trailer, they found a folding knife, an empty pack of

MURDER BY GRAVITY?

Djarum clove cigarettes, two plastic grocery bags containing spray paint cans of various colors, and several pieces of wire. There was literally junk everywhere. The contents of Richard's truck cab were methodically and arduously itemized by the other officers in attendance. The camper shell had been removed previous to their arrival and was not on the property. The truck bed was loaded with Richard's work materials and tools, all soiled by the black residue that remained from the fire. There was a long wooden box with hand tools inside, a 12-volt air compressor, auto repair manual, broom, grease gun, fishing gear, a leather tool belt, handsaws, jumper cables, and among several other items, a red plastic gas can and a plastic sheet with purple paint remnants on it.

Incredibly, the glove compartment in the truck contained over fifty different items. Most noteworthy of the contents was a copy of the New Testament, a cassette tape by "White Snake," a black billfold with miscellaneous photos, four books of food stamps, one pair of boxer shorts, three wire cutters with different colored handles, a purple garter, plastic bags, a chrome pry tool, a disposable razor, two toothbrushes, a comb, shampoo, a compact, vitamins, a ring with a pink stone, a watch, a yellow hair band, three lighters, and four pens.

The console area carried keys, coins, Ace bandages and the notes Richard had written the previous summer at Joyce's insistence about his sexual fantasies involving Ruby and Joyce. There was also a copy of an Electronic Monitoring Services report.

The bench seat was scattered with copies of the flyers Richard had made up to post around town. Joyce's smiling face dominated the pages, under the word "missing," in large capital letters. Joyce was dressed in sparkling evening clothes. Under a small, brown pillow was a packet of informative brochures from the National Cancer Institute and miscellaneous personal papers of Richard's.

St. Jons stepped outside the trailer door and said to Richard, "The phone number you gave me for Ruby is no good. A kid answered and said she moved in with Red and didn't know the phone number. Do you have it?"

"I don't know. Joyce might have it in her purse," Richard said.

"I've got it right here," Graham said, stepping out of the door with Joyce's purse in hand. Richard took it from her and rummaged around until he produced a little pink address book.

"Here it is . . . Red Pollock." Richard handed the open book to St. Jons.

"Red Pollock, the *cop*?" David St. Jons gasped and verified that the house address was the same one with which he was familiar. "Ruby's living with Red Pollock? Didn't you say she's a drug dealer?"

"Hey, I don't know where she's living. I called Mike Deere's house last week, looking for Joyce, and Ruby answered the phone, so I thought she was shacked up with *him*. I can tell you for a *fact* that Ruby does drugs and sells them to her friends . . . and she has a lot of friends!"

If it were true that Red Pollock was living with a dealer/druggie and had been present when she sold his murder victim drugs the night before she disappeared, St. Jons could be opening up a very large can of worms in the Yuma Police Department. He went inside Richard's trailer with the pink book and called the phone number on Richard's phone.

Richard and Graham waited as the other officers had Richard's truck towed to the Material Management Yard. The tow truck driver took the keys from Richard and gave him a receipt with a case number on it.

When St. Jons returned from using the phone, he gave Graham an exasperated look and shook his head. Graham was curious, but had faith that he would tell her what was said when the time was right.

St. Jons took Richard's arm and guided him to a standing position and cuffed him. "Mr. Handcock, you are under arrest for the murder of Joyce Handcock."

"Are you crazy? My wife isn't dead! But if she was dead, there are other people who hated Joyce. I loved her! If you investigated at all, you'd know that. Check out Mike Deere and Phil Seward. They both had motives for wanting Joyce dead," Richard explained. "Where are you taking *me*?"

"You are going down to police headquarters with us. I need the keys to your trailer so I can lock it up. It's being seized in addition to your truck and will be towed to the same place. I'll have the paperwork for you later on."

MURDER BY GRAVITY?

Once at the station, they escorted Richard to a locked examination room and left him there alone for half an hour while St. Jons and Graham got a cup of coffee and had a chance to talk privately. They took their coffee cups and went into the room next to the one Richard was in and watched him through the two-way mirror.

St. Jons kept his voice low and explained to Graham, "Ruby Vasquez was Joyce's best friend, according to Richard, and now she's living with a retiring cop named Red Pollock. She answered his phone when I called earlier and admitted that the night before Joyce disappeared, Red drove her and a friend over to the Handcocks' trailer to sell Joyce some crystal meth. Can you beat that? I'm going to have to investigate my former boss now!"

"Maybe we can find a way to keep his name out of this," Graham replied. "How about I go in there and soften Richard up a bit, ask him if he wants something to drink and play 'good cop' for a while. Give me about ten or fifteen minutes, then you can come in and raise holy hell with him. Okay, "bad cop?""

"Yeah, fine," St. Jons said, but he worried about the potentially explosive situation involving retired Lieutenant Pollock. St. Jons found himself in the middle of an impossible situation. Rumor was that Red started drinking heavily after his wife left him and soon thereafter, he was taking acquired time off before he retired from the force. St. Jons felt sorry for the guy, but he couldn't believe that anyone with Red's ethics and authority would sink that low. He forced himself to think about the lies with which he was about to confront Richard. St. Jons saw liars every day on the job and hated them with a passion. He thought about that and let nature take its course as adrenalin pumped and readied him for the "bad cop" role.

When he entered the interrogation room to join the others, St. Jons sweetly asked, "Mr. Handcock, may I call you Richard?"

"Whatever," Richard replied insolently. "Look, you say you found Joyce . . . if that's true, why didn't you let me see her to identify the body?"

St. Jons, still smiling, looked at Graham briefly and said to Richard, "*You* don't get to ask the questions here. I'd like to know why you told us that you were gone the morning of January 11th from 8:00 AM until just before 11:00, when your electronic monitoring device logged you out at 7:41 AM and didn't log you back in until 12:44 PM. Didn't you think two additional hours worth mentioning?" St. Jons asked sarcastically.

"Well, I don't remember exactly. I didn't think I was gone that long."

"You said you and your wife planned to meet at the trailer at noon that day to go shopping and *she* didn't show up, when in fact, you were 44 minutes late arriving home," St. Jons stated flatly.

Richard's voice became whiney, "I don't wear a watch. . . ."

"Of course you don't, but you had one in your glove compartment and it was set for the correct time," St. Jons pointed out. "Now, just going by what you already told us, you've made some changes in your story."

Richard shifted in his chair as the detective paced back and forth across the room while he spoke. "For one thing, you originally told me that the day your wife disappeared, you had sex with your wife. . . ."

Richard interrupted him, "Made love with my wife," he said, correcting St. Jons.

In a supreme act of indulgence, St. Jons said, ". . . . You said that you 'made love with your wife' while Nickie was down at the showers. Then the next time you told the story, it was after she left for school. In the first version, you neglected to mention that you stopped at a gas station before you went to the Foothills. Then you couldn't remember when you went to the various construction sites that day. First you said you went to two sites, then three, then you went straight home and the next time you stopped to buy a drink."

"I told you, I don't remember exactly . . . . I didn't know at the time it was going to be such a red-letter day, if it was, or I would have documented my whereabouts better for you!" Richard was getting tired and irritable.

"You had the *opportunity* to murder your wife that morning, and we have a witness that says you attacked Joyce at her work the night before," St. Jons pointed out.

"Your witness saw nothing! And my wife isn't dead! Why don't you listen?"

St. Jons leaned across the table nearer Richard's face, "Oh, we know it's her, alright. Why would Joyce leave home to go shopping without her purse? Think about it and stop acting like everybody but you is stupid. We'll have the DNA results for the record in a few days, but we all know it's her, don't we? We found wire similar to that outside your trailer wrapped around your wife's wrists and ankles and you had *three* wire cutters inside the cab of your truck!"

"So, what? I'm in construction and I use them all the time. You've got jack!"

"What did you burn up in the back of your truck, Richard?" St. Jons asked, keeping the pressure on. "I saw wood pieces like the ones found at the crime scene in the bed of your truck the day before Joyce's body was found."

"I didn't burn anything. I wasn't there when it caught fire, I just put it out. Look, this has been fun, but I think I'd like to call my court-appointed attorney now," Richard calmly said and simply quit talking to them and looked away.

St. Jons stormed out of the room, Graham on his heels as he led her to his supervisor's office. Graham was introduced by St. Jons to his supervisor who treated her like a lady, pulling out a chair for her to sit in. She hated it when other cops treated her differently than they did each other, but she nodded her thanks to him.

"What's going on, guys?" The chief folded his hands together on his orderly, over-sized desk and listened attentively as the two detectives poured out the highlights of the story to him.

"You don't have enough evidence to keep him, David," the chief said, lowering his bushy eyebrows. "If the body were found a day sooner, before the husband set fire to destroy the evidence in his truck that might have been a different story."

St. Jons hung his head and said pointlessly, "But we know he did it." The small office filled with silence.

"Wait a minute," Graham suddenly came to life. "All we have to do is hold him until we can get a judge to revoke Richard's assignment to Electronic Monitoring Services!" The young detective had their attention. "He's already serving time, remember? We just hold him until we can get him remanded back into custody. That'll buy us some time to look for more evidence and more witnesses. What do you think?" she asked, searching their faces. They smiled in response to her quite obvious solution.

CHERIE HUYETT ACHTEMEIER

* * *

While St. Jons took Richard to the nearby jail, Graham headed over to question Jeff Dupre, Ruby Vasquez's former boyfriend, with whom she lived prior to moving in with Red Pollock. Jeff had called the police department to give them information that he said, "might be important."

The house Jeff owned was nicer than most in the area. It was set back far from the road and had a long, curved asphalt driveway that split the lawn roughly in two and had large willow trees on either side. Several huge Mexican bird of paradise and purple sage bushes under the window were neatly trimmed. Two well-used mountain bikes were laying on the asphalt near the front porch. Detective Graham stepped over them with little difficulty, then pressed the door bell. She listened, unsure if the bell rang inside the house, then saw a figure approach through the stained glass of an Early American door. The man who opened the door was tall and slim; his boyish face sported a neatly trimmed brown mustache as if to testify that he were truly an adult. Long, curly eyelashes framed beseeching light brown eyes. He reminded Graham of a tall Johnny Depp, and she had to remind herself why she was there. She produced her badge and introduced herself.

"I was told that you have information regarding the Joyce Handcock murder," she stated.

Jeff invited her inside where they sat in his spartanly furnished living room.

"So, it was murder, then?" Jeff said with sadness.

"That was fairly obvious when we found her body. Haven't you read the newspaper yet?" she asked.

"A friend of mine called me earlier and told me basically what it said; that she was found tied up in the gravity canal and had weights attached to her, but I don't believe everything in the newspapers, Detective," Jeff replied. "It's a damn shame. She was such a terrific and pretty lady."

"Mr. Dupre, can you tell me about your relationship with Joyce?"

"Yeah," Jeff said, looking relieved to talk about Joyce alive rather than deceased. "Joyce and I go way back to about 1988. We went out together a couple of times, but we were always just good

MURDER BY GRAVITY?

friends. My fiancée was a very close friend of Joyce's. We just recently split up."

"Ruby Vasquez?" Graham asked just to be sure.

"Yeah. Joyce's daughter, Nickie, used to baby-sit for our kids all the time. She's still young enough to be a real good baby-sitter. You know, usually when kids get to be 14 or 15 years old, they tend to forget everything they knew when they were 12."

Graham chuckled at that comment, "I know what you mean."

"I called the police right away when I heard about Joyce being dead. I think I seen something that you should know about," Jeff started. Graham nodded at him, readying her pen to her notebook.

"The day Joyce went missing, I went over to Joyce's trailer to ask if Nickie could baby-sit for my kids. That day was some kind of school holiday in our school district. All the kids were out of school and mine didn't want to be trapped at my shop all day and they're too young to leave alone. I have an air-conditioning business that I started twenty years ago."

"Really?" Graham said with surprise. "You don't look old enough!"

"Thanks," Jeff said smiling, "Anyway, I remember that day because it was a day that I worked and the kids were off and it was ten days before they found Joyce's body. The details fit too closely to be any other day."

"When I knocked on the trailer door that morning, Richard answered and I asked him if it would be okay for Nickie to baby-sit. Richard left the door open and went back to talk to Nickie while one of my kids and I waited outside. When he came back to the door, he said, 'Yeah, she'd like to, but she needs a minute to get ready.' I walked about fifteen feet back to the car, and while I was standing there waiting, Richard was changing clothes in the doorway of the bedroom. He looked up and asked me if I'd seen Joyce around and I told him, 'No.' He said that she didn't come home from work the night before and said if I seen her, to tell her that he was looking for her."

"He was standing there, shivering, and out of the blue says that he'd had to get in a canal that morning. Then about ten seconds later, Nickie come through the door and she told Richard she'd be back later. He leaned down and she kissed him on the cheek." Jeff continued, "I couldn't help wondering as we drove away, what would he be doing in a canal on a cold and windy day?"

"Do you remember what holiday it was?" Graham asked.

Jeff shook his head, "Sorry, I don't know what or if it was a holiday. Maybe it was just a day off. I also have a vague recollection of Joyce or Richard coming by my place to get whatever concrete blocks they could use to support and level their trailer. I had a couple of dozen of them and one pyramid-shaped concrete block."

"That morning you came by, about what time was that?" Graham asked.

"I'm not sure. I had taken the kids out to breakfast first, so it was probably some time between 9:00 AM and 11:00 o'clock."

Graham consulted her notes then said, "We know that Joyce used drugs. Do you know if Richard did also?"

"I never really hung around Richard much, but I figure they were birds of a feather, you know? I only consider him a friend because his wife was one, and if there was anything I could do for him, he was entitled to it because of Joyce."

"Uh-huh. Your ex-fiancée, Ruby, admitted to my investigation partner that she sold drugs to Joyce the night before she disappeared. Do you use drugs at all, Mr. Dupre?"

"No, I don't feel that I need them, besides, I'm a single father and role model for my kids. If Ruby used drugs, she didn't do it around me or the kids," Dupre lied.

"That's very commendable, Mr. Dupre. But do you have *any* friends who do drugs?" Graham said with a slight sarcastic edge to her voice.

"I'm kind of a 'live and let live' person. What other people do is their business," Jeff replied, ignoring her sarcasm. It almost felt like his father's words were coming out of his mouth, but he thought it sounded pretty good.

She was about to throw his "Birds of a feather" line back at him but found it counter-productive. Instead she asked, "Do you know a man named Red Pollock?"

"I don't really know him, but as I understand it, Ruby is living with him now," Jeff said.

"I see. Do you remember anything else about Richard's actions that were unusual?"

MURDER BY GRAVITY?

"He was very controlling of Joyce and they hadn't been married long when I heard that he slapped her around and he had to spend the night in jail for it. He was always very jealous."

"Last fall, Richard came over to our house, Ruby was still living here then, and he was crying real hard and he said that he had caught Joyce red-handed, cheating on him. I thought he'd walked in and found her in bed with someone else, but he just had this tape recorder that he'd hidden under their bed and the only things you could hear was the television and closets opening and coat hangers being moved around. It sounded to me like she was just housecleaning. Then he'd say, 'Right there! Do you hear it?' He said that he could hear her having sex with somebody on the tape in their bedroom. We didn't hear anything at all like that. We tried to calm him down, but he just left, and he was mad at us because we didn't believe anything happened. In fact, at one point, he even said, 'That sounds like your voice, Jeff!' Ruby and I couldn't believe it."

Jeff took a cigarette out of his pocket and a disposable lighter. "I also heard that Richard had given Joyce some jewelry for Christmas or something, and after four or five months, there was a burglary at their residence. I had given Joyce a small gun for protection several years before she met Richard, and then it was gone and so was the jewelry. Joyce told us that six months after the jewelry was stolen, Richard had given her the same jewelry back, as a gift in a new box! She never let on that she knew it was the same stuff. He thinks everyone else is an idiot, that guy does. Joyce was only staying with him because he has incurable cancer, you know."

"Cancer? No, I didn't know that. This is very interesting, Mr. Dupre. It's not often we get people who just telephone us to volunteer information, like you did, unless they think there's a reward, or they do it to get even with somebody that they're mad at. Do you, yourself, have any reason that you'd like to see Richard in jail?"

"You've got to be kidding me, lady! No, I don't especially want to see Richard in jail unless he did something to put himself there. I just told you, Joyce was a good friend and I'm just trying to help."

"Sorry, I wouldn't be doing my job if I didn't ask," Graham said, getting to her feet. "Thanks for your time," she said extending her hand to him. Jeff reluctantly took it and said, "You're welcome."

CHERIE HUYETT ACHTEMEIER

* * *

The last stop Donna Graham made that day was the Perrons' house. She had made arrangements to interview Joyce's parents and her daughter while she was there.

Lori Perron recognized her immediately and invited her inside the park model and led her to the dining room table where she had a pot of coffee, cups, spoons, shortbread cookies and napkins laid out.

"Please go ahead and help yourself, Detective, I'll go get Nickie so you can talk to her first," Lori said and left the room. In seconds a very pretty young girl entered the room carrying a diet soda.

"You must be Nichole," Detective Graham said and introduced herself to her. "How old are you Nichole?"

"Twelve. Everybody calls me Nickie," she said.

"Okay, Nickie, I have to ask you some questions about your mother, so we can find out who hurt her," Graham began.

"My grandma told me already," Nickie replied, picking out a cookie for herself.

"Good. I understand that you didn't always live with your mom. Can you explain that?"

"I'd been living with my mom for the last three months or so. Before that, my brother and I spent the summer at my aunt's in Phoenix," Nickie explained. "I lived with my dad for a while too, but mostly with my mom." She was nervous and occasionally tearful.

Detective Graham kept her voice soft and pleasant and was careful not to upset Nickie, if at all possible. "How well did your mom and Richard get along, Nickie?"

"It's been worse since I came back from Phoenix. I heard them fight about every other day. When they were fighting, I came over here to get away," Nickie answered.

"I see. What did they usually fight about?"

"I heard my mom tell Richard that some girl left notes at her work for him, and her name was Hazel. Mostly, Richard was being jealous because he thought my mom was too friendly with the guys in the bar where she worked and he didn't like the clothes she wore. Sometimes Mike Deere brought my mom home from dumpster diving for craft supplies early in the morning, but it was still dark and Richard didn't like her to do that or go anywhere with him."

"Did you ever see Richard hit your mother?"

"No, I never saw a physical fight, but my mom had a lot of bruises on her arms and legs."

"Did you ever hear anything about Richard having cancer?" Graham asked.

"Yeah, he told me that he had it. He went away for a couple of weeks for therapy and when he came back, he was bald," Nickie stated.

"Could he have just shaved his head?"

"No, he looked bald, not shaved," Nickie insisted.

"Did you ever see clumps of his hair around the trailer?"

"No, I didn't. He was bald already when he came back."

"I see. Nickie, did you ever see any green strapping at your trailer?"

"Yeah, I saw it around in the shed behind the trailer."

"When your mom painted her crafts, how and where did she do it?"

"Lately she usually painted outside, up against a chair or a crate."

"Tell me about the day your mom disappeared," said Graham.

"I woke up at 5:30 and went to the showers and got ready for school. I asked my mom for a brush because I couldn't find mine, and I left at 7:15."

"Was your mom wearing anything when she handed you the brush?"

"I don't know, I just saw her arm and it didn't have anything on it," Nickie said.

"What happened when you came home from school?"

"I came home at five o'clock and Richard said she was gone. My mom always got ready for work at 4:30; she took her shower and got dressed real nice so she could be at work at 6:00. I was surprised when she wasn't there, so I came over here to ask if my grandparents knew where she was at and they didn't know either. At 9:30, I had to leave to baby-sit for Jeff's and Ruby's kids that night and I didn't get back until after midnight," Nickie said.

"You're sure you had school that day?"

"I'm very sure."

"Did Richard look for Joyce that night while you were there at the trailer?" Graham asked.

"I didn't see him look for her or call anybody to ask about her," Nickie answered. "He didn't seem worried."

"What about the next day?"

"The next day I didn't see Richard ask anybody where Mom was or call anybody either. On that day, I came over to stay at my Grandma's, because Grandma didn't want me to stay with Richard alone."

"Then on Friday, the 13th, I walked over to my Grandma's work after school with some friends and asked my Grandma if I could go home and she said I couldn't. She wanted me to move in with my Aunt Lynn, so I got really mad and left. I thought Mom would be back and she would want me to stay at the trailer and wait for her," Nickie explained.

"Is that the aunt that lives in Phoenix?" Graham asked.

"No. This one lives a few blocks from here. That's where I'm staying now."

"When you came back from taking your shower the day your mom disappeared, where were your mother and Richard?" Graham asked.

"Richard was sitting on the edge of the bed and Mom was sleeping."

"Nickie, did you ever see cement pylons or a milk crate outside your trailer?"

"Pylons? What's that?"

"You know, like some people use to make bookcases out of?" Graham offered.

"All the time," Nickie replied.

"One more question, then we're done. Did your mother usually carry her purse with her when she went somewhere?"

"Mom never left the house without it. She kept everything she needed in there," Nickie responded.

"Okay, kiddo, that's it for now. We may need to talk with you again later on, though. Will you go get your grandma for me now?"

* * *

When Lori came into the dining room, she poured them each a cup of coffee and dropped two sugar cubes into hers. She was obviously trying to cope with the loss of her daughter and at first, seemed very uncomfortable and about talking.

Detective Graham asked Lori to tell her about Joyce--what kind of a person she was and about the brief marriage between her daughter and Richard.

"This last year has been a nightmare," Lori said, looking at the tablecloth thoughtfully. She told Detective Donna Graham of her first meeting with Richard at Christmas at her daughter Lynn's apartment and the quadruple bypass her husband had right after Joyce's wedding. She shared her concerns that she had when Joyce started having bruises on her body and to the best of her knowledge, listed chronologically the times Richard and Joyce split up and got back together.

"I haven't really discussed all this with anybody before. I normally would talk things over with my husband, Bill, but the doctor said to try to keep things calm around him and not let him worry. Sometimes I wonder, if I hadn't been so busy working and taking care of my sick husband, if Joyce might have shared her feelings and fears more with me. I think that's why she spent so much time with Mike Deere the last few months. I asked her once if they were having an affair and she said that she wasn't sexually attracted to him. It was hard for me to believe because he's an attractive guy."

"Mrs. Perron, don't think that because you were busy taking care of your sick husband that any of this is your fault, don't think that for a minute," Graham said.

"I did tell her that I thought Richard was lying to her about having cancer, though," Lori said.

"Richard told *us* that he didn't have cancer," Graham said.

Lori was stunned at her simple words. "Joyce was beginning to wonder about it, too. She was going to confront Richard with her doubts and insist that she join him on his trip to Tucson to talk to his doctor about it that day—the day she came up missing. She would have left him when she found out the truth. You wouldn't believe to what lengths he went to make it seem believable."

"Let me ask you this, because I've been wondering about it. Did those people that Richard used to work with at Swift Sales actually kidnap and whip him?" Lori asked Graham.

"When would that have occurred?" Detective Graham asked her.

"Early to mid-December, I think. I know there was a police report. Can you check that out for me?"

"Sure thing," Graham said, writing down the details.

"Richard had Joyce and Nickie thinking all that time that they were in danger too. He said that these guys from Swift Sales were responsible for some break-ins at their trailer. The girls were really scared about it. He wanted them to believe they needed *him* to keep them safe," Lori recalled.

"When was the last time you spoke to your daughter, Mrs. Perron?" Graham asked.

"Tuesday night. The night before. On Wednesday afternoon, Nickie came over to ask us where her mom was. It wasn't like Joyce to leave without discussing it with Nickie. Right away, I called Mike Deere's house and Ruby answered. I guess she'd left Jeff and was staying at Mike's for a while. She said neither of them had any idea where Joyce could be. Then I called Richard and he didn't know where she was either. I asked him if he had cancelled his doctor's appointment and he said it was postponed a week. He didn't seem too concerned about it at the time. He rented a movie and got a pizza for him and Nickie that night before she left to go baby-sitting for Jeff, and Bill and I went looking all over town half the night for Joyce. We went to her work and checked to see if she had been to her storage unit and nobody had seen her. We went to The Show Place, which is the sister bar, and she wasn't there so then we drove by Mike's and then we drove by Jeff's."

"The next day, I had to go to work, but Bill talked to Richard two or three times. I came home for lunch and asked Richard if he had reported Joyce missing to the police yet and he said he was waiting for them to get back to him on the phone. We kept looking for police cars at their trailer, but they didn't come," Lori said.

"After the kidnapping, we didn't think the trailer was a good place for Nickie to stay, so we had her pack up her stuff and come to our house. That was the *first time* I ever saw Richard get emotional and he protested saying, 'Nickie is fine here,' but he didn't have much say in the matter as far as we were concerned."

"That afternoon after I got off work, Bill and I went to Joyce's post office box and asked the postmistress if anybody had checked on or picked up Joyce's mail. She said there didn't appear to be movement, but would keep her eye out for us. We went back to the bars again that night looking for her, but none of her friends or customers had seen her. Then we talked to Richard about getting some missing person flyers made up to post around town and he said that he would if he could get some time off on his electronic monitor to do it, but that he didn't have any money, so my husband gave him some. We asked him if he'd filed a missing person report yet with the police and he said he was going to whenever they got around to calling him back."

"By then, we were getting truly concerned about Joyce. Richard told us that he got some time off the monitor to go look for her and he said he was going to post up some flyers. He told us that he didn't need or want our help. He said he was going to call around and do everything himself. On Friday, we had to go out of town, and Richard assured us that he would take over where we left off, looking for Joyce. My husband was scheduled to judge an Elk's ritual program and he'd already made a commitment. We had a cell phone with us and kept in touch with Joyce's sister, Lynn, and Richard. We stayed in our room the whole time, waiting for any news. We ended up leaving Lake Havasu early Sunday morning, explaining that we had some personal problems. I was a nervous wreck by then."

"Shortly after we returned, I saw the article in the Yuma Daily Sun and saw that Richard had given the police the wrong description of my daughter. That's when I called Detective St. Jons and corrected it. I was so mad at Richard! Up until the body was found, we kept asking Richard if he'd heard anything, and he told me that he'd heard from some woman at The Dark that Joyce had gone off with some biker. I knew that had to be a lie. I didn't believe Richard about anything anymore, not after the way he was acting. It was like, Joyce is gone, and why don't the rest of us just go on as usual? You know, like, she'll turn up eventually. My husband and I kept going out to look for Joyce, everywhere we could think of and we didn't see any of the flyers Richard had printed anywhere except at The Dark, where Joyce worked. There was a small stack of them on the bar. We looked in laundromats, convenience stores, and other bars and never saw any of the flyers posted."

Lori had been fighting tears on and off, but was determined to tell Graham everything that might be helpful. Lori finally asked, "How long does the medical examiner usually keep the bodies he autopsies? We want to plan a small memorial and we'd like to have her body cremated pretty soon."

Graham replied, "I guess it depends on how much evidence they need. Richard's in police custody now, you know."

"Yes, we saw you take him and the truck and trailer away. Has he admitted anything yet?" Lori asked.

"Not yet. I was going to interview your husband, but it sounds like he's been kept in the dark about much of this, so we'll hold off for now."

"Would it be possible for me to find out periodically how the investigation is going?" Lori asked.

"Sure, here's my card," Graham gave her the Sheriff's department card and thanked her for her time. "Call me if you think of anything else."

CHAPTER 27

The responsibilities of more than a dozen other ongoing cases caused Detectives Donna Graham and David St. Jon to slow down their work on the Handcock murder case, or at least put it occasionally on the proverbial back burner. St. Jons and Graham split up the list of people, who had been involved with the Handcocks. They would interview some people separately and some primary individuals together. They planned to have telephone conferences with each other twice a month or more often if something important broke along the way.

Within days, St. Jons was visited by a fellow officer who told him that his snitch had informed him that he had witnessed goings on at the Handcock residence. The snitch's name was Roy Bounder. Roy lived in the same recreational vehicle park as Joyce and Richard, and had spoken to Richard on several occasions. St. Jons asked if his snitch was any good and was told that he was about as good as any.

On the way over to talk to Roy, St. Jons tried not to get his hopes too high. A regular snitch that the police used might have a good idea of what information was worth sharing. On the other hand, the typical reason one became a snitch was to get someone out of their existing trouble with the police.

The woman in the park's office directed St. Jons to an area directly behind the office where Roy was working on the motor of a gas-powered golf cart, which he used while attending to his other maintenance duties there in the park. He was a part-time employee who did cleaning and repairs in exchange for a free rental space.

Roy was a man in his late twenties who had seen his fair share of tough times. That day, while working on the motor, Roy was dirty and tired and wondered if the free rent was worth it. Roy told the detective that the manager instructed him to tell the Handcocks on several occasions that they must clean up all the junk outside their trailer. He said that often when he was in the vicinity of the Handcock trailer, that he heard loud arguing and smelled marijuana. Roy said that because the park was almost all elderly, one of his duties included knocking on their door to tell them to keep the noise down because it was disruptive.

"From thirty feet away, I heard Richard say, 'Joyce, you're an f-ing bitch!'" Roy repeated in a more pleasant manner than the way he had originally heard Richard say it. "Another time, I heard him say, 'You dress like that to attract men!' Why, one time when I had to knock on their door to get them to quiet down, Richard told me, 'I should slap the bitch' and he said 'I wish she was f-ing dead!' too."

"When did he say that?" St. Jons asked.

"Gosh, it was early in January sometime," Roy said, removing his baseball cap, exposing lush brunette curls. He scratched his neck where sweat trickled down to form a dark area on his gray T-shirt.

"Did you ever personally see any milk crates, cement blocks, or wood pieces around their trailer?" St. Jons asked, hoping for collaboration on the wood pieces that he himself had seen in Richard's truck the day before the fire.

"Heck, yeah! That stuff and all the trash is what the manager wanted them to clean up," Roy replied.

* * *

Ruby's pulse quickened as she locked her car in the parking lot at the Yuma Police Station. She had received a phone call from Sheriff's Detective Graham, who requested her presence for a taped interview in regard to the Joyce Handcock murder case. Graham had explained that the police and sheriff's departments were conducting a joint investigation.

After Ruby checked in at the front window, St. Jons came out to the waiting room and showed her back to the video room where Graham was waiting. They were introduced and Graham started talking about the weather to relax Ruby, while St. Jons fetched a pot of coffee and Styrofoam cups for all of them. For a woman who was not being investigated as a suspect, Ruby was very tense. Both St. Jons and Graham attributed it to her drug use.

MURDER BY GRAVITY?

St. Jons asked Ruby if she would be comfortable with the video equipment and she said that she was camera shy. St. Jons told Ruby to just pretend that it wasn't there then turned the camcorder on anyway and made a brief statement as to whom they were interviewing, the case number, and the date.

Graham began the questioning by asking Ruby how long she had been friends with Joyce.

"I first met Joyce in the spring of '93 when we both worked at P. J.'s as bartenders. She worked the shift after mine and we went barhopping together sometimes," Ruby said.

"When did you first meet Joyce's husband, Richard?"

"When he came to P. J.'s to work as the bouncer, which was in the summer of the same year, I guess," Ruby said.

St. Jons asked, "Did Joyce seem happy with Richard?"

"At first, yeah, they both were really happy and he brought her flowers all the time . . . but, before they got married Richard dropped her off at work a couple of times and Joyce was crying. I guess they'd had a fight, or something. I asked her how well she really knew Richard and she said that she admitted that she didn't know him very well, but she loved him. It always seemed weird to me, because she could have done a lot better for herself than Richard. He's not good looking or rich, and she could have had anybody she wanted. Then the next thing I know, they got married. Joyce was happy and excited. They rented a nice house and Joyce's daughter, Nickie, came back to live with her and Richard," Ruby stated.

Graham asked, "Were you friends with Joyce up until she disappeared?"

"Yes, I was, but not that close of a friend. She never told me anything, you know, *personal* about herself," Ruby lied.

St. Jons was surprised by that statement, but concealed it and instead asked, "How did Joyce dress when she came to work?"

"Well, you know, she tried to be a total knockout and she really was, too. She is. . . I mean, she *was* a very beautiful woman who loved to wear sexy clothes."

"Did Richard seem jealous of Joyce being around other men at the bar?" St. Jons asked.

"Not that I could ever tell. He didn't want Joyce to hang out with certain people. That's why she got fired or quit, or whatever. He just didn't want her working there because of some of the people that came in there. I was the only friend of hers that Richard really approved of her being around. One time, he brought her over to my house and he left her there for a week! Joyce was crying and very upset. Eventually, he came back and then soon after that, she came into P. J.'s and started giving me her clothes, because Richard thought they were too provocative and he didn't want her to wear them anymore," Ruby said.

St. Jons observed, "He wasn't a jealous guy, but he didn't want her wearing provocative clothes. Is that right?"

"Yeah," Ruby said, not catching the sarcasm in his voice.

"Was there a time when you noticed that Richard changed?" Graham asked her.

"When he came back to Joyce last fall and he had colon cancer," Ruby said. "He shaved his head and wore hunting clothing all the time, jumpsuits, I think. He was saying he lost his hair, but you could tell his head was shaved. Once, he even lifted up his shirt to show Jeff and me that he didn't have any hair on his chest, either. Joyce said she wanted to do everything she could to help Richard in his last days," Ruby added.

"Did you ever see Joyce or Richard use drugs?" Graham asked.

"To the best of my knowledge, they didn't use them," Ruby said.

St. Jons jumped on that. "Didn't you tell me on the telephone that the night before Joyce disappeared, that you came over with Red Pollock and another woman and sold some meth to Joyce?"

"As long as that camera's on, I'm not saying anything without a lawyer!" Ruby stated flatly.

"Ruby," Detective Graham said gently, "This is a *murder* investigation, and according to the deceased's husband, you were her best friend. This is more important than any drug charge."

"Red says you have to give me immunity before I say anything that might incriminate me," Ruby said, crossing her arms across her chest.

St. Jons and Graham stepped outside the room to have a conversation. When they came back, St. Jons turned the camera off and thanked Ruby for coming in and said that he would see what he could do about getting her immunity.

CHAPTER 28

Regret and trepidation grabbed at St. Jons' gut as he sat in his car looking across the shady tree-laden lawn to Red Pollock's front door. His mind turned back the clock to not so long ago, and he remembered the many parties and potluck dinners that he and his wife, Rachel, had enjoyed behind that same door with his other colleagues from the police department. Red and Sally's house had been a popular gathering place for the Yuma Police Department, primarily because Red had built a large den onto his house with a tavern-sized bar complete with draft beer. The Pollocks' had loved to entertain friends. Now with Sally gone and Ruby in her place, he couldn't imagine how the old house would feel to him.

David St. Jons knocked on the door and wasn't surprised when it was Ruby who opened it. She was dressed in a low-cut spandex halter top and low-rise sweatpants that exposed her navel and a washboard-flat stomach, maintained, no doubt, by her methamphetamine use. Ruby was curt in her manner toward St. Jons, but led him through the still sparingly furnished living room to the shade-drawn and darkened den where Red was seated behind the bar watching a small color television.

When Red saw St. Jons, he clicked the television's volume low with the remote in his hand and said jovially, "Hey, big guy! Long time, no see, Davey!" St. Jons shook Red's extended hand and smiled halfheartedly. His former boss seemed genuinely glad to see David and had shook his hand forcefully. Red wasn't going to make the reason for his timely visit any easier.

After St. Jons took a seat opposite Red at the bar, Ruby tiptoed around the back of it and said to Red, "I'm off to the grocery store, sweetie," and firmly kissed Red in front of St. Jons, causing him to feel even more uncomfortable, which was her intention. He missed Sally and the homey feeling the house used to have whenever he visited in the past. Sally always had something cooking in the oven that smelled wonderful. St. Jons was sure that the void he was feeling was nowhere near what Red must have felt during the time after Sally left him. Red's loss had been great, for Sally was a wonderful woman and Red had only himself to blame for the breakup. Both men fell silent as Ruby's golden, high-heeled sandals clicked on the parquet flooring as she walked out of the room.

"It's really great to see you, Red," St. Jons began. "I wish it were under different circumstances. I'm sorry, this is a little awkward for me." St. Jons tone was almost contrite.

"Relax, Davey, I can't fire you anymore, remember?" Red joked with a tired smile. "Just ask me what you need to, and I promise not to bite."

"Okay then, how did you meet Ruby?" St. Jons asked.

"After Sally left me in January of last year, the next summer I met a woman by the name of Leigh Gerard. I was having a rough time living alone and Leigh was going through a divorce at that time too, so we naturally gravitated together. After a while, she moved in with me. Ruby was the bartender at the neighborhood bar where Leigh and I hung out and Ruby introduced me to Joyce. I assume you're here because of her disappearance. Anyhoo, Ruby was living with another guy named Jeff Dupre at the time. When she split with Jeff, I told her that she could stay here with Leigh and me. One thing led to another, and Leigh moved out and Ruby stayed. That's about it," Red said.

"Were you aware that they were using drugs?"

"When I met Leigh, she wanted to get away from the drug scene, and she stayed in my spare bedroom and agreed not to use drugs inside my house. After a few days, I wasn't sure, but I thought she might still be using. We talked all the time about her problem and I encouraged her to clean up and she always said that she was trying and she was getting better at leaving it alone. She never used drugs in my house to the best of my knowledge. Everybody knows I don't go for that."

"What about Ruby's drug usage?" St. Jons asked, sensing Red's discomfort at talking about the subject.

MURDER BY GRAVITY?

"Ruby doesn't use drugs, as far as I know," Red maintained. "For a while, during the time Joyce disappeared, both Ruby and Leigh were living here with me. We used to go out around midnight for last call at The Dark Place. I was taking acquired time off before my retirement was final in that time frame."

Red continued, "Ruby and Joyce did crafts together. In fact, it was Joyce who taught Ruby how to make flower arrangements and decorate baskets when Joyce was staying at their place with Jeff and her back when they were still together. I guess things were bad between Joyce and Richard at the time. I've never met him, by the way."

"You were still watch commander at the time, if I remember right," St. Jons mentioned.

"Yup, but like I said, taking time off. Ruby and Leigh began to have jealousies about me and Leigh moved out," Red explained. "It was sure great while it lasted, though!" Red said with a sly grin. "They're good gals, both of them," Red lamented. "Ruby and I are planning to move to Las Vegas shortly. I have a buddy up there that can get me a management job in security at one of the casinos."

"Well, that's really sounds great. I'm glad for you, Red. Now, can you tell me what occurred the night before Joyce disappeared, when the three of you went over to the Handcocks' trailer in the wee hours of the morning?" St. Jons asked, trying to return to the subject at hand.

"Ruby wanted to take some craft stuff to Joyce's, so I drove her and Leigh over there after the bar closed. I guess it would have been about 1:30 in the morning. I waited in the car alone for three, maybe five minutes, and then we left," Red stated simply.

"You didn't see Ruby give drugs to Joyce?"

"When she came back to the car, she had some craft stuff that they'd gotten out of Joyce's shed together," Red replied.

"Are you saying, then, that *both* women got out of the car and you waited alone in the car?" St. Jons remembered a discrepancy. Richard had told him that Ruby was the only one to get out of the car.

"Sure, why?" Red asked.

"Ah, nothing, probably not important anyway," St. Jons pondered. "Hey, thanks, man. I hated to bother you with this, but you know how it is . . ." St. Jons said, shaking Red's hand and rising from the bar stool.

"No problem," Red replied and walked David to the front door.

"Still," St. Jons said on the stoop as if it were an afterthought, "strange time of night to be delivering craft materials." He kept walking after he saw Red's fair face flush blood red.

CHAPTER 29

The world watched as Judge Lance Ito ruled that the members of the families of Nicole Simpson and Ronald Goldman could be present during most of the Simpson murder trial. In a major blow to the defense, Ito also ruled that many of the allegations of domestic violence would be admitted during the trial of O. J. Simpson, including potentially damaging 911 calls made by his ex-wife, Nicole. On January 24, 1995, opening statements in the Simpson case got under way when prosecutor Christopher Darden told the jury that they would find out why Simpson killed his ex-wife and her friend Ronald Goldman.

On January 25, 1995, Johnnie Cochran began the defense's opening statements by saying that Simpson was an innocent man wrongfully accused. That was the same day that would have been Joyce and Richard Handcock's first anniversary. Richard had said that they were planning to renew their wedding vows in a ceremony. No one other than the police who interviewed Richard had ever heard about such plans. There had been no preparations made for a vow ceremony locally. In fact, they could ill afford any official wedding reenactment. When asked, the people who knew the couple could not imagine there was any truth to Richard's declaration.

Detective St. Jons kept in touch with Joyce's mother, Lori Perron, throughout his investigation. He decided it was time to speak with the Handcocks' neighbors who all lived in the same recreational vehicle park as Joyce's parents. Lori told the detective that a neighbor named Rachel Hammer had become friends with Joyce.

David St. Jons found his way to Rachel's space and noted it was across the park from the Handcocks, most likely unable to have any visual access to their trailer. Rachel Hammer's park model was directly opposite the Handcock trailer, with a block of RVs and motor homes in between.

The detective knocked on the door and introduced himself to Rachel Hammer. She said that she had seen him at the Handcocks' trailer earlier in the week and that she figured someone would come to talk to her eventually. When she opened the door of her pretty, petite park model to let him inside, St. Jons was overcome with a sense of nostalgia. Either it was the subtle breeze of the White Shoulders perfume she wore, the print on her crisp dress, or the dainty crocheted doilies and antiques she had in her home; but somehow, briefly, St. Jons felt like he was eight years old all over again visiting his grandmother's house. Rachel was about the age his grandmother would have been if she were still alive. She was taller than he; stately and her every move a study in grace. Once inside the living room, she directed him to a tapestry-covered straight-back rocking chair. She offered him coffee, which he gratefully accepted. St. Jons sometimes garnered immense amounts of information over coffee, so he usually accepted the invitation during an investigation. People seemed more relaxed then, plus they were generally committing themselves to a minimum of a ten-minute interview just by offering him a refreshment.

In minutes they were settled down with Rachel's delicate gold-leafed coffee cups on her antique coffee table. St. Jons asked how well she knew Joyce or Richard across the park.

"Well, actually, when they first moved in with just the camper shell, I didn't see either of them much, except occasionally I saw Joyce at her parents' house, or walking to the laundry." She stopped to laugh and explain, "I know they're really park models, but we call them houses, because most of us own houses somewhere else and just spend the winter here, and they feel like a house too. Just a smaller one! I live here year-round now. Lori may have already told you that Joyce's father, Bill, had serious heart problems and an operation just a year ago, I believe. Since I'm a retired nurse, and because I've known them both for years, I volunteered to help Lori out and watch over Bill while she went to work. I was an overqualified, unpaid private nurse, you might say." she laughed engagingly. "I made them an offer they couldn't refuse."

"To get to your point, Detective St. Jons, I have seen Richard walking around the park, and so forth. I knew who he was. I got to know Joyce better when Richard moved out and Joyce bought the trailer they live in now. I can see their place through my kitchen window and I saw Joyce's father, Bill, outside their trailer the first day the trailer was towed in and he was helping his daughter move some heavy things. I ran over there to get after him about not working. That's when Joyce and I got to know each other better. She said she was so happy when Richard moved out and she was on her own. She had such fun fixing up her own place. I couldn't believe the amount of junk that was in that trailer when she bought it. There was a huge pile of junk in the yard that she'd taken out of it before she could even move in, including a mummified cat. Bodies preserve well in the desert, you know."

St. Jons glanced towards Rachel's kitchen and was puzzled. "How can you *see* the Handcock place from here?"

Rachel stood and asked him to follow her into the kitchen. Looking out her dining room window, he could see between the two monstrous motor homes parked across the street, two fifth wheels behind them, which were smaller, and straight through to the Handcocks' cement pad next to where their trailer was parked. In fact, she had a near-perfect, straight-on view of the area to which their trailer doors opened out. She would be able to see *anybody* come and go from their home.

Rachel said, "In the summer, when all the recreational vehicles are gone, I have a great park-like view of their space, which is usually empty in the summer. That's how I got to be friends with the Perrons. We were part of the small, motley group that stay here year-round." We have monthly pot lucks and so forth.

Detective St. Jons stood there looking out and nodding his head. They both started walking back to their coffee cups and St. Jons asked, "Have you ever seen a beige Jeep come by their place?"

"Oh, yes indeed. It has a roll bar on it. I've even seen Joyce drive it around several times while Richard was gone. Her friend who owns it is a real cutie. Joyce said his name is Mike Deere, I believe. I remembered because it reminded me of the Disney movie, "The Lady and The Tramp." Lady's 'parents' were named Jim Dear, and Darling. Those were the only names Lady had ever heard them use while speaking to each other. So, Jim Dear . . . Mike Deere, see? At my age, any trick that can help you remember something is a good thing in my book."

"How often did you see the Jeep?" the detective asked.

"Ten to fifteen times, I guess, and always in the daytime. Detective St. Jons, in my mind, the only reason Joyce let Richard back into her life is because he convinced her that he had colon cancer. Later on, when she and I were talking, I asked her if he had abdominal scars and Joyce said that he had no scars. Well, I told her that he would have abdominal scars in order to be diagnosed with colon cancer. We spoke about it again a couple of times, and she told me that he said that his cancer had spread to his stomach and another time she said that he told her that the cancer was in his bladder. It just didn't sound right and I had the feeling that Joyce was beginning to doubt that Richard had cancer at all."

"One time when Richard was out of town, Joyce told me that she'd received a phone call from Richard and he said that he was in Tucson and that he'd had his *first* chemotherapy treatment and he'd *already* lost *all* of his hair! When he came back, she told me privately that it looked like he'd shaved his head and she kind of chuckled. I know that Joyce seriously doubted that Richard really had cancer before she died." Suddenly, Rachel's eyes swelled and her nose turned pink on the sides. She tried to blink back the tears and go on. "Poor girl," Rachel said, choking back a sob. St. Jons offered her his fresh handkerchief which she declined as she reached for the tissue box on the end table. "Thanks, anyway," she said. "I would usually talk to Joyce when I did my daily mile walk in the park and I'd stop for a few minutes at her place to see how her redecorating was going. She was a very talented and beautiful young woman."

The detective gave Rachel a minute then asked if she had seen Richard on the day Joyce disappeared.

"As a matter of fact, I was eating lunch and looking out the window. I saw Richard go to the laundry room carrying a load of wash. To answer your next question, I usually eat lunch sometime between twelve o'clock and one o'clock."

"Was that a common thing for Richard to do . . . the laundry?" St. Jons asked.

"I'd seen him do it maybe three or four times, but always in the evening . . . after work," Rachel said. "Since the laundry and showers are right next door, they would walk by my house anytime they went

MURDER BY GRAVITY?

to the laundry or to take showers. So I saw them frequently on this side of the park, too."

"What are the laundry hours here?" St. Jons asked.

"Seven o'clock in the morning until ten o'clock at night."

St. Jons was thinking that he knew Richard's electronic monitor reported his return at 12:44 PM. He asked her again, "What time was it you saw Richard go to the laundry?"

"Most likely, sometime between twelve noon and one o'clock," Rachel said. The detective finished his coffee and thanked Rachel.

Emerging from her front door, he looked around to see who else might be home that he could question. Across the street from the Handcocks' trailer, he knocked on the door of a fifth-wheel trailer; one that has an extra area that goes over the bed of the truck pulling it which is usually a small sleeping area. A 75-year-old woman by the name of Irma Stebbins answered the door and stepped outside to speak with him, leaning heavily on the stair's railing. St. Jons asked her how well she had known the Handcocks and she said that she was a "snowbird" from Canada and didn't know some of the local residents that well. She had seen them, of course, across the street, and had not become aware that Joyce was missing until *two days after her disappearance. It was that same day, the day she found out about Joyce, that she saw Richard moving some of his property into the back of his truck from out of their trailer.* The truck didn't have the camper shell on the back and she said that his truck had been backed in over the pad instead of the dirt driveway next to the pad, so it was *right next* to the trailer doors. The awning had been taken out of the way, so he didn't have to carry things across the pad to his truck. She couldn't see what he was putting in the truck, but as he drove away, she saw in the bed of the truck some kind of yellow material, that looked like an egg crate or convoluted foam rubber mattress cover, rolled up and tied in a big roll. She couldn't see the surface of the bedding; only the exterior. She said it was very unusual for Richard to back his truck into his space, and never had done it before or since then.

Mrs. Stebbins also told him that she had known Joyce's parents for fifteen winter seasons and, when asked, she had never seen Richard going door to door asking people if they'd seen Joyce and had never seen a single flyer posted about her disappearance.

CHAPTER 30

The heavy mahogany door was closed in St. Jons' office and the din from the hall and other offices grew softer as evening enveloped the public building. St. Jons rocked back in the worn leather chair with his feet crossed on his desk and soon realized that it felt too good. Though he knew he was tired, he let his feet drop down from the desk noisily and forced himself to concentrate on the Joyce Handcock murder case. It was just another very long day.

He looked for his puzzle again in the wood grain on the back of his door. More pieces there now; lots more. Even his former boss was there, who had been third in the chain of command of the Yuma Police Department. The round-knot design that came to be known to him as Richard seemed in his imagination to be smirking at him. It was his job to see how the pieces fit together and, as he knew too well, there were always pieces left over at the end of these matters, but they all had to be collected and examined for their possible worth, significance, and credibility. He was sure that as the investigation continued that there would be even more pieces that he would uncover and, hopefully, place rightfully together.

Richard had said that the morning his wife disappeared, he went to look for construction work as a carpenter. According to the detective's notes, Richard said that he had received permission from the Electronic Monitoring Service to look for work at 8:00 AM, at which time he went to see a man named Dick Kidd whom Richard had said was in charge of the construction site behind The Grocery Store, where he waited for forty-five minutes, but Mr. Kidd never showed up. Then he said he went to a Mesa Del Sol site to see a man named Hernandez, who was the superintendent of a company that had been subcontracted to build a future Jack in the Box, off I-8 and

MURDER BY GRAVITY?

Fortuna Boulevard, but he couldn't remember in which order he went to those two places. In either case, he went to The Bottoms Up Pub afterward to see a man about used tires, whose name he didn't know, but Handcock claimed that he did speak with him. He also said that he saw his ex-girlfriend there, who was the bartender. St. Jons looked up the addresses and made plans to check out Richard's alibi in the morning.

* * *

The next morning, St. Jons tried to keep his mind on the other cases he was working on until it was time to leave to investigate Richard's story. He hadn't slept well, so he arrived at his office at six o'clock and against better judgment brought a dozen doughnuts.

In the newer version that Handcock had given him when Detective Graham was present, he remembered that Richard had changed his story and said that he had left his trailer at eight o'clock in the morning to look for work, *then* went to get gas at the station on Pacific Avenue. St. Jon's office was on the same side of town as the Handcocks' trailer, so he allowed time that Richard would have needed to get his truck filled and proceeded to the Foothills.

St. Jons reached the construction site behind The Grocery Store on Foothills Boulevard without delay. The traffic was light at that time of day in the direction in which he was headed. He looked at his watch, and saw it was only 8:28 when he arrived. The time may or may not be significant because Richard couldn't remember the order in which he visited these places; nevertheless, it seemed worthy of note because the other construction site wasn't far away. The construction activities were in full swing by the time he arrived. He parked as closely to the store as was possible; to do otherwise would guarantee a layer of dust on the austere, white undercover vehicle that he drove. His presence was noted by some of the workers in the area and St. Jons approached the closest one.

"What're you guys building out here?" St. Jons asked.

The worker stopped what he was doing and said, "That's going to be a car wash out back there, and the front one here is going to be an auto repair, at least, that's what the plans say," he said good-naturedly.

"Do you know where I can find a guy named Dick Kidd?" St. Jons asked.

"I doubt it. He's hardly ever here!" the worker replied.

"Isn't he in charge around here?" St. Jons asked.

"Ha! That's a good one! No, not even remotely. That would be Jared Andrews. He's the superintendent of the job. You should find him over in the first building on your left," he said.

"Thanks." St. Jons headed for the building as directed and nobody was there. He looked around as he waited, and in a couple of minutes a man walked in from behind the unfinished plywood walls. St. Jons asked him, "You wouldn't happen to be Jared Andrews, would you?"

"Matter of fact, yeah . . . who would you be?" Jared asked dubiously.

David St. Jons displayed his shield and introduced himself. "I'm just checking out some facts in a case I'm working on." St. Jons glanced at his notes, "I was told that a guy named Dick Kidd would be the person to see out here about employment."

"That's very amusing. Who told you that?" Jared quizzed him.

St. Jons wasn't worried about giving up too much to this man, so he answered honestly, "A fellow named Richard Handcock. He told me that he came out here on January 11th and waited around to see Dick Kidd about a job," St. Jons said. "Said he waited the better part of an hour and he never showed up."

Andrews said, "The part about him never showing up is true, all right, but the rest is bull. Dick Kidd is just one of the hands out here; a carpenter, that's all, and not a very good one at that. He frequently didn't show up for work and that's why I fired his ass. It happened that same week you were asking about, too, if I'm not mistaken. You can ask our bookkeeper who is just inside that construction trailer over there, if you need to verify that."

"Do you know Richard Handcock or did you ever get a message that he was looking for work?" St. Jons asked.

"Never heard of him. Sorry," Andrews answered.

St. Jons mumbled his thanks and headed over to the construction trailer, stepping carefully around the debris on the ground. Once inside the compact trailer, he saw two desks immediately in front of him. One of the two older women inside asked if she could help him.

MURDER BY GRAVITY?

St. Jons identified himself and asked about Kidd's work record. The woman who was the bookkeeper looked him up in her accounts book.

"The last pay period that Dick Kidd worked here ended on January 12th. I can't tell from the pay documents whether he worked the 11th or not, but he only put in twenty hours total that week," she said trying to be helpful. "I understand that's the reason they let him go."

St. Jons thanked them for the information and headed for Mesa Del Sol construction office. It only took him seven minutes to get there. He had not seen any construction around the nicely landscaped building and he had a feeling he was in the wrong place. Nevertheless, he entered the door to pleasant surroundings with a bubbling fountain and soft music. There was a young woman at the front desk. Her nameplate read simply, "Claudia." St. Jons could smell the new carpet on the floor then Claudia's heavy perfume. She was dressed ultrafemininely in an outfit befitting an uptown New York City office. When she stood to greet him, her gold bangle bracelets clinked distractingly. St. Jons had not noticed that the rest of the office staff was discreetly observing him as the recently divorced Claudia flirted with almost all the men who walked into the office. Claudia's co-workers referred to her as "fluff n' stuff" behind her back. It was always interesting to see how quickly her normally unpleasant personality morphed into sweetness when an attractive or affluent man walked into the office.

St. Jons had become so amused by the Latin and exotic-looking Miss Claudia that he almost forgot why he was there. When he found his voice he said, "Ah, I must be in the wrong place. I'm looking for a man named Hernandez who's supposed to be building a Jack in the Box in the area. Would you happen to know anything about that job?" St. Jons asked doubtfully.

Claudia's lovely face had a voice just as smooth and beguiling as the rest of her. St. Jons eyes feasted on her. She told him that Hernandez was a subcontractor employed by Mesa Del Sol and he was indeed building a Jack in the Box. To find him, however, he would have to go to another location on Fortuna and the I-8. She gave him the directions, since he was unfamiliar with the area. He thanked her more than necessary before leaving.

On his way to the new site, he wondered if Richard had the same problem that day finding his way to the construction location. This might help Richard's alibi gel, if he had been as misguided as St. Jons had been.

St. Jons arrived at a vacant lot next to the freeway where two men were talking by their trucks. St. Jons pulled in and asked the men if this was where the Jack in the Box was going to be built. One of the men identified himself as Hernandez and said that they had a setback and they weren't going to begin construction there for another month. When asked, he said that he knew Richard Handcock and that he'd worked with him a few years earlier in '92 or '93, he wasn't sure when, but that Richard had been a good worker and he would have hired him if he'd come around looking for a job. His company had another construction job where they had passed their prospective date of completion and he was looking at daily penalties because of it. Hernandez said that he would have put Handcock to work immediately if he'd seen him.

"The job we're on now is heavy work that requires a lot of strength on the part of the carpenters. Those guys have to be in pretty good shape to do the work and they have to know how to use tricks to lift heavy loads," Hernandez explained.

St. Jons asked, "If Richard had come around on January 11th, would he have been able to find you here?"

Hernandez said, "I'm not so sure about that. But if he'd asked around a little bit, he probably should have been able to find me."

* * *

St. Jons wondered what to expect if Hazel was in The Bottoms Up Pub when he arrived. It was still early, so it was difficult to believe that this kind of business would even be open; and yet it was as Richard had said.

The bar was in an L-shaped strip mall. The businesses faced the parking lot, with the exception of a hall between a chiropractor's office and The Bottoms Up Pub. The hall led to the entrances of the pub, an insurance office, and a dog grooming business. This odd mix of businesses was an example of the Foothill's early new growth.

St. Jons entered the pub and saw a cozy place with an informal

MURDER BY GRAVITY?

neighborhood feeling. It was decorated as if to imitate a British pub. There were two pool tables, booths for seating, and stools at the bar where St. Jons sat and ordered a cup of coffee.

When the bartender came back with the coffee, St. Jons asked her if her name was Hazel.

"Yeah," she responded. She figured him for a cop, but played dumb. "How did you know that? I mean, I haven't seen you in here before, have I?" She managed to give him a small smile.

"No, I'm Detective St. Jons." She verified that after scrutinizing his badge. "You know Richard Handcock quite well as I understand," he said.

"Yeah, we dated for a while a long time ago. I read in the newspaper that his wife disappeared," Hazel stated and gave the definite appearance of what St. Jons referred to as "the wall." He frequently saw the walls go up when he questioned people. Some people just didn't like or trust cops. Some only put up the wall when they had something to hide.

Hazel said, "How can I possibly help you?" She was trying to sound pleasant in spite of the hostility she was beginning to feel, unsure at whom just yet. St. Jons saw through her and she knew it.

"Richard said he came here on the day his wife disappeared, that was on January 11th. Can you verify that?"

"Probably. Richard and I are still friends and he comes in two or three times a week, whether I'm here or not."

St. Jons said, "I'm here because we found his wife's body in a canal a couple of miles from here with her head bashed in and straps attached to her arms and legs with rocks in a crate and a cement pylon to weigh her body down." St. Jons wanted to see the effects of his blunt statement.

"My God!" Hazel brought her hands to her mouth as she gasped. "I didn't know that," she said. "What day of the week was that . . . the 11th, did you say?"

St. Jons said, "Yes, the 11th was on a Wednesday. He said he was looking for a guy to buy used tires from."

"Oh, yeah, I remember. It was the day Mary had lunch here. She had to leave early because her daughter had a club meeting that day. She'd probably remember the time better than me, but I think it was 10 o'clock or 10:30."

"Isn't that a little early for lunch?" St. Jons asked.

"Well, whatever it is she eats. Brunch, maybe? The kitchen isn't really open that early, but my boss knows her real well and fixes something for her. She does the cleaning around here in the mornings three days a week, too. The kitchen opens to the public at 11:00 o'clock." Hazel continued, "Richard said he was looking for used tires and he talked to a guy about it. The guy's name is Bud Dockter, but he was quite intoxicated that day," Hazel remembered. "Bud was, that is."

"A little early, eh?" St. Jons commented.

"Well, maybe it was later than I was thinking. He usually comes in about that time of day," Hazel said.

"Kind of early for a kid's Brownie meeting, too. Wouldn't that be in the middle of a school day?"

"Well, with year-round school, who knows anymore, ya know?" Hazel said.

St. Jons asked, "When you were dating or whatever with Richard, did he ever get rough with you? Did he ever assault you?"

"No, never! I wouldn't let him live with me if he did something like that. We hardly ever argued, but when we disagreed, he usually went for a walk. He's not a violent man," Hazel said adamantly.

"Is your boss here today?" St. Jons asked.

"Yeah, but she doesn't know Richard." Hazel unconsciously started biting her lower lip.

"Where can I find her?" St. Jons asked.

Hazel motioned to a door behind the bar and said, "She's in there."

* * *

St. Jons poked his head in the door and saw an older, tough-looking woman seated at a desk, going over some office work..

"Excuse me," St. Jons said to her. "You must be the manager of this fine establishment."

She stood and straightened out her skirt as she said, "Yes, my name's Jimmy, what can I do for you, *officer?*" Her husky voice got a pitch higher when she inquired about his credentials, but she seemed good-natured.

"Guilty as charged," St. Jons smiled and introduced himself. He asked if she had ever met a customer by the name of Richard Handcock--a friend of Hazel's.

"Well, no, I haven't met him, but I seen him lots of times. He used to come in and sit at the end of the bar. Once when he did, Hazel came up to me and says, 'That's Richard!' I could tell she was excited. That man sent her so many flowers, it looked like a freakin' funeral parlor in here once, but I don't mind none. He was blond and had a long pony tail."

"Would you know if he was here the morning of the 11th of January?" St. Jons asked.

"I'm usually back here, takin' care of the book work and I'm done by noon."

"But you know who comes in, right?" St. Jons asked.

Jimmy raised her heavy eyebrows then winked. She knew.

"Did Richard come in that day before you left here?"

"Nope," she said concisely.

"Hmmmm," St. Jons was thinking out loud, "What shift does Hazel usually work, Jimmy?" St. Jons asked.

"Hazel always works day shift, which includes happy hour. Richard always comes around in the afternoon."

"Thank you, Jimmy." St. Jons extended his hand to her. "It's been a pleasure meeting you!"

St. Jons left the pub and waved at Hazel with a smile on his way out. It was a smile that really worried Hazel.

CHAPTER 31

St. Jons called Detective Donna Graham at the Sheriff's office across the valley and up in the Foothills, making sure to get her up-to-date with his findings. He asked her to check out Mary, who did the cleaning over at The Bottoms Up Pub in the mornings when she got a chance, and try to speak with a regular customer by the name of Bud Dockter, to find out if he had spoken with Hancock on the 11th of January about buying some used tires.

Graham didn't say anything as she jotted down the information he had given her. In the silence, St. Jons wondered if she was still with him and asked, "So, how's it going on your end?"

"I've been busier than a one-armed wallpaper hanger," she said with a sigh.

Her statement sounded to St. Jons like she was making excuses and said, "Well, same here, but the sooner you can get to these two potential witnesses, the better." In an effort not to sound too pushy with her, he added, "I'd really appreciate it."

Graham was rightfully vexed, the thought of this man ordering her around. She was a detective just like he. There was a pause on the telephone line and St. Jons sensed her hesitation to work with him further. He knew from other people that he had worked with in the past that he tended to bulldoze his way over other detectives. He wasn't a team player, though he tried many times to change that fact. Whenever they told them, "There is no I in the word TEAM," St. Jons would always respond, "But there is an M and an E!"

"I hope you don't mind," he said, "that I went out to the county which, I know we agreed, is your turf, but I had time to check out Handcock's alibi this morning, so I just went.

MURDER BY GRAVITY?

"So I gathered," Graham, said not worried if he knew she was miffed.

"Anyway, her name is Mary; sorry, no last name yet, shouldn't be too hard to find since she works there, and this guy, Bud Dockter, neither one was at The Bottoms Up Pub at the time I was there," St. Jons explained.

After waiting very briefly for a response and not getting one again because Graham was still writing her notes, he said, "Look, what do you think about the two of us planning a time to get together to do a luminol test inside the Handcock trailer? I can do it alone, but I thought you might want to be in on it. Also, I was hoping you could bring the pictures of the crime scene and the pictures of Mrs. Handcock's body, taken at the scene and at the morgue. And I'd like to go through Joyce's purse that you should have in your evidence lockup," St. Jons said.

"No problem," Detective Graham began, "I didn't know if you had done this yet or not, so I went ahead and clocked the time Richard spent traveling on the 11th. Even with road construction going on now, it took me only eighteen minutes to get from Richard's house to the construction sites and it was a distance of twelve miles. The time between the two construction sites is five minutes. So, I figure total travel time for Richard that day was forty-five minutes, plus a couple more minutes for getting gas. They also sell gas behind The Grocery Store, too, where that one construction site was, so he could have even purchased gas there, you must have noticed that when you went there. But still, you figure Richard Handcock was gone that morning almost *five hours*," Graham reminded him.

"*Also*, when you told me about the egg crate being rolled up in the back of Richard's truck," Graham continued, "I spoke with Nickie and she said that her mother and Richard had several pieces of it on their bed. Apparently, the bed was so hard they had bought or found the thick foam egg crate so it would be soft enough to sleep on. But the size wasn't big enough for the whole bed, so they had two or three pieces of it to cover it. We both saw it was gone by the time we questioned him, remember?" she said rhetorically.

"Then I went to the American Mine, or whatever the name of it is, where Mike Deere works and I spoke with the office staff about

Mike's alibi for the 11th, and guess what?" Graham said.

By this time St. Jons figured she was being rhetorical again, so he remained silent.

Graham went on, "I found out that Mike's work hours were ambiguous for that week. The time cards were turned in at the end of each day and so was Mike Deere's, but I spoke with the foreman personally and *his* time sheet shows that Mike took a paid personal holiday on the 11th. The foreman figures that one of Mike's buddies turned in his time card for the day, and he trusts his time sheet over any other paperwork the office has on Mike Deere. He said that the guys do that all the time when one of them is missing. They just turn in another guy's time card and usually nobody catches it." Graham said, and finally took a deep breath.

"Well done!" St. Jons said, surprised that she'd done anything at all on the case.

Graham took even his "Well done" remark as condescending. "I'm not done yet," she said. "Did you know that Joyce Handcock filed charges of sexual harassment against a man by the name of Phillip Seward, the owner of the house that Richard and Joyce rented when they first got married?"

St. Jons said, "I remember the name. Richard said when we initially interviewed him that Seward had a reason for wanting Joyce dead."

"He might have been right. Did you know that Joyce was supposed to testify against Seward in court *just two days after* she went missing? That was Friday, the 13th, as a matter of fact. The case was dropped because she didn't appear in court as scheduled. Difficult to testify when you're tied up with weights and dropped in a canal. This guy, Seward, is a prominent realtor in Yuma, by the way," Donna Graham said, fairly certain that St. Jons didn't know about this one yet. Her competitiveness was satisfied when she said, "Oh, that was in the *City* of Yuma, which we agreed is your territory, not the *County*. I hope *you* don't mind, I went against our agreement too."

Despite her negative personal feelings about St. Jons, she agreed to meet with him the next day at the Yuma police impound yard to go through the trailer.

MURDER BY GRAVITY?

* * *

That same afternoon Detective St. Jons received two strange phone calls. The first was from a woman who claimed that she heard a man named Gary Cox say that he and Phil Seward had tortured and mutilated a woman bartender until she was dead. The female caller added that Cox said that he had a torture chamber in his house and that he said he had cut off the bartender's arms and legs in a satanic cult sacrifice.

After he spoke to Cox on the telephone, St. Jons drove to Gary's home immediately with his forensic evidence-gathering kit. Mr. Cox was home and let St. Jons inside without a search warrant. He said he was just trying to psych-out a couple of broads at a bar when he was drunk one night, and he had nothing to hide.

"There ain't no torture chamber in here either. I just wanted to freak them out." St. Jons, who was trained in the use of luminol, a chemical spray that is used for illuminating blood evidence, tested Gary's house for blood traces and found nothing out of the ordinary. St. Jons was almost positive there would be no evidence. While admittedly luminol is *not* a 100% fail-safe test for blood evidence, his money was still on Richard Handcock. Besides, he already knew that Joyce was not mutilated and there was no scene for a cult sacrifice where her body was found.

There was that name, Seward again. "The informant said that Phil Seward also tortured this woman bartender," St. Jons said.

"Don't know the man," Gary Cox said.

St. Jons no sooner walked into his office when the phone rang again. This time it was Mrs. Joyce Handcock, Richard's mother. St. Jons was puzzled as he sat down in his chair and asked how he could help her.

"My son is still in jail and I don't guess he's going to be getting out anytime soon," she began. This felt awkward to St. Jons as he began to imagine what she was going to ask. But she didn't ask anything. Instead she said, "After Joyce went missing and before my son was arrested, he brought a lot of Joyce's and his stuff over to my house. He had to get rid of all the junk outside of his trailer fast, because they're pretty snooty over at that RV park where they was at. I let him move their things over here for a just a while and gave my son a check for $240 for rent because they was always broke, ya know. Turns out it was a waste of good money, because Richard and the trailer got taken away. The thing is, I'm selling my house and I need to get all of his junk out of here before the realtors can show the place. If you want to, you can come over and take a look at this stuff before it goes to the garbage heap. You can take it all away, as far as I'm concerned."

St. Jons couldn't believe his ears, he tried to act nonchalant about it, as he didn't want to spook her into destroying any potential evidence, so he said, "As a matter of fact, we would like to take a look at it with your permission. Would tomorrow afternoon be okay for you?" he asked, as he pulled out his notebook to write her address on.

"Yes, that's just fine," Mrs. Handcock said.

"I'm sure that if you speak with the RV park's manager, you'd be able to get some of that rent money back," St. Jons suggested helpfully. Visions of little wood blocks that he'd seen that day in the back of Richard's truck danced in his head. They actually had a shot at getting their hands on some of that stuff that he hid at his mother's. He hadn't even thought about looking for evidence there. What great luck!

CHAPTER 32

The next day, Graham and St. Jons met at the City of Yuma impound yard as planned. As David St. Jons led the way to the Handcock's trailer, Detective Donna Graham told him that she had caught up with Bud Dockter over at The Bottoms Up Pub.

"Dockter said that he goes to The Pub at least two or three times a week. He says that he remembers talking with Richard sometime between ten and twelve o'clock. Dockter said that he started the conversation with another guy, you know, talking about buying some used tires, and Richard comes over and said he might have some for sale. He said that Richard wasn't the one who wanted to buy used tires; it was the other way around. Then Richard left and said he was going to call him back at the bar after he checked his yard to see if he had any, but he never called. This guy said he ended up buying his tires somewhere else."

"So?" St. Jons asked.

Graham went on, "So, here's the kicker; he says the conversation took place around the *first of the month* . . . not the 11th. Dockter says he knows this for sure because he just got paid, and he gets paid on the first of the month. He said he would have been broke again by January 11th," Graham said.

"So what do you think about the guy? He sounds like a real winner," St. Jons said sarcastically. "Is he reliable? You know, when they take this case to court, they're going to have some pretty colorful witnesses. So, I guess what I'm asking is, will he hold up in court as believable?"

"These are all bar bums; who the heck knows what a jury will think? Besides, it ain't over 'til it's over."

"And here we are; the Handcock home in all its glory," St. Jons said, guiding Graham to the silver trailer on the left side of the lot.

"Joyce's country-blue written words survived her," said Graham referring to Joyce's inscription on the side of the trailer, "I love you, Richard!" "It's so sad," said Graham, "She had so much hope and love when she wrote that."

St. Jons looked at Graham's pretty, sun-lit face and felt her sympathy was about to wash over. It happens sometimes in the business, if one hasn't become too hardened by the job, so he changed the subject. "Have you ever used luminol before?" St. Jons asked her.

"No, I assumed that *you* had," Graham replied, suddenly worried that she had assumed too much.

"Yeah, I have. It's pretty cool stuff," St. Jons said with enthusiasm.

"How does it work?" Graham asked, anxious to learn new techniques whenever possible.

St. Jons had enjoyed chemistry in high school and always signed up for classes offered by the department in crime solving through the use of scientific approaches, which had become very popular, particularly in the last decade. He said, "The process is known as chemiluminescence. It's the same phenomenon that makes fireflies and light sticks glow. The basic idea of luminol is to reveal traces of light-producing, chemical reactions between several other chemicals. Luminol is a powdery compound mixed with hydrogen peroxide and other chemicals and poured into a spray bottle. First you have to close the doors and windows, then darken the room. Find an area that you suspect to have blood residue, spray the luminol and look for a bluish-green light that glows where the hemoglobin is; which is an oxygen-carrying protein in the blood. In this reaction, the original molecules have more energy than the resulting molecules. The molecules get rid of the extra energy in the form of visible-light photons, which are quantum of electromagnetic energy . . ." St. Jons stopped to take a breath and looked at Graham who was staring at him blankly.

"Anyhoo, tiny particles of blood will cling to most surfaces for years and years without anyone knowing they're there. That's the only part you need to remember, really," St. Jons smiled kindly at Graham.

"Why don't you *show* me how it works," Graham suggested.

All morning long, they spray, and waited. The luminol only lasts for thirty seconds at a time, so it must be done repeatedly.

While they sprayed and waited, primarily in the bedroom because they both believed the assault probably happened there, St. Jons asked, "Didn't Dr. Andrews, the M.E. in Tucson, say that Joyce had been hit *three times* in the head?"

"That's what I heard," Graham responded. They both looked up at the ceiling at the same time. "If she was hit more than once," Graham theorized, "Richard must have taken the blunt object up and over his head at least once, most likely spraying cast-off blood on the low ceiling in the bedroom." So they sprayed and waited on the ceiling, too, but no glow. Not anywhere in the trailer; not on the ceiling, walls, floors, or cracks.

Graham said, "Thanks for this fine demonstration of luminol!" And they both laughed. The small trailer had become hot with the windows closed and they were happy to get back outside.

St. Jons said, "I forgot to tell you what we're doing this afternoon! Let's go get some lunch and I'll tell you about the telephone calls I got yesterday. I sure hope you can clear your calendar on this short notice."

CHAPTER 33

That afternoon when St. Jons and Graham arrived at Mrs. Handcock's house, she stepped out on the front porch to meet them.

"Most of this junk out here is his," she said with disdain. "Like I said, feel free to haul it all away."

The two wandered toward the small, rickety trailer at the end of the property. As they approached and saw its contents, they were both struck with awe. It was like divine intervention. They remembered the square frame that had been cut out of one piece of plywood and left in the fire campsite where Joyce's body had been discovered. It had similar flaws and the same country-blue paint flecks on it. This small, square piece of wood seemed to match the center of that square frame and was lying on the top of the pile of junk in the trailer. Richard was, unquestionably, tied to the crime scene.

In the detectives' minds, Phil Seward couldn't be tied to any physical evidence in the case and he was dropped as a person of interest even though his sexual harassment motive was compelling. The strapping tape and wire that were on Joyce's arms and legs were consistent with that found at Ron Gene's lot where Richard and Joyce had lived earlier and Richard was suspected of stealing some of their inventory. This in addition to other evidence was sent to a forensics lab in Phoenix. St. Jons and Graham did what they felt was their due diligence.

CHAPTER 34

As the time for a speedy trial came and went, Richard lost his first attorney because counsel complained that the court paid less than sixty percent of his general fee and it would be a hardship for him to keep his practice afloat. Richard's next attorney, Finch, represented him on theft and drug charges and Richard was incarcerated on those charges during the two-year period prior to Joyce's murder trial, conveniently tucked away from society.

At pre-trial, Richard's new court-appointed attorneys, William Millington and Dusty Wheelwright sought equal pay as co-counsels and said that they would need air fare and expenses for ten to twelve witnesses to travel to Yuma to testify on the defendant's behalf and for a detective's services. They also found a forensic pathologist on the east coast who would debate the cause of death spiritedly against the findings of the medical examiner in Tucson who said that Joyce died due to drowning. This was after they had asked not to represent Richard because their secretary knew one of the witnesses. But Judge Hale cited rule ER 1.7 concerning conflict of interest: *"A lawyer shall not represent a client if presentation of that client may be materially limited by the lawyer's responsibilities to another client or third person."* Judge Hale found that there was no conflict. Richard stated that he was uncomfortable about the situation, but said, "There's nothing I can do about it." He then waived his Sixth Amendment right to a speedy trial so his new counsel could prepare for court.

The new defense counsel would perform a reenactment, which also required payment. A diver, a witness and a volunteer who was the same size as Joyce took off in an inflatable boat and put it forty feet off of the point where Joyce was found, the hypothesis being, that the prosecution would say that Richard used a small boat on his mother's property to dump the body. They marked the spot using buoyancy-control techniques. The diver went down first and hovered above the bottom of the gravity canal without disturbing the bottom and took photos. The volunteer had a crate of rocks that weighed thirty pounds in her arms and in her mouth was a device called "Spare Air" which is a tiny air tank with about twenty breaths of air in it. Their evidence showed that Joyce would be covered in sediment that is two feet deep in that location.

Richard's co-counsel stated that the defendant never gave his approval for his wife to be cremated and that Richard claimed that he didn't believe that she was really deceased since he never saw the body. He claimed to have objected three times to two mortuaries and they refused to cremate because he wouldn't give his consent until he alone made his identification. Mr. Millington argued that there is a statute which requires a special certificate to be issued by the medical examiner and that there has to be no evidence of foul play before a body can be cremated. Defense argued that if there hadn't been a cremation, another autopsy could have been performed; one that would exonerate his client. The medical examiner must not have thought it was death by foul play, or that the body was Joyce Handcock and that he and her family had conspired to frame Mr. Handcock by proceeding with the cremation without his consent. Either way, it had to mean freedom for Richard. Defense counsel moved for dismissal. It was denied.

***

Judge Hale ordered that Richard be allowed to attend trial in street clothing, but the subject of media attendance was argued. This was a significant case for Yuma County. It was expected to last five weeks minimum (the longest in Yuma's history at that time) and was the first to be based solely on circumstantial evidence. It could make careers.

"I'm unaware of any authority I have to regulate the media in terms of what they broadcast according to the First Amendment," Judge Hale stated.

Co-counsel, Ms. Wheelwright agreed to some access, but said, "It's clearly the media's intent to prejudice this trial by continuing to broadcast. My client can't get a fair trial. The intent should be taken into consideration when new rules are set."

"Their intent is to receive as high of a rating as they can," Judge Hale said squarely. "As long as attorney-client privilege isn't breached or the jury shown, I don't have a problem with television cameras in the courtroom.

It was decided that microphones and cameras would not be allowed in Richard's face as he entered or left the court building. Ms. Wheelwright didn't want anybody taking pictures of his hands in cuffs or chains around his ankles or waist. This would be prejudicial.

There was a skirmish over what pictures of Joyce Handcock before and after death would be shown to the jury. Most were objected to by the defense, naturally.

CHAPTER 35

This is where I blundered into the picture, so to speak. My husband, Butch, and I had been working and traveling around the country after the younger of our two daughters married and began a family of her own in Nebraska. We left our house in southern California and sold the contents three years earlier and enjoyed recreational-vehicle living and working together while traveling around the country. It had been a dream of ours to work and see the country. Butch had previously worked as a construction superintendent, overseeing the building of resplendent hillside homes, but on the road he went back to being an industrial electrician, an ability he learned while serving in the Navy many years earlier. Electrician jobs were the most abundant at the time but it was a major decrease in pay. Fortunately, we no longer had a mortgage in California to pay. I had previously worked as a columnist at a local newspaper and was the secretary of our local Chamber of Commerce, and was the founder of a non-profit teen outreach group. But on the road I was able to work as an administrative assistant or some other job where Butch worked.

As the subcontracted jobs began and ended, we moved on to new jobs in different cities and different states and sometimes with a regular crew. Butch was the foreman. It was a great time, although Butch and I were not using the skills we had acquired while matriculating in college. He had a bachelor's degree in business administration while I majored in English. Although I went to college for six years, most classes were lower division, so I couldn't graduate; wasn't even trying. Back in those days, in my family women weren't expected to work, but waited until the right man came along to find us, get married and have babies. I know I'm dating myself and the middle-class social traditions here. I was raised and indoctrinated with this belief system.

My mother kept at me to take English and secretarial classes in case, God forbid, something should happen to my husband. I also managed to get a medical assistant degree later on. Thank goodness my mother insisted some of those classes. Something did happen to my first husband. I divorced him when my daughter was two months old and raised her alone until she was eleven. At the time of the trial, I was in my forties and Butch had just had his fifty-fifth birthday; making it possible for us to move into an exclusive senior five-star resort. We had been through a lot the months prior and were excited about the move.

Butch had an industrial back injury in November 1994 and in January 1995 he was the recipient of a "failed back surgery." The doctor had accidentally cut the nerve in his back while operating and he's been continually going downhill since that day. His surgery in Long Beach, California, was on the day Joyce Handcock's decomposed body was found.

After many more doctors and worker's compensation hoops, Social Security red tape, it was evident to all that Butch could no longer work and would end up in a wheelchair eventually. Though we had lived in several states, the move from where Butch was injured was the state in which we'd started out. Our final move was to be from Huntington Beach, California, to Yuma, Arizona, because it was much less expensive and also most importantly--because Yuma is beneath the jet stream and the lack of clouds helped me with my sinus headache-like migraines over a period of years. The heat helps Butch's aches and pains too. We could have chosen to live almost anywhere in the country. It is beautiful living here in Yuma, but I do miss living near a body of water. Our two swimming pools and spas will have to suffice. We had to wait two months before any barn, shack, shanty, park, or hotel had an opening to buy or rent. We were shocked that Yuma was so popular! And the city had at least twenty-five RV parks at the time!

When we arrived, I worked for a few months at the post office until Butch's workers' compensation and Social Security Disability payments started coming regularly in the mail. We traded our RV for a new park model and added a large room. It wasn't life like we knew it in California with the big house, but while it is about one/fifth its size, it's surprisingly lavish. The living spaces are similar in size to those of most homes, but only has one bedroom. That interior decorating class I took in college helped along the way, Butch's knowledge of structure added dimension, coupled with my art classes, that inspired the first of many murals I painted making a unique difference. I enjoy decorating and have taken on the occasional decorating job by referral. Butch likes to work on his model railroading hobby. We added a room just for that, too. (No, the subject didn't come up when we were dating!) One of the neighbors is always picking his brain on how to build something, repair, or someone needs construction advice.

In October 1996 Butch and a family friend named Zack (a guy we had picked up as a "family mascot" while working in Corpus Christi Texas) both met me at the Phoenix airport after I had a week-long visit with family. While I normally treasure my time with my daughter and only grandchild who was five years old at the time, the visit with my daughter had been fraught with tension and arguments like we never had before or since. She was going through a divorce and I think I was a safe place for her to vent her anger. I had been sick and too upset to eat or sleep.

Butch and Zack and I had planned a short detour trip north before heading home southward. So we went up to the Grand Canyon to unwind. Zack had never been out of Texas before we talked him into moving to Yuma. We stopped at the Anastazi Indian cave-dwelling remains known as Montezuma's Castle on the way. It was there in the solitude of the mountains and timeless surrounding area awash in fall colors and in its silence that I began to stop shaking all over. We listened to a John Tesh CD in the car and the music seemed to perfectly illustrate the countryside as if it were written to describe musically what we were looking at. That's what I was thinking when Zack said it out loud. Zack and I rarely think the same things. We checked into a beautiful hotel suite in Sedona, with a balcony over looking the picturesque red rock formations, domes, and fingers carved out by an ancient artist.

We made instant cocoa in the kitchenette and turned on the timer on the automatic gas fireplace. At my stage in life, I like simple things like that.

Zack was already on his balcony next door as we took our mugs outside to watch the breathtaking sunset. The artist in me, trying to memorize the changing colors for the next time I would be with my paintbrush in hand.

The next day we visited several of the fifty art galleries in the scenic city and ate rattlesnake and steak at The Cowboy Restaurant. We took a helicopter ride around the huge monuments dressed in burnt umber and sienna and fell in love with Sedona.

On the way home we stopped in Prescott, Jerome (an old mining town on a mountain top), and another museum in Wickenburg before returning home which is where I found my jury summons waiting for me. My peace was brief.

CHAPTER 36

On Halloween 1996, two hundred and eleven of my fellow voters and I were gathered in the largest jury pool in Yuma County history. They asked us to sit in the biggest court room available in the old courthouse that has since been replaced. But while most of us were seated, many stood along the walls or sat on the floor.

First we were asked if any of us were related to or knew any of the people involved in the case. A lengthy list of names was circulated among us. Several people raised their hands and were asked to explain their relationship and some were asked if it would influence their opinions about the case. I remember one young woman was excused because she had been a baby-sitter for a number of years for one of the prosecutor's children.

Then the judge stated that they expected this trial to last for about five weeks, and then asked for a show of hands again on how many people this would cause an extreme hardship. A single mother was excused. A disc jockey at a local radio station explained that his boss and another co-worker were on vacation and he was the only one left who could read the news on the air. He was excused. Several others were also excluded; especially sole-income providers. I searched my mind. In the past, I would have done the same, but this was basically the first time in my life that I could honestly say it would not be a problem in one way or another. I insanely forgot about my chronic migraine headaches for the moment. I had medication that sometimes worked and it was working at the moment. It was the time of year where Yuma gets a cloud or two. The whole change of seasons can be tough for migraine sufferers. I listened, thinking of the eleven years I was the sole provider for my daughter, Chriz (pronounced Krizz) working through migraines before I met my wonderful

MURDER BY GRAVITY?

husband and, then suddenly it was the end the first day of jury selection.

When I came home that evening, I said to Butch, "They're not going to pick me, what are the odds?" It started out about 1 in 17.8 and that night was about 1 in 12.

My all-wise husband said, "They *are* going to pick you."

And, of course I said, "No, they aren't. The case is about spousal abuse and a man murdering his wife! The defense will never okay me!" Butch knew that my first husband abused and almost killed me in a relationship that ended in 1972, two months after Chriz was born. I raised her on my own before marrying Butch and becoming stepmom to his sweet daughter, Tina, who is two years older than mine.

* * *

Day two of jury selection began with questionnaires being passed around. They were intensely personal. It asked about arrests, opinions about alcohol and drugs and usage there of, and (surprise!) if I'd ever been the victim of spousal abuse or an assault. We were sworn in and under *oath* before filling out these questionnaires, so it wasn't to be taken lightly. I wondered who would be privy to my information as we turned them in and went to lunch. I assumed it would be both sets of counsel. Clusters of prospective jurors gravitated together and picked restaurants in which to walk that were plentiful near the courthouse.

When we returned at the prescribed time, we saw the two county attorneys, the two defense attorneys, and to my horror, the defendant, reading through our questionnaires! Whether he was guilty or not, I didn't feel that he had the right to know all about our personal lives. Maybe I'm wrong, but I sure wasn't expecting that. We were here to discuss *him*.

The Assistant County Attorney, or A.C.A., would pick up a questionnaire and ask appropriate questions, followed by defense questions. There were a few problematic areas for some prospective jurors like, "Did you read about this case in the newspapers when it first unfolded?"

I thought, hey, *I had another get out of jury duty free card* because I had read about some of the Handcock case when we first moved to Yuma. But then the following question, "Would any news article that you read taint your views when presented with other facts that displayed the accused's innocence in court? Would you *still* keep the same views from a news article if shown other evidence to the contrary here in court?"

That question shot down most intelligent life forms. Except one-- a lady actually sat through that and said her mind was already made up that Mr. Handcock was guilty *from reading the newspapers!* Even after the judge re-phrased the question, the woman stood by her answer. It worked, too, because she was immediately dismissed.

One questionnaire after another was examined. The defense asked me about the newspaper. I answered that I vaguely remembered reading something about the case when we first moved here, which was the exact truth. I used to write for newspapers and I know better than to always believe the spin. He asked me briefly about the assault without going into detail that happened over twenty years ago and would I be able to separate those experiences from that of the victim? He had me by my pride; my need to find logic in all things and cease to be all things hysterically feminine. Of course, I should be able to detach myself from the past and approach the subject with more maturity. My husband understood this before I did. And so it was that I was seated as number seven on the jury of twelve plus two alternates.

* * *

Opening statements began at three o'clock the same day after we were sworn in and the other prospective jurors sent home. I was still pinching myself in disbelief that I was still there at all. The county prosecutor began telling us that he and his co-counsel would provide us with enough circumstantial evidence to find Richard Leon Handcock guilty of the murder of his wife, Joyce Ann. He told us that he would explain that he was not only being charged with murder, but premeditation of that murder and kidnapping as well.

The prosecutor told us that the couple's marriage was a rocky one and that Handcock was insanely jealous of his wife. Richard was the last person to see his wife alive and he had five hours he couldn't account for on the day she disappeared, and that there was evidence found at the crime scene such as wood, cinder blocks, and blue paint that matched materials found at the Handcocks' home.

Co-counsel for the defense had to wait until the following morning to give their opening arguments. We were then told by Judge Hale that this was *not* a death penalty case and that the judge would fix the sentencing, not the jury. I was relieved. We were also made aware that only twelve out of the fourteen of us would deliberate. The last two jurors chosen weren't necessarily alternates.

Judge Hale told us not to speculate or guess about any facts, but to determine only what we could from the evidence. He said we should not be influenced by sympathy or prejudice that we had to follow the law. He further told us that we were to be the judges of the facts gleaned through witnesses, documents, exhibits, facts stipulated; that we must accept and decide the credibility and weight to be given to direct or circumstantial evidence. We were instructed to disregard objections that were sustained and not guess the answer. The judge said that we could accept all; or part; or none of what a witness said. We were to also observe the witness's manner while testifying and whether or not the witness contradicted himself or seemed reasonable, or if he had a motive. We were to consider all evidence in the light of common sense and experience.

Hale said that we would make our decision at the end of trial based on what we remember; that we would not get a transcript, so we should pay close attention as the testimony was given. The judge said we could take notes, but we had to leave them in our seats whenever we were out of the courtroom. He didn't want our notes to distract us in such a way as we would miss any testimony.

Since school, I've always been a compulsive note taker. My former shorthand is now blended into a personal speed writing. I follow ideas better when I take notes. When I was the secretary of the Chamber of Commerce, the president would look at me and say, "That's a good point; put that in the minutes."

And I'd say, "I already have." He always looked incredulously back at me. But I'd learned to sort out the important facts to be noted and wrote them almost simultaneously as they were being said. I'm fairly certain the judge didn't think I was distracted. I just think and remember better with a pen in my hand.

Judge Hale then admonished us with jury do's and don'ts:

- Don't talk to each other about the case or anybody else connected to it.
- Do not talk to attorneys or witnesses until the end of the trial.
- You may tell people what case you're on.
- Do wear your juror badge at all times.
- If someone tries to talk to you about the case, stop them or walk away. Report it to the judge.
- Do not visit locations where the events of the case took place.
- Keep an open mind; don't form an opinion until the end of the trial. (And they wonder why juror's faces are so difficult to read!)
- Do avoid the news media coverage. If you read the newspaper, have someone else cut out clippings about this case so you can't read them. If it's on the television news, leave the room.

The court rules require the proceedings be televised in such a way that no jurors can be recognized. Hale said the jurors were prohibited from asking questions directly, but if we had a question for a witness, we could write it down without signing our name and give it to the bailiff. This was a relatively new procedure at the time. (As if no one would notice who wrote the note!)

Judge Hale explained to us what the direct examination, cross-examination, and re-direct procedure was and that we had to wait until both sides had all their questions asked and answered before we could ask our questions. (I want to add here that while this *sounds* like a good idea, you can sit there in the jury thinking *somebody* is surely going to ask the question you have, but by the time re-direct is over and you realize no one has asked your question, the witness has been dismissed!)

* * *

Judge Hale read the following instructions:
"The crime of first-degree murder consists of both first degree

MURDER BY GRAVITY?

murder by premeditation and first-degree felony murder. The crime of first degree murder by premeditation requires proof of the following three things:

1. The defendant caused the death of another person.
2. The defendant knew that he would cause the death of another.
3. The defendant acted with premeditation.

Premeditation means the defendant's intention or knowledge existed before the killing long enough to permit reflection. But the reflection differs from the intent of knowledge that contact will cause death; it may be instantaneous as successive thoughts in the mind and it may be proven by circumstantial evidence.

The crime of first-degree felony murder requires proof of two things. Mr. Handcock committed or attempted to commit kidnapping and in the course of furtherence of this crime or immediate flight from this crime, the defendant or another person caused the death of any person.

Kidnapping requires proof of three things:

1. The defendant knowingly restricted another's movements.
2. The restriction was accomplished.
3. Moving the person from one place to another.

* * *

The opening statement of the defense was succinct and delivered by the senior; masculine half of the co-counsel, William Millington, who told us that Richard Handcock loved his wife, that their marriage was not rocky, and that in fact, they had been planning to renew their marriage vows on their first anniversary, at Richard's behest. Millington further stated that Handcock had an alibi for the morning his wife disappeared and that he had not been the last one to see her alive . . . her killer was, if indeed she were dead. He was not permitted to see his deceased wife's body even though the medical examiner's office kept it for six weeks before allowing Joyce's mother's signature to send her to a crematorium for final resolution in Yuma.

The police had kept Richard locked up like an animal and unable to see if this unfortunate woman was his Joyce. Richard still hadn't let himself believe that she was really dead. If he were a guilty man would he have fought off her cremation so hard and so long? It was Joyce's parents who said she wanted to be cremated, not Richard. He had nothing to hide.

CHAPTER 37

The prosecution began its case by calling Sam Sayers, who told of finding Joyce's body in the Gila Gravity Canal that chilly January day. Sam explained how he had gone fishing with his son and came to urinate in the bushes, discovering the white object in the water area behind where they were fishing and how difficult getting a good look at the floating thing was. Sam said that once he'd discerned it was a body, he'd gone to take his son home and make the phone call to the Sheriff's office to report a possible body. He then came back to the Gila Gravity Canal to lead the body recovery team. It was his opinion they might not have found it otherwise.

Sam Sayers came across as a good father and good citizen. Then the fit, fair-haired and fifty-something, Mr. Millington began asking his questions for the defense.

"You make it sound as if you and your son were alone on that day, Mr. Sayers. Is that what you're saying?"

"Well, no, I had a friend with us also." He glanced toward the prosecution as if for help. "We both had been laid off and were killing some time that day."

"And why didn't you mention this third person before when you gave your account to the police?" Millington asked slyly.

"Because he wasn't supposed to be there," Sayers confessed.

"And why is that?"

"He's on intensive probation. If he wasn't at work, he was supposed to be home or looking for work, I guess."

"And you didn't think another witness might be important for the police to know about?"

"They had *me. I led them to the body and I never lied about nobody else being with us*. I just didn't volunteer the information."

"So when you took your son home, you took your friend home."
"Yes. And I dialed 911."
"How long ago did the police find out about your friend being with you that day?"
"Two days ago."

Millington seemed disappointed not to catch the police in a lie. He muttered, "You wait almost two years . . ." he then turned a page over on his legal pad and said, "It says here that you told the Sheriff's Department to come in a four-wheel drive vehicle. That it was necessary to navigate the roads out there."

"That's right."

"Nothing further," Millington ended abruptly. He looked satisfied at his co-counsel, Dusty Wheelwright, an ample matron in her early forties with a slight mustache, and an attractive man in his late thirties who usually sat behind them during court hours. Speculation ran wild among the jury as to what his function might be.

Knowing that Handcock drove a standard pick up truck and catching the direction in which the defense was going, Assistant County Attorney Stephen Russell stood for re-direct and asked Sayers if a regular, standard truck could make its way over the dirt roads to the Gila Gravity Canal and Sayers. "Sure, it could make it."

Russell looked at his second chair, Josh Schulmire, and a smile played lightly at the corners of his mouth. It was a good thing too, because the man was so gaunt and chalky he looked like he belonged in a casket. Through the weeks ahead his merry blue eyes and wry sense of humor saved us from some of the unrelenting tension surrounding the case. It did take some getting used to for the man who looked so ghoulish to be also so unexpectedly funny. Russell and Schulmire made a good team. They were both small-framed men, but well-built, and must have been terribly overworked to have avoided the sun so completely. There are only a dozen or so overcast days a year in Yuma.

There was another party at the County Attorney's table--a trim, attractive blonde woman. Each of the jurors wondered who she could be. She was Russell and Schulmier's little ray of sunshine, or so we thought.

* * *

MURDER BY GRAVITY?

The prosecution called Dylan Sopher to the stand who testified that he was one of the divers for the Sheriff's Department and Joyce Ann was his first body retrieval. He stated that he drove a Ford F-150 with standard clearance to the Gravity Canal that day without difficulty.

Millington asked Sopher if there was a transfer dump station near the site and Sopher answered in the affirmative. "So a person going out there wouldn't have an expectation of privacy?" Millington asked.

"There aren't any houses there or anything," Sopher replied.

Steve Russell called Robert Larson, the more experienced diver, to the stand who was asked for, and gave, a list of his experience and training as if it were a pedigree. When taking the stand professional witnesses are generally asked for a list of their credentials so the jury may value or not value their testimony and interpretations. Larson testified that Joyce's body was nude, except for a black bra that was pulled up on one side. That the water was so murky they never thought it was a murder and didn't realize at first that the body was weighted down with wires, straps, crates, and rocks. It was only after several unsuccessful tries that they tried to pick her up and found the attachments. He said her body was so bloated, he didn't see the wires that had dug into her skin. They saw the head wound and blood still oozing from it. They then carefully removed the body and Detective Graham took several photos of it and the attachments.

Larson continued, "There was one milk crate with rocks in it tied to a wire that was wrapped around both of her wrists. And a wire and strapping went around both ankles and were secured to a cement pylon."

Russell theorized, "So one person could carry her, put her in the water, then attach the weights to her feet and then to her arms, right? How long do you think that would take for one person to do this?"

"Oh, I'd say, about ten or fifteen minutes." This was just one of the many times I thought Richard's attorney might not be paying attention to the testimony.

Larson also testified to the "small search" that was performed just before dark at the body discovery site. He said that they had taken into evidence from the fire pit location something resembling a picture frame that had some blue paint on it, some pieces of flat wood, ply-wood and something that looked like fish guts and bagged it for the lab. He said they used the metal detector and found nothing. They took the weights that were attached to Joyce and bagged them as well. Detective Graham photographed everything.

When Millington asked if they stopped searching when it got dark, Larson said they used flashlights at first but they were shortly ordered off the search. He then asked Larson if he thought that a thirty minute search of the area was adequate and Larson admitted that he thought it was odd they didn't return for another month to look around again.

* * *

Steve Russell called Joyce's sister, Lynn, to the stand. Lynn stated that she was Joyce's younger sister and that they were close. She said she was shocked when Joyce had married Richard after the family had only met him the one time over Christmas and a month later they were married. She said she had never known her sister to do things that spontaneously before. Joyce's first marriage took a year to plan. She asked Joyce before the wedding if she knew what she was doing, but Joyce seemed to have her mind set.

Joyce's sister was pretty in a more subtle way than Joyce. The prosecution had put up on an easel a giant photo of Joyce that was to be in the courtroom during much of the trial. Lynn described her sister as being full of life and fun to be around. One could sense that about her from the photo. Lynn said Joyce had always taken good care of herself. She wore pretty clothes and had her makeup, nails, and hair done whenever she went out.

Lynn said that in her opinion the marriage was great at the beginning, but after March or April of that same year, Richard told Joyce that she couldn't work in the bar anymore. That he had accused her of having affairs and Joyce began getting bruises the size of grapefruit on her legs. Lynn said that Richard told her confidentially that Joyce didn't understand how to be a wife and that he was going to move her and Joyce's daughter, Nickie, to

Phoenix "so she would be away from all of the men she knew."

"So Richard and Joyce went through a period of time when they were on and off together?" Schulmire prompted Lynn.

"Yes. In the fall of 1994, Richard and Joyce were living in a trailer on the lot at Swift Sales. Joyce walked over to my apartment. She said the night before, Richard had kicked her out of the trailer and she was trying to calm him down and she almost had him talked into letting her stay when Mike Deere drove by. She said he wouldn't even let her in to get her clothing in the morning after she'd slept outside there. She stayed for about a week that time and at my place and with another friend after that. I'm not sure about the details, but she did go back to him."

"Did you notice anything different about Richard's appearance after that?" Schulmier asked.

"Well, his hair was cut real short, like military or boot camp, and he was wearing fatigues all the time. They were real baggy, like he'd lost a lot of weight too. Joyce told me he had cancer. I heard about doctor appointments from her, but not from him. Joyce's friend, Mike Deere told me that around the first week of December Richard had told Joyce that the doctor had given him like eight weeks to live. Of course, Joyce would not leave him under the circumstances. It had a profound effect on her in conjunction with the kidnapping and whipping Richard had suffered."

"That was when Richard was kidnapped by . . .?

"The people he used to work for at Swift Sales."

"Is that what Richard told you?"

"No, Richard told Joyce and our whole family that he was kidnapped and whipped. We saw his arms and legs."

Steve asked Lynn, "Your sister came up missing on Wednesday. How were you informed?"

"My dad called me on Thursday and asked me to come get Nickie to stay with me because Joyce was missing. Joyce wouldn't just leave and not call her work or tell Nickie that she was leaving."

"And you understood that your family didn't want Nickie staying alone with Richard?"

"That's right. He was upset about it, too. He wanted Nickie to stay!"

"So, Richard didn't call you to see if you knew where your sister was on Wednesday the 11th, even though he knew that your sister had a history of going to your house?"

"No, he didn't call."

"Did he ask on Thursday the 12th when you came over for Nickie?"

"No."

"Or did he call Friday the 13th looking for Joyce?"

"No, he *never* called me asking if I knew where Joyce was," Lynn said flatly.

"Can you repeat for the jury what Joyce told you on New Year's Eve, just eleven days before she disappeared?"

"She said, 'If I don't get out of this marriage, he will kill me,' and she said that he was obsessive and jealous and more specifically, *"He's going to kill me!"*

Bill Millington jumped to his feet to object strenuously.

CHAPTER 38

Both sides of counsel approached the bench and the jury was escorted out of the courtroom.

An interesting thing happened on the last day we deliberated; the bailiff took all of our notebooks away from us. I thought by the end of the trial it was a matter of public record, but the bailiff said it was against the rules for us to take our notes home. So the only way for me to see the transcripts of the trial was to go to the County Clerk's office after the end of the trial and plow through twenty books that were two to three hundred pages each in length. I was unable to take the transcripts home, so I became a regular fixture at the Clerk of the Superior Courts's office.

One of the benefits of reading the transcripts, of course, was finding out what happened when we, the jury, were out of the room!

When both sides of counsel approached, Judge Hale was upset and said, "I want to know why we spend untold hours in pre-trial and *never* reached these issues! Do you have others who will corroborate the victim's admonishment?"

Russell said, "Well, yes, we have another witness, the owner of the bar who said that Joyce told her, 'If I don't get out of this marriage, he will kill me,' and we know that the timing of her disappearance is significant because she was going to insist that she accompany her husband to his cancer specialist in Tucson the very morning she disappeared."

Hale said, "What about the *State vs. Charo*? Pursuant to that case, the victim stated she feared for her own life as evidence to the identity of the murderer was admissible."

Millington quickly countered, "But in the Charo case that rational for allowing it was overruled. A few other points of law enter into this: Joyce wanted the world to know they were renewing their vows on their anniversary eleven days after her death. She had changed her mind."

"Richard had fantasized that they were about to renew their vows! There is no evidence anywhere of his allegations."

The judge asked Russell, "What do you think happened?"

"I think she said she was leaving him. Look, we don't know what was the straw that broke the camel's back, but we will continue to lay out a series of bizarre behavior by Richard and the circumstantial evidence that ties Richard to the crime."

Hale says," *Okay, the bar owner's testimony that Joyce told her that Richard was going to kill her is inadmissible."* What a system!

The jury was out for fifty-five minutes on that day, which had taken some of the wind out of the sails of the prosecution, who was working with only circumstantial evidence.

* * *

Millington stood to cross examine Lynn. He laid the foundation that Joyce was her big sister and Lynn would do anything for her, even lie for her. "Joyce called you many times when she was going to Mike Deere's house and asked you to tell Richard if he called that she was doing laundry at your house, right?"

Lynn looked down at her hands and said, "That's right."

"She also worked at The Dark after her husband asked her not to work in bars, isn't that correct?"

"Yes, but that was after he disappeared. She needed a job. When he came back, she took care of him."

"Isn't it possible that Richard wouldn't call you after Joyce disappeared because he knew you would lie to him?" Before she could respond, Millington said, "I have no further questions at this time, Your Honor."

CHAPTER 39

Who would have thought that staying still and quiet in court would be such a chore? Oh yes, a kindergartner! At the end of each day, I would be so stiff and tired and my mind was jammed up with mental pictures that I couldn't make go away. I tried to sleep, but that was useless. I couldn't eat. I prayed each night that we would be able to see the truth. My mind wouldn't shut off. I heard someone else mention later in the week that they were having trouble sleeping too.

My husband dutifully cut out the pertinent articles from the newspapers before I read it each morning before court. I left the room at night when the news came on. By Friday, we had the day off and I went to a ceramics class at the resort where I live. As I chatted with the other ladies and sanded down my green ware, I slowly became less stressed. I started to realize that I was beginning to feel like myself again. The ladies in the resort were much older than I at that time and I remember a sweet retired school teacher asking me what my grandson did in Omaha.

I responded, "He's in kindergarten!" and laughed.

She said, "I keep forgetting you're so young!" It made me feel great that they forgot about the age difference, because I always did.

After class, I still felt the burden of my jury duties, but I could function again on a daily basis. I started to eat again, but I started Ben & Jerry's ice cream too, which I normally don't indulge in daily and of course I started to gain weight. But I felt like I needed to spoil myself a little under the circumstances!

I had worked for an attorney many years earlier and now I found myself wondering how they sat through long court trials day after day. The courtroom was so quiet, that one would draw attention to themselves if they coughed or sneezed. Any decent attempt at levity was greatly appreciated to lessen the stress.

The jurors began mingling in groups. Still being one of the few dreaded smokers in the world, I would go outside during breaks in exile. This practice alone puts you in the company of people with whom you might not normally select to associate yourself. When I came inside I would normally talk to the other women sitting in the halls. Two jurors in particular were both housewives and fretting that they didn't have appropriate clothing to wear to court for more than a couple of days. I believe both finished high school, but got married right afterward and had several children at a young age. Both were still married to their high school sweethearts and never worked outside the home. Yes, that is what my parents wanted for me, as a matter of fact. I am glad for the college experiences and intelligence. I wouldn't trade that. We mostly talked about our children. They were younger than I, but they reminded me of my mother--typical stay-at-home moms. It's difficult when you're in a trial and the one thing on your mind you're not allowed to discuss. So we got to know each other. We talked about everything under the sun. They quizzed me for hair and makeup tips. For lunch I usually ended up going with the men, I don't honestly remember why or how that came about, but it was four or five of the men on the jury and me going to lunch regularly. Probably because they were more my age and we talked about interesting subjects and had another smoker or two in the group. We tried all the local restaurants that we could walk to. I remember one time going to Mexico on my own to get medicine during lunch break and I wondered what judge would think if he knew one of his jurors was out of the country!

In the hall I also got to know that one of the alternates was the manager of our local office equipment store, to put it generically. She had obviously been educated. There were two other professional women there who were middle management and a school teacher. Some of the men and women worked for Yuma Proving Ground and received their regular rate of pay while serving on the jury. Some days we got off or got off early and they still had to go to their jobs.

Our jury consisted of one black man who dressed in a suit every day. He was a Baptist minister. During our down time he read The Bible while sitting in the hallway. He rarely spoke to anyone.

Two of the men knew each other distantly through work at the

MURDER BY GRAVITY?

Proving Ground where they test military and other assorted equipment out in the desert. They were civilian workers, with great benefits, I might add. One of the men had formerly been an owner of a local mortuary. He was interesting to talk to. He had a wonderful sense of humor. He was also into local politics. One of the men sold paint at a local hardware store. I still see him now and then working at Wal-Mart. The man who was to be our fearless leader later on was number six, who sat next to me in the jury box. He was a bit older than I with silvering hair, a little Latin, and he walked with a cane. He was very distinguished and handsome to be sure. He was disabled and that was why he was free to be in the jury and why he had the cane, although on him the cane looked like a prop for a movie. In marked contrast to his distinct appearance he told me one day that his family in California whom he had little to do with were still grieving over Jerry Garcia and were Grateful Dead-heads to the end. He smiled with amusement, though. I found the mental picture of a family reunion intriguing.

While the jury chairs were quite comfortable, tilted and swiveled with a bar to put up our feet, the gallery was not so comfy. Butch would have liked to watch some of the trial but he would have a tough time sitting on the wood benches for very long.

After our first week, juror number one, who was a very young lady, only nineteen years old, called in sick. Our first alternant was placed, leaving only the manager of the office equipment store, number fourteen, as alternate for the remaining weeks ahead. They would be drawing names at the end and one of us wouldn't be on the jury. Any one of us could have been selected at the end to be out of the jury pool.

We were severely spoken to by the judge regarding our civic duty and that none of us could take any sick days. I wondered with my migraines how I would manage to get through this trial. I usually had an ice pack on my face at some point during the day to help suppress the blinding pain I got in my maxillary sinuses and eyes.

When I had this book about half done, I became seriously ill with an electrolyte imbalance and nearly died. I was in the ICU for eleven days and in the hospital for a month. My calcium spiked and my magnesium plummeted. The doctors weren't sure if I had a prolactinoma—a small tumor in the pituitary inside the brain. When I came out of the ICU, I was like a three-year-old with amnesia; I didn't know where I was or what the year was or how to say the word for the bathroom. I didn't know how to work the telephone or the can opener. I had to relearn verbal skills and even a year later I was stammering, had twitching of the face, and was biting my tongue when I tried to talk. Then I would have poor impulse control and get flustered and cry. I didn't get dressed except to go to the doctor's office and I had insomnia every night. I watched the same three movies over and over again, because they were the only things I understood. The floor moved when I looked down, so I walked with a cane. I still have no memory of 2003. It was a long two-year recovery. My husband, Butch, took wonderful care of me. I had much of the book done and looked for another writer to finish it for me. Before I found one, I started getting better!

It was a year into that recovery process that I hooked up with a doctor out of Barrow's Neurological Institute in Phoenix who knew how to treat my migraines and was instrumental in the development of a medicine that finally gave me relief from the torture that plagued my life. I feel like a new person. Apparently migraines can mimic other kinds of headaches. For me it was like sinusitis. Who knew? But at that time and for years, I often went through weeks and months of non-stop, mind-numbing pain. I was very good at not showing it; only those really close to me could tell I was hurt or those I would confide in, which was rare.

When I prayed at night during the trial, I also asked for the physical ability (it can be difficult to concentrate during a migraine) to complete the trial and the wisdom and discernment to find the truth. I also hoped the Baptist preacher would be on the same side I was at the end, because I figured he was praying too.

CHAPTER 40

Steve Russell called Roy Bounder to the stand for the State. Roy said that he was currently working as a cab driver but used to live and work at the recreational vehicle park where Joyce and Richard Handcock lived in December of 1994, where he helped the manager with maintenance, repairs, and clean up.

"Did you ever hear any voices coming from the Handcock trailer, Mr. Bounder?"

"Yeah, I heard arguing and sometimes I smelled marijuana and had to tell them to clean up the area. The park is mostly elderly, so I had to tell them to keep the noise down because it was disruptive. Several times I heard Richard, and others did too. You could hear him from thirty feet away. He'd say that she was an f-ing bitch and she dressed sexy to attract other men. One time when I told him to keep it down he said, 'I wish she was f-ing dead!' That was early in January of 1995."

"Was there anything else, Mr. Bounder?"

"On occasion, I heard Richard say that he should slap the bitch."

"Russell asked, "What kind of things did you see around the outside of the Handcock trailer?"

"I saw wood pieces, cement blocks, square milk crates, and trash strewn outside."

"Did you ever see Richard doing laundry?"

Roy shifted in his chair and said he never did.

Russell now sat on the end of his table and crossed his arms and stated, "When our office subpoenaed you, they found a couple of criminal matters. On April 13, 1989 you were convicted of theft. Later, in Arkansas, you had a felony conviction for writing bad checks. And on October 9, 1996 you were convicted of a misdemeanor: that being of *giving false information to the police!*

But now today your testimony given here is true." Russell figured it would be better for him to bring up the messy background of his witness than for the defense to do so.

"Yes, sir, it is the truth," Roy looked sincere enough as he could under the circumstances, although a bit like a rabbit stuck in front of the oncoming headlights.

On the cross examination Bill Millington asked if the police had asked Roy not to leave town during the investigation and during the trial and he answered, "Yes."

"I may have questions for Mr. Bounder at a later time, Your Honor," Millington added.

"That's fine, Mr. Bounder, you're excused for now."

* * *

The State called Beth Kimberly to the stand, and she was sworn in. Beth worked at the sister bar of The Dark--The Show Place. Beth stated that she was thirty-four years old and had lived on and off in Yuma since 1979, but left in '86 for Japan with her husband, a Marine, and that she was his dependant wife. Since then, they had also lived in Hawaii, England and South Carolina. She stated that she first met Joyce when Joyce's last name was Martinez some time prior to 1991. The next time she saw her was around the fall of 1994 when Beth returned to town.

"Mrs. Kimberly, were you friends with Joyce Handcock?"

"No, I'd say we were more *bartender to bartender*. It was not a friendship. I would see her when she came to help out at The Show Place or vice versa," she said.

"Now when you saw Joyce this time did you notice anything different about her?" Russell questioned

"When I saw her in '94, I couldn't believe the difference. She just wasn't the same at all! She seemed unhappy and distant with people. As a bartender, we're supposed to be happy and cheery. I remember thinking that her tip moncy must have fallen off horribly."

Russell casually asked Beth if she'd ever met Richard and she said, "I met Richard in December of 1994 and I thought no way is she married to that guy! He wasn't cute like her usual boyfriends."

MURDER BY GRAVITY?

"Did you ever observe how Joyce was when Richard was in the bar?"

"Some of us were barhopping as a group in separate cars and we went to The Dark near closing time." Beth then asked for a glass of water because she was losing her voice.

"Did you know the people there?"

"Me? No, I remember faces and drinks, and sometimes the regulars' names. Anyway, while we were there, Joyce was happy and joking with us like old times and then Richard walked in and she just clammed up and got tense. She wasn't her usual self. Richard sat at the end of the bar giving everybody dirty looks. I was really uncomfortable around the guy," Beth said.

"Did Joyce ever discuss her relationship with Richard with you?"

"Yeah, we had a couple of ladies' gripe sessions. Joyce told me that she wanted out of the marriage but she couldn't leave because Richard had cancer. I overheard Joyce talking to other people on New Year's Eve that year and she was upset and said, 'If I don't get out of this marriage he's going to kill me,' and she was crying," Beth said, she then gave Richard a defiant look across the room. Richard seemed nonplussed.

Millington stood immediately to object and he was *overruled!* Apparently Judge Hale had changed his mind about allowing Joyce's words from the grave into testimony. Of course, we the jurors didn't know about that, but it caused me to begin observing the defendant more. His blond hair was cut short for the trial and he showed up every day in court in a button-down-collar shirt and a cardigan sweater, looking much like a would-be school teacher. One with white, ashy skin tones much like those of the prosecutors. From where I was sitting, which was to his right past the County Attorney's table and facing his side, and I was on the end of the front row. I had to turn my head to the extreme right to see the witnesses. After talking to the other jurors, I was glad I was sitting where I was, because he would practically have to turn his chair to the side to see me. The other jurors in the front of the room were complaining during brake that he was looking at them and that he was "so creepy."

Steve Russell pressed on for the County Attorney's office, "Now, while you were working at The Show Place, did you ever hear of any phone calls regarding Joyce coming into the bar?"

"The phone calls started three or four weeks before December in 1994. The first call was in the daytime. Some man called and said, 'Joyce had AIDS,' and hung up. In three or four days another call came in saying, 'Joyce is a dead bitch,' with the same male voice. There was a lot of noise or traffic in the background so it might have been a mobile phone or a pay phone. Between November and the first week of January we got about five or six calls saying, 'Joyce is a dead bitch,' or, 'Joyce has AIDS.' After Joyce disappeared, the calls stopped."

"Did you report the calls to the police?" Russell asked.

"I reported them to the bar owner, Stevie Lynd."

"What happened on the day Joyce disappeared?"

"Stevie went into work for Joyce. She wasn't too worried because Joyce was supposed to go to Tucson with Richard that day to see his doctor. Joyce had told Stevie that she'd be back in time to go to work, but Stevie thought it would be a stretch. But then when Joyce didn't call her to let her know she wasn't going to make it to work, she got worried the later it got with no word from her. If Joyce didn't come to work she always had solid excuses and she *always* called in ahead. The next day Stevie talked to Richard to see if he knew where Joyce was and to tell him to report her missing and he said that he was going to. I had a strange feeling that we should check to see if he really did it."

"Mrs. Kimberly, during the last month of her life, did Joyce ever express fear of any one other than the defendant?" Russell asked poignantly.

"Not that I know of." Beth answered.

Russell thanked her for her testimony and Millington stood for cross-exam.

"Mrs. Kimberly, isn't it possible that the Joyce that was the subject of the phone calls was some one other than Joyce Handcock? Isn't that possible?"

"That's possible, I guess."

"Nothing further."

* * *

MURDER BY GRAVITY?

While the jury was out, the players played. In the transcripts were:

Stephen Russell and Bill Millington approached the bench simultaneously. When the handyman, Roy Bounder, who worked at the RV park where Joyce and Richard lived, was dismissed from the stand previously, they were all in agreement that he was to be arrested in the hall by Detective Donna Graham, who was overheard and seen shaking his hand and saying, "Let's go have a beer," as a ruse to get him to jail. When Dusty Wheelwright went to the jail to visit him the previous night she was very upset to discover that he had not been arrested.

Schulmire said that their Arizona arrest warrant wasn't honored because California didn't want to extradite, so Y.P.D. was unable to hold him. Detective David St. Jons shared with Dusty Wheelwright Bounder's California address, so they could talk to him, to see if he would volunteer to testify or give a deposition. He was just over the state line and about two miles from the courthouse.

Josh Schulmire said that, if anything, this should help Richard because Roy might believe they had penalized him for coming forward.

Judge Hale told the defense to make arrangements through the county prosecutor's office to interview Roy and not to wait too long.

At that point, Millington complained that being in court all day long was wreaking havoc with his practice. Judge Hale said that we would take Friday afternoon off to accommodate him.

* * *

Mr. Russell was still sitting in his chair as he said, "The State calls Robert DeVore." In lumbered a man of pleasant girth with a back brace on and a look of some swallowed pain. He told us he was permanently disabled; that his back had been broken and he couldn't work anymore. Bob said that he'd been living in Yuma for ten years and met Joyce at The Dark Place when she started working there; it was his neighborhood bar. Bob testified that Joyce was a pretty lady and was a fun bartender.

"People came in just because Joyce was the bartender there. She was popular. We had lots of conversations at the bar and we played darts when she had the time. Joyce was always happy-go-lucky until Richard came in and she'd button up."

"What about phone calls?" Russell prompted him.

"She would make comments about Richard calling her at work. Sometimes I was there, and I heard her cry and call him names or hang up on him. Her voice was very angry. When Richard came into the bar a couple of times, Joyce and him went into the back room to talk. They were fighting about something. Richard would come in three to five times a week and sit in the back of the room and, like, glare at everybody. I felt like he hated me and he didn't even know me! Then later on, he stopped coming in, and just hid in the back of the parking lot and watched everybody that came in until it was time for Joyce to get off work. Around the twentieth of December, Joyce asked me to stay until she got on her bike to leave. She wanted me to make sure that Richard wasn't in the parking lot first. I did that a few times for her. One night somebody wrote graffiti spray paint on the side of the building saying, 'Joyce has AIDS,' and I got some paint and I painted over it."

"I asked her one time, 'If you're so unhappy, why don't you just leave him?' and she said he had cancer and that he was dying and that she would stay with him until then. But that was before the graffiti."

Bob DeVore told us about the last Sunday that Joyce came to his apartment and that she was planning to approach Richard on Wednesday about going to Tucson to meet his cancer doctor.

Russell asked DeVore, "Did you ever notice any bruises on Joyce's legs or anywhere?"

"I never saw any on her legs, but she was usually behind the bar. But I did see some once like somebody grabbed her; bruises on her neck and above her breasts. Joyce said she got it moving stuff into storage and it fell on her. But Joyce was never particularly clumsy. And I know she was strong, because I saw her picking up cases of beer and trash and she wouldn't accept help."

"Did you ever see any flyers around town with Joyce's picture on them?"

"Oh, no. Once I saw a pile of about twenty of them on the bar at The Dark. I didn't see them anywhere else. I went to The Show Place and didn't see any there either," Bob said.

"Mr. DeVore, did you ever see Richard in The Dark after Joyce disappeared?"

"Well, somebody brought in the flyers, but I never saw him once after she disappeared."

"Was Joyce afraid of anyone else that you know of besides her husband before her death?"

"No."

"Did some people think that you and Joyce had more than just a bartender/customer relationship?"

"If so, I can't imagine why. The only time she ever came to my apartment was that Sunday afternoon I told you about. We didn't talk on the phone; only at the bar. We were just friends."

When Bill Millington began his cross-examination, he asked, "Isn't it possible that Mr. Handcock parked in the rear so that customers would have a better place to park when they came?"

"That's possible, but he didn't usually come in and there was plenty of parking. A lot of people parked on the side or next door at the liquor store. He just sat out there in the dark at The Dark," he smiled at his joke.

"Did you ever observe Joyce flirt at work, Mr. DeVore?"

"She was good at her job!" Bob insisted.

"I see. Did you ever meet any of Joyce's fiends?"

"I met Mike Deere and Ruby and some others. They seemed friendly and like they'd known Joyce forever."

"What did you think about Ruby Vasquez and Mike Deere?"

"I only met Ruby once and I thought she was a pretty, but a flake. I don't usually come into the bar until about ten o'clock at night and she's gone by then as a rule. I got the idea that Mike Deere might be an old boyfriend. He was good-looking."

On re-direct Russell asked DeVore if he ever met Danny Brooks before.

"I had never heard the name until the Detective who was investigating Joyce's disappearance brought the name up."

CHAPTER 41

Steve Russell called Stephanie Lynd to the stand where she was sworn in and testified that she had lived in Yuma since 1972.

"I first met Joyce in 1994 through my friend, Tammy, who owns P.J.'s. Joyce was a good little worker; very reliable and friendly."

"Was there a time that Joyce shared some personal information with you about her husband?"

"Yes, she said that Richard had cancer and she was concerned. There was about three times when he didn't come in to pick her up from work that I came in to take her home and we had conversations. I offered to give her a ride home every night so Richard wouldn't have to but she said that Richard liked to."

"Now did there ever come a time when Joyce told you that she and Richard were having problems?" Russell asked.

"Well, I knew at the get go that they were on and off. Around the end of December of '94 I had the impression things were not as they should be. Joyce told me that Richard didn't like her working in a bar, but she said somebody had to pay the rent and he wasn't working. On New Year's Eve, Joyce had told Richard that she was going to her sister's to drop something off and came to The Show Place instead to wish everyone a happy new year. She made the comment, 'By this time next year I'll be a widow.' I gather it was because Richard would be dead or maybe she'd be divorced. I only had the impression she was staying because he had cancer."

"Can you tell us about the Sunday before Joyce disappeared?"

"She came by in the early afternoon and wanted to get an advance on her paycheck to pay her rent and told me that she might need Wednesday off in addition to her regular time off so she could meet Richard's doctors in Tucson to find out more about his cancer. I asked her if Richard knew she was going with him and she said that he didn't."

Stevie verified that Joyce had a great attendance record and always called in advance if she couldn't make it. Joyce also sometimes filled in at The Show Place for some of the other bartenders if necessary. When Joyce hadn't shown up for work Wednesday night at 6:00 PM, Stevie had opened the bar and wasn't worried. She had thought Joyce would be late. But by 7:30 PM when Joyce hadn't called in, Stevie got worried and called Richard at home and asked if they made it home from Tucson okay. He said that he had that morning when her daughter went to school about 7:00 AM and that he had gone to look for a job and returned at 11:00 AM and she wasn't there and he hadn't seen Joyce the rest of the day. He said somebody was supposed to pick her up to do errands and pay bills, but he didn't know who. Stevie thought that was odd since he always wanted to know where she was and who she was with, since she had to make up an excuse to get to The Show Place on New Year's Eve. Also, when Joyce picked up her check on Sunday she asked if Richard had called because apparently she was gone longer than she was supposed to be.

The next night Stevie said she called Richard to see if he'd heard from Joyce and Richard said he had not. Richard had never called her looking for Joyce. Several people came by the bar because they were concerned about Joyce. Stevie said that Richard never came in looking for her. When asked by the Assistant County Attorney, Stevie Lynd stated that graffiti was not a common thing in the area.

William Millington shuffled papers and briefly conferred with Wheelwright. Without getting up he said, "Haven't you had graffiti on your building on other occasions?"

Stevie replied, "There were two other occasions, two and four years earlier. One was gang related and the other about another bartender named Delia LaRose. It was something crude; I don't remember what it said now. That was before Joyce came to work. We painted over it and never caught who did it."

"Did the police ever ask you who Joyce's friends were?" Steve Russell asked.

"Within a week after she came up missing, they came in asking about Joyce. They didn't ask me who her friends were. They didn't ask who they could contact."

"If they did ask you, who would you have told them to contact?"

"I would have told them about Mike Deere. He came in almost every night to check to see if anybody had heard from her."

"Did Richard bring in missing flyers after Joyce's disappearance?"

"It would have been sometime on Saturday."

"Did Joyce *always* call in before missing a shift?"

"The last time she missed work, she called twice. And when she was an hour late she called a few hours earlier to let me know. One night Joyce called me at 8:00 PM after she was at work and she was very upset. Richard had beaten her up and she had to leave so one of my other bartenders, Marcy, came in to cover her shift. That was sometime between October 1994 and January of 1995. Joyce was normally a very reliable worker." Stevie was adamant about that.

"So Joyce had Sunday off and Monday off. Did she work Tuesday night?"

"Yes."

I'm guessing Millington was trying to dig himself out of a hole and he suddenly decided to leave it alone.

Russell stood for re-direct. "On that Tuesday night that Joyce came in, can you tell us what happened?" Then Stevie Lynd told the story of when Joyce ran into the bar and into the bathroom with her shirt neckline pulled to the side and Joyce holding her bra together because it had been broken. Stevie told us that Richard had followed Joyce inside the front door and she could tell he was really mad, but that he left. She told us that she'd offered to stay with Joyce and she didn't feel good about leaving her alone there.

"She was really shook up! Joyce's skin was red where Richard grabbed her. Joyce had a safety pin in her purse that she gave to me to fix her bra for her. When I left, Richard was gone."

"This exhibit entered into evidence is a black bra with a safety pin on it in a plastic bag. Do you recognize it as the bra Joyce was wearing that night?" Russell asked Stevie.

Stevie took the plastic bag and examined it. She began to cry when she answered that it was one and the same. Russell stated that the bra was found on the body of Joyce Ann Handcock, the single article of clothing she was wearing when her body was found in the Gila Gravity Canal strapped down to weights.

CHAPTER 42

During a conversation with a friend of both of my daughters, I mentioned this book and the local history. Marc is a recent re-plant, as are so many in Yuma these days. He mentioned the trial to his brother who had lived in Yuma for several years and his brother knew who Ruby Vasquez was and that she had testified in the Handcock case. It turned out that Ruby stayed with a friend occasionally who lived just across the street from Marc.

Shortly thereafter, Marc had a long talk with Ruby and she told him that she is still distraught over losing her "best friend" and that she knew "that Richard killed Joyce." Ruby said that her life was permanently altered because of Joyce's murder. Ruby also gave Marc a scrapbook to give to me to help me in this endeavor. It had newspaper articles about the incident, some I didn't already have from when Richard was first arrested, and pictures of Joyce. (My husband had cut out the news articles and saved them for me during the trial.) The scrapbook itself was ultra-feminine and made by Joyce. It was padded with paisley fabric and trimmed with lace and ribbons.

Keeping what Marc had learned from Ruby in mind, her testimony during the trial is particularly confusing. During one of the times that the jury was out, it is mentioned that Ruby spent twenty to twenty-five minutes talking to the private detective who was working for the Handcock attorneys just before she testified. The private detective was the good-looking man who sat behind defense council during the trial. I can speculate that he may have influenced her testimony or that she was threatened by someone else like some of the other witnesses were, as I later discovered.

Assistant County Attorney Russell called Ruby Vasquez to the stand. After she was sworn in, she stated that she was thirty years old, divorced, and had two kids. She stated that she first met Joyce in 1993 at P.J.'s and that later she met Richard there. She said she asked Joyce if she was happy that she was getting married and was concerned because she'd only known Richard for such a short period of time. Joyce conveyed to her that she knew what she was doing. A couple of times Richard dropped Joyce off at work and she was crying and that had been before the wedding, she was quite sure. Ruby said she asked Joyce if she knew anything about Richard and Joyce had said no. Ruby said she was Joyce's friend until the day she disappeared.

"Can you tell us about Joyce and Richard's on-and-off-again relationship?" Russell asked.

"Joyce was always upset when Richard would leave. One time Richard dropped Joyce off at our house just for the afternoon and never returned for weeks or a month! It seemed like months," Ruby told us.

"So you're saying that the marriage wasn't going well."

"I never got any information that the marriage wasn't going well," Ruby said, acting curiously obtuse.

"Did Joyce ever tell you that Richard had cancer?" Russell tried again.

"Yes, she said she wanted to do everything she could do to help him in his last days."

"Did Richard limit Joyce to associating with only certain people?"

"Yes. He didn't want her around certain people. That's why she quit P.J.'s. He told her that I was the only one that he would approve of her being around."

"One day, she told me she was going to give me a lot of her clothes. She told me that Richard said she didn't need to be so greedy and to clean out her closet."

Russell observed, "You and Joyce were pretty close friends."

"She never told me anything really personal, but when she was with him she was happy. She'd cry when he was gone." Ruby crossed her arms.

"Richard was a jealous man, wouldn't you say so?"

"No, I really don't know him to be jealous."

"Ruby, did Richard's appearance change during the time you

knew him?"

"When Richard came back, when he said he had cancer, he lifted his shirt to show me and Jeff that his chest hair was gone and his head was bald, but you could see that he shaved his head. He used to dress in nice shirts and slacks, but a few weeks before Joyce disappeared, he dressed in camouflage every time I saw him; like a jumpsuit like guys wear when they go hunting." Even though I was reserving judgment, that last comment sent a little chill up my spine.

Ruby told us about the incident when Richard came over with the tape recorder and that he said he had heard Joyce having sex with some other man in their bed and that she and Jeff didn't believe it, but that Richard was absolutely convinced of it. She said the night before Joyce vanished she got a ride from Red and Leigh over to Joyce's trailer after the bar closed to drop off some *drugs*.

Judge Hale stopped Ruby immediately and advised her of right to remain silent and that she could invoke her Fifth Amendment right. He asked Ruby if she wanted to continue answering at that time and she said no, but that she could answer questions that didn't implicate her.

"Anyway, I was there to drop something off and I had a booze buzz and Joyce was in her bathrobe. She came outside and she looked so tired. I didn't want to get her into trouble with Richard or cause an argument. I asked her if she was okay. She said she was, and that was the last time I ever saw her."

"Did Joyce ever say anything to you about renewing her wedding vows with Richard?"

"I don't remember her ever saying anything about it."

"Did Joyce ever have any of her jewelry missing?"

"Joyce told me some of her jewelry was stolen out of her house. She said Richard had pawned or sold it probably to the owner of P.J.'s. She said later that the only things worth anything that was left, she was wearing during the burglary. The real gold earrings, and her wedding band."

"Since you were the only friend Richard approved of, did Richard call you looking for Joyce after she disappeared?" Steve Russell inquired.

"He asked if I had seen Joyce the day after she disappeared. But he called me at Mike Deere's house, so he wasn't expecting me to be there. I was between residences. He never called me specifically."

Dusty Wheelwright began her cross-examination of Ruby with a lot of discrepancies to work with.

"Now, Ruby, isn't it true then that Richard would have no way of knowing where you were to ask you where Joyce was?"

"Yes."

"The last time you saw Joyce she wasn't unhappy, correct?"

"Correct."

"Didn't you come inside the trailer?"

"No. She came outside. She kept telling me to be quiet because I had a buzz on and I kept forgetting to be quiet."

"Did Joyce ask for help or say that she was afraid of Richard?"

"No."

"Did she ask for a ride or look unusual?"

"She just looked tired and she didn't ask for a ride."

Ms. Wheelwright asked, "Now, Ruby, you say that you were the only friend that Richard approved of, yet when you visited with Joyce, Richard wasn't around and you rarely went to her trailer, isn't that true?"

"True."

"You were approved of, but you were *not* her best friend. Is that right?"

"Right."

"Then who would be her best friend?"

"Maybe Mike Deere?" Ruby speculated. I stole a quick at Richard at the defense counsel table, and he looked impassive throughout.

Ruby continued to tell us about the time Richard came home to the house after he left and Joyce begged him to stay and Joyce held onto his legs while he dragged her to his truck and she was crying and he refused to stay. Ruby said that Joyce loved Richard, and later when he came back to her trailer, she had written on the outside of it, "I love you, Richard!" Joyce had been depressed while Richard was gone. She also told us about the time Joyce had to file charges against Richard for assault at least once.

At this point, Judge Hale called for lunch recess, but for counsel to stay in the absence of the jury. Ruby Vasquez was still seated in the witness seat.

Judge Hale said, "With the exception of Richard and Joyce, all the other

MURDER BY GRAVITY?

witnesses should be referred to as Mr. or Mrs. And Ruby Vasquez is now married to Jeff Dupree and shall by referred to as Mrs. Dupree. Years of experience have tended to show it's usually females referred to by their first names; men are referred to as Mr. It is suggested that it is condescending toward women. So please be more professional."

(On a personal note, yours truly voted for Judge Hale for re-election.)

Also while the jury was out, Assistant County Attorney Russell wanted to bring up a subject regarding the immunity of Mrs. Dupree. After she invoked the Fifth Amendment, both prosecutors wanted to explain her immunity defense to her and that she had a right to counsel, but it would not be appropriate for them to discuss it with her unless she initiated contact with the state.

Russell explained that Mrs. Dupree is willing to testify under a grant of immunity, as is her husband, Jeff Dupree.

"I will file *The Use and Derivative Use Immunity* petition with the court. There will be four or five other witnesses for the state that will have similar potential problems with testifying."

Judge Hale said, "I am concerned about setting precedence here and perhaps not having the authority."

Russell added, "In the matter of methamphetamine, Mrs. Dupree was present at a number of places because of drug deals. Mr. Millington, will you agree that immunity is in the best interest of justice?"

All were in agreement that everything was in the best interest of justice.

"Granted, as long as someone doesn't confess to murder so the immunity is limited to drugs," Hale stated.

Millington stated that Phil Seward may be called and it would involve a charge of a possible attempted rape and he would be taking the Fifth Amendment. Judge Hale tells him to wait and see. He also advises Ruby, "They cannot charge you because that would be derivative use. The jury will be notified of the immunity use."

Russell said that they would go over the testimony again on re-direct.

Ms. Wheelwright objected to the open of re-direct, but they agreed to limit it to drugs only.

Judge Hale further admonished Ruby that she could be prosecuted for perjury, false swearing, or contempt or failing to answer.

After lunch, the judge advised us of the immunity of the witness and future witnesses on the subject of drugs and we were instructed to draw no inferences from the witnesses who invoke.

ACA Russell again asked Ruby about the last night she saw Joyce.

Ruby said, "I asked Red and Leigh to take me to Joyce's. I told Red that I was going to pick up flowers from Joyce. Joyce had asked me earlier for some meth; a quarter gram of crystal. And I did bring flowers, too."

The judge interrupted, "I have a question for the camera person. Is that camera positioned so it doesn't film any jurors?"

The camera man from Yuma's local CBS affiliate replied, "Yes, your Honor." He and the various reporters had become constant fixtures in the courtroom.

"Please continue."

"Red and Leigh stayed in the car. Joyce and I went to a flower shed next to the trailer and she kept shushing me because Nickie was sleeping. I asked if it was okay for me to be there because I didn't want to start a fight. It was 2:30 AM when Joyce said, 'Thanks and good night.'"

"So Red Pollock didn't know about the meth?"

"That's correct."

Wheelwright got a chance to continue her cross-exam.

"So, you were doing Joyce a favor?"

"Yes."

"You didn't usually sell it?"

"No, I just did her a favor a couple of times."

"Did you ever know if Joyce stayed with Mike Deere?"

"Yeah, once she put her things in storage and stayed with him a week or so."

Ruby told us about Joyce's dumpster diving and how they went together at night and Joyce taught her how to make floral arrangements and crafts and that Joyce was talented and people bought what she made as fast as she made them. She said they found baskets and she drove Jeff's car even if he said no. She said sometimes Joyce would borrow Mike's Jeep.

Dusty asked, "You saw Joyce do meth all the time, right?"

"Well, actually, I saw her take a couple of hits. It seemed to me that she did it very little. Sometimes Richard brought her over and they'd stay and party. He used meth too at first."

"Who asked you for the cement pylons?"

"Joyce said that Richard needed them to level their trailer. Jeff gave him a couple of them and some strapping for towing."

"Did Joyce ever tell you about her and Richard's sex life?" Dusty asked.

"She told me that he liked to ff-screw. One time he got arrested or pulled over and Richard had some pictures of Joyce naked. She was embarrassed because the officer gave the pictures back to her and the cop had them in his wallet!"

Dusty asked, "Do you remember in your taped interview with Detective Graham, the transcript reads, 'The worst part was she could never get satisfied. We talked about our fantasies and Richard's was a threesome. She loved him a lot and would do anything."

"How did Joyce act, as a bartender?"

"She was courteous and nice. From what I observed, she was *promiscuous* but she was flirting with customers and that's all I meant by that."

"Did Joyce know another Jeff besides your husband, Mrs. Dupree?"

"Yes. Before she met Richard, she had a boyfriend named Jeff Warren, who was an ex-Marine and he scared her. So she asked my Jeff to get her a gun. She'd had enough and wanted him to leave. He even busted the windshield of her car with her inside it! Or maybe it was because she was scared of being alone, I don't remember. It was for protection."

"Was Joyce scared to be alone or afraid of anyone besides Jeff?"

"Yeah! Joyce got a note in her mailbox and she was very, very afraid of Phil Seward."

"Did Joyce ever speak to you about making out wills because of Richard's cancer or renewing their vows?"

"Yeah! Joyce did talk about making out wills. She may have mentioned vows . . . I don't remember."

On re-cross by Russell, he asks, "Did Richard ever come over to your house that you shared with Mr. Dupree before you were married to use drugs?"

Ruby replied, "Several times."

"Mrs. Dupree, isn't it true, and I don't mean to upset you, that you don't like testifying?"

"It's true."

"You had a lot of tragedies personally hit you at the time Joyce disappeared. You lost some loved ones and it makes testifying difficult."

Wheelwright objects and was over ruled.

"Thank you, Mrs. Dupree. There will be no further questions at this time."

CHAPTER 43

Josh Schulmire called Ron Gene to the stand for the State of Arizona. Ron stated that he had lived in Yuma since 1936 and was self-employed. Ron was old-school Yuma and more of a country man versus a city man such as Yuma has become. He stated that he owned Swift Sales, a heavy-equipment and salvage dealership on Arizona Avenue.

"I know Richard because he was referred by another carpenter for some carpentry work I was doing years ago. The work was heavy-timber construction which includes things bigger than 2" X 4" and even 8" X 10". This is work like bridge builders do. If you don't have a crane, it can involve heavy lifting."

Josh says with a laugh, "So you wouldn't hire Mr. Russell or me for the job?"

"Probably not," laughs Ron, visibly feeling more at ease.

"Now, you and Richard had a barter agreement in May of 1994. Richard needed a place to stay and a job and he asked you about working something out, is that correct?"

"That's right. I thought he was divorced or single. I let him stay in a trailer on Araby in exchange for fixing it up. By mid-summer I found out that he was staying with his wife in a motel because the trailer was too hot because it had no air-conditioning."

"Is that when you offered to let them stay in a trailer with air at the salvage yard in exchange for fixing it up?"

"Yes and that was when I met Joyce."

"Can you describe the salvage yard for us?" Schulmire requested.

"It's a lot 80' by 800' like a storage and equipment lot; I have an office that's about 150' from the street. Richard still worked on the Araby trailer, but was working on the lot too."

"Did you see Joyce Handcock very often, Mr. Gene?"

"Well, yeah."

"Did Joyce and Richard get along?" Schulmire asked.

"She came in to use the phone and was crying a number of times. Richard would see her at the office and then complain to me that they were having problems. I overheard arguing 100' away also numerous times. Joyce would cry on someone's shoulder or mine. She frequently left on a bike. Once she came back with a car and loaded it and left. But she came back eventually. You could hear her voice when she was pissed off! A lot of yelling about moving out. I guess that qualifies for not getting along, Mr. Schulmire. Sometimes we saw her at the chain-link fence and she'd be hanging on and just crying. Joyce talked on the phone to her sister and she tried to comfort her."

"Did you ever see Joyce sleep outside in the lot?"

"Sometimes Joyce slept outside in a chair when Richard locked her out at least on three occasions. She'd come into the office in the morning and her language was rough and derogatory about Richard."

"On October 4, 1994 did you have occasion to ask Richard and Joyce to leave?" Josh asked.

"But I don't think I really had to. He was quite upset. There was an investigation. After the authorities brought him back, I wanted to talk to him, but he didn't want to talk with me. He turned around and said, 'No!' and went out to the trailer house. He was back there about fifteen or twenty minutes and some people came by my office because there was a fire. I came to see what they were talking about because a lot of noise was coming from back there. It sounded like a wrecking crew! Several of us walked back to see."

Ron Gene continued, "Joyce and Richard were taking everything of theirs and packing it into his camper and moving out. Richard got violent with me when I approached him to ask what was going on. Here's Richard *stuffing* this camper and it was full, and he couldn't get it all in. And if it wouldn't fit in, Richard tore it up, broke it and threw it on the ground. Then he had this big hammer and he began beating the stuff. He was hysterical! And he had a big knife and slashed the seats that he'd taken out of his own camper because there wasn't room for them. Whether it was his or just in his way, he was violent! We decided to stay about twenty-five feet away from him during all of this. We were all amazed! I've seen people upset before, but nothing like this."

Schulmire brought out some evidence from the crime scene and asked Ron to examine it all. "Have you seen any of this stuff before?"

"Yeah, the nylon strap and wire tubing is from my salvage lot, and was about twenty-five to thirty feet from Richard's trailer."

"Now you said in your taped interview that you had seen Mike Deere drive by in his beige Jeep many times and Richard became anxious, correct?"

"Yes. I also saw Joyce driving it."

"Did Joyce dress modestly?" Schulmire asked.

"Yes, most of the time, but in the summer she wore a bikini. I had to tell her not to wear it because it was distracting my workers."

"The wire that was on the body seems stiffer than the wire that Richard carried on his tool belt. Do you have different types on your lot?"

"Oh, yes. 95% of my salvage is bought from government surplus and I re-sell it. My wire is on pallets or boxes. They come in pieces and in rolls."

"Nothing further."

Millington cleared his throat and looked up at Ron Gene. "What kind of wire is this and do you cut it to length for people?"

"This is #18 wire that has been cut with some loops on the end. We will cut to lengths by the foot, but we don't have much call for this bigger stuff. I haven't bought any in six years."

Millington, clearly set on digging his hole deeper said, "I suppose somebody could probably buy this type of wire all over town if they wanted to," Millington scratched his head.

Mr. Gene said, "No, sir. I'm the only place in Yuma County that carries it."

I would like to interject here that Yuma's nearest city is an hour away, with nothing but desert in between. I'm no expert, but even I've heard that you don't ask a question in court unless you already know the answer to it. Again I searched for any sign of *anything* on the faces of defense's council and co-council. Nothing! And they say jury faces are hard to read.

* * *

The State called Officer Rolland De La Bree who stated that he was thirty-two years old and had four years experience before being hired by the Yuma Police Department for eleven months before responding to the "delayed kidnapping" on December 7, 1994. He explained that it's called a delayed kidnapping because it already occurred. He assumed it was Handcock that called it in and he responded around midnight.

"Mr. Handcock was sitting in his truck across the street from the mobile home park where he was residing. His head was down to the side with a towel wrapped around it. As I approached, Mr. Handcock fell out of the truck, but stayed on his feet. Richard said he didn't need any medical attention and he was covered up, so I couldn't see."

"All of a sudden, he pulls his shirt up and drops his pants! Then I saw a number of linear deep gouges or lacerations, with scratches on his chest, arms, legs, and back. He seemed intoxicated and his speech was not clear."

"He said he was in his storage locker on 24th Street getting stuff to put up for a yard sale. While he was sorting, he heard a voice that he recognized but didn't seem threatening, so he continued and started to load up his truck. Then all of a sudden he was struck on the right or left side of his head and knocked out and fell to the ground. When he regained consciousness, he was in the back of a truck with his arms and legs bound behind him and was stripped down to his boxer shorts," Officer De La Bree continued to read from his extensive notes.

"He said two Hispanic men dragged him out of the back of the pick up and threw him down to the ground and started whipping him with a wire rope. (They had his truck there and another truck and transferred him, I was told later.) Mr. Handcock indicated that they never said why they did this. Then all of a sudden, Handcock got one of his hands free and grabbed a stick lying next to him and fended them off. He untied himself and got in his truck and drove back to Yuma. He did not explain how he had the key and no clothes."

"Mr. Handcock had no other details, which seemed odd, but said the truck was a 1970s Ford, dark color, and he didn't know the attackers' names. Then they began to chase him. This occurred out by the Cocopah Indian Reservation. He claimed they shot three times

MURDER BY GRAVITY?

at him but there was no evidence on his truck. Then he went to The Dark Place to tell his wife about what happened and she convinced him to get clothed and phone the police."

"It was then that Mr. Handcock informed me that he had cancer and was going through chemo. All of a sudden he balls up into a standing fetal position. My supervisor arrived and we went to put a blanket on him and he jumps up and yells, 'Don't f---ing touch me!' and, 'Stay away.' My supervisor took him to Behavioral Services after that," De La Bree finished his report and was excused.

Detective Jack Moer, the supervisor, was called to the stand next and stated that he was in the Yuma Police Department for fifteen years.

"After Behavioral Services released Mr. Handcock because it was their opinion that he was *not* dangerous, I took him to the station," Moer said while shaking his head.

"Mr. Handcock speculated that the two men who attacked him were from Swift Sales where he used to work. Handcock said that the owner and him had some possible litigation coming up and they were trying to intimidate him. So then I had him remove his shirt and pants and took several pictures of his lacerations."

Russell asked, "Are these those pictures that I'm showing you now?"

Moer looked them over and answered affirmatively.

Russell showed the pictures to the bench and asked for permission to show them to the jury. It was pretty obvious to me, anyway, as the pictures made their way around one by one, that from the pictures of his back, the scratch marks were in the directions that one would make if they were self-inflicted. There were none in the center because he wasn't very agile. The scratches on the arms and legs were all completely vertical; on the front, sides, and back. None were overlapping. There were hundreds of deep scratches. On the chest the marks were a little more random and there were two or three hesitation marks in the center. It was a curious thing to look at. It was difficult not to be repulsed.

Moer told the same story as that of Officer De La Bree, but had more to add.

"I told Mr. Handcock after I saw the injuries that they were not consistent with someone else whipping him as he described; that I did not believe he was being truthful with me and that people often make false reports to the police department when they have family problems. It was then that Mr. Handcock admitted that he did it to himself because he was hoping to get his wife's attention, since they weren't getting along very well. He thought that maybe she'd feel sorry for him. Mr. Handcock told me that unless things changed he was afraid he was going to lose his wife. He also told me that he was undergoing chemotherapy and his cancer was causing trouble at home. Mr. Handcock said he used a large nail to inflict the wounds and he never mentioned having any pain or discomfort, which I thought was strange. Mr. Handcock said he had *not* been hit in the head, but that he had slipped in the blood and fell while getting back in the truck . . . he hit his head on the ground."

Russell asked, "Did he admit anything after that?"

"I was walking a fine line, trying not to offend Richard, but I needed to get the whole truth because there could be people arrested if he lied. He admitted he lied about Swift Sales and showed no remorse at all; he seemed to think it was an appropriate response and an appropriate way to keep his wife."

CHAPTER 44

The next morning before jury convened, I had a dilemma that I wasn't quite sure how to handle. My husband had told me after the news the night before that CBS had shown my face and those of some of the other jurors on television, which is a big no-no. I was incensed that they could be that sloppy! I thought, as had the judge on the previous day, that the camera looked as though the lens was trained on the jury as well, even though the operator had denied it and then somehow it got by editing and was aired. I, in the number seven position, was closest to the camera. The morning before I left home, some neighbors told me that they saw me on television as I left for court. Of course, I didn't see it; I wasn't allowed to watch that part of the news! I felt that my privacy had been violated.

When I was seated before the judge arrived I wrote a note and sent it to my right toward the bailiff. Judge Hale stated that he received a note from a juror whose husband had seen jurors' profiles on the news. (I was miffed that the judge had even given away my gender.) The bailiff also informed him that she had been told informally by other jurors that their families mentioned the news incident as well.

"It is a direct violation of the court's orders regarding media coverage. The news station will be excluded from the courtroom and today's proceedings. If it happens again, you will be excluded from the remainder of the trial. The note will be received and filed, but the juror's name will be blacked out." A slap on the wrist, I thought. But my name was blacked out in the transcripts.

"I'd also like to make it known that these witnesses are allowed to remain in the court room during proceedings: Lori Perron, Bill Perron, and Ed Martinez, Jr. as pursuant to the Victim's Bill of Rights."

I had wondered if some of those people in the gallery were Joyce's relatives, now I wondered which ones they were. I would have to wait a little longer to find out.

The State called Marcy Montgomery to the stand. Marcy stated that she was thirty-two years old and had been living in Yuma for the last twelve years.

Russell forgot himself for a minute, "Marcy, uh, may I call you Marcy or would you prefer Mrs. Montgtomery?"

Even I was surprised when she said, "I'd prefer Mrs. Montgomery."

Red faced, Russell continues, "Were you a bartender at The Dark in 1994 and was Joyce a friend of yours?"

"I worked there two nights a week and Joyce was a co-worker. We really didn't have a relationship. I just knew who she was, but we never had conversations. She was a very nice person. She gave me a box of Christmas decorations when mine didn't make it back in time from Japan. She just said, 'Here, you can have them.' I worked her shift when she came up missing in January."

"Did you ever see the defendant in the bar, Mrs. Montgomery?"

"He brought her in a couple of times. I didn't feel comfortable leaving her there with him. He was just *glaring*. It was eerie and I was intimidated by him. Sometimes he would stare at the customers. Finally, Joyce told me he was Richard. Joyce wouldn't talk to any of the customers if he was there."

"Did you ever see milk crates at The Dark Place before?"

"Yes . . . oh, my God!" Marcy began to cry as she realized what the prosecutor was leading to. "The crates disappeared just before Joyce did! She said she needed them and took them home."

"Nothing further," Russell stated.

Dusty Wheelwright stood with all her girth and stature and dark discolorations under her un-made-up eyes and face and pounced on the wee Marcy Montgomery.

"Isn't it true that when you were first interviewed you weren't emotional; that in fact, you were laughing and joking at times during the interview?"

"That was when we were talking about Joyce's dumpster diving and arts and crafts. I've worked in a lot of bars and it's *very unusual* for somebody to stand in the doorway like Richard did and say nothing and glare at people."

In Russell's re-direct he asked if anybody left messages or a note on the bulletin board for Joyce and she said they had two or three times.

"Do you know who Danny Brooks is?"

"I don't think so."

"Why did you start to cry a little while ago?"

"Well, it's a lot different talking with a few people in a small office than testifying in court and I had been waiting for days to do it so the stress built up. This is a formal setting with a microphone and jurors watching. I didn't want to cry and make a fool of myself! Also, I just realized that one of the milk crates that were in The Dark could be one that was used to weigh her body down in the water! I read about it in the newspaper!"

* * *

Steve Russell stood and called Rachel Hammer to the stand. A sweet-looking and surprisingly statuesque, elderly lady in a prim blue suit was escorted inside and up to the witness stand where she was sworn in. Rachel stated that she retired from nursing just a few years earlier and that she was a neighbor of the Handcocks.'

"I was a registered nurse for thirty-seven years and I was helping to take care of Joyce's father after he had his bypass surgery. I lived in the park for nine years and knew Joyce. I never actually met Richard, but I knew who he was."

"Did Joyce ever tell you that Richard said he had cancer?"

"She did. The first time she said colon cancer. Then I asked her if he had any abdominal scars because they couldn't make the diagnosis without making incisions. Joyce told me later that he didn't have such scars and that then he said it was cancer of the stomach. And another time she said it was cancer of the bladder. I got the feeling that gradually Joyce was convincing herself that Richard did not have cancer at all."

"Later, Joyce told me that Richard had received his first chemo treatment in Tucson and had already lost all of his hair. She said it looked like he shaved his head. It was a statement with a smirk and a chuckle. She seriously doubted the cancer story."

Russell stood and rubbed his palms together as he paced slowly, "Now, do you live next door to the Handcocks?"

"No, I live across the park from them. If I'm standing in my kitchen, I can see between RV's and see their space. Also, I walk around the park once a day and they have to walk by my house to get to the laundry facility which is next door to me."

"Have you ever been inside their trailer?"

"Yes, Joyce showed it to me when she was redecorating it. She was wonderfully inventive and talented. That was before Richard returned, of course."

Millington began to cross-exam by asking, "Mrs. Hammer, do you know Mike Deere?"

"I know him by name only. I've seen Joyce drive his beige Jeep around with the roll bar. I've never seen him. That was in the day time only; never at night.

"But how well could you really see anything over there when you are fifty-seven spaces away and in January the park was full?"

"Like I told you; I'm not fifty-seven spaces away, I'm directly across the park from them. The day Joyce disappeared I saw Richard doing laundry The laundry facility is right next door to my house. And I was eating my lunch, which I do between twelve o'clock and one o'clock. I never saw Richard do the laundry often and when he did before, it wasn't in the day time. That day he walked by with a full laundry basket."

Russell's re-direct, he asked again if Rachel was absolutely certain that she saw Richard doing laundry between twelve and one on the day Joyce disappeared. Rachel looked him dead in the eye and said she sure was.

* * *

Josh Schulmire called Luis Figuroa to the stand for the State. He took the oath and testified that he is a Yuma Police assistant and had worked there two and a half years. Luis states that Richard Handcock contacted him on Thursday, January 12, 1995. As he consulted his notes, Russell told him to put down his report and that he wanted him to answer from memory! I thought that was asking a lot since the report came in nearly two years earlier. Nevertheless, Figuroa managed to press on, I assumed that he must have read his notes before coming into court.

Figuroa explained that there is some delay between the time when a person calls in until he actually gets back to them to take a full report. He tried to call Richard three times and he wasn't home. One of the questions he asked Richard was if they were having marital problems.

"I told him that if they're just separating, it's not unusual and eventually the reporting party will hear from other friends or family that their spouse is okay. He said they weren't having problems. In fact, he told me that they were supposed to get remarried that same month. I asked him if they owned a vehicle and he said, 'No.' And I told him that I needed an accurate description, which he gave to me. He also told me that she was last seen wearing black Levis', black boots, and a blue jacket. He said he had last seen her at 0745 hours the same day. Handcock said he'd tried to find her and he didn't mention if she worked or if she might be with anyone else."

"Thank you," Schulmire said.

Millington brought his eyes forward from his detective sitting behind him. "How many missing person's reports have you taken in the last two and a half years?"

"About thirty. There are other people beside me who take them. I also report theft, fraud, etc."

"You are *not* a certified police officer?"

"Correct."

"My detective has supplied me with the transcript of the conversation you had with Richard that day. You said, 'Is she driving a car right now?' and Richard answered, 'No, she doesn't have a car.'

"If the report says they don't own a vehicle, it is possible it's incorrect. I don't save my original notes," Figuroa concedes.

Millington continued from his transcript, "The next time was still on Thursday, January 12, 1995 at 1435 hours, or 2:35 P.M. Richard called and asked if you'd found her yet and was told no. He called again on Friday, January 13, 1995, to see if there was anything reported yet. And you told him, 'If we find anything we'll let *you* know. So we're not flooded with phone calls. He also told you then that he was going to look for his wife again, because he'd just been told that no one in the Police Department was even looking for

Joyce. Isn't that right?"

"If we see the person, we'll stop and talk to them, but we don't try to track people down! If Richard had told me about her friends or relatives, cops would have checked it out at the time, given they had the time. An 'Attempt to Locate' was put in, but not actively seeking. *The only priority for what an officer pays attention is if someone comes into the police department they will be helped sooner than a phone call.*"

"Is it possible that when Richard gave you Joyce's description that it was an honest mistake?"

"Sometimes people give the wrong information about the characteristics. People get nervous and make errors."

"Since Richard was told to only call if he had any new information to add, are you surprised that he didn't call back?"

"No."

"What did you do with the report you took that day?"

"I put it on Detective David St. Jons's desk."

Schulmire stood and asked one question for re-direct: "Isn't it true that if a person came into the station, they would probably bring a picture of the missing person with them and wouldn't be able to give an inaccurate description as easily as over the phone?"

"That would be true," Figuroa said nodding his head.

CHAPTER 45

Steve Russell called Edward Martinez to the stand for the State. This was a name we recognized from previous testimony and he stood up from the gallery to be sworn in. Ed stated that he was thirty-seven years old and had lived in Yuma his whole life and was Joyce's ex-husband. To me, he resembled the actor Eric Estrada, who played Ponch from the old television show, C.H.I.P.S. Ed was much more attractive than Richard, clearly.

"We were married for four years and have two children, Ed, Jr. and Nichole Ann. At the time of Joyce's disappearance, I had custody of Ed, Jr. and Joyce had custody of Nickie," Ed stated.

"Did you see your daughter regularly?"

"Yes, I had Nickie for the weekend every six weeks," Ed responded.

"Now, let me back up a bit. Did you ever meet Richard Handcock?"

"No, but we knew who each other was."

"How did you find out about Joyce's disappearance?" Russell prompted.

"Joyce's sister, Lynn, called me three days after she disappeared to see if I knew where she was."

"During the nine days following Joyce's disappearance, before her body was found, did Richard phone you to see if you knew where she might be?"

"No."

"And would he have your phone number?"

"Yes, of course."

"Now, during the time Richard returned, oh, let's say, October 1994 to January 1995, did Nickie ever come over to your house when she wasn't supposed to come over?"

"Yes, often. And sometimes she got in trouble for it. Sometimes Richard dropped her off or picked her up. As far as I was concerned, she was welcome all the time."

"Did you ever visit Joyce's trailer?"

"No, never."

Ed was not cross-examined and he was admonished as were all the other witnesses not to discuss the case.

* * *

Joshua Schulmire called Edward Martinez, Junior, to the stand for the State. Ed, Jr., stated that he is Joyce's son who was at the time of the trial barely fifteen years old and lived with his dad at the time of his mother's disappearance.

When Schulmire questioned him about his visits with his mother he said, "I would come over to visit at my grandparents and my mother and sister would come over to their house. I was there a lot, but sometimes not for a whole week. I only went to my mom's trailer like twice. I met Richard like every time I was at my grandparents or at the first house my mom lived in with him after the marriage."

"When did you find out about your mother's disappearance?"

"Three days later; when my dad did from my Aunt Lynn. The last time I saw my mom was before Christmas," he said sadly.

"Did Richard ever ask you if you knew where she was?"

"No, he didn't."

Millington stood to cross examine, "Can you describe your relationship with Richard?"

"I helped him clean up around the house they had; moving shelves, washing dishes. He asked me to do it when my mother wasn't there and I was spending the night. We didn't do it together."

"How many times did you sleep at your mother's house after she married Richard?"

"Four or five times and only once when my mom wasn't there. He didn't spend much time with me. That was when they had the house. I was only in the trailer for ten or fifteen minutes." Not exactly the warm and fuzzy picture Millington was trying for, I'm sure.

CHAPTER 46

Assistant County Attorney Russell called William Perron from the gallery to the stand to be sworn in. Again, a face we had seen daily and only now realized he was Joyce's step-father. He stated that he goes by the name of "Bill" and was sixty-three years old and had been in Yuma since 1974. He spent two years in the Marine Corps Air Station in Yuma. And that after twenty-five years in the military, he was a Master Gunnery Sergeant, retired.

When Bill Perron retired, he began selling life insurance until he retired again after fifteen years in 1990. Since then, he began his own computer software company and has a strong work ethic. He stated that he thinks work is an important part of life and he can't understand people who don't agree.

Russell asked Bill if Richard had ever complained to him about Joyce flirting on the job.

"Affirmative. He told me that she did it and he didn't like it. I told Richard that since he'd worked in construction before, that maybe he should do it again so that Joyce could quit working at the bar and he could afford to take care of his family. Joyce quit working there shortly after that."

"Were you also employed part-time by the RV park where you live?" Russell asked.

"Affirmative. I was the summer manager. At one point Joyce asked me if they could put a cab-over camper to live in permanently in the park. They were about 120 feet away from our park model."

"Richard had a one-ton pickup truck with a camper attached. I found out later that at some time that they'd been living at Swift Sales; a *junk yard* in a trailer. We agreed not to butt in if they moved into the RV park."

"One day Joyce called about three o'clock and asked if Richard was at our house. She said he was having problems with the truck and was out by the Cocopah Casino and she hadn't heard from him. When she called again at seven o'clock, I went looking for him and couldn't find him. Then when I came back, he was there with the camper off the truck and loading boxes in the back of it. We told him that Joyce was waiting for him to pick her up at Ruby's and he never did. He just left her for like three weeks."

"While he was gone Joyce traded her car for the trailer. It was a real mess! I couldn't believe it, but she said, 'Dad, it's *mine.*' She fixed it all up. It had a leaky roof and a broken window. She had to take all the trash out before she could fix it up . . . it even had a dead cat in it. She wouldn't let me help her."

"Eventually, Richard called her and told her that he had cancer and said he was coming back home to her. I saw that she had written, 'I love you, Richard' on the side of their trailer in anticipation of his return and I asked her why she was going back with him and she said, 'Dad, he's dying of cancer. He's my husband. I can't just leave him.'"

"She said the reason he had left was because he was going to be sick and spitting up blood and he didn't want her to see him like that. That's why he went by himself to therapy. Later on I found out that Richard had to go back to Tucson for treatment and at the time they were having problems with the truck, so I offered to help or give him a ride. This was a few days before Joyce's disappearance. Richard said he may have to spend a week or two there and that he might already have transportation. He said his mother or a friend might take him. He tried to talk me out of helping him. After Joyce disappeared, Richard told me that he'd cancelled his treatment."

"Did you think that was odd behavior?" Russell asked him.

"Affirmative. Richard said that he didn't know what hospital it was at because the doctor booked it. Joyce could never get the name of a doctor from him. She never knew who was paying the bills either. She never got any bills in the mail. Richard never asked us for any money for doctors."

"Were you in town on Wednesday, the day Joyce vanished?"

"Yes, that morning, I drove my granddaughter to school somewhere between 7:15 and 7:30 in the morning and then I had errands to do. When I returned around 8:30, Richard's truck was there, *backed in* and under the awning next to the trailer. The big padlock was on outside, so I figured they must be over at the manager's, because they were supposed to talk to her about cleaning up the rest of the area and give her money for rent. They still had paint cans, bricks, milk crates, metal boxes, and a tool box lying out there and it made the park look dumpy. The campground owner was still not happy with their progress. Joyce used to paint crafts out there and she used the blocks and milk crates to prop stuff up."

"Was there a point at which you noticed that Joyce should have been home and wasn't?" Russell asked him.

"Affirmative. Joyce would take her shower at 4:00 PM and stop by to say hello to us and then get dressed for work after. So when she didn't come by, I went over and asked Richard and Nichole if they'd seen Joyce and they said they hadn't. Richard said she might be at the storage locker. They each had one. I suggested we go look for her and Richard said he couldn't because he was on monitor."

"Later, we decided to call The Dark to see if Joyce was there and then they started to get worried too. Lori and I drove to both storage lockers and no Joyce. We went back to The Dark and she still wasn't there. Richard sounded like he couldn't get any more time off his monitor to look for Joyce, so I kept asking him to file a missing person report. Richard just acted like Joyce wasn't there and life would go on. He wasn't concerned. So we got after him to make 'missing' flyers and asked him if he had a picture for it and he said he did and he made some copies. The flyers had Joyce and Nickie together! We told him that he couldn't do that to Nickie. So he took black Magic Marker and took Nickie out of the picture. We kept looking for the flyers and Richard said he didn't have enough money to make more than six copies, so we gave him some money. After that, we looked everywhere locally and still didn't see any flyers."

"On the next day, we had Nickie leave Richard and move to Joyce's sister's since he had all the problems with the kidnapping. He also had somebody set fire to his truck later on, plus the burglaries prior. We believed that whoever was after Richard could have Joyce too. We didn't mention it to Richard because we didn't want him to think it was his fault. Richard never told anyone but the cops that it was fraud. The whole family believed Richard until later in the investigation."

"On Friday, Richard said that he received time away to go look for Joyce, so Lori and I went out of town. I was scheduled to judge an Elks ritual program and had already made the commitment. We had a cell phone and kept in touch with Lynn. Lori stayed in the hotel room the whole time and called eight or nine times. We came back on Sunday from Lake Havasu early and told them we had personal problems and just left."

"When we got back we saw Joyce's description in the newspaper and saw that it was all wrong and just couldn't believe it! Lori was visibly upset . . . she was mad as a hornet. You could have passed Joyce on the street with Richard's description and not recognized her. Joyce was 5 feet 4 inches, and Richard said she was 5 feet 8 inches! We both went over to Richard's and he said that the Yuma Daily Sun got it from the cops and the cops got it wrong."

"Up until Joyce's body was found, we kept asking Richard if he'd heard anything and he'd say, 'Yeah.' He'd heard that she was seen at a bar on 8th Street with some biker, but he didn't check it out because of his monitor. He'd say, 'That person told my mother or my aunt, it wasn't first-hand.' Then another time he told us that she'd been seen at The Dark Place with a biker. And another time he told me he heard she was living in an apartment on Virginia with some individuals. That was just around the corner, so I said that I'd check on it and what was the name of the person she was living with? He said, 'Frank or Jason or something.' Lori kept calling Joyce's friends and people we know. Nobody could believe that Joyce would leave Nickie without instructions on where to go. *Everyone knew something was wrong,* but we couldn't prove it. Richard never accepted our assistance. He said he'd make phone calls and get the guy's last name. It just felt to me like Richard's attitude was 'she's gone and that's it.'"

"When we saw the Yuma Police Department cars around Richard's trailer, we went over there and Detectives St. Jons and Graham wouldn't let me come in. They told me that they recovered the body and they were charging my son-in-law with the murder of his wife. They said they were pretty sure about the I.D. Graham asked Lori about identifying marks. They asked us to come and identify facial pictures."

When Millington began his cross-examination, he asked Bill about all of Joyce's old boyfriends, going back to Jeff Warren before

Richard. He asked about Joyce's relationship with Mike Deere and Bill said they were friends. He also asked how many people had access to the cinder blocks near Joyce's trailer.

"Well, they were part of an old wall there; I suppose several people could have gotten back there."

"And what about the cement pylons, Mr. Perron?"

"I gave them to her to hold down the awning down."

"Did you know that Joyce used drugs?"

"I knew that she did in the past, but I was surprised that she was while she was at the trailer. Lori and Joyce kept a lot from me because of my health. But I know that Joyce *never* left for a day without letting someone know."

Russell asked Bill Perron when Mike Deere came over to see Joyce.

"He only came by when Richard moved out."

"Would a casual observer know all that stuff was under the Handcocks' trailer?"

"No, the fence obscured it. You would have to know it was there to see all of that. You'd have to dig that stuff out from under the trailer to find it."

"What would happen if Joyce hadn't made arrangements for Nickie's care in her absence?"

"Ed Martinez would have immediately been down to the court filing an order trying to get custody of Nickie. They'd had custody battles because they each wanted both of the kids. Joyce wanted to keep her daughter and would have done nothing to give Ed a chance." Mr. Perron seemed to have temporarily forgotten that his step-daughter was using illegal drugs.

* * *

Josh Schulmire then called a young woman to the stand, who stated that she had known Joyce for four years and met her when she worked for her mother, who was the owner of P. J.'s Tavern and met Richard when he went to work there.

Schulmire addressed the young woman who looked obviously pouty. "I understand that you are a reluctant witness for the State. Is that correct?"

"Yes," Ellie replied quietly.

"Will you please tell the jury what happened in roughly September of 1994 when Richard Handcock came to your door?"

"My mom said Richard was a nice guy when I met him. Richard needed a place to stay and I let him crash at my house. He said that he and Joyce were having problems and he needed to get away for a while. He didn't say what problems. He just stayed for a week and he was only a friend."

"And how long had you known him?"

"A couple of months."

"Did you know if Joyce and Richard did crystal methamphetamine?"

"Yes. They snorted or smoked it; both of them."

"How many times did you see them do that?"

"More than ten times. I'd see Richard do it in the bar while Joyce was working."

"Did Richard watch Joyce? Did you see a change in her behavior?"

"He watched her, but I didn't see a change in her behavior."

Schulmire tried again, "Do you remember in February telling Detective Graham that you observed Richard jealous and brooding?"

"Yeah."

"Was Richard ever acting sick at your house? Did he have a good appetite?"

"Yeah, he ate everything I cooked!"

"Did he ever tell you that he had cancer?"

"No, he never mentioned it and he never looked ill to me."

Bill Millington asked on cross-exam if Joyce had talked to her during the time Richard was at her house.

The young woman's voice changed. She said, "Joyce came to me crying because she couldn't find Richard and she was worried because she loved him. I told her that he was at my house and not to worry. The next thing I know, I get a phone call at work from a neighbor telling me that Joyce is at my front door pounding on it and yelling for Richard to come out! After that, I never saw Joyce and Richard together again. Later in September, I think, Joyce called me and said she was relieved to know that Richard was at my house."

MURDER BY GRAVITY?

"In your opinion, was Joyce a flirt at work?" Millington asked her.

"A good bartender knows how to make a customer feel welcome and pleasant. It's good for business. I'm a bartender too. Joyce was flirtatious with customers as part of the job. Bartenders know how to read people."

"And how did you read Richard Handcock?"

"I read Richard as jealous, but he never did anything *overt* about it."

Schulmire asked her if there was a difference between somebody sitting quietly in a bar and not looking jealous rather than how Richard acted and looked when he was in the bar with Joyce.

She said, "Richard's body language was different; he brooded."

CHAPTER 47

Steven Russell called Lori Perron to the stand from the gallery. After she was sworn in, she gave much the same background as her husband, but was thus far the only person who didn't have to give her age, which I deemed thoughtful. Lori said that Bill was the only dad that Joyce really ever had since he'd been her step-dad for so long. She told of meeting Richard first at the Christmas party at Lynn's apartment and that she was surprised that Joyce hadn't brought Jeff.

"Do you mean Jeff Dupre or Jeff Warren?" The prosecutor asked for definition.

"Oh, Jeff Warren. The two Jeffs are completely different. I had asked Joyce about Richard and why she broke up with Jeff and she said the Jeff thing was going nowhere and Richard brought her flowers and told her she was pretty and made her feel like she was the most important person in the world. Joyce said he was so romantic and that he wined and dined her and nobody had treated her that way for a year and a half. In the past, when I thought she'd found the right guy, she wasn't ready to get married. And then when she decided to get married; the guy wasn't ready. Richard brought her enough flowers for two men! I said, *'This sounds like an okay guy, maybe you ought to hang on to this one'.*"

"Around the middle of January, Joyce called and said she had something to tell me. When I asked her what, she said she was thinking of getting married. I asked to who! I hadn't heard any more about Richard since Christmas. So when she told me Richard, I was shocked because it was so sudden! Joyce's relationships always took much more time."

"So I asked her, 'What does he do? Does he work?' Joyce said he was still working as a bouncer with her and did maintenance and

MURDER BY GRAVITY?

carpentry. And I said that she hadn't known him long. She said what with working together, they'd gotten to know each other real well already. Then she told me that Richard was from a good family who had lived in Yuma forever and they were in construction."

"I had my husband's upcoming angioplasty on my mind a lot. I just asked her if she was sure. I couldn't believe it when she said that they wanted to plan the wedding for the following week. I told her that was no good. That was when her dad's angioplasty was taking place and we'd be out of town. I asked her where would they get married? Where would they live? Had they done blood tests?"

"I asked her why the rush and she said she was *afraid she would change her mind*. I told her that was why she should wait. She said she'd done that before and missed out. She was happy. He seemed like a nice fellow and she *liked* him a lot. They ended up scheduling it for the 25th of January. Three days before Bill's procedure. The angioplasty turned into a quadruple bypass. He was in the hospital a week."

"Do you think that Joyce *loved* Richard, Mrs. Perron?"

"Joyce was a happy newlywed; very much in love. They rented a three-bedroom house in a good neighborhood, with nice furniture. She was happy and we were pleased that this man took care of Joyce and cared so much about her."

"So, early in 1994 you believed that your daughter had done well for herself?"

"Very well. He was good to her."

"Did things change later on?" Mr. Russell asked.

"March was when I noticed the happy picture change. Bill was doing better and Richard wasn't as friendly as he had been. Then the tone of voice changed between Richard and Joyce and finally, I began noticing bruises on Joyce's legs. She'd say she ran into something at work. Then she'd get new ones and new excuses. In fact, there was hardly a time when there weren't bruises there of one degree or another; new and old. Then she didn't want to discuss it with me."

"By April it was far worse. They had lots of arguments and Richard rarely spoke to me. Richard got laid off because he got in a fight with one of his supervisors. One day Joyce was really nervous and upset but said she didn't have time to talk. She did say she didn't know where Richard was. She said that they had gotten into a fight and he didn't like her working as a bartender and she came home from work and he was gone. I found out a week later that he was still gone. Finally, Joyce told her boss that when it came to her husband or her job, her husband won and she quit working at P.J.'s. He wanted her to stay home and be a housewife and he came home and she did it. They seemed happy again for a while."

"What happened then?"

"Well, things started missing around the house. Joyce's jewelry; unless you were looking you wouldn't notice. It was small-item stuff. They had some break-ins. Nickie had fifty dollars of her baby-sitting money stolen and she blamed Richard. Joyce was mad and thought that was pretty low. Richard was the only one who could have taken it."

"Then Nickie and Ed, Jr., went to their aunt and uncle's in Phoenix for the summer and Joyce and Richard weren't working. From May until August, I know that Richard and Joyce weren't happy, but Joyce became resentful of my interference and she thought I was being too nosey and she could take care of herself. She knew how I felt about physical abuse because of my first husband and the way he treated me. Joyce and I always had a close relationship. I told her that Bill and I would help her, but she was determined to make the marriage work. Joyce didn't call me all summer and we worried about her. Lynn told me in August that Joyce and Richard were living at Swift Sales and that Richard had gone missing again and that there were more arguments about money or because Mike Deere would drive by. Richard locked my daughter outside all night."

"What was your daughter's relationship with Mike Deere?"

"He was a good friend. She depended on him for transportation and she'd clean his house and he'd pay her storage fees."

"How do you know that they were just good friends, Mrs. Perron?"

"Because I once asked Joyce about it. She said she just liked him; that he didn't, 'turn her on' which was a pretty defining ingredient for her."

"When did you hear from your daughter again?"

"When she wanted to move into our RV park from where they were staying at Mittry Lake. We had to come up with some money to help them out, but I was glad to have her close by again. But they were living in the camper over his pickup truck. It really shouldn't have been allowed in the park, but Bill let them. He put them far enough away that we wouldn't hear them fighting. We asked them to dinner every night because it was so cramped in there, but Richard kept refusing. He took the camper off and that's what they lived in! Joyce is a good cook, but he wouldn't eat much. That's when he told her that he had colon cancer, after living in the park for two weeks. He said he couldn't keep anything on his stomach and he'd eat a little and run next door to the empty lot and throw up. Joyce said he was using marijuana for the cancer and it wasn't helping. Shortly after that, Richard took Joyce to Ruby's house one day, came back and put the camper back on the truck, and he never came back to get Joyce. Joyce called the next day and said they hadn't been fighting, but he was gone for three weeks then."

Lori's accounting of the time frame in which Richard comes and goes and when his cancer began doesn't jibe with other witnesses, but the essence is the same. She said that she believed early on that Richard was being untruthful about having cancer and eventually she made a point of sharing her suspicions with her daughter. Lori said that Joyce became upset and looked away from her but later Joyce said that he looked healthy one day and Lori was sure that Joyce, too, was beginning to believe that Richard was lying about having cancer.

Even still, Joyce had called her once, very distressed about Richard being kidnapped by the men who worked at Swift Sales and that they had taken him out into the desert, whipped him, and shot at him, and she was afraid for the whole family. Joyce told her mother that Richard had been hurt and that they had called the police and Joyce believed that until the day she died.

"After Joyce didn't show up for work, right away I called Mike Deere, but Ruby answered. Neither one of them knew where she could be. We called Richard to see if he'd heard from her and when he said he didn't, we drove around all night looking for her. I had to go to work the next morning, but Bill talked to Richard two or three times. He said he was waiting for the police to get back to him. He just didn't seem as motivated as Bill and I were. Because of the kidnapping, we were afraid for Nickie too, but Richard said, 'Nickie is fine . . .' That wasn't good enough. So we took her to Lynn's. That was the first time we'd seen Richard show any emotion."

"We went to Joyce's post office box and there'd been no activity, but they said they'd keep an eye on it."

According to Lori, the trip that she and Bill took for the Elk's ritual was in Glendale, west of Phoenix, not in Lake Havasu. After she saw the description of Joyce in the paper, she called the police to make sure they got a correct one. She also made sure that they knew about the lump in Joyce's shoulder from a broken clavicle, the ear piercings, and that she'd had her tubes tied.

"Can you tell us how you know a man named Phil Seward, Mrs. Perron?"

"Phil's been a personal friend since 1982, a friendship which is now strained. I never spoke with him about the problems between him and Joyce. Joyce was upset, but it was an *emotional injury, not a physical one and it made Joyce mad as heck.*"

"Bill and I sold him a car before Joyce got married to Richard and Phil had been working on it. Eventually, he refurbished it and needed to get a license and needed the paperwork from us saying that it had not been on the road. He called to see if he could come over. If we had any thought that Phil had really harmed Joyce, we wouldn't have let him come to our house." The jury remembered Ruby's testimony that Joyce was afraid of Phil Seward.

It was Millington's turn to grill the witness at this point. I wasn't truly sure where Joyce's parents' stood regarding Richard. They were seemingly emotionless and just reporting the facts. But I'm sure they were doing their best to be that way.

"Wasn't Joyce due to appear for a deposition regarding felony charges against Phil Seward the Friday after she disappeared, Mrs. Perron?"

"I believe so, yes. But the charges against him were dropped due to *lack of evidence.*"

"Well, I should think so, since the primary witness against him was missing!"

"Objection!"

"Is there a question, Mr. Millington?" Hale asked.

"Did you know your daughter was using methamphetamine and other illegal drugs?"

"I knew she was using them occasionally, though Joyce didn't

MURDER BY GRAVITY?

tell me. But Joyce hung with Jeff and Ruby; *those type of people.* Joyce told me that Richard had been in prison, I knew that. I didn't know that Mike Deere ever supplied Joyce with drugs. Lynn says that Joyce used drugs recreationally for three or four years, maybe once or twice a month. But I certainly couldn't tell anything by Joyce's behavior."

Lori went on telling us that Joyce had been divorced from Ed for ten years before marrying Richard and that she'd been married to Ed twice. He asked her again several times since then to remarry him. At one point, they stayed with Ed's folks and shared the kids.

"*Nichole was living with Joyce when she met Richard.* Ed and Joyce had disagreements about custody and both had filed court papers about their ideas. There was a home study done and they felt that Joyce was not using drugs at the time because she *wanted* the kids. I had the impression that Joyce was using drugs in January when she married Richard, not by behavior, but by comments. If Ed knew, he would have taken steps to get custody of Nickie and there would have been *no visitation.* Ed remarried and had other kids that also live with him." Nickie wasn't living with Joyce until after the wedding. (But Lori conveniently forgot this and refused to discuss it with me during my telephone interview with her. The idea that Joyce married Richard to get custody of Nickie was a touchy subject.)

Millington said to her in court, "It sounds like you and your other daughter took good care of keeping track of Joyce."

"Yes, because we never knew if her husband was going to be there to do it."

(i.e.) I'd just like to interject my own thinking here that if Joyce couldn't take care of herself, as an equal adult, how could she possibly be responsible for a pre-teen daughter in her care?

"Mrs. Perron, what if Joyce was spending nights with Mike Deere and he was supplying your daughter with drugs?"

"Mr. Millington, my daughter was a real good-looking girl, okay? If she was going to stay with this guy, he was going to have to really impress her. Mike didn't. He was a friend. She didn't want to stay over there at night and spend a whole lot of time there because she was still concerned about her daughter. I already said I don't know if he supplied her with drugs."

"Okay. Joyce's trailer had two doors; one in the front in the living room, and one in the back in the bedroom, both on the same side. Is that right, Mrs. Perron?"

"Correct."

"So, when Richard's truck was there, you couldn't see in the doors."

After no response, Millington moved on to ask who made the arrangements with the medical examiner's office to have Joyce's body released and taken to the mortuary for cremation.

"We did. The family had a memorial service for Joyce *before* her body was released and cremated."

"So, it wasn't Richard that had her remains cremated, correct?"

"That's correct."

When Russell began his re-direct, he asked Lori what the charges were that Joyce filed against Phil Seward.

"In my age group, we call it 'grab-ass.' He was groping her and she did not like it. She came to me and said she wanted to do something about it. Seward never forced her to disrobe. The grope was all that happened or unwanted touching over the clothes."

Was this an effort to keep suspicion off of Seward, or a mother who couldn't believe that behind closed doors people might do things that their friends find distasteful and a breach of trust? Lori herself called her daughter a good-looking girl.

CHAPTER 48

Dr. Rolland Andrews was sworn in on a Monday morning and quite frankly, compared to some of our bar hounds, was very easy on the eyes; sturdily built, solidly alert, and oozing confidence. Andrews had a young, but accomplished, professional air about him. The County Attorney asked for his experience and education and Andrews began his pedigree by telling us that he was a forensic pathologist and assistant clinical pathology professor at the University of Arizona Medical School.

"We don't work out of the hospital at all to try to determine the cause of death in possible unnatural causes. Deaths that are violent in nature, such as homicide, suicide, accidental death, don't occur in hospitals, but occur out in the community from either violent or unknown causes. The prime method of determining why someone died is to perform an autopsy. I attended McGill University in Montreal, then five years of residency in pathology at the University of Arizona in Tucson. My fifth year was a forensic path fellowship. I served in the Marine Corps before college for four years. After my fifth year of residency, I began work training at The Forensic Science Center and am currently serving my third year."

Andrews was a Board Certified Pathologist and was to take his exam for the Forensic Pathology Board the following year. He explained that one must work as a forensic pathologist before becoming Board Certified. He estimated that he participated in fifteen hundred to eighteen hundred autopsies and assisted in twice that many. He stated that he did seven or eight autopsies a week and has served as an expert witness in sixty to seventy cases and he is a qualified expert in Yuma County.

"Joyce Handcock's autopsy was performed at The Forensic Science Center. I found the moderately decomposing body of a young woman was bound by wrists and ankles with two types of ligature materials. A ligature is something which generally wraps around a body part in order to either secure it or produce compression. Detectives St. Jons and Graham and two assistants were present."

"There were also three significant wounds to the right side of the victim's head from a blunt force trauma."

Andrews described the broad, ribbon-like fabric and thick wire ligatures and green plant-like material on her skin. He said the ligatures were complex ties around the wrists and ankles and were very tight. He said that Joyce couldn't possibly have done this to herself. He said there was no evidence on the skin surface because it was washed away. The autopsy photos were handed to the jury for inspection. Judge Hale asked that in no way should the photos "accidentally" be viewed by the spectators.

The photos weren't like in the movies or television. The bloating and marbling was real and awful. Some of her skin had slipped off during the cleaning process. I was glad her parents didn't have to see the pictures. I'll never forget how Joyce looked that day. The three lacerations to her head had been shaved and a close-up picture taken. Each of the lacerations was the same size and about the same distance apart; chevron-shaped. There was bruising around the whole area, but when the scalp was reflected back, I could see that, though the wound had been deep, it hadn't cracked or fractured her skull. My old nursing background told me that it was primarily a severe subdural hematoma (bad bruise) in addition to the lacerations. It probably bled like hell. Dr. Andrews said that it probably knocked her unconscious.

"These were not caused by being left in the water by rocks or debris. All of the lacerations have the same orientation, so random postmortem injuries are not a possibility. *These wounds were caused by three separate impacts to the left side of the head.* It's unlikely Joyce could have fallen to have three separate, but similar wounds clustered in the same area. These are *classic injuries* from a linear object, which most likely was intentionally done to the right side of her head. A blunt trauma of which origin the possibilities are too numerous to determine. Perhaps a piece of wood, brick, tire iron, would have to be fairly heavy and have some velocity behind it. The wounds are lacerations as opposed to cuts. Cuts are by a sharp object, like a knife, and have to have a smooth border. There were no abrasions or scrapes; it was a clean, blunt force. It was obviously murder. She had been in the water more than one to two days; rigor had come and gone. The canal water acted as a preservative so decomposition was slower."

"Joyce's organs were removed for further study. There was no laceration on her skull, but there had been significant bleeding within the temporal muscle. *Joyce was alive."*

Andrews continued, "To get this amount of hemorrhage certainly would imply there was blood actively pumping into the area of the scalp. The wound to her head did *not* cause her death. *There is a 50/50 chance that she became unconscious* with wounds such as this over the side of her head."

I held my breath and looked at Richard. I saw no trace of an, "Oh, shit!" moment there. He could have taken her to the hospital instead of the canal, if he thought she wasn't dead. *If* that was what he thought. Had he heard before that very moment that Joyce was alive when she was put in the canal? I couldn't tell by looking at him. *If* he were the one who did it. Maybe he knew she was alive and was afraid of going back to prison and that's why he didn't take her to the hospital. He thought that nobody would miss Joyce; she was a party girl. He was wrong.

Andrews was asked, "Wouldn't a layman know if she were alive or not?"

"Probably be seeing simple breathing or a heartbeat. But there is a real spectrum, you know *a person can be anywhere along the spectrum from completely alert and aware to a little bit foggy or almost intoxicated appearing, confused or unconscious. Normally, if someone is conscious, they would not allow themselves to be bound and attached to weights and we would have seen signs of a struggle around the wrists and ankles.* She was most likely to be unconscious when she was bound and I'd say 99% chance that those wounds alone did not cause her death."

"We also did toxicology reports, which are difficult to interpret on a victim who is as decomposed as this one was. There are disagreements among medical professionals because there are no controls to know the time of death. Some tissues and organs retain toxins at different rates. The brain can concentrate a drug over a long period of time."

"Joyce was using methamphetamine at 1311 nanograms per milliliter; pretty much the level you would find in the blood of someone who uses the drug recreationally. 95% of all people wouldn't die with this amount of the drug in them."

"Besides the wire and wrapping on Joyce, we also found her wedding ring still on her finger. The wire looked as though a tool might have been used to shape it and cut it. If the tool could be found to perhaps match it. Someone wanted to make sure she didn't get free. If she had become conscious, we would have seen some fresh wounds on her wrists. Based on all the findings including where she was found, *Joyce was drowned after being knocked out. Drowning is a diagnosis of exclusion. It's not this or that. Less that 5% of drownings are not due to water getting into the lungs causing anoxia or lack of oxygen, but due to trachea spasms called dry drowning. It doesn't allow water in. It takes three to four minutes to drown and the heart to stop.*"

Ms. Wheelwright stood to cross-examine the doctor and asked him again how many autopsies he'd performed. How the specimens are collected and that he was responsible for sending them to the crime lab. She then asked him why he hadn't sent or performed a possible rape kit for evidence.

Andrews explained that the time had degraded any possible evidence for that to happen.

Then Ms. Wheelwright asked if it weren't remotely possible that Joyce could have passed out from using too much methamphetamine and fallen and hit her head. (And tied herself up?) Andrews looked at her incredulously and so did we.

"How did you identify the victim as Joyce Ann Handcock?"

"There is no one way. We go to physical characteristics; i.e., brown hair, missing ten days, young, decomposing, time frame, fingerprints weren't good enough. Dental charts were unavailable, we did find the shoulder injury; a prior fracture for I.D."

"There is no way you would definitely be able to say if postmortem pictures were Joyce. An ADNA test request range put her death at five days to two weeks. The first death certificate is required when the body is released. The mortician needs a death certificate to take care of the body. The death certificate is filled out by ten to twelve different individuals. I only do my part."

There was a juror question read by Judge Hale: "Could the ligatures have been placed on the victim's wrists and ankles after death?"

Andrews responded, "That's a good question. I looked for major areas of hemorrhage in the ankles held by strapping fabric, and I did not see it. The wrists had deep furrows, due to the wire. I saw some hemorrhaging with my naked eye, but not much. Then sections under the microscope yielding a few red blood cells outside of some vessels."

"The process is not very helpful because, a) people can be alive and bound and receive no major injuries of hemorrhage or, b) if they are unconscious, one might not even suspect areas of hemorrhage, or c) she had a little bit but not much. Bleeding can occur even in postmortem bodies a little bit . . . probably not worth trying to figure out what it means. *She was alive because she drowned.*"

CHAPTER 49

Stephen Russell called Yuma County Sheriff's Department Detective Donna Graham to the stand and that was when the pretty blond who had been sitting at the prosecutor's table every day of the trial stood and walked to the witness stand to be sworn. Ms. Graham stated that she'd been with the Sheriff's Department since 1977, which was hard to believe, looking at her. She was quite feminine and looked younger, not toughened by the job. I was surprised that the Sheriff's Department did without her every day during the forecasted; and what was in fact, a five-week trial.

Detective Graham said she was dispatched to a "body found" call where she met Mr. Sayers who didn't seem to be withholding information. She described the divers having trouble finding the body and that she had to direct them to the site. Once the body was brought up, she began taking photos and checking the area. They found the fresh piece of wood in a fire pit where everything else had been burned. The wood had paint and grooves and they sent it to be fingerprinted, which made the wood slightly darker when they treated it for fingerprinting. She then testified that she put evidence tags on everything, but they'd been removed, but she recognized them. The tags were removed when they were given to the defense, she said. The body had no identification, but she remembered that a bartender was missing and contacted Yuma Police Department; which she described as her, "*sister* in law enforcement."

In State's evidence was a cinder block with country-blue paint in a semicircle, followed by strapping, wire, and a milk crate.

Graham said that she requested that the body be taken to Tucson for forensic examination for which she was present. She took more photos on a different camera and told Dr. Andrews about the circumstances in which the body was found. She observed the

MURDER BY GRAVITY?

earring holes on the body as Detective St. Jons had learned from the victim's mother and other forms of identification.

Graham and St. Jons began by splitting the investigation; St. Jons worked inside the Yuma City limits and Graham in the Yuma County jurisdiction. She assisted St. Jons when he executed the search warrant on Richard Handcock's residence on 28th Street.

"When we first arrived, outside was a lot of garbage; wood, paint cans, milk crates, speckles of paint, paint on the trailer, spray paint. Inside the trailer was a lot of clothing and a saw in the living room and other tools. It was unkempt. I took more photos and Richard's pickup was present. There was no noticeable blood in the trailer."

"I talked to Richard after the search and made a report. We advised him that a body was found and believed it to be Joyce's. We told him about the circumstances of the paint where Joyce was found and paint around his trailer and that we felt he had something to do with her disappearance. We asked him when the last time he had seen Joyce was and what was he doing that day. Richard seemed willing to talk. He answered coherently, rationally. We told him he was a suspect. He was not injured or intoxicated. I explained that he didn't have to talk to us, but he was still willing to. Our guns were holstered the whole time."

At this point, Millington asks for permission to voir dire the witness and Hale granted it. Millington asked Graham if she had advised Handcock of his Miranda rights and she told him that she did not, but that St. Jons did read said them to him.

Graham continued with her narrative. "Richard said the morning he had last seen Joyce, he woke up and Nichole had gone to have a shower and while she was gone, Joyce and he made love, then Nichole came back and talked to her mother and left for school at 7:30 or 7:45 AM and then he left to look for work at 8:00 AM. He said he had gone to the Foothills area said he had gone to the Foothills area but first went to a gas station on Pacific. Then he went on to the Foothills to look for work. He cited two places where he had gone and who he waited for but did not see and then he went to a bar where he saw his old girlfriend, Hazel Mess, at a place called The Bottoms Up Pub in the Foothills."

"Richard said he was at The Bottoms Up Pub between 10:00 and 10:30 to 11:00 to 11:30 AM Then he went home and Joyce was not there. So he went to a neighbor's house, "Cricket" and asked her if she'd seen Joyce and she said that she hadn't. Richard said that he returned home between 11:00 and 12:00 noon. He said he was surprised that Joyce wasn't there because they were planning to meet up at noon to go to the store and they were supposed to contact the manager of the park. After he talked to Cricket, he went to his in-law's park model, the Perrons', and asked if they had seen Joyce. He said he contacted the bar that evening to see if she'd gone to work and he said the last thing he saw her wearing was sweats."

"I then contacted Lori and asked if she had any kind of dental records of Joyce's. That turned out to be a dead end because Joyce had gone to Mexico to have her dental work done and they don't keep records there. Lori also told us about the shoulder scar and that Joyce's tubes were tied for identification purposes."

Russell asked, "Did you check on Richard's alibi?"

"Yes, I went to the two construction sites looking for the people he said he went to see. Nobody remembers seeing him that day. Richard's old girlfriend, Hazel, came in and we did a taped interview with her."

So what did Hazel say? Donna Graham didn't say because nobody asked her then. But what was driving everyone in the courtroom to distraction was the fact that Detective Graham had her legs crossed and her upper leg was bouncing her entire body up and down and she was chewing gum. Gosh, this did make it more difficult to take her seriously, but we were determined to focus as a jury . . . most of us.

"When Nichole came home that day she told us to investigate the state of the marriage and the use of illegal substances. She said when she came home that day her mother was missing, she found Richard in the bedroom and he had a hammer and he appeared to be doing something to the ceiling."

"What did you think he was doing?" Russell asked her.

"Objection; calls for speculation," Millington said.

"Sustained," Hale reasoned.

"Then what did you do?" Russell asked.

"We searched for the bedding based on Nichole's statement, and never found it. Sergeant Pijanoski, Yuma County Sheriff, in the Foothills said somebody had reported finding clothing in an area near a canal bank several miles from Joyce's body. Lori and Nichol said it wasn't Joyce's, though."

"Five to seven days after Joyce's body was found, I spoke to Mr. Kidd's at his apartment on Virginia Drive. On the front porch was a rubber boat or a float. Then I went to Mr. Mulissin's residence to obtain a boat. It was a silver, small aluminum boat. We searched Joyce's storage and found lots of craft items, clothing, furniture, and lamps. Richard's storage had strapping similar to that found on Joyce. The ends were cut."

"And did you send any of the strapping off to be tested?" Russell asked.

"I don't remember sending it off. It wasn't in the report."

Millington requested a voir dire again, citing that Detective Graham could only recognize the bag of strapping tape, not the tag she put on it, because it was gone.

There was a discussion at the bench after which Detective Graham could only say that the strapping tape was only similar to that found on Joyce. That tape which was photographed by the medical examiner.

Millington questions the chain of evidence. Though there are no tags, there were marks on strapping, none made by her, and she identified it as the evidence with the ends cut in a sealed bag. She identified the bag under oath. Graham agrees there are lots of rolls of bags at the Sheriff's evidence locker and *that anyone could use them*. She had brought this one over from the evidence room and it had been inside the milk crate.

"I went to Swift Sales to speak with Ron Gene because I knew that Richard and Joyce had lived there. This nylon strapping tape was laid 15 to 20 feet from the trailer they lived in and there were two pieces with the ends cut. There was also wire similar to that which was used on Joyce in a big spool and laying around all over dirty and rusty; in the area where the Handcocks' lived."

Russell asked, "Did you do any further interviews?"

"I interviewed Nickie, Mr. Kidd, Hazel Mess, Mr. and Mrs. Perron, Lynn White, and Joyce's brother, who's name is also Richard. We had blood drawn for DNA tests requested from Lori, Nickie, Ed, Jr., which were all obtained by the DPS crime lab to identify Joyce beyond a doubt. I also spoke to Mike Deere at length and asked for other contacts and looked for other boats that Richard might have used."

"We also went to the Yuma County Detention Facility and talked with a Mr. Marsano Cordon who reportedly had information regarding what he may have overheard Richard talking about. I also spoke with Richard's mother."

Graham told us about Richard's mother calling Detective St. Jons to come get Richard's things out of her house because she was moving and that was when they found the two small pieces of pressed plywood that looked like those found at the gravity canal. It was then the outer square, frame-like piece of wood was exhibited to the jury followed by the piece that had been cut out of the inside of the frame that had been left at the crime scene. Though the outer piece was a little darker because it had been processed for fingerprints, there was no doubt after seeing the grain and the flecks of country-blue paint on the inner piece, that they had once been part of the same piece of plywood before the frame had been cut. The inner piece found at Richard's mother's house and the outer piece found at the crime scene definitely put Richard Handcock at the location where his wife's body was found. It was very compelling evidence indeed.

We were excused and admonished not to talk about the case for the evening. Counsel remained behind and discussed how much they would let in from the future witnesses from the electronic monitoring devices company. An earlier judge had ruled that it be unrestricted. Hale wanted to check further and therefore put off the employee's testimony.

The next morning, Detective Donna Graham returned to the stand. Gone were the gum and the bouncing leg. Someone must have tipped her off.

Russell asked, "Would you please tell us where your investigation took you next?"

"I spoke with Richard's mother about him having cancer and about his previous relationships and jealousy over Joyce. She seemed truthful and answered fully. Then we received a call from a woman who said that she heard that the lady bartender had been put in a torture chamber in somebody's house and it had something to do with the occult. The injuries did not match up with Joyce, but the caller did not seem like she was trying to mislead the investigation. I also spoke with Susan Shotz, Richard's ex, and the people who lived across the street from the Handcocks. Then I spoke to Mr. Cody Hatch, an investigator for the Naval Intelligence Service to see if he had any aerial photos of the canal for a certain date and he didn't. I spoke to the people at the mine to see if Mike Deere had an alibi for the date Joyce came up missing."

"I also went to the places Richard said he went to during the five hours his electronic monitor said that he was away that morning Joyce came up missing and my total travel time was twenty-five to thirty minutes."

"I have no further questions, Your Honor," Steve Russell finished.

Bill Millington seemed to come out of his own world and asked Donna Graham, "What hours were Richard Handcock gone that day?"

"The monitor says 7:45 AM to 12:45 PM"

"Are you aware that a witness puts Richard doing laundry at noon?"

She was non-responsive. (Actually, the witness said she saw him when she ate her lunch between 12:00 and 1:00 PM. If he picked up his laundry in his house at noon, the electronic monitor would have noted him there earlier, unless he kept his laundry outside.)

"When you were retracing Richard's steps on January 11, 1995, how long did it take you to get from one job site to another?"

"Five to seven minutes."

"Isn't it true that if you took surface streets it would have taken longer?"

"Another ten minutes tops."

"You did it in November, in January there would be more traffic from tourists."

"It wouldn't take five hours."

Millington asks her to lay the groundwork of how she found the body and how they pulled Joyce's body out of the canal.

"What did you do then?"

"I took a lot of pictures and we searched the area."

"That sounds good. Where are the pictures?"

"None of them came out. They were all black."

"I see. And how long did you search?" Millington asked, his voice dripping with sarcasm.

"About an hour. It got dark then. We used flash lights, but we couldn't find anything more than what we already found in the fire ring and the pink glob that was probably fish guts that we bagged."

"So did you send out the glob for testing?"

"I don't think anyone bothered to send it in."

"Did you come back in the morning to search?"

"We had a deputy, a sergeant, and a detective come out a couple of months later to search the area," Detective Graham said without looking embarrassed at all.

Millington was enjoying himself. He asked, "What did Richard say when you came and told him that the body was Joyce?"

"He started crying and said, 'Oh no, not Joyce!'"

"What does your report say that Richard told you she was wearing?"

"Dark pants and black boots; not sweats. *I admit that I made some mistakes!* Richard was arrested that afternoon."

"Richard told you about Joyce dumpster diving and the person who went with her might be involved with illegal drugs, right?"

"That would be correct."

"After Richard's arrest and the autopsy, you had occasion to speak with Lori Perron, Joyce's mother, several times, yes?"

"Yes."

"Did you ask Lori if Joyce had an old boyfriend who abused her?"

"I don't remember."

"Doesn't it seem that it would have been a good idea to ask the mother if there could have been a physical altercation with an old boyfriend?" Millington quizzed her.

"Probably, yes," Graham said, not looking too smart.

"But you didn't even bother to ask who?"

"I may have. I don't recall."

"Wouldn't it be in your police report?"

"Sometimes, yes. Sometimes I forget things."

"Like the names of suspects," Millington loved digging at her further with good reason.

"No."

"If there's not a name in here, you didn't get a name?"

"If there's not a name, I didn't think they were suspects."

"Lori mentioned that Joyce had gotten her shoulder dislocated?"

"Yes."

"That was when she was having this altercation with an old boyfriend, right?

"Yes."

"Your main reason for being there was to learn of identification marks Joyce had, correct?"

"Yes," Graham struggled for her footing. She shifted often in her seat.

"You weren't concerned with who else might be a suspect?"

"I would always be concerned."

"Did you find rebar at Richard's trailer?"

"I don't know. St. Jons may have been notified. It was a joint investigation."

Millington continued, "There were several YPD at the search and from the Sheriff. Have you reviewed all the evidence found?"

"Not all of it, no. Only what I had."

"Like what?"

"Things out of the storage locker, the wood. I didn't take anything from the trailer."

"So you and Detective St. Jons haven't compared notes to see what kind of evidence each has?"

"No, I'm sure if it was significant we would have told each other."

"On January 21st you reported interviewing Richard at YPD and you advised him that he was the last person to see Joyce alive. But according to your report you did not speak to other residents to find out if anyone had seen Joyce leave or someone come over. You just thought YPD did it. Your report says that none of the residents had seen her, but that's what they told *Richard!* Isn't that true?"

"I suppose."

"Now when you spoke with Nichole, she told you that Richard had a hammer or some tool to fix something high up on the wall. She even mentioned a shelf, not the ceiling. She also told you that she didn't recognize the cement pylon or cinder block from around the trailer. She mentioned Joyce using silver paint, not blue. You also started looking for evidence that Richard had access to a boat and you even seized one that belonged to Richard's cousin. Is that right?"

"Yes."

"And you discovered that it hadn't been moved in a long time. Then you found the piece of wood at Richard's mother's house in the front of her property, isn't that correct?"

"Correct."

"He wasn't trying to conceal it. Then you found out that Mike Deere delivered the blue paint to Joyce, but you did not go to his place to take samples, did you?"

"No, we didn't. I hadn't heard that until the trial started."

"Now you had two conversations with the witness that told you about the occult torture of the lady bartender and she told you that the Naval Intelligence Service was investigating Gary Cox because he refused a urinalysis test. And Detective St. Jons was given this information by yet another witness. Both witnesses said that this happened to Joyce because she was supposed to testify against this person in a sexual assault case that was coming to court soon. Both witnesses said Gary Cox was the one who did this to Joyce because she was taking someone else to court and neither you nor Detective St. Jons thought it was important enough to investigate Gary Cox. Why was that?"

"I reviewed the *Yuma Daily Sun* articles and found that charges against Seward were *dismissed because a key witness failed to show up. I didn't go to Seward to find out where he might have been on the day Joyce disappeared.* I was aware that Seward would lose his realtor's license if convicted of a felony and we did not search his home to look for blue paint." Oh, my God! As a fellow blond, I was sorely embarrassed by this woman.

Millington consulted his notes, I thought stalling purposely letting us absorb the Seward detail. He then asked Graham if there were some occasions when she noticed some evidence missing from their locker.

"Yes, recently we lost the picture of the strapping tape, but it showed up again."

"And what else did you lose?"

MURDER BY GRAVITY?

"The victim's purse and a denim bag with personal papers in it and her personal notebook are missing. Nickie told me the affidavit submitted to the judge for the warrant was in Joyce's purse. Even though Mike Deere was paying for Joyce's storage, we don't believe he had access to it."

"Did you read everything you found?"

"No."

"Would an AIDS testing card be something that might pique your interest?"

"No."

"Did you seize an answering machine?"

"No."

"If you seized evidence, it would be in the Sheriff's evidence locker?"

"Yes, if it pertained to this case."

"So, if there were an answering machine in that locker along with other evidence in this case, you would have seized it?"

"Yes."

"But you don't recall?"

"No."

"As soon as Joyce was properly identified, you went to lock up and told Richard it was Joyce's body, correct?"

"Yes."

"And what did he say?"

"He started crying and then turned and walked away. So after I determined that he didn't have any questions, I quickly turned and left too."

"How many times did you speak with Mike Deere?"

"Two or three."

"And where did you meet with him?"

"Once at his home and twice in the Yuma County Detention Facility."

"How many murder investigations have you been involved in, Detective Graham?"

"Twelve or fifteen."

"Was there any evidence in the boat you took as evidence?"

"No. St. Jons did a luminol test with a black light sometime in 1996 and it was negative. I haven't been trained for that test. I do know there was no blood found."

"So it was impounded for quite a while! No further questions, Detective."

Stephen Russell began his re-direct by asking Graham if Richard ever mentioned being stuck in traffic the morning his wife disappeared and she said he absolutely didn't. She said that he never said he used Highway 80 to get to the Foothills either as opposed to the freeway.

"Why didn't you go back to the crime scene to search the day after the body was found?"

"We had search warrants and interviews and didn't have time. Also, we had to wait to borrow an underwater metal detector."

"The DPS chemists would not appreciate you sending them any old item to analyze," Russell prompted. "What do you think happened to the film in the cameras?"

"It's common for photos not to come out and officers have problems with pictures just like everybody else. There are a number of things that can go wrong."

Sitting on the end of the front row of the jury box, next to two steps above the spectators, it was difficult to keep a non-judgmental face when she said that. I could see a couple of shots not turning out, but two different cameras, two different rolls of film, with two different people taking the shots? That was really tough to buy. I looked at the spectators and they looked back. I put my best jury face on. I was reserving judgment for the end of the trial, even if I thought Detective Donna Graham blew it. Maybe Detective St. Jons would be better, I reasoned.

"About the altercation Joyce had with her old boyfriend . . .?"

"It was over a year earlier and Joyce injured herself when she grabbed onto a truck."

"Why do you think that Richard didn't bother to hide anything at his mother's?"

"He never told us he had anything there. His mother called us!"

"Was there another reason that you were so quick to leave after you told Richard that the body was his dead wife?" Russell asked.

"Yeah, because I felt his crying was phony and it made me sick."

"When you tested Richard's trailer for blood, even though the bedding was missing and lots of stuff was at his mom's. The test was negative. How do you account for that?"

"A lot of cleaning was done before Joyce's body was found and we never found any of the bedding."

To the best of my knowledge here is that a lot of cleaning can be done, but getting all the blood or traces are nearly impossible even if one uses bleach; there's usually something the human eye doesn't see that will show up, according to the television shows my husband and I watch and consider ourselves amateur sleuths of sorts. I also have read all the medical examiner crime novels, etc. I'm no expert, to be sure, but somewhat educated. I confess, I also researched extensively on many subjects for this book. If Joyce were struck *three* times, there should have been cast off splatters on the ceiling as well as the walls. It would have made a mess and not just on the bedding.

One juror submitted three questions that couldn't be answered at that time because the judge said that they were objectionable for one reason or another. He did say they would be answered later at some point. My curiosity was piqued but I didn't see who turned in the question!

CHAPTER 50

Josh Schulmire of the Yuma County Prosecutor's Office, who had been sitting second chair, called Nichole Martinez to the stand. After being sworn, Nichole reported that she was a freshman in high school and Joyce Handcock was her mother. Nichole seemed very composed and between her father's Hispanic olive complexion and dark hair and her mother's features, she was a very beautiful girl. Incredibly, Nickie tells us that she never met Richard before her mother married him! She stated that after the wedding, she lived with her mother and Richard most of the time during the following twelve months.

"Miss Martinez, did you ever hear any arguments or fighting between Richard and your mother?"

"Yes, the last three months especially. They fought approximately every other day. I would go outside or to my grandparents' house when they were fighting."

"What did they fight about?"

"I overheard that Richard was mad at my mom because he thought she was too friendly with the guys at the bar and my mom was yelling about some woman calling the bar asking for him and that her name was Hazel. Mostly it was Richard being jealous."

"Did you ever see a physical fight between them?"

"No, but I saw a lot of bruises on Mom's arms and legs. She always made an effort not to get bruised up so she could wear pretty dresses."

"Did Richard ever tell you that he had cancer?"

"Richard said he had cancer and he went away a couple of weeks for therapy and came back with his head shaved. I mean, I thought he looked bald, not shaved, but I never saw any clumps of hair falling out or anything," Nichole said, trying to touch bases.

"Did you ever see any green strapping tape at the trailer or paint?" Schulmire quizzed.

"Yes, I saw the tape in the shed behind the trailer and Mom used to paint crafts outside against a crate or a chair."

"Nichole, please tell us about the day your mother came up missing," Schulmire asked gently.

"The day she disappeared, I woke up at 5:30 and showered and got ready for school. I asked my mom for a hairbrush and then I did my hair and left at 7:15. All I saw was Mom's arm from the upper bicep down. I didn't see any clothing but the bed sheet and blanket were on her."

"After I came home from school that day, I noticed that the sheets and blanket were gone. Richard was walking out with them and said he was going to wash them. I came home later at 5:00 and asked Richard where Mom was and he said she was gone. Normally, she would have started getting ready for work at 4:30 or 5:00. She always dressed nice and took her time getting ready. My mom never went to work without first coming home to get ready. She had to be at work by 6:00. I was really surprised that she wasn't there. At no point that evening did Richard ever make an effort to locate Mom. I went to Grandma's and asked if they knew where Mom was and I told them that I had to baby sit for Jeff and Ruby's kids at 9:30 and I was there until after midnight. Jeff drove me back home."

Schulmire sat on his table and crossed his ankles. He asked about the following day and Nickie told us that Richard never looked for her mother and that night she went to live with her Aunt Lynn because her grandparents didn't want her there alone with Richard.

"On Friday, the 13th, a neighbor in the RV park asked if I could spend the night and I was told, 'No.' I was really mad because I wanted to be nearby because I kept thinking that Mom would be home soon."

"Nothing further."

Defense strategy had Dusty Wheelwright cross-examine the poor child.

"You met with Detectives St. Jons and Graham several times at their office and at your grandma's house for thirty or forty minutes at a time, right?"

"Yes," said Nickie, looking confused at Schulmire.

"You also spoke to County Attorney Schulmire today at lunch. Didn't you usually speak with them when no one else was there?"

"Y-yes," she answered.

"And how many times were you interviewed by them?"

"Five or six times."

"Didn't you spend at least two and a half months with your aunt in Phoenix in the summer of 1994?"

"Oh, yeah."

Nickie told us that Mike Deere brought Joyce home from dumpster diving early in the morning, in the dark after she was married to Richard. She said Joyce had dated Kirby and Sparky and that somebody had broke out her windshield and she didn't know who. She said that Joyce was always trying to quiet Richard down during their fights and sometimes they fought about Mike Deere, but never about drugs.

"Do you remember telling Detective Graham that Richard was working on a shelf in the bedroom?"

"I don't remember saying that or him doing that."

"What were your mother and Richard doing when you came back from the showers the day your mother disappeared?" Wheelwright asked.

"Richard was in bed, but sitting on the edge and Mom was sleeping."

"You don't remember telling Detective Graham that Richard called your mother's work around 6:00 PM asking if she came in?"

"No."

On the re-direct Josh Schulmire asked, "Did anybody tell you what to say during your testimony or were you threatened?"

"You just said, 'Just tell what you remember.' My grandparents didn't tell me what to say either. They just said to tell the truth."

* * *

County Prosecutor Russell called Dale "Red" Pollock to the stand where he was sworn in. Mr. Pollock told us that he was forty-eight years old and that he had been living in Costa Rica for the previous five months and that he was a retired Yuma Police lieutenant after being on the force for twenty-five years. When he retired he'd been a lieutenant for eight to nine years and that he had been in third place from the top of the chain of command. Pollock stated that he had not been subpoenaed to come to court, but he received a call from his daughter just that previous Wednesday and *she was the only one in Yuma who knew where he was living.* He said he retired to Costa Rica because it was cheaper to live there and that he only needed twenty years in to retire, but he didn't retire for another five years after that. Red said he was married for twenty-six years and had two kids. His divorce had become final in January 1994, but he didn't want the divorce. He had been devastated by it. He dated for ten months before retiring.

He told us that in the summer of 1994 he met Leigh Gerard, who had been in a bad marriage, was young, poor, and using drugs. Red told us that Leigh wanted to get away from the drug scene, so she stayed in his second bedroom at his house with the agreement that she would not use drugs or bring drugs inside his house. He said that after her departure, he was pretty sure she was still using them.

Leigh Gerard introduced him to Ruby Vasquez, barkeeper. This was his story, not necessarily *the* story. Red said he took earned time off from work for a month before he retired; around December 1994.

"Ruby came to stay with Leigh and me at my house. Actually, she spent about half her time there and the other half with Mike Deere. I began a sexual relationship with Leigh Anne two or three weeks after she moved in, but it was not exclusive. I had sex with Ruby the first night she came to live with me. It wasn't long-term and we both knew it. At 11:00 to 11:30 PM we used to go to last call at the bars and the girls said they wanted me to meet Joyce at The Dark Place. Ruby introduced me to Joyce and the night before Joyce disappeared, we took craft stuff over to Joyce's. I waited three to five minutes *alone* in the car and I never met Richard. At that time, my two women were okay with our love triangle, but then jealousies developed, Leigh Anne moved out and Ruby moved in full-time. Then in February 1995, Ruby and I moved to Las Vegas. I was never involved in Joyce's investigation, but Detective St. Jons asked about my visit to her trailer that night. *I had been the watch commander at the time."*

Nobody asked the question: Didn't Red think it was weird to take craft materials to somebody's trailer at 1:30 in the morning? Most people would have waited until the next day. Or is that just my take on things? Also, after living and working in Yuma for twenty-five years, why didn't Red want anyone other than his daughter to know where he was at? I thought that was fishy to be sure.

Red continued, "In February I was security at the Mirage Casino. By June or July, Ruby and I argued and split up. I drove her back to Yuma and left her at her boyfriend's. That would be Jeff Dupre's house."

"I suspected Ruby was into drugs because of her friends, but I never asked her. In January, she told me it was crystal meth and she wanted to quit. In Vegas, Ruby was drinking more and said she needed to get drugs and was antsy. I told her, 'No, I won't get them for you.' She also had a gambling problem and I'd let her use my credit cards. When I came back to Yuma in August, I was having financial problems and got work managing Mansky's (a local bar) to supplement my retirement. I had to file for bankruptcy. Ruby and Jeff and Mike Deere are all into drugs so I didn't hang with them."

"Did you ever report any of these people to the authorities?" Russell asked.

"My *intuition* told me that Jeff's house was a place the cops should be watching or investigating. Mike Deere was afraid to talk to me."

"Do you know who killed Joyce Handcock?"

"I don't know."

Russell sat back down and Millington took his cue, "Did Leigh Anne stay with Mike Deere too?"

"Yes, but it was okay with me if she was home or Jeff's or Mike's. She was twenty-four years old."

"Why did you leave Yuma?"

"I told you; cheaper to live in Costa Rica. But I stayed in Yuma for something to clear in my bankruptcy before leaving."

"How were the reports on your performance at work before you retired?"

"In '94, because of my divorce, I got a bad performance report at work. Actually it read that I had not met their expectations and that there was possibly a personal problem," Red now was able to say casually.

"Mr. Pollock," asked Millington with a sparkle in his eye, "isn't it true that these girls are not the kind that you would bring home to your mother?" Millington was now smiling.

Red blushed, "No, sir, not the kind I'd bring home to my mother."

CHAPTER 51

Josh Schulmire called Ike Groves to the stand for the prosecution and he was sworn in. Groves graced us with his rich Texas accent and said that he had been working at Yuma Pre-trial Services for two years.

"Can you explain what your job entails, Mr. Groves?" Schulmire probed.

"Yes, I gather information for the judges to help them make release determinations and to supervise persons under our care. There are four levels; one, two, three, and four. Level four is the electronic monitor, which is the *most restrictive*. Level one is the least."

"In January 1995, I was supervising Richard Handcock in an unrelated case (drug, spousal abuse, and speeding). The defendant wore a little transmitter around his ankle and there's a unit attached to the phone and it is always looking for the transmitter. When the unit cannot find the transmitter, it will send out a signal through the phone line to our monitoring center that the person is away from the phone or away from where they're supposed to be and we'll get what we call an alarm away."

"It is house arrest. If the person is out for any reason other than what is authorized, we'll be notified. I've worked with up to five hundred individuals. I make notes regularly and report aberrations from their release conditions to the judges."

A juror question was read, "If a person leaves the trailer, would an alarm go off?"

Groves answered, "It depends on if the door is closed or not, if the microwave is on or a TV or radio equipment on. It depends on if it's in a house or a trailer. Sometimes a person can't even go through their entire house due to rebar and the signal won't pass through it. If they re-enter, but do not get close enough to the machine, it will register as continually away."

"What can you tell us about Richard's schedule?"

"According to my notes, on January 6th, '95, Richard was allowed out from 12:00 AM to 2:00 AM the nights his wife worked because she didn't drive and she was worried that someone was stalking her. As of December 9th, his schedule was Monday through Saturday, 11:00 AM to 7:00 PM and 11:00 PM to 2 AM, then Sunday 8:00 AM to 2:00 PM for church. Once he set up the schedule, he didn't need permission to leave during the allotted time for the correct purpose. If he went shopping and not to work, he would need to inform me; it's required. On the other hand, unless he was caught, he could be just about *anywhere*."

"In my notes for January 10th, 1995, Richard said he had to work on the eleventh and would leave around 0730 and it was okayed. I had gone on a field trip the night before Joyce disappeared and Richard mentioned that he needed to change his schedule that night. He told me that he had a job already and that he was not looking for work. If he said he was going to look for work, that would have been noted and he would have been given an allotted time frame to seek work. We encourage people to look for work; we usually give six hours, two times a week, to do it on Mondays and Wednesday for interviews. Defendants always say my notes are incorrect, so they'll look better in court, by the way."

"If the machine is tampered with, it sends an immediate notice. I, um, on the date Joyce vanished, Richard left at 0008 or eight minutes after midnight and returned at 0124 or 1:24 AM. The next entry is an alarm away at 0741 because I hadn't faxed Richard's new schedule into the office yet, so there was no reason to be concerned. The alarm company called Richard's and let it rang ten times to see if he actually was home and, of course, he wasn't. Then they phoned me."

"So Richard left at 7:41 A. M. and returned at 12:44 PM. So he was gone a total of five hours and three minutes. At 1423, or 2:23 PM he left again and returned at 1501 or 3:01 PM. He was out for thirty-eight minutes that time."

"Could you continue telling us his movements for the next few days until I tell you to stop?" Schulmire asked.

"Sure. On Thursday January 12th, he was gone from 12:37 PM until 1:36 PM, a total of fifty-nine minutes. There are no notes saying that Richard wanted to look for his wife. On Friday, January 13th, he left at 3:12 PM until 3:57 PM; uh, forty-five minutes. On Saturday the 14th, he left at 1:18 PM and returned at 2:06 PM, that's forty-eight minutes, but then he left again that day at 4:43 PM and returned at 11:53 PM, that's seven hours and ten minutes and the alarm sounded because he was outside of curfew and had not asked permission. On Sunday the 15th, Richard left home at 10:52 AM and was back at 11:40 AM; forty-eight minutes again, Monday the 16th, he left at 11:05 AM and returned 12:18 PM That would be one hour and thirteen minutes, and he left again that day at 12:20 PM until 1:35 PM; an hour and fifteen minutes. On Tuesday," Groves paused for a drink of water and looked at Schulmire to verify if he was still to continue and got a nod, "the 17[th,] Richard left at 10:57 AM and returned at 2:08 PM. That's three hours and eleven minutes. The first time Richard requested extra time to look for his wife was on the 18th of January!"

"Mr. Groves what was the reason that Richard Handcock was placed on electronic monitor verses being in custody in the first place?"

"Because he had a medical condition, cancer, that required him to get out of town for treatment," Groves stated. "There was a dispute between the Sheriff and parole who would pay for the trips so they decided to release Richard to Pre-trial Services so he could do that."

"How often did you visit Richard's home?"

"About three times a week."

"Were you able to verify if Joyce was being stalked or not?"

"No. Richard told us that the people who beat him up were the ones he allegedly stole stuff from. They were the stalkers."

"Nothing further at this time," Schulmire said.

Dusty stood up as her usual for cross examination, and asked how the ankle bracelet is sized appropriately.

"The ankle bracelet is sized and has room for two fingers and it requires heat. It can't be slipped over the heel. If it's cut off, I'm notified within three or four minutes that the device has been compromised. Everything the machine does is logged. The average person on electronic monitoring has it for two to four months, some a year. This is *never used in lieu of a jail sentence; only pre-trial.*"

"Of four hundred people, the only guy who ever was quazisuccessful at getting the monitor removed had it put on by a man with big fingers; more like the space of four fingers, then the defendant took a hair dryer and heated the rubber up and splashed water in it; heated it, stretched it, heated and stretched. All that time we were getting proximity alert. I requested an officer go out because the device was not being worn against the skin, but ended up going out myself. I knocked and the defendant's mother said he wasn't there. And I said, 'Well, my machine says he's here.' So we checked and found the unit on the counter and we were able to pick him up because he hadn't gotten far."

We broke for lunch and after I came back from lunch with the guys, I sat in the hall with the other women. That day, one of the two housewives said to me and I'll never forget it, "Did you know that one of the ceiling tiles in the courtroom has one hundred and forty-four holes in it?" I was stunned. I couldn't believe she hadn't been paying attention to the testimony!

During the testimony I was acutely aware that all were talking to the one person in the jury with the least intelligence in our group. I had to keep reminding myself not to feel offended by the attorneys', judge's, and expert witnesses', constant over-simplifications and fifth-grade vocabulary. Now if only they could get this woman to pay attention!

When we filed back into the courtroom, Mr. Schulmire began his re-direct examination of Ike Groves. Ike explained to us why he thought that the electronic monitor is a good strategy. He said that if the defendant leaves unauthorized, he can be placed back into custody. If they leave for an extended period of time, they can be charged with escape.

"The defendant signs a contract that explains the rules."

"Did you see Joyce when you visited Richard?"

"Yes, about fifteen times, but I don't know anything about her personal life."

"Isn't it true that on December 16th, 1994, you received a phone call from Mr. Mendoza from parole that stated that Richard did not have cancer, but probably had AIDS and Joyce beat him up?"

"Yes. Joyce was present when I had that conversation with Richard about AIDS and she was shocked! Richard's reaction was, 'Who said that?' Richard and Joyce said it was absurd and I reported it to my boss."

There were two questions from the jurors:

1)Q. "What about call forwarding? Can you tell when they are at another location?"

A. "They are not allowed to have any special features on their phone, but if they did, the devise would report it as away from home when they weren't."

2)Q. "Can they bathe with the bracelet on?"

A. "The bracelet is completely watertight."

* * *

Stephen Russell called to the stand Christy Shannon who stated that she was a paralegal who worked at Jeff Richard's and worked at Pre-trial Services from October 1994 through March 1995.

"Can you identify Richard Handcock?"

"He looks different now. His hair is now thinner on the top and it's not long and in a ponytail."

Russell smiled and asked how it was that she came to know Handcock.

Christy said, "Yes, Judge Mancini leaned over and said to me that Pre-trial would be accepting Richard for electronic monitoring. I told him that I didn't think that Richard was appropriate and the judge said Richard was ill and that's why he was on Pre-trial. On January 11th, 1995 there was a note that Richard called to confirm he could be away for work. He had a job; not that he was looking for a job."

"Nothing further, Your Honor."

The defense said, "We have no questions for this witness."

Christy Shannon was excused. But wait! I wanted to know *why* she didn't think Richard was appropriate for Pre-trial Services! That seemed like the next obvious question, but nobody asked it and Christy was gone and the jury was excused suddenly.

While we were out, the state told the judge that they were calling Jeff Dupree next and requested immunity for him as to any drug or drug cases he testifies about; the same as Ruby Vasquez got. Russell said that many of his contacts with the defendant and victim were in the context of using or supplying drugs. Jeff already told them that he'd take the Fifth Amendment if he was asked about his drug usage or dealings. Most of his testimony was to be about drugs and he supplied drugs to Richard and Joyce.

"Judge, when you're tryin' the devil, you don't go to heaven to get witnesses! We'd just like the court to extend the use immunity to Dupree as well," Russell pleaded.

While waiting in the hall, somebody said, "Hey, do you notice how you can always tell which ones waiting to testify are going to be witnesses for *our* case?" Darned if they weren't right. There was something about them that was different. Not just the clothing; it was something hard about the face, I guess, but you could always tell which ones they were. Some had to wait all day in the hall to be called or even for a few days. They tried to read our faces too.

After waiting briefly in the hall as we often did, we were asked back inside the courtroom. Jeff Dupree had been called to the stand and sworn in. He testified that he had been an air conditioner contractor for twenty-three years and had lived in Yuma since 1980. Jeff said that he had kids, two were his and two were Ruby's. He said he was currently married but separated from Ruby. He also said he had temporary custody of all four children.

"I first met Joyce in 1988. We went out a couple of times, but we were just great friends. We weren't compatible romantically. I first met Richard just before the wedding and Joyce seemed happy. Ruby was a close friend of Joyce's and Nichole baby sat for us. Joyce and Richard hadn't been married long before I heard that Richard slapped Joyce around and spent the night in jail. Richard behaved jealously at our house, which was the only place he would let her go to without repercussions."

"In the fall of 1994 Richard came over and he was crying hard and said that Joyce was cheating on him and he had proof because he'd planted a tape player in the bedroom. We listened for ten minutes and didn't hear a thing except somebody cleaning and the TV. We tried to calm him down and he left."

"Did you ever see Richard at The Dark Place?" Steve Russell asked him.

"Yeah, but I never saw him acting jealous. I wasn't a regular there. I never noticed Joyce behaving differently when he was there."

"Did you hear about them being robbed?"

"Oh, yeah, Joyce had some jewelry missing, birthday and

Christmas gifts. After three to four months, there was a burglary at their house. A small handgun I bought for her years ago was missing and some jewelry. She wanted the gun for protection from a former boyfriend she was afraid of. He was loud and unruly and Joyce thought she might be harmed physically. That was about eighteen months before she met Richard. Six months after her jewelry was stolen, she'd gotten the same jewelry back for a gift in a box as a new gift from Richard! We never heard anything more about the handgun."

"After Joyce traded her car for the trailer, she asked different friends for rides. She kind of spread it around, so one person wasn't breaking their back. Then Richard returned. Joyce told me several times what Richard was going through with his cancer treatments. One time he left for Tucson for chemo for three or four days and came back bald."

"In the last six or eight weeks Joyce was alive, every time I saw Richard, he was dressed in camouflage jumpsuits and combat boots."

Judge Hale interjected with an instruction to the witness, "You can go ahead with your answers, but know that your answers would be admissible in some other proceeding. If you aren't granted immunity, Jeff, take the Fifth."

"Your Honor, the dates in question, I was arrested and pled guilty to possession of meth and have done my time and I'm paying a fine. I've been on probation a year and I've been through treatment and put my life back in order."

Judge Hale pointed out that Jeff had "use immunity" and it was limited to drugs.

Steve Russell asked Jeff how often he did drugs with Richard and Joyce.

"Mostly I did it with Richard, and more than once with Joyce. Generally it was meth and the occasional joint. One or both would come to my house and if they had anything, they'd share; like offering a beer at a barbeque."

"Did you ever see bruises on Joyce after she was married to Richard?"

"Yeah, they were plum-size."

"Now didn't you see Richard on the day Joyce disappeared?"

"The day after. The reason I remember, I had my oldest daughter with me that day and her school had the day off. The details fit too closely to be coincidence, so almost immediately after Joyce was found, I went to the detective on the case and offered the information that I had to them. I recounted it over and over."

"Please tell us everything you remember, Mr. Dupree," Russell implored.

"On that day, I asked my daughter if she wanted us to go get Nickie to baby-sit rather than be in my air conditioning shop with me all day. It was a weekday, but she was out of school for some reason. We went to the trailer on 28th Street to pick up Nickie and when I knocked, Richard answered the back bedroom door and I asked if it would be alright if Nickie baby-sat Jennifer. Richard turned and spoke into the trailer and said it was me and if she wanted to come baby-sit Jen. He turned back to me and said, yeah, she'd like to; just give her a few minutes."

"I was standing by my car; about fifteen feet from the trailer door, and Richard was in the doorway changing clothes and he asked me if I'd seen Joyce and I told him no. He said she didn't come home from work the night before and if I saw her, to tell her that he was looking for her."

"He was standing there shivering and out of the clear blue sky, he said he'd had to get in a canal that morning and ten seconds later, Nichole emerged through the door and told Richard she'd be back in a while. He leaned down and she kissed him on the cheek."

"I couldn't help thinking as I drove away, what would he be doing in a canal? It was a cold and windy day; clouds too."

Russell asked if Ruby and he were having spats at the time and Jeff said that they were arguing and Ruby was not living with him at the time Joyce disappeared.

"We still hung with the same crowd and shared information. She asked me if I'd seen Joyce."

Russell stood then sat on the table's edge; the table more than strong enough to bear his thin frame. "Do you own a boat, Mr. Dupree?"

"I have a custom-built 16' aluminum with a center console boat with twin motors."

I kept wondering why all this talk about a boat? The divers established her body could have been dumped from the water's edge and that was where they found the wood piece evidence.

Jeff said he had a vague recollection of Joyce or Richard coming by his house to get whatever concrete blocks they could to use to level and support the trailer. He said that he had two dozen cinder blocks and one pyramid-shaped concrete block.

Dusty Wheelright stood for her cross-examination. She was wearing a long, dark purple full skirt with a pretty pink shirt and black blazer with short sleeves. (Blazers with long sleeves are a waste in Yuma. You can only wear them a couple of months.)

"What time of day did this encounter with Richard happen would you say?"

"I had taken Jennifer to breakfast first, so mid-morning. Between nine and eleven," Jeff said.

"And why did you think this was important enough to call the police?"

"Well, after Richard's comment and the discovery of the body in the same time frame, I just added two and two and decided the canal dip was an important piece of information! I decided to call Detective St. Jons. I spoke with three to five other detectives too. That was about the third week of January. Three to six months later we did a taped interview. The next time after that, they asked me for a polygraph test; that was about four or five months ago. I did take the test willingly."

"Why was Nickie not in school that day?"

"I don't know; maybe it was a holiday. She went to the junior high and Jenny went to elementary school. Maybe it was a three-day weekend. I don't know exactly. It could have been a Friday or a Monday or a conference day, I don't remember."

"What was Joyce to you? Didn't you have a thing with her once?"

"She was a good friend and he was her husband and therefore entitled to anything I could do for him, because if he made her happy, then he made me happy."

"So you knew Richard well and you were good friends?"

"I don't know him very well, but I considered him a friend because he was married to Joyce."

"Isn't it true that you have a connection to the place where Joyce's body was found?"

"Well, I read in the paper that she was found in the Gila Main

Gravity Canal, which originates about 150 yards behind the summer house that my parents have owned since I was four years old. I spent the summers there my entire life."

Dusty went over his pedigree, "Isn't it true that you were arrested in March of 1995?"

"Yes, for possession of methamphetamine."

"And what was your punishment?"

"I got four months in the county jail, 30 days on electronic monitor and $3,000.00 in fines. I also am on probation for three years."

On re-direct Russell asked how many times Nichole had baby-sat for him and Ruby and Jeff supposed it was about eighteen times, but only twice when she was living at the trailer.

CHAPTER 52

All eyes turned to the door as the prosecutor asked the bailiff to show Mrs. Joyce Handcock to the witness box. It was Richard's mother, of course, but she was being called to testify against her own son!

Once sworn, Mrs. Handcock stated that she lived in Yuma for forty-five years, but she was currently living in Prescott.

"Richard went with Joyce for several weeks or so and came and told us he was going to marry her. I guess he knew her a couple of weeks or a month. I didn't go to the wedding; Richard brought Joyce over to our house about thirty minutes after the wedding so we could meet her. The next time I saw her was in the courtroom roughly the following September or October when Richard was involved with the case against Swift Sales. I never socialized with Richard and Joyce."

"In October or November of 1994, Joyce called me to ask if she could talk to my son or knew where he was at. They had a dispute. Joyce said he left at least once a month but he always came back home and laughed about it. She also told me that Richard had cancer and he went away to die."

"Later on, I asked him about his health and he said he would take care of his self and not to worry about it. He had seen doctors. I didn't . . . by looking at him, he was real thin and didn't have too much hair. I didn't think cancer at the time. I thought, maybe, probably, ulcers of the stomach. I offered to drive him to Tucson, but he said no, he'd take care of his self and not worry about it. Then we didn't discuss it anymore."

"Were you and your son close, Mrs. Handcock?" Russell asked.

"We called each other two or three times a day! After Joyce went missing, I saw Richard probably everyday or every other day. He came to my house. He was making flyers to put out and we talked

MURDER BY GRAVITY?

about what he should do; flyers or call the police department. I lived about ten or fifteen minutes away from him. He'd stay fifteen or twenty minutes to an hour. Sometimes he had a sandwich or I cooked him breakfast. The year Richard was married to Joyce, he did visit me. He had no reason not to contact me. After Joyce was missing he also started bringing their possessions or garbage to my house because he had to clean up around his trailer or be evicted and the rent had been paid. He brought two or three truckloads and they were put on the side of the patio. Joyce's craft stuff came into the house. He put some of it under my son's playhouse. He had tools, scraps of wood, plastic, sheet metal. There was a boat out there that hadn't been used for ten years. He also left a little two-wheel trailer."

"Detective Graham came to my house and looked through the items Richard brought."

Millington stood and asked Mrs. Handcock if she had intervened and talked to the real estate agent that handled the trailer park on Richard's behalf.

"Yeah, they said that Richard could stay if he paid up and cleaned up. This was after Joyce was missing. I gave Richard $200 or $240. Richard said for me to save his stuff until he could go through it. I moved to Prescott a year after Joyce was gone."

Stephen Russell asked how Mrs. Handcock had come to call the police about all the things in her yard that Richard had left there.

"Well, I was trying to sell my house. I tried several times to get hold of Richard to pick up his stuff. I knew about the investigation, so I figured the cops should go through it before I threw it out."

"Thank you, Mrs. Handcock," Russell said, smugly.

* * *

The jury was asked to take a ten-minute break. While we were out, Josh Schulmire brought to the attention of the court that Hazel Mess believed that she knew one of the jurors, Karl Koenig; third chair, was a customer and had known him for four and a half years. She used to work at The Bottoms Up Pub, but now is working at Mickey B's. Hazel claims to have met his wife and kids, but has never been to his house and he hasn't patronized her employer for at least two weeks.

CHERIE HUYETT ACHTEMEIER

* * *

Josh Schulmire for the prosecution called Irma Stebbins, who stated that she was seventy-five years old and a Canadian, and been a Yuma snowbird for four or five years.

"Joyce and Richard were my neighbors in the park. We lived across the street from them. Joyce was missing for two days before I heard anything about it. I just heard that she was gone."

"About two days after Joyce was missing, I noticed Richard moving property into his truck and out of his trailer. I just saw a yellow material in back of the truck, like bedding crates, and a rubber foam mattress rolled up in a big roll. I couldn't see the surface."

"Convoluted rubber?"

"Yes, that's what they call it. I call it eggshell cartons. I never saw Richard going door-to-door looking for Joyce and I never saw a single flyer posted either," Irma said and glanced directly at Richard, who froze.

Dusty stood and asked Mrs. Stebbins why she had waffled on the date she'd seen Richard move this alleged egg crate.

"You changed the date from five days after to the day of, isn't it true that you can't decide? Isn't it true that you saw this thing in Richard's truck as he was driving away?"

"Yes."

"Do you have any reason to hate Richard?"

"No, but I know what I saw!"

"Thank you, no more questions."

* * *

Prosecutor Russell called Jared Andrews to the stand. The good-looking, tanned man said that he was thirty-nine years old and that was how long he'd lived in Yuma. Jared described himself as a working supervisor of carpentry. He said that in December of 1994 and January 1995 he had been working for K. Lee Developers behind the Foothills Market. He said that Dick Kidd was on the crew, but he frequently didn't show up and had to be terminated. January 12th was the last day of his pay period and he worked twenty hours, instead of the required eight-to nine-hour days, five days a week.

MURDER BY GRAVITY?

"So if Richard Handcock said he came to the construction site and waited an hour to see Dick Kidd about getting a job on January 11th?"

"He'd be looking for the wrong guy! But somebody there would have noticed him or remembered him. They would have asked him what he wanted. Nobody remembers Richard looking for work."

"So you never got a message from or interviewed Richard Handcock?"

"Correct."

Millington looked up at Andrews and asked, "The company that you work for, they have other locations, other job cites?"

"True."

"If someone was looking for a job, they might not speak only to you, correct?"

"Correct."

* * *

The prosecution called Loren Waller, who stated that she'd been a bookkeeper for thirteen years and worked for K. Lee Developers in payroll. Loren stated that though the last pay period ended on January 12, 1995, she was unable to tell for sure if Dick Kidd worked on the 11th or not. She only knew he worked a total of twenty hours that pay period.

* * *

Steve Russell called Albert Hernandez to the witness stand to be sworn. Hernandez stated that he'd been a superintendent of construction for thirteen years and that he was *not* working on building the Jack In The Box in December 1994 or January 1995, because he didn't get the job. He had some relatives that worked there.

"I know Richard. He was employed previously by me in '92 or '93 as a carpenter. You have to be in shape for that kind of job and able to lift heavy weights. You have to know tricks to lift. I last spoke to Richard when we were bidding on a roof job. Richard asked for openings."

"I did not see Richard personally in January 1995 looking for work. I didn't want the job at Jack In The Box, so I didn't bid it. If a person went to the head office, and not to me, I suppose he would be told there were no openings. But my foreman would have told me if somebody was looking for work."

*　*　*

Dick Kidd was the next person called to the stand by the prosecution. Dick said he was thirty-six years old and currently worked at a Circle K, but for the past fifteen years he worked as a framer. That in December 1994 and January 1995 he worked at the car wash behind the Foothills Market as a framer. He told us that he wasn't happy there so he didn't often show up for work. He finally left the job by his own choice. He said he received his final check the following Friday after his last day of work and that Richard Handcock was an acquaintance and sometimes in the past they'd had beers together after work.

"Richard was at the job site looking for work sometime between 10:30 AM and 11:30 AM and stayed about forty-five minutes waiting for Jared Andrews. I came down off my ladder to borrow a tool from Richard. One or two days later I quit. Richard also lived down the street from me."

Millington asked only one question, "Isn't it true that you got rained out often in January?"

"That January was the rainiest in years, so yeah."

Russell asked on re-direct, "Why didn't you tell Jared Andrews that Richard was looking for work?"

"I think I did tell him," Dick said, as he shook his head to get his hair out of his eyes. He was dismissed.

CHAPTER 53

It was a beautiful late November morning. Gone finally was the dreaded heat of the extra-long summers in Yuma that dissolve into winter. There was a breeze blowing the leaves around the great lawns of the courthouse. I could wear my regular business suits from when I worked in offices in California. I seized the moment and wore long sleeves and they still fit because I had been dieting with a friend the previous summer. Ben & Jerry's hadn't caught up with me yet.

After the jury filed in, lined up in the order in which we sat, we waited for Judge Hale to be seated. Steve Russell called Hazel Mess to the stand. Richard's girlfriend! *This was going to be interesting,* I thought.

Hazel and Richard gawked at each other when she came in. Hazel stated that she tended bar for seven years and she was thirty-three years old at the time. Hazel said that she'd been in Yuma since 1987 or 1988 and knew Richard Handcock. She said she'd first met him in 1989 at a bar where she worked and they had a romantic relationship for two years.

"We remained friends after the breakup and started dating again in August of 1993. We lived together until December of 1993 when things didn't work out. I found out Richard was married in January 1994 just one month later!"

"Did you know Joyce?"

"Yes, I knew her as a customer."

"Did you start seeing him again after that?" Russell asked.

"I saw Richard again in April or May of 1994 at The Bottoms Up Pub. He dropped in occasionally once or twice a week, but sometimes not for a whole week at a time."

"Now, Ms. Mess, you spoke with Detectives St. Jons and me

three weeks ago and we made a tape of our conversation."

"Yes, and I got a copy of it from defense counsel yesterday," Hazel said defensively.

"Richard talked to you about his cancer and depression and his relationship with Joyce and he also sent you flowers, right?" Russell asked.

"I also get flowers from other people, not just him, and Richard only visited for twenty minutes," Hazel said, pouting. "He needed a friend to lean on; that's why he came to see me. He won't admit it. He had problems arguing with Joyce."

"When was the last time you saw Richard?" Russell asked just as nice as you please.

"The last time was before he was arrested in January of 1995. We remained friends during his marriage from April 1994 to January 1995. He told me that Joyce was becoming physically violent to the point of causing him injury. He said Joyce followed him and got in back of his truck and when he tried to get her out, he was arrested! She hurt herself or got hurt during it."

"Christmas of 1994 he said they got into arguments and Joyce had scratched his arms. He showed me his scratched arms!"

"Did you hear about Richard 'being kidnapped'?"

"It was in the newspapers but not about being injured."

Russell persisted, "Did Richard ever tell you he was jealous or threatened?"

"He mentioned one time about Joyce and Mike Deere and I didn't feel that he felt threatened or jealous."

"Are you aware that you told Graham and me that he was concerned and jealous?"

Hazel was non-responsive.

"You still like Richard, don't you? You tried to speak with Richard yesterday in the hall, didn't you?" Russell kept chipping away.

Hazel wasn't answering again.

"What kind of dates did you have with Richard while he was married to Joyce?"

"Sometimes we met at P.J.'s, or we played darts or talked and Joyce wasn't invited. I had sex with Richard only once while he was married to Joyce."

MURDER BY GRAVITY?

"Because you were just friends and he sent you flowers while he was married and spent time with you, yet he still just liked you as a friend?" Sarcasm crept into Russell's tone of voice. You could tell he was trying not to let it, but it bubbled up.

"Why was Richard losing weight, Ms. Mess?"

"I think he was using methamphetamine all the time and that's why he lost weight. He told me that he wanted to quit."

"Isn't it true that you had previously been convicted of a felony in regard to dangerous drugs, in fact meth, and that Richard was your co-defendant?"

Hazel began to pick and choose what she would answer and this was one question she wouldn't.

Russell approached the bench and said, "I believe this is a hostile witness and I am allowed to use leading questions." Hale agreed.

"On the tape you made with us, you said you were innocent when you were arrested with Richard. The offense occurred when you were in Richard's truck and you implied it was Richard's drugs. Yet you stayed with him after this conviction."

"That arrest was on our first date and we dated afterwards."

"Did Richard ever tell you that he had cancer?"

"I do remember Richard complaining of cancer," Ruby said stoically; like it was a blister on his hand.

"Did you ever go to the Mittry Lake area with Richard?"

"Yes, he liked to fish. When we lived together, we went fishing twice. He liked to fish all over the Mittry area. I'd get lost, but he never did. He went a couple of times a week. Sometimes he got in the water to fish or go on a belly boat; a tube you sit in like an inner tube. We used to do it together."

A real Norman Rockwell picture that. We recessed for lunch and when we came back, Hazel Mess had not returned!

* * *

In lieu of continuing with Hazel, the prosecutor called Jimmie Lowen, the owner of The Bottoms Up Pub in the foothills. Jimmie said that she'd been in Yuma eleven years and employed Hazel during 1994 and 1995 as a bartender. Jimmie said that she didn't know Richard, but she'd seen him many times.

"What can you tell us about the morning of January the eleventh?" Russell asked.

"I have a good friend who was my neighbor for six years. She's a self-supporting single mom who cleans houses, but on Wednesdays, we like to get together for breakfast or an early lunch. We eat before the kitchen opens at 11:00 AM, so I know roughly when she was in that day, and I know it was that day because she usually has a sitter for her daughter but that day my friend had to pick her daughter up at 12:00 PM for Brownies."

"Did Richard ever send Hazel flowers?"

"Oh, yes! She received lots of flowers. Everybody always remarked about it."

Millington began his cross-exam by re-laying a foundation, "So you never met Richard Handcock, but you'd seen him?"

"Yeah, he'd sit at the end of the bar and Hazel came up to me in the afternoon and said, 'Jimmie, that's Richard!' At the time he had a ponytail."

"Is it possible, Jimmie, that he came at other times of the day?"

"99% of the time he's in the bar, it's after lunch."

Hello? Don't ask a witness a question on the stand if you don't already know the answer, Millington! I learned that as a legal secretary many moons ago. I also have a colorful past.

* * *

Steve Russell recalled Hazel Mess who had mysteriously returned. She was dressed for Richard, I thought. It was an "after five" suit rather than a business suit. It was gray satin and tight at her trim waist. Her hair and make up were done precisely. She made a lot of eye contact with the defendant and he with her. She had on black stiletto high heels and was really quite pretty in her own way. Her hair was dark blond; the color most blonds, like me, usually end up high lighting somewhat because it's a little "mousey."

Russell tells the court that Ms. Mess has requested that she not be filmed, so the TV cameras were ordered off.

"Ms. Mess has her tapes with her (tightly clutched to her chest,) which she requested from our earlier interviews. She admits that she had a romantic, sexual interlude with Richard which occurred prior to

MURDER BY GRAVITY?

January 11, 1995, maybe as much as two weeks prior."

"Do you remember your discussion with Detective Graham when she came to the Pub to ask you questions?"

"Yes, she came at a very busy time; during happy hour, so I tried to answer the questions quickly. I told her that I didn't remember the last time I saw Richard come in. When she pressured me, I didn't think it was an important question!"

"I see, do you remember Jimmie and her friend having lunch that day?"

"No, I thought it was the next day. They figured it was the 10th or the 11th of January and Richard was there at 10:00 AM. He could have been there as late as 10:30 AM I didn't give Donna Graham the date. It could have even been before 10:00 AM! I served him and we had a little conversation like I do with all the customers. Richard was there until 11:30 AM or so."

"So what was he doing for a hour and a half?"

"He was looking for someone to buy tires from, uh, Bud Docktor. They talked about it. This occurred on Wednesday, not the day Richard was there for an hour and a half."

"Didn't you tell Graham that the tire guy was quite intoxicated that day and that happy hour is from three to five in the afternoon?"

"People come in before happy hour." Hazel was getting petulant again.

Millington stood and greeted Hazel from the defense. It was his turn to question her. "What did you say to the defendant yesterday in the hall?"

"Hello. The last time I saw Richard was the last time he was in court on this case. We didn't speak. The last time I had contact with him was before his arrest in January 1995 and he called me from jail a few times. We never talked about the case at all. He never asked me to help him. I spoke to the police and attorneys at least ten times and another time face to face just before this trial!"

"Did you receive some threatening phone calls and did you make tapes of them?"

"There were several phone calls and they were threatening, so I recorded them."

"Were you trying to deceive Graham by the intent of those calls?"

"Richard never physically assaulted me and we never argued. If we disagreed, he'd take a walk instead. It was a good relationship."

"Did you ever visit Richard in jail?"

"No. He wrote to me and I didn't write to him. The tapes were made of conversations with the County Attorney. I was being careful."

"And to cooperate with Mr. Russell you brought the tapes back today in case he wanted to listen to them. Didn't he mention it to you several times?"

"Yes. I wanted the tapes back so my boyfriend could listen to them prior to all this which never occurred either." What?

"He was concerned about me being involved in this. Richard wrote me several times from Yuma then from Perryville."

Millington asked, "So you always tried to cooperate with the police?"

"That's what I'm sayin'."

Russell stood for his re-direct and asked, "During your conversation with Schulmire, two of your friends were there. You didn't mention any letters from Richard."

"Nobody asked and I didn't say," Ruby said defiantly.

Russell put on his chagrined face and said, "No more questions."

CHAPTER 54

Joshua Schulmire called William Nagel to the stand to be sworn in for the prosecution. He stated that he was forty-eight years old (but looked older) and had lived in Yuma for twelve years.

"I'm a tree trimmer and I do yard work and I'm a customer at The Bottoms Up. I walk three-quarters of a mile to get there and it takes me about twelve to fifteen minutes. My wife changes the TV channel to her soaps at 11:00 AM and that's my excuse to go to the bar." A chuckle came from some of the jurors. "I had a conversation with Willie about tires. I found out two days ago Willie's other name is Richard Gates. He needed tires for a truck in January 1995. That was about noon, because the soap starts at 11:00 AM and then my walk time. It was 1:00 PM at the latest. Richard said he could supply tires, but Willie told me later he didn't come through. He wasn't a regular there. Near the end of the week he still hadn't got them. The conversation was early in the week, like Monday or Tuesday. Near the end of the week Willie hadn't gotten the tires yet."

Millington asked for the defense, "You spoke for fifteen to twenty minutes?"

"And did Willie ever buy tires?"

"He did buy used tires on January 15th."

* * *

Josh Schulmire called Detective David St. Jons to the stand for the State. David, a man in his prime, said that he had lived in Yuma for twenty-two years and was a Yuma Police Department investigator and had been dealing with major felonies since 1982. He had a forty-hour investigating class, thirty-two hours on death by itself, etc. (I guess we would have to rely on his experience, since education seems lacking.)

"I was very busy investigating other crimes in 1995. I had a huge caseload. I had to prioritize my cases and had not time for a shotgun case that can take a wrong turn. I didn't speak to everybody about everything. After January 20, 1995, I worked with Detective Graham at a Sheriff's joint investigation because of the different locations in the investigation. We communicated back and forth on our progress."

That sounded to me like perhaps Detective Graham or someone in the County Attorney's office had discussed her testimony with him before he took the stand because he certainly covered all his bases without provocation.

"The missing person report I found on my desk January 16th and her husband reported her missing on the 12th. It had Joyce's general description on it and initially I did nothing with it. On the 17th, I got a phone call from Lori Perron and after that I took steps to find her. I went to The Dark Place and asked several people if they might know where Joyce could be. I also spoke with Bob DeVore, Stevie Lynd, and others. Other than a couple of blind leads, there was nothing. I spoke to Richard Handcock at his trailer unannounced on January 19th and I did not arrest him. I wanted to ask him where she could be and if there were any problems between them. Richard was sober and helpful and cleaning up the outside of his trailer."

"Richard said that the last time he saw Joyce was 8:00 AM on the 11th before he left. In his version of the morning, while Nichole was in the shower down the street, he and Joyce were intimate. Nickie came back and ate and left for school. Then Richard called Pre-trial Services to see if he could go look for a job and left the trailer at 8.00 AM. He said Joyce was wearing a gray sweatshirt and off-gray sweatpants. I noticed that Richard had given the original officer a different description of what she was wearing; he said a black shirt and levis."

"Richard then said after he left at 8:00 AM, he drove to the Foothills to meet Dick Kidd about getting a job. He said he got there at 9:00 AM at the site behind The Grocery Store, also known as Foothills Grocery or 38th Street construction site. Richard did not say he was working on the 11th. He was looking for work and waited around for forty-five minutes for a boss who never showed up. Then he said he went to Mesa Del Sol or K. Lee Development and was looking for Albert Hernandez, who was not there either, so he left and went to The Bottoms Up Pub where he met his former girlfriend, Hazel Mess. Once he was there, he had a V-8 and stayed there for thirty to forty minutes."

"He told me he got back sometime before 11:00 AM. Then he went and spoke to Lori and Bill to ask if they had heard from Joyce. He did not explain the time between 8 and 9:00 AM."

"Richard said that before he left home that morning he'd had a discussion with Joyce about doing errands she needed to run. Richard said it was possible some friend took her. He said that there was no fight the night before and that two girlfriends came over late. He looked out and saw a man with a nice new car and that the women were Ruby and Leigh. He said when the friends came over, the ladies went behind the trailer, got some tin foil and they were involved in the usage of illegal drugs. He also said there was nothing missing of Joyce's except a pair of black shoes. I asked him if he'd ever assaulted her and Richard said that he never had. When I asked him if anybody didn't like Joyce, he said it was Mike Deere. It was obvious that Richard disliked Mike. Richard said that he had *two* former wives and there was never any violence in those marriages."

"On Friday, the eve of the 20th, there was a call from the Sheriff asking if we had a missing female reported. It was Detective Donna Graham. There were some similarities, so I went to The Gila Gravity Canal and first I saw the vehicle from the mortuary. I saw Joyce in a body bag. I noticed the body had been in the water at least twenty-four hours and there was nothing but a bra on her. Her hands and feet were still bound to milk crates with rocks in them and a ring of paint on it."

"I identified the pylon and photos and the blue paint ring. It was a crescent on a cinder block. All the evidence was identified the same as Graham said earlier. The red glob looked like fish intestines to me--not human. There were two picture frames in the fire ring with jagged edges and large grooves clear through. That was when we decided to do the joint investigation. We got a search warrant for the home before the autopsy. We found purplish paint drops on the asphalt and on the frame and the trailer and the wire; spatter on everything, really. We found everything except the strapping tape at the trailer. We did find that later at Swift Sales where Richard once lived and worked."

The jury was dismissed again briefly. Fifteen minutes, just enough time for a quick smoke and restroom break. I had wondered how my abnormally small bladder would do, but we had plenty of breaks and I drank very little.

Mr. Millington brings his problem to the attention of the court while we were out. "Your Honor, we are having problems with Roy Bounder. There could be a mistrial if we can't find him to cross-examine. We'll need him before the defense rests."

Judge Hale ordered Bounder to present himself Friday at 1:00 PM and Millington requests a short day because he was coming down with the flu.

The jury returned and Schulmire returns his direct examination of Detective St. Jons. "How did your investigation proceed from that point on, Detective?"

"We sent Richard's wire cutters to the lab and after our search we took Richard to the station for an interview. Richard said his statement was the same as Thursday night and was not arrested at that time. We spoke to Mrs. Perron and told her that we had four pieces of wood that matched and put Richard at the crime scene, which shot gunned our investigation as far as I was concerned. Plus he had similar wire that matched visually."

"I spoke with Phil Seward and there was no way he could be tied to the physical evidence. I checked out the guy who supposedly had tortured and killed someone in a devil worship sacrifice, but he didn't even know Richard or Joyce and we found no evidence of a torture chamber in his basement. We spoke to residents in the Handcocks' R.V. park and Nichole. What's more, we did luminal tests in the trailer, which were negative for blood." St. Jons added pointedly, "Richard was the last person to see Joyce alive."

Millington stood and adjusted his tie, "How many investigations were you running at that same time?"

"About twelve at a time. Richard said that Joyce and he were planning on going to K-Mart or Wal-Mart and when she was still gone, he figured that she went with someone else. He didn't go immediately to the Perrons'. Nobody told me that Richard called Joyce's work."

"Did you provide copies of everything you were doing

MURDER BY GRAVITY?

independently to Detective Graham?"

"Yes."

"Did Richard have permission to be gone the morning of the 11th?"

"He had permission to be gone that morning. I also told Graham about the cigarette brand Joyce smoked which was a unique brand because they were clove."

"Did you investigate to find out where they sell it?"

"No. And Richard didn't tell me he stopped for gas on his way to the Foothills that morning."

"Did you talk to Red Pollock?"

"He didn't give me any confirmation about the drugs being delivered to Joyce the night before she disappeared. I got it later from Ruby and Leigh."

"Did you re-read your reports to prepare for your testimony today?"

"No, I did not." That seemed neglectful to me; and not fair to Joyce or her family.

"How do you decide which missing person cases to work on?"

"It's only when people have major concerns that we dig a little deeper."

"Did you ever tell Dr. Rolland Andrews that Joyce's body had been dragged by the divers across the lagoon with weights?"

"I don't recall."

"Not even when he noted the damage caused by the wire?"

"There wasn't much."

"Didn't you have a big discussion with Nichole about whether or not she'd seen the green strapping at the trailer? And didn't you ask Nickie who she thought might be involved?"

"Yes."

"And didn't she say Phil Seward who had been accused of grabbing Joyce? That Ruby told Nichole about it--not Joyce? You knew about Seward before your talk with Nichole and yet you played it down? You *never* spoke to Seward, did you?"

"There was no physical evidence and it was dismissed."

"Yeah, sometimes things happen to witnesses . . ." Millington let it drop. "You didn't even speak to Jeff Dupree until June of 1995. He has a pickup truck. Dr. Andrews said there would be a lot of blood, but he would have had plenty of time to clean out his truck by June."

"Blood would depend on several variables. . . "St. Jons began.

Dusty approached Bill Millington and whispered something. Millington said, "Your Honor, I would like to dismiss this witness at this time, subject to recall. We have an expert witness who just arrived from Atlanta, Georgia to testify as a defense witness."

CHAPTER 55

The decks were cleared for Dr. Kris Sperry who stepped up to the witness stand, looking just a shade short of dignified. Sperry stated that he was the current Deputy Chief Medical Examiner of the Fulton County, Medical Examiner's Office in Atlanta since 1991; that he was second in command there and before that he was in Albuquerque, New Mexico, and his pedigree was plentiful. He said that he had performed, supervised, or reviewed nineteen to twenty thousand autopsies. He had provided expert testimony as a forensic pathologist 325 times in 22 states. He also performed all of the autopsies of the people who died during the Olympic bombing in Atlanta and in other Olympic-related deaths. Ninety percent of his testimonies were in criminal matters and only ten percent civil.

It was very impressive and since that time I have seen this man several times on television in his capacity of testifying in trials as an expert witness. I saw one trial in which his expert testimony *alone* convinced a jury whether or not to convict.

"Dr. Sperry, do relatives ever misidentify loved ones?" Millington asked.

"Family members identify the wrong bodies because of the emotional state involved. I have to authorize, release, and have no room for errors. There are investigators who assist, but leave the time of death blank because it's almost impossible to know in a vast majority in reality. Not like TV."

"I reviewed the file from the Pima County Medical Examiner's Office and tissue samples, lake water samples, photos, forms, and documents. I also read the Grand Jury transcripts and telephoned Dr. Rolland Andrews in Tucson. The samples were in formaldehyde but still break down, you can tell by the smell."

"Joyce's body was cremated, so I had *no direct examination*. I was retained in March of 1996 for the Handcock case. I was not asked to prepare a report for this, nor was this a consult case. I did make myself available for the County Attorneys to interview me. I spoke with Steve Russell at least two hours. I haven't spoken to Dr. Rolland Andrews after my review for professional purity."

Millington was looking more awake today. That was a good sign. He asked, "Were you able to identify a cause of death in this case?"

Sperry cleared his throat and took a drink of water. "Forensic pathology has limitations. I was not able to make a definitive cause of death in this case."

"What could have been done to help determine the cause?" Millington asked.

"A second autopsy; look for other injuries, bruises. Anything hidden deeper in the tissues of the arms or legs or back that was obscured by decompositional changes. Extensive dissections. If Joyce hadn't been cremated, but embalmed instead, there would be more tests that could have been done."

"Is there anything else you would have done in this case to assist you in determining the cause of death that Dr. Andrews did not do when he did his autopsy?"

"Yes, during the removal of the neck organs, the larynx and hyoid bone at the base of the neck is routinely done to look for injuries. I would have removed the tongue. The tongue itself is very important; especially in strangulations or blunt trauma or seizure related to drug toxicity (they may bite the tongue). I don't find that Dr. Andrews did that."

"Because of the nature of this case and the suspicions; just because of the circumstances and because of the decomposition, it would be prudent to dissect and remove the skin or the arms, back leg, buttocks, and the back of neck. When I teach class I say, 'If you don't look, you won't know.' If he'd done this and still had not cause, then he should have considered toxicity."

It was time for lunch break and believe me we had food for thought. Not that we could discuss any of it. Pete graced us with his impersonations of famous people while we dined at Lute's Casino, which wasn't a casino anymore, but made great stuffed jalapeños and combination hot dog/hamburgers are the specialty of the house. I

MURDER BY GRAVITY?

hadn't yet discovered that their old fashioned malts were to die for.

* * *

When we returned, C.A. Russell said that the State could hopefully finish its case that day if we stayed beyond five o'clock and hopefully be done before the Thanksgiving recess. And somehow, we were back in gear for Russell's direct of Detective St. Jons.

Russell reminded us, "Now, Richard was connected to the area where the body and other items were collected, right?"

Millington interrupted and said that the defense would stipulate that Richard was familiar with the Mittry Lake area.

Russell mentioned that he was having voice problems due to a cold, but he struggled onward. "The physical items linked to Richard; the paint drops at the trail and items found with Joyce might have come from their home. Didn't Nickie say that Richard told her that he left at 7:15 AM and he told her he was back by 11:00 AM?"

"I could not confirm that anyone other than Richard saw Joyce after Nichole went to school on the 11th."

Russell sat on his table again, his voice dripping with sarcasm. "Let's talk about Mr. Red Herring. Excuse me, I mean Red Pollock." Many chuckled. Somebody had to say it. "He was not at the trailer between 7:15 and 11:00 AM. He had no motive."

"That's right."

"And Danny Brooks? The man Joyce left a love note for?"

"He could not be connected to the physical evidence. The note was a dead-end lead. In general, it said she invited him to come to her trailer and made comments that she loved him and for the note to be given to him when he came in to The Dark Place. It was still at the bar when I found it on the 17th of January. Brooks hadn't been in the bar yet and he never saw it. I talked with his probation officer and the Yuma County Jail about Danny and his whereabouts. He was incarcerated from July 1994 through January 9th, 1995. Then he went on work release program and was only out of jail for particular hours from morning to mid-afternoon, as on the 11th."

"I spoke with Detective Graham about Mike Deere's whereabouts. She was able to confirm that he actually worked that day according to the people he worked for."

"And what about Phil Seward's whereabouts that day?" Russell inquired, to put the issue to bed.

"Seward did not have access to Richard's trailer between 7:15 AM and 11:00 AM. We never received information that he even knew where Joyce was living. He wasn't linked to the wood pieces."

(Personally I think it's conceivable that Seward may have known where the Handcocks lived. According to Lori Perrons' testimony, Phil had purchased a vehicle from them. It isn't far fetched that he could have seen "I love you, Richard" and maybe seen Richard's truck and figured out where Joyce was living. Maybe Lori even let it drop in conversation with Phil).

"We had several wacky leads we had to check out. Mrs. Willingham was a source. She said there had allegedly been some type of physical mutilation done to Joyce; that her arms and legs were missing, so based on the physical evidence, there wasn't much validity in the lead there. We also looked for the torture chamber she told us about and there wasn't one"

"I was trained in luminal and it's not 100% fail-safe. I knew when we did the bedroom in Richard's trailer that part of the bedding was missing."

"And what did Nickie say when you interviewed her?"

"She told Detective Graham that she was scared that the man who put Richard in jail and kidnapped him and cut him had her mother too. She said this man also grabbed her mother and made a pass at her. We explained to her that that was two different people and that the kidnapping was a false report and that Richard had done that to himself. It never happened; even admitted it to the police. We told her to put her mind at ease and said she didn't have to be afraid anymore."

"Now Dupre says he picked up Nickie in the morning, but she puts it in the afternoon. That was the day Richard had to get in the canal and it was cold outside."

St. Jons explained, "I figure that Nichole is more accurate about the time of baby sitting. I called the school and found they were in school but recessed early at 1:00 PM that day."

Mr. Russell asked, "After you served two search warrants on

MURDER BY GRAVITY?

Richard you arrested Richard. Where was he when you arrested him?"

"He was in the Yuma County Adult Detention Facility on another matter. That was why he couldn't retrieve things from his mother's house. We also seized everything--all of Richard's property on January 23rd, 1995."

Millington stood for his cross-examination for the defense, "Was there a shed by the trailer?"

"There was no shed. It was more like a lean-to behind the trailer."

* * *

The State recalls for the cross-examination for the defense Mr. Roy Bounder. That eliminated Handcock's hope for a mistrial.

Dusty stood and asked Bounder about the fights he over heard at the Handcock trailer.

"Did you ever witness any physical fighting?"

"No, I didn't, but I heard Richard say, 'I should slap the bitch.'" Did anybody ask the judge to instruct the witness to answer the questions with a simple yes or no?" No.

"Isn't it true that you didn't come forward with this information until March of 1996?"

"That's true. I spoke with St. Jons and my own attorney and then St. Jons again."

"Why then, did you wait so long to come forward?" Dusty asked incredulously.

"I didn't feel it was important to come forward with possible threats sooner than fourteen months later. I spoke to St. Jons again Friday night after I testified. Handcock's private investigator was coming for an interview too. I was helping another officer with another case. They call me a 'cop wanna be' according to my former probation officer, Alma McCullough."

"Do you know Mike Rose, Jr.?"

"He's the son of City Cab's owner where I work now."

"And didn't you in fact call the police and tell them that it was possible that Mike had marijuana?"

"Yeah."

"And didn't you plant marijuana on Mike Rose for them to find?"

385

"I did."

"You did this in order to get him in trouble?"

"Correct. It was how he treated his father; and his father was more of a father figure to me. Mike had been impossible before, but the cops wouldn't do anything".

"You were convicted of a felony in 1989 in Yuma County?"

"Correct."

"Felony theft?"

"Correct."

"And you were placed on probation for three years but it was revoked because you were not at the address where you were supposed to be. You were not actually picked up until five years later on a probation violation warrant."

C.A. Russell stipulates that Roy had a prior felony conviction.

"Very well. Let me see if I have this right, Mr. Bounder. You were released from probation which was a mere sixteen days after *you were convicted of giving false information to the police* in which case you planted evidence on Rose?"

Judge Hale hit his gavel a few times and said for us to clear the courtroom. Gee, just when it was getting fun. No worries! Remember I read the court transcripts and this is what was said when the jury was out:

Judge Hale wanted to know if Ms. Wheelwright was implying that Roy was receiving special consideration.

"That's a serious allegation!" Judge Hale was incensed.

Dusty said that in 1989 Roy was placed on probation for three years. Within less than a year he absconded and was caught five years later and put back in probation. He never did complete the original three years. He was on probation again. In less than a year after violating probation once, twice, three times and more, he indicated Mike Rose Jr. didn't have anything happen to him because he was on probation.

Dusty also said that she was not accusing Detective St. Jons or the court. Judge Hale had been the prosecutor at that time and was involved. Roy failed to pay his court assessments, probation fees, and changed his residence. Five years later he appeared in court unsupervised, and made full restitution.

In the end, Hale ruled all of this irrelevant, asked the jury to return, and instructed us to disregard the last several questions. All we needed to know was that Roy Bounder was currently on probation and works as an informant for the Police Department in Yuma. He has provided information about drug cases and the State has not made any promises or deals for him to testify.

*　*　*

Josh Schulmire called Bill Morris Jr. to the stand for the State of Arizona. He stated that his age was fifty-four and that he was the supervising criminalist at the Arizona Department of Public Safety Criminology Lab in Phoenix since 1972. He was currently on the board of directors for The Association of Firearm and Toolmark Examiners.

"Did you look at the pieces of wire found at the crime scene?"

"I studied two pieces of wire and two additional pieces of wire, a pair of Stanley needle nose pliers, a Klein diagonal cutting pliers, a pair of Fuller diagonal cutters and numerous wire fragments and also containers of tape and nylon webbing that St. Jons submitted through the usual chain of custody for a tool mark comparison."

"Can you tell us about your findings, Mr. Morris?"

"A mark that is made on a relatively soft object by a relatively hard object, that's what we look for. We first examined the wire because it had a high potential for identification, then compared them to the shape of cuts that he made in some lead material with each of the pliers. The defects on the cutting edge scrape the surface as it cuts through."

"All those tools submitted may be used to cut wire. I mounted wires in comparison microscopically; which is essentially two microscopes hooked together then compared to see if I could find tool marks similar to the pliers from Richard's trailer."

"I was able to conclude that the shapes of the cuts are similar to each of the tools, but there was an insufficient amount of individual information to either exclude or identify any of the tools as cutting the wires."

"The wires looked to be the basic same type of steel wire. Some appeared narrower in diameter than those from bundles. I used a digital caliper to measure them. The wire fragments of item four were dissimilar and smaller in diameter."

"Tools can pick up individual characteristics during use, wear and abuse. I did not know where the wire was seized from, but I got a list of items."

Judge Hale said, "We have three different sets of numbers here and it gets confusing."

Morris replies, "Items 4, 6, and 7 are all pieces of wire found around the trailer. Items 25 and 26 refer to the wire taken from the wrists and ankles of the victim. Three sets of wire from the trailer and two from the victim. Two were similar in diameter, two pieces were dissimilar. This wire is very common. Ankle bindings end cut by typical pliers have class characteristics. To do a comparison you need a known and an unknown."

A juror has a question. "Were any tests conducted to determine if any of the wires were composed of the same metal or alloy?"

Morris answered, "No. It was not performed because of a lack of database to compare with, there's not much meaning derived. A piece of wire that's made today can have essentially the same metallic compositions of a wire made a year ago."

We then took our second afternoon recess because we were staying late because it was the last day before the weeklong Thanksgiving recess.

Judge Hale made an announcement before we left the courtroom, "I have taken the liberty of stopping by the bakery this morning and purchased a couple of pies. We will cut those up and you may partake, if you want to. There is coffee provided too." Yes, I definitely voted for Judge Hale again, though it is my habit to turn down pastries, since I'm usually on a diet.

* * *

When we came back from recess, the State called the accountant from the mine where Mike Deere worked at the time Joyce disappeared.

"Could you explain how the time cards are done at the mine?"

"Yes, there are daily time cards that are filled out at the end of the shift and must be turned in by morning. Mike Deere's time card dated 1-11-95 has the hours of 7:00 AM to 3:30 PM and it is signed by his foreman at the end of the day to verify he was there."

Dusty stood and asked if she was personally aware if Mike Deere was there that day or not and the accountant said she wasn't.

* * *

The State called Mike's foreman from the mine, who identified Mike's time card with his signature. He said, "Inside our line-out room, we had just a rack there and the cards deposited at the end of the shift. Then they get checked again as they go in and out the main gate."

Millington asked about Mike's job. "He did mill maintenance, tech, pump repair, crusher, conveying systems, and was basically just an all-around mill type mechanic."

"Do you remember if Mike took any personal time off? Here are two time cards; one for the 13th and the 14th. On the 14th, it shows that Mike had a paid personal holiday."

"I keep a time sheet in correspondence with time cards. Mike Deere's name is not on the time sheet. There's a notation down at the bottom that he had the 14th, Saturday, off confirmed on his time card."

Russell re-directs by asking the foreman, "Don't the time cards show that Mike worked eight hours on Wednesday the 11th, Thursday the 12th, and Friday the 13th?"

"Yes."

A juror has a question and is read by Judge Hale, "Does anyone monitor the time card rack to verify who puts their card in?"

The answer was no. "I work side by side with Mike Deere and I know when he's there!"

CHAPTER 56

Josh Schulmire called Michael Eyring to the stand for the prosecution. Eyring stated that he was a forensic scientist and a criminalist at the Arizona Department of Public Safety in Phoenix. He said he had been an expert in the microanalysis of fabrics, fibers, polymers, and electromicroscopy since 1977. He was given the items of paint and materials that paint had adhered to and was reportedly associated with the suspect. There were cans of spray paint and a lid from a can of paint.

"They were sent to me for comparison to see if I found any association between the materials found with the victim and materials found at the victim's and suspect's house."

"There was paint on a cement block. I applied spray paint to the concrete block and let it dry. The paint can had dried paint on the lid that was found to be physically and chemically similar to the paint found on the concrete block. Then I looked to see if the items looked dissimilar microscopically and I analyzed it to look at the paint pigment. I used another instrument to analyze polymers that made up the paint to hold it together."

"The paint lid was identified to be physically and chemically similar to some glue-gray material associated with the victim. Exhibit 22, the outer side of the lid, has adhesive with the label, B-E-H-R custom tint and name. I could not discern anything to tell them apart."

"On the four pieces of plywood, they looked different because they were sent to the latent print unit first. But on the edge you can see the original color. This was a simple wood comparison. This turned out to be a picture puzzle."

"The two larger pieces were found in the same general area and the two smaller pieces found in another general area. By way of the flow of the grain, a big cut in the bottom, a slot, wood splinting on bottom edge, and two cracks put together, the two smaller sections of wood if placed properly, fit perfectly together. They were originally one piece of wood. Everything matches up. The same was true for the other piece of wood. You can see that the fractures in the wood fit together and that *all four pieces of wood came from a single piece of wood."*

The wood pieces were passed to the jury for our inspection.

"Thank you, I have no further questions at this time."

Wheelwright stood for her cross-examination. "What kind of tool would you say cut these pieces of wood, Mr. Eyring?"

"A circular saw."

"And did any circular saws get sent up to your lab for inspection?"

"No, I didn't receive any saws to compare with the cuts in the wood."

Dusty stepped up closer to the witness, "Can you say absolutely that the paint on the concrete block came from the actual paint can?"

"No, I can't say for certain."

"Now, in item number one, the purple paint chip material associated with the victim from the cement pylon, were you able to match any of the six spray cans from the Handcock house to it?" Wheelwright asked.

"No, they were excluded. There were indications of more than one color on the lid. Purple was on the edge of the lid and the paint had separated partially in storage. The purple turned out to be a portion of a flower blossom that was stuck to the edge."

Russell stood for re-direct, "Isn't it true that some items don't get sent because they can be seen by the naked eye whether they're the same or different?"

"That's true. The paint of the pylon was different than the paint on the lid."

At that time we recessed for the entire week for Thanksgiving. I never had a job that gave me that much time off, but I gratefully took it. The tension of the trial after almost a month was weighing on my shoulders. We hadn't lived in our resort long and decided to have Thanksgiving with our new friends at Sun Vista Resort. The park provided a huge turkey for each table of twelve and the residents signed up for the table of their choice and each table had a meeting to decide what each person was bringing to the table. It was a lovely sit-down dinner for five hundred in the clubhouse. We're still friends today with our tablemates from that night.

* * *

When we returned, Dusty Wheelwright told Judge Hale that they still had additional evidence to be presented and they wanted to continue with Dr. Sperry, who was back in town from Atlanta.

"Can you explain to the jury how a hemorrhage occurs?"

"A hemorrhage can only occur in someone who is alive. Blood will still leak by gravity, though it can be a great deal. There was no hemorrhage under Joyce's wrists. I only saw the photos, but Dr. Andrews said there was minimal subcutaneous (under the skin) hemorrhaging. I didn't see enough evidence that Joyce was alive when she went in the water. Andrews' report says the number-one explanation of death is probable drowning, number two is blunt-force trauma, and number three is methamphetamine intoxication. It would have been useful to know the temperature of the water, if the body was found in the sun or the shade, the air temperature and what was inflicted on the body upon its' retrieval. Two blunt-force, one superficial injuries. All three separate injuries, relatively closely spaced on the left side of the head were small. There was no fracture of the skull or bleeding of the brain. This particular area is the thinnest point of the skull and this attack was not life-threatening. It could have caused unconsciousness; there's no way to know for certain. Joyce could have fallen on a single irregular object such as like large gravel. Not a flat surface."

"Joyce had 1,311 nanograms per milliliter of methamphetamine in her system. A nanogram is a billionth of a gram. Some parts of Andrews' report says he took fluid from the cavities although the autopsy report claims there was no fluid in the cavities. Meth and amphetamine were found. A percentage of meth converts to amphetamine. The cavity is the empty space where the lungs sit; the thoracic area."

"*The level of meth in Joyce could have caused her death.*" Sperry stated.

I was incredulous about this line of thinking. I thought, and then what? She tied herself up?

Sperry continued, "Some people die when the level is low from complications frequently. *Death can occur in a wide range of blood levels. You don't need to know if a victim was a regular drug user or not."* What? "The lowest range that could cause death would be six hundred to eight hundred nanograms per milliliter; less than one half of Joyce's range. I can not state what definitely was the cause of death, *most likely she died as a consequence of meth abuse."*

"For a forensic pathologist or medical examiner to use the phrase, "probable drowning," basically means it's a guess. In other words, he can't prove it. He also used the word, 'pending,' under the cause, in the original certificate. He was waiting for toxicology reports. If it were probable drowning, why would he need tox reports? *I saw no implication of drowning."*

Wheelwright asks, *"Does a person actually have to be alive to drown?"*

Was it just me, or did anybody else think that was a stupid question? Sometimes it took a supreme act of patience to sit in that jury box.

Sperry stated the obvious, "You cannot drown someone who is dead already. Most often people who drown have water in their stomach and Joyce had less than one ounce."

"Now *there is such a thing as dry drowning* in a small percentage of the people who drown. When they go into the water, they are drowning in the act of breathing in the water will cause the airway and larynx to spasm and shut. As a consequence, they asphyxiate. *Joyce might have dry drowned, but most likely meth killed her."*

Schulmire stood for his cross-examination. "When you are an expert witness, your travel expenses are paid for, as is your time. Is that correct?"

"Sure."

"Of the 325 times you testified, you said that ninety percent are criminal matters and five to ten percent of that ninety percent your testimony on behalf of the defendant, is that correct?"

"Correct."

"And isn't it true that that percentage has increased in the last few years?"

"Probably."

"And defense counsels hear of you through word of mouth?"

"Correct."

"And this is the third time that you've been called to Yuma to testify for defense cases fairly recently?"

"Yes."

"And what did you do for the defense and how did you bill them and what did you get paid?"

"I put six to eight hours on Handcock and was initially paid $1,500 which was applied for my expert review and I rely on others to assist me. The defense has never instructed me to make a report. If I were to write a report, it would have to be disclosed to the State. I wasn't even aware that according to Arizona law I was required to disclose my notes. At any rate, this is all from memory. I didn't take notes."

"Weren't you taught to take physicians notes like everyone else?" Schulmire asked.

"No, I only take notes on living patients. I read things and remember them. Why would I need notes?"

"You have testified in forty-five cases this year and with all those cases, wouldn't notes be helpful?" Schulmire walked up close to Dr. Sperry. "Well, wouldn't you agree that thirteen hundred nanograms is not a common cause for death?"

"Yes, it's usually higher. The highest living patient I've ever seen had twelve to sixteen thousand milliliters or approximately ten times the amount Joyce had. *Over a long period of time, drug tolerance builds.* The *defense* never supplied information about Joyce's drug habit. Meth can be ingested a number of ways: snorting or smoking or by IV, which could be very dangerous because the blood level rises rapidly and can cause a sudden death at a lower level. I was not made aware of her administration. It would make a difference in the danger."

He had said previously that he didn't need to know if a victim was a regular drug user or not. Too bad he didn't take notes; he would have found his contradictions.

"You did a test on the decomposition fluid, not the blood?" Schulmire asked.

"Yes, chronic users could affect the rate of absorption. According to Derek Pounder in <u>Forensic Science International</u>, his article entitled 'Post Mortem Drug Redistribution, A Toxicology Nightmare,' says. 'The concentration of a drug in an autopsy blood sample may not reflect the true blood concentration at the time of death by a factor of several fold; there is a real danger that an individual taking a therapeutic dose of a drug, with an elevated post-mortem drug level may be misinterpreted as a lethal dose.' And I agree. Joyce's level was higher than if she had taken an amphetamine tablet. But in order to know levels, *you must know prior usage as a baseline.*"

Sperry continued, "Decomposition fluid is different than levels reported in the blood. Organs and tissues have stored-up levels of concentration. The levels remain for a long period after the use has ceased. Meth can cause incapacitation, not just death. Dr. Andrews' report is good, but there are other things he should have done. In fact, far better than most reports I see."

Dusty Wheelwright stood for her re-direct of Dr. Sperry. "Where did you get Dr. Andrews' report from?"

"The defense."

"And how does your experience differ from that of Dr. Andrews?"

"I've been doing this longer, I've written more articles and attended and given more lectures that Andrews."

"And would it be rare for someone to die of thirteen hundred nanograms of meth?"

"It is not rare. It's in the potentially lethal range."

"Nothing further. Thank you, Dr. Sperry."

Isn't it moot if she's tied up with wire and drowned?

* * *

Detective St. Jons was called back to the stand for a cross-examination by Bill Millington. "In your search warrant affidavit, you wrote it as if the tests for blood could in fact detect the presence of blood in Richard's trailer."

St. Jons explained, "Dr. Andrews told us that there would be lots of blood and that's what what we looked for in the trailer, but we didn't check his sewer lines. We found nothing."

"Wasn't the person who you investigated with the reported

torture chamber telling people that Joyce had gone swimming with cement shoes?"

"He had no connection to Joyce, we checked him out thoroughly."

"Isn't it true that you didn't do a complete investigation because you thought that Detective Graham was investigating some of the other people? That you didn't ask a lot of important questions?"

"No. We didn't look for the cement pylons at Jeff Dupree's house because he moved."

"How convenient. Nothing further, Your Honor."

The jury was dismissed but Wheelwright stayed behind, "But I would like to ask again for permission to take the jury to visit the scene."

"Your Honor, my name is Hunter, I'm representing Mr. Phil Seward who is present in court today. I have directed my client to plead the Fifth Amendment about questions about the victim, or the previous case."

Millington said, "I believe there are no incriminating statements here to put Mr. Seward on the stand and ask him about his business relationship with Richard or Joyce. What were the circumstances of them moving out? He can't claim the Fifth on all that."

"Mr. Seward came over to the Perrons' to their home trying to get them to get the charges dismissed by having them talk to Joyce. Many of the walls in that house were blue and blue is an important color in this case. But there's no way to get it in because according to the police, he did nothing. There is no testimony or evidence and we're going to take the 5th unless we are granted immunity."

"The case against Seward was dismissed without prejudice at the time before Joyce's body was found. No one was certain how to proceed." Judge Hale said that it would be a proper invocation of the Fifth.

Schulmire said they were left with a nullity. "If he invokes the Fifth, there's no testimony at all. If it can't be said to be relevant to the case and can't be said to be depriving anyone of favorable or unfavorable testimony because there is no testimony; if that's the case, there is no reason to put Mr. Seward on the stand. Juries are not allowed to draw inferences on the legitimate exercise of constitutional rights but that appears to be exactly what the defense counsel wants them to be able to do in this case, it's totally improper."

"The only way to really prevent that from happening is not allowing Mr. Seward to get on the stand unless there's some relevant area that they need to question him about, which he doesn't have an appropriate Fifth Amendment right to. If there is, they can put him on the stand for that purpose. I haven't heard of such a purpose yet."

"The only purpose for Seward to take the witness stand in front of the jury is so that Millington can ask incriminating questions," Judge Hale continued. I'm glad that I didn't know about this at the time, because I would have been angry that he couldn't have been questioned. I think it's only fair that we know pertinent details. Ruby knew about Joyce's attack from Seward, but nobody asked her

Millington said, "I think everyone knows the County Attorney has no intent to refile that sexual abuse charge against Seward. They don't have a case without Joyce."

Hale stated, "I just don't think that putting him on the stand in the position where he will almost undoubtedly invoke the Fifth to all of your questions is appropriate."

I would have liked to seen Seward and the expression on his face and his tone of voice when he took the Fifth. All these little things can make a difference!

Hale said, "I'm going to grant the State's motion to excuse Seward."

Then Bill Millington moved for a *directed verdict*. If granted, they wouldn't need any other motions. This is important because a lot of what is said here is the essence of closing arguments for both sides.

Millington began, "Because there is no eye witness to put Richard and Joyce together after Nichole left for school. No one will say there was a big fight; nothing to require Mr. Handcock to kill his wife. It's all circumstantial. The bricks and the common paint on the pieces of wood in the fire ring and at his mother's house are all circumstantial. No one can say when or who put them there: There's nothing that puts him at the scene!" Millington declared, "Premeditated and felony murder because she was kidnapped is a stretch. They don't have evidence to show beyond a reasonable doubt. They can't prove there was a murder. Based on this, I believe counts two and three need to be dismissed. I would even argue count one should as well."

Russell countered, "Richard had motive, and bizarre manipulations that were no longer working. Richard had opportunity. The defense doesn't take into consideration the whole package. Even though he'd been granted permission to go to work, there was still an alarm away and nobody answered the phone and no one else was there. So it had to have occurred between 7:15 AM and 7:44 AM. And when Bill Perron returned between 8:30 and 9:00 AM, there was a padlock on the door. Access to objects used to weigh Joyce down that Richard had access to--the wire and strapping--and they admit Richard was familiar with the area. The paint was chemically indistinguishable, the wood found ties everything together beyond a reasonable doubt. It all fits like a puzzle. Richard's mother said he alone had brought materials and no one else had disturbed it. Joyce only had a bra on and no articles of clothing were at the scene, indicating strongly the attack took place at her home before she got ready for the day."

"If other people decided to dump her body because she overdosed why would she be naked? It wasn't just a few bindings to weigh her down, these multiple bindings were to restrict her movement. Also, the missing bedding Nickie testified to and that Irma Stebbins saw Richard taking away in the truck . . ."

Russell continued, almost out of breath, "Your Honor, the only theory of this case that makes sense is that the attack took place in that trailer shortly after Nickie left and after he was done incapacitating her with blows to her head. He wrapped her in the blankets and eggshell mattress cover and took her away. That's why she had no clothes or earrings on and that's why the blankets and egg crate mattress could not be found. He got rid of them."

"Clearly there was premeditation shown in the gathering of materials to weigh her down and during the lengthy transport to get her to the scene. More than that, premeditation is shown abundantly because of the manner in which this man chose to kill her by. Because unlike stabbing her or shooting her, this method took time. It takes four or five minutes to drown. Every second after he put her head under the water, he absolutely knew that what he had done was going to kill her. Every second that he waited and decided not to pull her head back up into the air, was a second that he premeditated."

MURDER BY GRAVITY?

Millington's response was, "It seems to me that the State, through their own case, pointed out some potential defendants or people who could be involved in this. The man whose house they checked for a torture chamber; so the State argues that that's for the people to decide. We will forget about the other people in view of the poor investigation. That clearly can be pointed out in this case, still it makes it difficult for me to believe that a jury would find beyond a reasonable doubt that Mr. Handcock is the only person who could have committed this crime."

Judge Hale remarked, *"The court concludes there is substantial evidence from which a reasonable juror could find beyond a reasonable doubt that Handcock is guilty of all three crimes.* It is ordered that the court is denying the defendant's motion for directed verdict on all three counts." (Didn't the judge just say that he thought a *reasonable* juror could find Richard guilty? I guess there would be no question what he believed but we never heard this, of course. I discovered it later in the transcripts.)

Millington asks again for permission to take the jury to the crime scene. "I think that the trip out there would prove to the jury beyond a reasonable doubt that the State's theory doesn't hold water. There's simply no way it makes sense. We will present aerial photos and a one-hour video. All the State's witnesses testified differently about what the area's like. The jury needs to see how many people are out there. The road is a clearly well-traveled, well-worn area where lots of people go."

After taking a copy of the video from Millington, Russell said, "As soon as "Monday Night Football" is over, I will plug this in and I'll enjoy it, I'm sure. For the record, we don't disagree to the trip, only it's difficult to manage. I don't think the video is irrelevant and it doesn't create reasonable doubt."

"Anybody could have picked up Joyce that day and then put her in the water where she was killed," said Millington. Did that mean that Millington didn't buy the death by meth story his expert spun? Or that she wasn't dead already when she hit the water?

Judge Hale asked, "They had all these items with them at the time?"

Millington responded, "Joyce might have brought it. There are more explanations. Why would someone hog-tie her, throw her in the truck where blankets could blow off and hope no one saw? That, plus the fact that the truck was mechanically unsound. The trip is what's important, not the site."

Russell said, "We believe we will have a witness available to testify that to call someone a rat in jail is a very strong threat. A rat is the worse thing you can be in jail. It could bring physical harm or death if other inmates believe someone is a rat. *Also, last week Officer Humphrey overheard Richard Handcock's brother threaten Mike Deere and say, 'Who are you going to snitch on today?' He later called him a rat in the elevator. Another defense witness told Deere, 'Bad things happen to snitches when they go to prison.' In a report from Officer Jones, the detention officer, an inmate named Williams told him that Richard told him he wanted his brother, Ben, to get next to an inmate named Deere. That's usually for intimidation purposes. These are four threats. The defense would like to bring up Mike's drug dealing. In* State vs. Contreras, *the defendant sought to influence testimony by threatening a witness as relevant.*"

Wheelwright said, playing it all down, "*I have a couple of brothers that say something all the time and I'm not aware of everything. Deere indicated that he didn't want to testify because he was in fear of his life. He's been told by people he will not name that there's $1,000 on his head if he testifies. There's no indicator that it was Richard.*"

Of course the jurors were never told about this situation during the trial. All we knew was that Mike Deere, the one person we were looking forward to seeing and hearing from did not testify. We kept waiting, but no Mike Deere.

CHAPTER 57

The defense began presenting its case by calling Mrs. McKelvey, who was a real estate broker for twenty-three years in Yuma. She also stated that she worked for the property management company that was involved in the property rented by Richard and Joyce Handcock in January 1995.

"They were residing in a mobile home park I have managed for years. The on-site manager for the off-season was Bill Perron and Richard and Joyce lived there for four or five months."

"Were you aware of any problems the winter manager was having with the Handcocks at that time, Ms. McKelvey?" asked Bill Millington respectfully.

"They had a lot of debris around their trailer and we were trying to get them to clean it up. It was unsightly. The owner and I worked with the Handcocks the whole time to clean it up. It was a sensitive issue because Bill was working for me and I didn't want to offend him or his wife."

"How did you 'work with them'?" Millington asked.

At first we sent written notices and they did clean it up some and it was better, but they were still working on it. When Joyce disappeared, there were still problems with the cleanliness issue. Richard did some cleaning and then the trailer was impounded."

"Did Richard ever telephone you?"

"Oh, yes, on January the 11th, Richard and Bill called me. Richard asked to see if Joyce had been in to pay rent and Bill's call came the same day."

"Did they have appointments?"

"Lord, no. It would be very unusual for them to come into the office to pay the rent. When Joyce was discovered, I took a written message from Bill and called the Yuma Police Department and asked for Detective St. Jons. He wasn't in and he didn't return my call even though the woman who answered said that I had information that might be possibly significant about the Handcock case. So I called St. Jons again two weeks later and told him the information I had and he said, "Thanks," and hung up. I kept the message for one year then tossed it."

"That would be the tape of Richard asking you if you'd seen Joyce, right?" Millington reiterated.

"Correct."

"The State does not wish to cross-examine this witness, Your Honor."

The witness asked if she could stay and watch the proceedings and Judge Hale agreed to it.

* * *

Dusty Wheelwright recalls Roy Bounder to the stand and asks him to tell about his connection with the Southwest Border Alliance.

"I'm an informant. I had been incarcerated and expressed that I wanted to work again with this sergeant that I knew there, who was a detective in 1995, and he debriefed me and made arrangements with California and a judge to try to get a position for me to work as an informant. I was on probation at that time. So, I was approved, and they sent me on two reliability buys; it's controlled, the buyer is patted down and the observed goes in low to the residence and returns back with a purchase of narcotics. I am no longer an informant. During the informant time I spoke with another officer who wasn't involved in the Handcock case. He said that if I had information about the Handcock case, I should have written to St. Jons. Nothing was said about comments I might have heard made by Richard prior to Joyce's death. The only information I gave the other detective had to be out of *the newspaper*. I did not approach the prosecution for a deal for testifying."

* * *

Roy Bounder's sergeant friend from the Yuma Police Department took the stand after being directed to do so by Ms. Wheelwright.

"Can you tell us about this discussion you had with Roy about Richard and Joyce's arguments? She asked.

"This discussion was not documented. If Roy told me he'd heard Richard say he 'wished his wife was dead,' or he 'should slap the bitch,' he would still be referred to the detective on that case and that detective would have documented it."

"Nothing further." But wait! He told *us* the same thing! So, the informant was not a snitch--just different sides of the same coin.

* * *

Millington called Kathleen Waltney to the stand who stated that she had lived in Yuma for fourteen years and was the property manager for the River Park Apartments for eleven years.

"Red Pollock lived there and he moved in the summer of 1995. He vacated without notice on June 10th, 1996. He left a note saying he'd filed for bankruptcy and had no money to pay his rent." He owed $1,120 in back rent."

"Thank you, Ms. Waltney."

Russell asked, "Isn't it true that Officer Red Pollock was trying to lease out the unit before he moved out and was unsuccessful?"

"That's correct."

What was that about? Oh, yeah; the "Red herring" again. The defense was trying to throw off the scent of the hounds during the fox hunt.

* * *

Bill Millington stood and recalled Albert Hernandez to the stand again.

"Mr. Hernandez, you testified a couple of weeks ago."

"That's correct."

"What kind of an employee was Richard Handcock?"

"He was a good employee; very reserved. He got along with people."

"Didn't you used to have a supervisor that yelled at everybody and nobody got along with?" Millington asked.

"That's true, most employees would talk back to him before they got used to him, but Richard; he rarely talked back to him."

* * *

Mr. Millington recalled Detective St. Jons to the stand and the judge reminded him that he was still under oath.

"In January 1995 did you investigate a fire in Richard's pickup truck?"

"Yes, it looked like clothing and debris had been burned. It was next to Richard's trailer park. I was also involved in the impounding of the trailer and clean up. There was no shed. I was told it was dismantled and hauled away. We also did a search of the bed of Richard's truck on January 20th; not everything in the bed was destroyed."

CHAPTER 58

During the process of selecting the jury, one of the questions we had to answer under oath was, "If the defendant did not take the stand in his own defense, would you think that was a sign that he was guilty?" I answered no because I realize that most attorneys advise their clients not to take the stand because the prosecution can confuse them with the questioning. Because of that question, I incorrectly assumed that Richard Handcock would not be taking the stand in his own defense. But I was wrong. It was a complete surprise to me and to many of the jurors when he was called to the stand by Bill Millington. I found out later on that it was Richard's decision alone to take the stand; to be his own star witness.

It also happened to be the one day my husband decided to attend court. He would have come more often, but because of his failed back surgery, sitting on a hard bench for long stretches was painful. Butch had to get up often, but he heard most of the testimony that day.

Richard was sworn in and stated that he lived in Yuma all forty of his years on this earth. He admitted that he told people that he had cancer when he knew he didn't have it.

Mr. Millington asked, "Why would you do such a thing?"

"If you have a severe medical problem the county jail doesn't want you. They will kick you out and I didn't want to go again, so I made up a story. I'd heard that the jail doesn't want to be responsible or liable for what would happen while an inmate is there and also, there's no cancer treatment facility in Yuma and the county would have to pay for the treatment. I was in jail at the time for stealing some items from a previous employer."

"And that would be Ron Gene at Swift Sales?" Millington asked.

"Yes," Richard confirmed. It was now established that Richard was a thief and a big-time liar with no fear.

"Could you please tell the court about your criminal history?" Millington asked, to my surprise. I guess defenses' strategy was that it's best if they mention the warts and all first, rather than being sandbagged by the prosecution.

"I was convicted in 1974 for burglary and possession of drugs and defrauding an innkeeper and I went to prison. Then I was convicted in 1989 for possession of meth and forgery and got out in July of 1993, when I met Joyce. Later on, because of Swift Sales, I was convicted of trafficking stolen property or attempted possession of stolen property and attempted possession of dangerous drugs."

Millington asked, "And you pled guilty on those occasions?"

Richard said, "Yes. I made up the story of the cancer when I was arrested. When I first told Joyce about it, she didn't know if I had it or not."

"To your knowledge, did she actually believe you did have cancer?"

"No, not after the beginning," Richard said in his button-down Beach Boys shirt and beige cardigan sweater. With the demeanor of a school teacher . . . until he spoke.

"But Joyce did go to court personnel to try to get you out of jail because of your cancer. She contacted Judge Mancini and talked to someone in his office."

Richard said without skipping a beat, "I know she was escorted once out of court for making a scene. She talked to Pre-trial Services and my parole officer at the time."

Russell stood up and said, "Objection! Your Honor, he can't know this!"

"Sustained."

"Joyce told me about it over the phone and I could see what was happening from my window in the jail at the entrance at the courthouse. She was being escorted out. We discussed over the phone that the cancer story was the only way I could get out of the detention facility."

I made a mental note to myself: don't smoke on the North side of the courthouse. The inmates *can* see out of those skinny jail windows.

"And you were released?" Millington asked.

"I was released to Pre-trial Services in spite of the fact that I had prior convictions and charges because I said I had cancer. It was a level-four release with an electronic monitor."

"Did anybody ask you for proof concerning your claims of cancer or medical records?"

"No, I had no medical records or documents or anything to support my medical problem."

"Pre-trial maintained supervision over me. I was also released so I could make scheduled medical appointments to Tucson. After I got out of custody, I told no one I'd made up the cancer story to get out of jail. I had to act like I was leaving town for treatment because I had to go along with the story! I was afraid if it got out I'd be incarcerated again. Joyce told my ma about the cancer. When I pretended to go get treatment, I camped out at Mittry Lake and once I went to Wickenburg and stayed gone two or three days. I never stayed with anyone local during those times."

"I still didn't believe that Joyce thought that I had cancer, but we had to abide by the story. I didn't expect Joyce to tell as many people as she did."

"Did somebody kidnap you at the end of '94?" Millington asked him.

"No, sir," Richard said.

"Why on earth would you make up that story?"

"At the time I was hoping to create enough pressure saying Mr. Gene had done it, so he'd drop the charges. I got Gene involved by giving a description of an employee vehicle. No one kidnapped or beat me. I scratched myself with a nail. It hurt a little, but they were just superficial scratches. I don't have any scars. They took me to the hospital and they didn't even look at them. They looked at the pictures and did a blood test. I wasn't bleeding at all!"

"So you admit you made up the story?"

"Yes, I made it up."

"And what happened with those charges?" Millington continued.

"Ron Gene didn't drop them like I hoped and eventually I ended up pleading guilty to it."

"On January 11th, when Nichole came home and you were fixing the light in the bedroom, can you tell us what happened, Richard?"

"Yes, there's a little neon light there. Earlier in the day, the shelf fell off that's located above our bed. I put it up, it's homemade. One piece is screwed into the wall and the shelf just sets on top of a little bracket."

"I'd set one of those forty-four ounce Thirstbusters on the corner of the shelf. There's not enough on one side to hold it and it all fell on the bed. Everything got wet! I stripped the bed and put everything in the laundry. It seemed like the natural thing to do . . . we always used the same sheets."

Previous to this point in time, I had been reserving doubt about Richard, but this story sounded pretty ridiculous and I stole a look at my husband in the gallery. His walking cane was between his knees and his forehead was resting on the top. I noticed his shoulders shaking. *He was silently laughing*! I thought if he makes me start laughing while I'm sitting up here on the jury, I'm going to be furious! I fought it hard for a few minutes before I regained my decorum. When Butch finally looked up, his face was red and I think he had tears in his eyes. Richard was a professional carpenter who couldn't build a decent shelf above his own bed?

Richard continued with his story, "We had regular box springs and mattress and no foam pad or anything lying on the top. Previously we had some foam; three or four pieces of egg crate. Joyce had gotten it *out of a dumpster;* three narrow strips about eighteen inches and one 2' by 4'. It didn't work out though, because it bunched up. Nickie gave me two blankets after school because I had forgot to put mine in the dryer that day. But when the cops came, that's why there was nothing on the bed."

"Now later when the police came *back,* and had a search warrant on another date and they arrested you, what happened to the bedding that time?" Millington asked, hoping for a better answer I guess.

"The same thing happened again and the bedding was in the laundry!" Richard said, straight-faced.

I stole another look at my husband and saw the shaking shoulders again. This defendant was obviously thinking everybody in the world was an idiot except him and that was from questions by his own attorney!

Millington asked, "So, did you think that you should fix this shelf?"

"Yes, sir. In the couple of months I was there, it was a constant hazard. On the morning of the 11th, when I got ready to leave, Joyce went outside with me. I made sure the truck started and took off the battery charger and she kissed me good-bye at the door of the truck. I left to head out toward the Foothills and that was the last time I saw her."

"Did you kill your wife, Richard?"

"No, sir."

"Please tell us about the fire you had in your truck."

"It happened two days *before* Joyce disappeared. It burned the camper shell completely and the entire contents. There was some foam bedding remnants, carpet, wire, tools, a bag of old clothes. The truck was still useable, but the items were burned or smoke damaged. I sprayed some primer to keep it from rusting."

"Richard, you made up some flyers after Joyce disappeared."

"Yeah, I went to my sister's; she has some computer printing things and we typed a description on a piece of paper then took a picture to Copytime and had flyers made up. There were three or four different kinds, and we ran twenty or thirty with different pictures, then the Perrons' said the pictures didn't look like her. So, with a different picture, we had twenty or thirty more made up. I took them all over town. Most of the bars that knew us and some that didn't and video stores we used and grocery stores we used. Joyce smoked only clove cigarettes which are sold only at Tony's pool hall and The Golden Cue, which was close to where we lived, so I checked with them daily to see if anybody was buying these cigarettes. I got permission to put flyers in the windows there and on the counters."

On a personal note, I too, smoke clove cigarettes and have never gone to a pool hall to purchase them. He was wrong about those being the only places she could have bought them in Yuma at the time. It is an expensive habit, but at least it smells sweet and very pleasant. Even my non-smoking friends tell me that they love the smell.

Richard continued, "I began to worry when Joyce didn't show up for work. I'd heard through other people that Joyce had taken off before with somebody to Vegas, Laughlin, or whatever. I didn't think this was the case, but I just didn't know. She'd never taken off on me. I didn't see her all that day. I began posting the flyers on Friday. On Wednesday, I called the jail to see if she had been picked up."

I glanced at Mr. and Mrs. Perrons' faces and they were hard to read. I know how I would feel after that statement about my daughter!

"I called the hospital looking for Joyce and then I called the police and they said they wouldn't take a report for twenty-four hours. The next day they took the report and I had trouble getting someone to help me at missing persons. They were out, they put me on hold, they referred me. But I called several times. Then I called the newspaper or Mr. or Mrs. Perron did or the police did, I don't remember how her description got in the news. I didn't get the paper and didn't see it until Lori showed it to me."

"Richard, why did you wear camouflage clothing?"

"I mostly only wore it to go to the showers because I could zip in and out of it easily and it was insulated. Joyce wore it too. We all wore it to the shower and back."

"Did you clean up to hide evidence, Richard?"

"No, I did clean up the area because it needed cleaning and I did not dump Joyce in the Gravity Canal or tie her up or hit her in the head. I know nothing about how it happened."

"Nothing further at this time," said Millington for the defense.

Steve Russell looked primed as he stood to cross-examine Richard Handcock. "Richard you lied about having cancer to everyone and you made no attempts until right now, just this very morning, to correct that lie, that impression. Is that correct?

"Yes, sir, *nobody asked.*"

"You lied to keep yourself out of jail, correct?"

"Yes, sir."

"After you'd been arrested again, there were hearings to determine the conditions of your release, is that correct?"

"Yes, sir."

"Are you aware whether or not testimony at those hearings is supposed to be given under oath?"

"*I didn't testify.*"

I think this is what they call in the political arena as "plausible deniability." Richard could run for president in another life. I looked at my spouse; shoulders shaking again.

Russell asked, "Your wife came to testify on your behalf, correct?"

"I don't believe she testified."

"And in fact, that was the plan, for her to tell people you had cancer. Isn't that what you testified to?"

"Yes, sir."

"At one point I thought you said, 'We had come up with an agreement and you didn't believe Joyce believed you had cancer. Isn't that your testimony, that you don't believe that Joyce thought you had cancer?"

"No, she knew I didn't have cancer."

"How did she know that?" Russell asked him.

"It was our agreement on the story to get out of jail."

"So now you are saying that she absolutely knew you didn't have cancer?" Russell was totally incredulous.

"That was the agreement we made in October," Richard said.

"Do you recall Ms. Mess said you first started going to The Bottoms Up Pub in April or May because you needed a friend and you were having problems with your family and were depressed over having cancer?"

"She's mistaken on the time. I didn't talk about the cancer at that time."

"Now, you're also telling us that the kidnapping never took place?"

"Correct."

"That you were lying to the officer about the kidnapping and injuries? That you were in fact lying about all of it?"

"Yes, sir."

"And lying to the other officer as well?"

"Yes, sir."

"You lied to Joyce when you told her you'd been kidnapped?"

"Yes."

"This wasn't a plan she was in on?"

"No, sir."

"You also lied to Pre-trial Services when you told them you'd been kidnapped and were fearful of these people?"

"I believe so."

"So, that was a lie?" Russell reiterated.

"Yes, sir."

"One thing we should always remember is that you know how to tell a story and keep with it. That's been your testimony hasn't it?"

"It's been the truth."

"Well, are you telling the truth today?"

"My testimony today is the truth."

"You have truthfully testified that when you tell a lie, you know how to stick to the story. Is that your truthful testimony?"

"Yes."

That was a thing of beauty and I couldn't suppress a small smile.

Russell was eating it up. "It appears from looking at these photos that you scratched yourself all over your body with a nail in an effort to make your kidnap story more believable?"

"Yes, sir."

"And these multiple superficial wounds didn't hurt all that much?"

"No."

"A small price to pay to make your lie believable, correct?"

"Yes."

I was beginning to wonder why Millington didn't plead his client guilty by reason of mental defect. That had a beat and I could dance to it.

"You told the officer that you scratched yourself to win back your estranged wife, isn't that correct?"

"No, I said it could possibly work," Richard mused.

"Now, let's go back to your statement in regards to how the blankets got dirty. Do you want the jury to believe you put a Thirstbuster on a shelf and it fell on your blankets and you had to wash them right away?"

"That's what happened," Richard turned and gave us his most honest face.

"When did you get the Thirstbuster?" Russell asked him.

"I brung it with me from the Foothills."

"Which Circle K did you stop at?"

"I don't recall."

"Is it fair to say you never told anyone in law enforcement of this story about this Thirstbuster until this morning?"

"Nobody asked before," Richard said evenly.

Russell turned away from Handcock and looked at all of the jurors as if to say, *'Do you believe this guy?'*

"When did you wash the blankets?"

MURDER BY GRAVITY?

"It was in the afternoon," Richard replied.

"Was this before or after you had asked your neighbors if they'd seen your wife?"

"I believe after."

"You said the same sort of thing happened again ten days later?"

"I believe that time it was a bowl of cereal."

"You just could never fix this shelf, I guess," Russell observed.

"No."

"Weren't you able to employ your carpenter skills to fix the shelf so your items didn't spill onto your bed anymore?"

"No, I never took the time."

"So it's a mere coincidence that you had bedding problems both days and that no one has seen the bedding since then? That's a coincidence, is that your testimony?"

"It's a coincidence. That's my testimony," Richard said.

"You were present when the police searched your trailer and truck, correct?"

Richard answered looking like he was beginning to lose his patience, "Yes, I was sitting outside."

"These officers took the time to search your mother's house, your storage locker, your trailer and truck, yet failed to find your blankets in the laundry room?"

"I told the officers they were in the laundry room."

"They just failed to get them?"

"That's apparent," Richard answered smugly.

"Did you hear your father-in-law testify that as manager of the park, that he or someone else had found the blankets sitting in the laundry room?

"No, sir, everyone had access to it.

"I believe you told the officers that while Nickie was at the shower building, you and your wife made love?"

"Yes, sir."

"Everything was real happy between you and Joyce?"

"Yes, sir."

"We know you left home at 7:44 AM because your electronic monitor gives us a recording when you left; isn't that correct?"

"Yes, sir."

"And you told the officers you drove out to the Foothills to look

413

for work, is that correct?"

"Yes."

"How far is your trailer from the Foothills?"

"I have no idea," Richard said evasively.

Russell mused, "Well, is it fair to say it doesn't take five hours to go there and back?"

"Yes."

"You said you were looking for work. Pre-trial Services has a note that you had work on that day. Are they mistaken?"

Richard replied, "I would assume so, because I had a lead on a job and was going looking."

"Now, you heard the gentleman who testified that he believed the conversation about the tires took place at the beginning of the week."

"Could be," Richard replied.

"I believe he said it was approximately eleven o'clock because he leaves home when the soaps come on. You have an enter on your monitor at 12:44 PM Is that the time you got back?"

"Maybe a little before."

"It does, in fact, give you plenty of time to go to the construction site, both the Car Care Center and Jack In The Box, doesn't it?"

"Could be, but I got in earlier than that. Somewhere around eleven and talked to Mr. Perron for five or ten minutes and Cricket for five or ten minutes and maybe another resident there."

"So it's your testimony that you knew your wife was missing before going into the trailer?"

"Yes. The padlock was on the outside of the door and you can't get in without removing it."

Russell seemed to be thinking for a minute and then asked, "Did you go straight to the Foothills on January 10th?"

"I believe I stopped for gas on the way out at the Texaco on Pacific."

"How long did that take?"

"Ten to fifteen minutes. There were other cars in line."

"Let's say fifteen. Driving time; where did you go first?"

"First, I went to the old car wash. I went to that place and realized it was the wrong place and drove to the other one they were building behind the Foothill Grocery."

"When did you get there?"

MURDER BY GRAVITY?

"Around nine o'clock."

"Now, even giving you fifteen minutes to pump gas, that's still an hour to get from your trailer to the first place you claim you went in the Foothills. Do you want the jury to believe it takes an hour to drive from Yuma to the Foothills?"

I had driven it that morning coming into court from the Foothills. By freeway, it was about ten to fifteen minutes. Several of the jurors were also from the Foothills.

Richard's response was, "That was not the first place I went. The first place was the other car wash which is behind the IGA."

"How many nanoseconds did it take for you to realize there wasn't construction going on?" Russell asked sarcastically.

"Possibly ten minutes. I drove around the area," Richard said with a straight face.

Yes, I looked at my husband and he openly shook his head by that time. Even I was becoming unaffected to the outlandish, one thing after another epic yarns this character spun.

Russell rolled his eyes and began again, "There were two grocery stores in the Foothills at that time and you went to one. Through the process of elimination, where did you believe you had to go to find the construction site?"

"The other grocery store."

"So it wasn't really a large amount of driving around to figure that out, was there?"

"Clear on the other side of the Foothills!" Richard exclaimed.

"How long would the drive be?"

"I didn't take the freeway."

"Ten minutes?" Russell asked showing remarkable restraint.

"I dunno."

"In your statement to the police, it took you approximately one hour!" (For the record, it only takes three to five minutes.)

"I guess so."

"How long did you stay at these sites?"

"Probably forty-five minutes waiting for Andrews to come back."

"Why did you leave?"

"I got tired of waiting so I decided to go through Mesa Del Sol to look for Albert."

"Why not wait at the construction site where you know the foreman is coming back?" Russell asked, throwing common sense into Richard's scenario.

"I didn't know when he'd be back!"

"So when you left, did you ever go back to that job site?"

"No, sir."

"How long did you look for Albert?"

"Probably thirty minutes."

"Why look for him there?"

"He works at Mesa Del Sol very regularly. He has an office out there on Frontage Road."

"So you felt if you just drove around you might see Albert?"

"Yes, sir," said Richard.

"You thought it was a better use of your time to randomly look for someone than to wait for someone who would actually be returning?" Russell asked, his voice getting higher.

"There was no set time when he would be back."

"Were you aware of a particular construction site that he actually had in the Foothills?"

"No, sir."

"Why did you drive around looking for Albert, if he has an office in the city?"

"They said he was in the field."

"And they couldn't tell you where?"

"I didn't ask."

"You want us to believe you didn't even say, 'Hey is there a job site in the Foothills?'"

"I just said, 'Thank you,' when she said he was in the field"

"You didn't ask where in the field?"

"No."

"This all happen on the 11th?"

"Yes."

"Now, at some point you gave up on finding Albert who was also your previous employer?"

"Yes."

"Where did you go?"

"The Bottoms Up Pub."

"Why?"

MURDER BY GRAVITY?

"To have a V-8 and talk to Hazel for about forty-five minutes. We talked about personal things, you know, how was her relationship going, mine, *personal things."*

"Well, I believe you testified earlier that you and Joyce were not having marital difficulties.

"Correct."

"Were you telling Hazel how happy you were with Joyce?"

"I wouldn't describe it that way. I was telling her that if Joyce would quit fooling around with all these other people and her involvement with drugs we'd be happy. We were happiest when she wasn't on drugs."

"Prior to marrying Joyce, you'd been living with Hazel, correct?"

"Yes," Richard agreed.

"You didn't break up the second time until December 1993, isn't that correct?"

"Yes."

"You married Joyce in January of 1994, correct?"

"Yes, sir," Richard said.

"And you want this jury to believe that when you spoke to Hazel in January of 1995 it was about Joyce's infidelity, Joyce's flirting and her involvement with drugs?"

"*Probable* involvement with drugs."

"You sent Hazel flowers that spring in 1994 when you started going back to The Bottoms Up Pub, right?"

"Her birthday and maybe two other occasions."

"Actually the records show five or six. Do you disagree?"

"No."

"Hazel says you sent flowers so often she has no recollection how many times she received them. Is she lying?"

"No. I sent the same flowers to Joyce, too."

The man was shameless.

"Did you court Hazel the same way you courted Joyce--with lots of flowers and attention?"

"I have known Hazel since 1989."

Mr. Russell asked Judge Hale if the jury might recess early for lunch while they discuss an issue that has come up.

I reunited with Butch and introduced him to my other lunch buddies. We walked to The Landing and I had the chicken salad (I have no idea why I remember that!), which was excellent. The men bonded. I knew Butch would like Karl, the former undertaker, and Pete, the great impersonator, and Walt, who worked at the hardware store, since Butch was always going there and Larry, who reminded me of Johnny Carson--glib. It was only until I was writing this book that Butch remembered that my lunch group was all men-folk. I hadn't actually paid much attention, but of course, he remembered. It may have been the smoker to non-smoker ratio, or non-objector factor. Isn't that the way society divides us even more so now? Even though my clove cigarettes make the air smell sweet like something in the oven baking, I'm still an outsider and, yes, I wish I could pay somebody else to quit for me!

During our recess Mr. Russell told the court that he thought Richard should submit to an examination to see if he did have scars from the self-mutilation. An officer was called upon to do the examination, since Richard wore long sleeves every day.

Millington expressed his concerns that the officer might not be able to tell a scratch from a scar.

After lunch we resumed with Mr. Russell's cross-exam of Richard, who stated that he first met Hazel in 1989 and within a few months, he moved in with her for approximately two years until he went to prison. He said they got together again afterward for about six months.

Richard told us that he met Joyce after he got out of prison and broke up with Hazel. By then, he said, he and Hazel were just friends, but he visited her regularly and sent her flowers a few times. He said that while he was married to Joyce and on the electronic monitor, he saw Hazel, but they didn't have any real dates. He admitted going to Mansky's and P.J's with her and he admitted to having sex with her, but *only once while he was married to Joyce.*

"I won't say we were lovers. I had two or three absences during the marriage and I was gone less than a month in November 1994. Two or three times prior to that, I stayed with Sherry Miller and Ron Worthing when there was an argument to save confrontations or make things worse. Isn't it better for one person to walk away? That's why I left often."

"Now, at that time, Joyce quit working at P.J.'s, correct?"

"I believe she quit in July."

"And she quit because you didn't like her working there, did you?"

"We weren't together when she quit."

"But one of the reasons she quit was because you didn't like her working there, did you?"

"I don't know. She went to work for 8th St. Tavern."

"Did you like her working for P.J.'s?"

"We worked at the same bar."

"Did you like her working?" Richard gave no response. *"Did you like her working there?"*

"It was her job."

"May I ask the court to instruct the witness to answer the question?" Russell was getting frustrated, with good reason.

"That was her job."

"Did you like that fact that your wife worked at the bar?"

"Sometimes no, and sometimes yes."

"When it was no, why not?"

"Well, her involvement with drugs."

"That was directly stemming from work at the bar?"

"Yes, sir."

"You worked at that bar. Did you have that same problem?"

"No, sir. I was told by the bar owner that there's no drugs allowed in the bar. I was to report any employees using drugs. The owners told me they thought Joyce was skimming from the cash register, dealing drugs over the bar. They wanted me to talk to her," Richard said casually. "That was in May 1994."

"Who told you that?"

"Tammy; she used to own P.J.'s. I told Joyce what Tammy said and we had another argument over it."

"How did you know she was doing that?"

"Well, when someone doesn't sleep four or five days and tries to tell you it's diet pills, I've been involved with drugs all my life; I can see those things!"

"So, she's stealing, taking drugs and you're seeing another woman and you don't see this as a troubled marriage?"

"It had its up and downs."

"When were the ups?"

"When she wasn't using drugs and working at the bar, we got

along fine."

"Did you like the way Joyce dressed?"

"She dressed nice."

"Did you like the way she acted with the male patrons?"

"Just the few involved with drugs like Mike Deere and Jeff Dupree and Ruby Vasquez."

"Okay, I'm going to shift here and ask you, isn't it true that there are witnesses that will say you were claiming to have cancer long before you committed any crimes against Mr. Ron Gene?"

"Whatever."

"Your manipulation was of the legal system, not your wife?" Russell thought out loud.

"That's right."

"When you spoke with Hazel for forty-five minutes, you discussed Joyce's drug problems and a rumor that Joyce had been unfaithful with Mike Deere. Didn't you also tell her that Joyce was sleeping with Bob DeVore? Did you play a tape for Jeff and Ruby?"

"Yes."

"Did you become emotionally upset?"

"Sort of, "Richard confessed.

"At one time, you suspected Mike Deere of having an affair with Joyce in May 1994."

"Joyce told me she wasn't having an affair. That's when she got the drugs. That's why she was always going over there. And I believed her," Richard said sadly.

"Didn't you also think Joyce was having an affair with Jeff Dupre?"

"When I forgot my wallet one time, I saw Joyce leaving in a car and I followed her to Mike Deere's house. Joyce later claimed she didn't go anywhere."

Russell walked away from Richard then looked at him; as if sizing him up for the first time." Are you a jealous man?"

"No more than anybody else."

"Did Nicole lie when she said you didn't like the way Joyce dressed?"

Richard leaned back comfortably, "She wore the same clothes when I met her. Nichole was mistaken."

"Nickie said you argued over Joyce's male friends."

"Because most of them were involved in drugs."

"During that time didn't you receive notes from Hazel on your truck?"

"Yes."

"And you and Joyce argued about this."

"She was concerned about the notes. An argument is different than a fight. Joyce got notes from Mike Deere and Jeff Dupree. But I wasn't concerned because I knew it was about drugs. Hazel's notes said she needed someone to talk to."

Richard would never admit to being more jealous than any other man, and he claimed that he never interfered with her work or argued on the phone. Anyone who said so was mistaken.

"Okay, I'm going to shift gears again. After you went to the Foothills on the 11th and you noticed the padlock on the door, you asked the neighbors if they had seen Joyce." Russell lapsed into a pregnant pause and crossed his arms. "Did you look inside to see if Joyce had left a note? Why didn't you just wait for her return? Why were you so alarmed? I mean, you waited forty-five minutes before opening the trailer door!"

"I wanted to use the rest room and the pay phone too," Richard replied, "and our toilet wasn't working in the trailer."

"But you had a phone in your trailer."

"Yes, sir."

"Why did you use a pay phone?"

"Because it had a phone book!"

Russell continued at him, "Why would you use a pay phone only ten feet away? Was there some other reason that you didn't want to go into your trailer?"

"No."

"Didn't you testify that you had a V-8 and a soda while you were at The Bottoms Up Pub?"

"Soda or tea, I don't remember."

"You must have been pretty thirsty if you had two drinks at the pub and you had to get a 44-ounce Thirstbuster on your way home."

"Yes."

Richard said that he became very concerned about Joyce around 4:00 PM and he was allowed away time until 7:00 PM. He made a couple of phone calls and stayed home. The next day he said he stayed close to the phone in case she called.

"The next day, on the 12th, I was gone for about forty minutes and I went to the grocery store to buy cigarettes. I couldn't look for Joyce because *where would you start?* I called everybody and they hadn't seen her."

Russell asked, "You already testified that Joyce lied to you about going to Mike Deere's. Why wouldn't you drive by?"

"I can't see through walls!" Richard exclaimed. "I checked to see if Joyce had bought clove cigarettes everyday. The 13th and the 14th was the same thing and I stayed close to the phone. Sunday or Monday of the following week I started cleaning up so I wouldn't get evicted. I also dropped off flyers."

"Why didn't you take one day to post up all the flyers you made?"

"I only had thirty or forty at a time. I made more when I ran out.""

"How long does it take to put up twenty flyers?"

"Sometimes an hour."

"Why didn't you post all that you had?" Russell persisted.

"I didn't stop at every street corner or every store because I didn't have that much money."

"Why didn't you post all you made?"

"I believe I had just made some more before they searched my trailer."

"That's an unlucky break!"

Millington objected and it was sustained.

"Where were you on Sunday the 15th and Monday the 16th and Tuesday the 17th?"

"I usually made a trip to my mother's and would take a different route home and put up flyers. I believe I also gave a flyer to your secretary, sir!" Richard explained.

Russell was forced to smile at Richard, who smiled in return. A temporary stale mate.

"Now, Richard, the only problem that you had with Joyce was her use of drugs?"

"Yes."

"Were *you* using drugs in 1994?"

"No."

MURDER BY GRAVITY?

"Wasn't there a single incident in 1994 where you were using drugs?" asked Russell, hoping to trip up Richard.

"I believe when they took the blood sample at the hospital, *it came up dirty.*"

"*Were you using in 1994?*"

"*No, not at that time. It was before then in December.*"

Judge Hale asked the jury to leave again. Richard was trying everyone's patience.

Bill Millington objected because he was concerned that Richard was hesitating to answer because he didn't want to admit under oath he was using illegal drugs in 1994. "We are still under the Statute of Limitations of that time. Richard would like immunity on any drug charges."

Russell said, "They brought up the drug issue. Richard pled guilty to attempted possession of a dangerous drug in the fall of 1994!"

Judge Hale responded, "A defendant has a right to decide whether or not to testify. He has a right not to. But once he takes the witness stand, he can't claim the Fifth to any relevant questions on cross-examination. Relevant is to prove his guilt or lack of guilt as to the offenses with which he's charged."

"It was indicated that the primary reason for trouble in the marriage was drugs. It only makes sense if he wasn't using drugs himself. It calls into question the sincerity of his concern. It is relevant and the defendant has opened himself up to that, by his testimony in that area. Richard was convicted of an attempt to possess in 1995, stemming from 1994 and the same in 1989."

Millington tried to plead again on the behalf of his client to be allowed to invoke and Judge Hale overruled him.

The jury was brought back into the courtroom and seated. We looked at all their faces as if we could determine anything that transpired during our absence. But this was to no avail.

Russell stood to continue his cross-examination. "During the time you indicated Joyce's drug use caused problems in your relationship, weren't you, yourself using meth and marijuana?"

"Not always, no. When I was arrested, they found meth and marijuana in my truck."

"Was that the only time in 1994 you were using?" Russell asked, getting irritated.

"I'd rather not say. I'll take the Fifth."

Judge Hale took off his glasses and addressed Richard directly, "Mr. Handcock, you don't have a right to take the Fifth. You must answer the question."

"That's the only time I was using; when they found it in my truck," Richard said with a straight face.

I don't think any person in the courtroom believed him; still, it made you realize that the man would lie no matter what. Before he testified, I had held an ounce of doubt about his guilt, but once he testified, there was no doubt, reasonable or otherwise. I wondered why his attorney put him on the stand at all.

Russell asked Richard, "Why did you want to take the Fifth just now?"

"Because you guys are prosecuting me again!"

"Mr. Handcock, when you were arrested in December of 1994, they took a blood test from you and you tested positive for marijuana, amphetamines, and crystal meth."

"I was not using at the time. It takes a long time to get out of your system," Richard declared.

"Did you ever ask Jeff for a substance called 'golden seal tea'?"

"Yes."

It was explained to us that it was for the purported purpose of obtaining a clean blood test--to wash out drug residue.

Russell asked Richard, "Have you ever smoked meth with Jeff and Ruby on several occasions?"

"No, sir."

"Was that a lie?"

"Yes, sir. I never smoked meth. I have snorted it, that's all."

"Then did you snort it with . . ."

"I don't remember," Richard said, enjoying the dance.

"You do have a history of drug abuse?"

"Correct."

"When they arrested you, when they found drugs in your truck, you actually wrote a statement claiming it was your drugs, didn't you?"

"Yes, sir."

"But I didn't use drugs for two weeks before my drug test in

MURDER BY GRAVITY?

December. I was arrested in November on the 22nd also.

"Dr. Sperry told us that the body disposes of crystal methamphetamine quickly."

"I hadn't used it," said Richard, sticking to the story.

Mr. Russell asked, "Was there a hearing for Joyce to lie at in your behalf?"

"No."

"And how did you get on Pre-trial Services?"

"They interviewed me and I got out of custody based on their recommendation."

"Why would Nickie and Jeff Dupree lie about the baby-sitting?" Richard just shrugged.

"Did Nichole baby-sit for Jeff that evening?"

"I'm not sure if it was . . . if it was *that evening.*"

"You followed up on leads for eight hours at The Show Place, Friendly Tavern, and 8th Street Tavern, but you didn't stay. You just asked people?"

"She was seen with a long-haired biker type guy, which fits Mike Deere's description. I got this information from somebody who called my mother, I believe. I went to Mike's place, but his Jeep wasn't there."

"This is the first time ever that you've said that you went to Mike Deere's house!" Russell just shook his head in amazement. "Thank you. Nothing further, your honor."

Millington began his re-direct by asking Richard, "Could you please take off your sweater and show the jury that you have no scars on your arms from the time you scraped them with a nail?"

Richard unbuttoned his white sweater and shirt that he wore everyday and walked up to me on the end then slowly walked toward juror number one. What with not having any tan at all, the scratch marks were nearly unremarkable beneath the thick fair hair on his arms and chest. It was amazing that he wouldn't have more scarring, after seeing the pictures of what he had done to himself that night. The human body is remarkable. Six years ago my doctor removed cancer from my nose that was the size of a quarter and more above my lip that was the size of a nickel. The doctor stepped back when he was done and said, "Zorro!" because it looked like I had a big red Z carved in the center of my face and my lip was held up in an Elvislooking snarl. Because I'm fair-skinned, it was almost indiscernible within six months.

Bill Millington wanted to make it clear that Richard was not accusing any witnesses of lying. Richard told us that the night before Joyce disappeared, he spoke with Dick Kidd and he told him that if he'd just show up, he had a good shot of having a job. He said that he'd been in construction as a carpenter since he was fifteen years old.

"I've worked with several local contractors and had a couple hundred jobs."

Millington, not wanting to dwell there asked, "Did the police ever ask you where your bedding was when they searched your home?"

"They never asked about the bedding or if I had disposed of anything or had anything in the laundry. I was told to sit in a chair, then they took me to the police station for questioning. After I answered some questions, they arrested me. Then I told one of the officers about the wash and he said they'd take care of it. I still don't know what happened to it because I've been in custody ever since."

"How was your relationship with Joyce? Did you ever argue?"

"I admit that we argued often and loud. Joyce was loud. I would usually go for a walk. I was concerned about Joyce's drug use and the possibility of her getting arrested!"

That was tough to swallow; the pot calling the kettle black, so to speak. But that was his story.

"Now, Richard, when you would take Joyce to work, how early would you get there?"

"About fifteen minutes or thirty minutes."

"And what was your behavior while you were there?"

"I just sat and waited for her to finish her shift. I didn't interfere with her work and I never told any guy to quit flirting with her."

"Now, why didn't you go drive around and look for Joyce?"

"My truck only gets six miles to the gallon and I didn't have the money and I really didn't know where to look! But I did make the telephone calls. I couldn't force Joyce to come home. I just wanted to know that she was all right."

"Did anybody help you look for Joyce?"

"Nobody helped me. The Perrons' didn't help me look for her or take flyers to hand out. Mike Deere or Ruby didn't help. None of her friends helped."

One of the jurors asked if Richard had ever sought professional help for Joyce's drug problem and Richard said that she had quit twice and they got along fine during that time period. But Mike Deere and Jeff Dupree would get her started again whenever she would hang out with them.

Another question was, "What was Richard doing Saturday, January the 14th from 4:43 PM to 11:53 PM?"

Richard replied, "Out, with approval of Ike Groves. I believe that day I called the police department on a rumor that someone had seen Joyce at 8th Street Tavern or the Friendly Tavern or some place like that. I called Pre-trial for permission to follow up on a lead."

Someone asked Richard why he locked Joyce out of their trailer at Swift Sales. He said that it was because the arguments were *potentially violent*. "I believe it's good to walk away." He said that he was aware of Joyce's bruises, but he never physically abused her. He suspected that she got them running into corners at work or crawling into and out of dumpsters.

One of the jurors asked Richard if he'd ever called The Dark Place or The Show Place and say the Joyce was a dead bitch or that she had AIDS and, of course, his answer was predictably, no.

Another juror wanted to know if Richard had ever disposed of Joyce's jewelry without her knowledge and he said that once she gave him back her wedding rings and he had pawned them. He didn't know who wrote on the side of the bar about Joyce having AIDS.

Richard was asked if Jeff Dupree picked up Nickie the day Joyce disappeared and Richard said no. Richard thought it was the following day.

Another asked how many frames Richard had made for Joyce and he figured somewhere between forty and fifty before Christmas.

Steve Russell began his re-cross exam by asking Richard, "Why would Nickie and Jeff Dupree lie about the baby-sitting?" Richard just shrugged.

"Did Nichole baby-sit for Jeff that evening?"

"I'm not sure if it was . . . if it *was that evening."*

"You followed up on leads for eight hours at The Show Place, Friendly Tavern, and 8th Street Tavern, but you didn't stay. You just asked people?"

"She was seen with a long-haired biker-type guy, which fits Mike Deere's description. I got this information from somebody who called my mother, I believe. I went to Mike's place, but his Jeep wasn't there."

Millington began his re-direct examination and asked about the baby-sitting. "Was it Wednesday or Thursday, Richard?"

"I believe it was Thursday when the Perrons came over and said I wasn't fit to take care of Nickie, so it must have been Wednesday. I don't dispute Nickie's Wednesday night testimony, but Dupre didn't pick her up in the morning. And *I didn't put pieces of wood out at the lagoon.*"

And with that final denial, Richard was released from the witness stand to the relief of all.

* * *

Millington called Thomas Jones for the defense who stated that he had lived in Yuma for fifty-one years and that he worked at the Federal Court Facility in Yuma, but had previously worked at the General Security Service Corporation, which is a subcontractor with the Federal Court. He stated that he was a licensed private investigator since March of 1996 and worked for the defense.

Mr. Jones said that he had spoken with Dee Willingham and her daughter, Bev Baker and Danny Miller, who is also a private investigator. He and Detective Graham received a report that threats were made by people who said they had disposed of a body. The people involved were Phil Seward, would-be rapist of Joyce Handcock, and Gary Cox, a.k.a. the neighbor who didn't have a torture chamber in his basement.

Schulmire cross-examined by asking the gentleman just what he remembered from the interview. He stated that he didn't really recall, except that they claimed a corpse was tortured and the arms were cut off, but they may have read it in the newspapers. It was a ritualistic devil-worshiping cult.

CHAPTER 59

Bill Millington called Wilburn McCurley to the stand for the defense who, upon being sworn in, stated that he'd lived in Yuma for thirty-eight years and that he was the County Constable and enforced Justice court orders, writs of restitution, and eviction notices.

Millington asked, "Isn't it true that you had followed Mr. Phil Seward to the house Joyce and Richard rented from Phil Seward, who was the owner of the house on 23rd Place?"

"Yes, I was there to serve notice. Joyce was upset with Phil, is what Phil told me on the phone previously and that she may be filing charges for molesting her."

"Did you ask Phil Seward to leave?" Millington asked.

"Yes. Joyce was quite upset with him and the fact that Mike Deere was there at Joyce's house. Phil Seward, Jr. showed up after Phil Sr. left. Joyce already had things in a truck and Joyce asked if I'd stay. She didn't want anyone else there and Phil did."

There were no other questions for the Constable from either side.

* * *

Dusty Wheelwright called Leigh Gerard in to witness for the defense. Leigh said that she'd lived in Yuma for twelve years and currently lived at the Crossroads Mission Women's Shelter and that she was in the recovery program for drugs and alcohol. Leigh stated that Joyce had been a friend for five years and that they had met at P.J.'s., a local bar. Leigh said that when she's not in her 120-day program, she was working as a secretary and that Richard was an acquaintance.

"I saw Richard the last day before Joyce disappeared. I was

living with Red Pollock and Ruby Vasquez and I'd been working at Johnny's Other Place and I needed a place to live and Red offered. I was twenty-seven and Red was old enough to be my father."

Russell asked the jury to step out. "I believe that Pollock and the drugs are irrelevant and the sleeping arrangements are irrelevant."

Millington said, "Red had to know about the drugs. They talked in front of him and he *lied under oath. He was with Ruby and Leigh when they delivered drugs to Joyce the night before she disappeared!*"

"It's moot."

Hale said to bring the jury back in.

Dusty asked, "So your relationship with Lieutenant Red Pollock was intimate?"

"Yes."

"The night before Joyce disappeared, you were at The Dark Place and you spoke with Joyce, correct?"

"Yeah, there were about ten people there between nine and ten o'clock and I was with Ruby and Red. Joyce wanted a storage shed and I was going to check if they had one by mine. She didn't say she already had one."

"Ruby said we needed to go somewhere before Joyce's. They'd already made plans with Joyce; Ruby said. When we left the bar we went to Skip's condo. Will the same Use Immunity be granted to Skip?"

Judge Hale said, "You will be held in contempt if you do not answer the questions."

Leigh seemed to weigh the judge's words then continued on cautiously, "They call him 'Skip-Eye' because he only has one eye. We went there to pick up a quarter-gram of meth. Only Ruby went in. Red knew where Joyce's trailer was. At Joyce's only Ruby got out of the car and delivered the crystal ice to Joyce. There were no craft supplies that night, except Ruby came back with silk and dried flowers in a bag from the shed."

"Mike Deere was in the bar that night. When I moved out of Pollock's, I moved in with Mike Deere. I'd been doing drugs at Mike's and nursed him through pneumonia. I stayed five nights and Red and I had a fight over it on the phone. Ruby lived at Red's off and on. I lived there for eight months before moving out to get

MURDER BY GRAVITY?

married. I still got drugs from Mike after that. *I hid my drugs from Red Pollock, but I did have them in his house.* He did know about it after I admitted it, though, and he could tell I was very high because I was very happy. He knew Ruby was too."

"Mike's was a place were people crashed at and stayed. I never got my belongings back from Red's. After I moved out of Mike's, Dee Seward moved in! She's Phil Seward Jr.'s ex-wife."

"Leigh, changing the subject now, would you say that Joyce Handcock dressed sexy?"

"She dressed provocatively, which is expected in a bar."

"After Joyce died, and you were living with Mike Deere, did he ever tell you anything about his sexual relationship with Joyce?"

"He said that he and Joyce used to play dress up--role-playing kind of sex games when she came over to get away from Richard."

"Since Joyce died, did Mike get a tattoo?"

"Yes, Mike has a tattoo of a naked lady laying on her back with a gravestone behind and roses and skulls underneath her and it says like, 'In Memory of Joyce,' on the back of his left shoulder."

"Why are you in detox right now, Leigh?" Millington asked.

"My husband and I got busted for weed and I went in voluntarily."

"No more questions at this time," Millington said.

Schulmire stood and adjusted his waistband and cleared his throat. "Did you tell Detective Graham that Richard had cancer between July and September?"

"Sounds right," Leigh said.

"Did you also tell her that Joyce liked to flirt and that Richard would get angry and that Joyce told you several times that Red didn't know Joyce until the night before she disappeared?"

"I had several drinks and crystal and pot that night."

"Did you mention the drugs to Red that night?"

"No."

"When did Ruby and Red start having sex?" Schulmire asked her.

Leigh was beginning to look miffed. She said, "The night she moved in with us."

"When did Mike have pneumonia?"

"About the time Joyce went missing," Leigh said, defiantly

431

sticking her chin out.

"Didn't Pollock make it clear to you that as a condition of you moving into his house that no drugs were allowed?"

"Yes. He told us not to use, so Ruby and I never used drugs in front of Red."

Dusty stood for her re-direct, "Leigh, isn't it true that the night of the 10th Joyce was tweaking in the bar and used drugs every day?"

"Yes, we all did."

* * *

Millington called Danny Miller, who had been a private investigator since April 1996 when he received his license. Prior to that he was a Deputy Sheriff and an investigator for twenty-two years and retired November 1995, was also the owner of Audio Einstein's Stereo on Fourth Street. Danny stated that he had posted a flyer at his store at the same time the Sheriff got them and didn't recall who brought the flyer in. He also stated that he had no involvement with Mr. Handcock but was authorized by the court to work for the defense. He was the attractive mystery man who often sat behind the defense counsel's table.

"Here is an enlargement of an aerial photo of the lagoon past the dump site, the photos of Hwy. 95 and 7E. The area is still much the same as it was then, though there is some difference in vegetation. We have a video to present of a recent trip we took by Jeep out to the area. It might make you sick if you watch for too long, I kept getting cramps in my hands." My house backs up to 7E., albeit a few miles away. This was getting too close to home!

We then were presented with a sixty-six minute video of a Jeep ride out to a wilderness area. Judge Hale said that if we felt sick to our stomachs it would be okay if we looked away. Millington gave a commentary as the film played, "The road goes down and around. This is the estuary (wide mouth of a river) and the concrete culvert; there are two pictures of the lagoon at the Gila Gravity Canal. A few houses were spotted from the area. (Far away and using the zoom, by the way.) This is where the fire ring was."

The defense was trying to show that other people used the area and Richard would have no expectation of privacy. But instead it

MURDER BY GRAVITY?

showed the houses were far away and there were two tunnels that the canal went through and a person could go in there and be hidden.

Russell began his cross-examination by asking Danny Miller how long it took them to make the trip when they were videotaping.

Danny said, "One hour and five minutes. We had a four-wheel drive and had to make two attempts to get through a rut at the bottom of the slope."

"And did you see anybody else while you were there?"

"We were there about fifty minutes before we ran into someone on the other side, then we saw them again five minutes later."

"And that was on the other side of the canal. How far is that past where Joyce's body was found?" Russell asked.

"About three miles. There are other areas, as well, where someone might have deposited a body."

"What are some of the difficulties with depositing a body just on the ground; even if you put bushes around it? If you don't want this body found?" Russell probed.

"Ever? You wouldn't just lay it on the ground . . . because a decomposing body smells noticeably and animals attack and destroy it; tear it apart."

"What about human beings discovering the body? Other human beings spend most of their time on land. If you leave a body just out on the land, someone prospecting or just hiking might stumble across it, correct?"

"Very possible," Danny agreed.

"In the water, animals and humans can't get to a body. Was the road to the Gravity Canal County-maintained?"

"It was not a County maintained road, no."

Millington stood to re-direct and asked if Danny remembered seeing people out there fishing three weeks before they took the video.

"Yes. And there are more people in January because of the snowbirds who take over the area. They think it's like the Old West. There are areas where the soil is sandy, some rocky, some clay. There are areas where a person could dig with a shovel and bury and cover up! That would be better than to leave a body on top of the dirt."

Bailiff: "We have a question from the jury:"

"On January 11, 1995, was County 5th St. a road on which the waste transfer site is located, paved?"

"It had been oiled." And you had to drive down that to get to the Gravity Canal.

* * *

Defense attorney Bill Millington called Debbie Nelson who works for the Yuma County Sheriff's office as the evidence tech. She stated that she had full custody and control of the property for the Sheriff's Department evidence that is seized and that which was seized in the Handcock case. Debbie said that others look at evidence from time to time, but the evidence was still secured there.

Millington asked her to identify a card identified as Exhibit E, found in Joyce's locker that read, "Free Anonymous AIDS Testing," and on the back said William Rockhouse. Nelson also identified books, papers, baskets, sleeping bags, and lots of other evidence and said that there was an answering machine, but she didn't know from where it was seized.

* * *

Millington recalled Detective Donna Graham, who re-identified herself as the agent in charge of the case.

"Before trial today, I asked you to look through the evidence to track the forms concerning a set of photos. No location was written on that document as to where they might have been taken from. There was no, 'Please print,' that you would normally write under that top part, correct?"

Clearly uncomfortable, Graham admitted that he was correct.

"Now, regarding the photos taken January 20th, 1995, it would be in your records department where the original report is the film of the fire ring and location of the body was on that roll of film. The pictures didn't come out. You were shown the negatives?"

"I don't recall if Debbie or the photo place showed them to me. I do know they couldn't make any prints out because they were all black."

"Did you ever interview Phil Seward?" Millington asked letting his irritation show.

"Even though he'd been charged of a crime by Joyce, I knew of Mr. Cox's statement and Bev Baker and the devil worship claims and that Phil's name had come up. I did interview Mike Deere five or six times and taped him. I spoke to everyone--the Perrons', Joyce's sister."

"Had you been told of Joyce's suicide attempt?" Millington asked pointedly.

"Yes."

"Didn't you discover that Joyce had tried to *drown herself* when she had a fight with Richard and he was arrested?"

"Mike Deere told me about that," Graham said softly.

"And wasn't the blue paint similar to the blue paint that is on the trim of Mike's house?"

"Mike said he gave her blue paint and poured it into a can for her."

"Did you check Mike's house for cement pylons?"

"No."

* * *

Millington recalled Detective St. Jons to the stand and after he was reminded that he was still under oath, he was asked about the property that he seized at Swift Sales.

"We took samples of rebar and wire and strapping. We also searched Richard's and Joyce's storage lockers. Nichole and Mrs. Perron had told me that Joyce's purse had disappeared after the locker was searched. Lori asked us about it before the search; the blue denim bag that Joyce always carried everywhere with her. It was never found again."

"Detective St. Jons, were you told about the use and distribution of drugs during your investigation?"

"Yes."

"Was anyone arrested because of it?"

"I was trying to solve a murder! I needed to keep my sources flowing with information. They wouldn't have done that if they thought they were going to be arrested for talking about drugs."

CHERIE HUYETT ACHTEMEIER

* * *

While the jury was out again Mr. Millington told Judge Hale that Dick Kidd was their last witness, but they were unable to locate him. He worked at the Circle K on Avenue C and he would testify that the day Richard came to look for a job was on the 11th and his pick up truck bed probably burned on the morning of the 9th.

Danny Miller said that he had spoken with Mr. Kidd the previous day, but now he couldn't be found. Judge Hale offered to file a bench warrant for Kidd but they declined.

Millington said, "We still thought he'd show up. A bench warrant doesn't do any good if we can't find him."

"Miller said he knew where Kidd lives," said the judge.

Millington said, "I was so busy this morning, it skipped my mind."

Judge Hale replied, "We are not going to recess today. You can close your case and still have the opportunity if he shows up later."

"That's acceptable, Your Honor," Millington agreed.

"If we need to issue a bench warrant . . .," began the judge.

Millington said, "I would ask you to do that at this point, Judge."

"Let's assume this is the close of your case and later on, if you want to make the same motion, you can do that to protect the record, I suppose. And what is the State doing at this point, Mr. Russell?"

"The State intends to call Susan Shotz, Richard's ex-wife, who alleges that in 1979, Richard flew into a rage and beat her up almost to death!"

CHAPTER 60

As I found out later, while reading the transcripts, Susan Shotz was not allowed to testify against her ex-husband because it showed prejudice. The court ruled it not admissible under Rule 403/Considerations.

The jury was returned to the courtroom and was told that the defense rested, subject to calling Dick Kidd.

Steve Russell called Dr. Rolland Andrews, the Tucson pathologist and the doctor who performed the autopsy.

Russell had a paper in his hand as he asked, "Dr. Andrews, you were asked to review medical literature in regards to methamphetamine intoxication. Can you tell us what you found?"

"Yes, I read a standard text by Cravey and Besalt called, *The Disposition of Toxic Drugs and Chemicals in Man,* which is the same book Dr. Sperry read and two others in addition. The highest recorded level in a living human who was *driving a vehicle* was 9,460. Joyce's was 1,309 but it was not a blood sample."

"Cravey and Besalt list research books which I checked out and they were incorrect on their authority. They said death can occur at 800, but that was specifically due to intravenous ingestion. Death results at a lower level as the body would be in shock if the body were getting all of the drug at once and the body functions are not able to buffer."

Andrews drew a picture on a chart of a bell curve. Like one many of us got graded on in school; the bulk of the class being at the top of the bell getting the "C" or average grade range.

"Generally, the range is 2,000 to 3,000; some as high as 18,000. Some people could even survive higher levels. Joyce had no needle tracks. Joyce was a chronic user since at least May 1994 and one can have a chronic level in the system all the time and a drug tolerance develops. Also, the longer a person is dead, the *higher* the concentration levels. Postmortem, the drug is released."

"Taking fluid from the lung cavity may make levels higher or lower. I had been given Dr. Sperry's testimony to analyze and asked to consider if it was right. Most people, who die of a drug overdose, use that drug routinely."

Russell asked Dr. Andrews, who drove four hours to defend his position; well, that and it may have been his job and he may have been served a subpoena, "If Richard took crystal meth on November 22, 1994, and his blood was tested on December 7, 1994, would you expect to see traces of the drug if he only used it on the 22nd?"

"No, the half life of meth in blood is about twenty-four hours. Meth would not be detected after about two days."

The bailiff announced that there were questions from the jury and the judge read:

"Dr. Sperry said that he would have done two more tests."

"Yes; removal of the tongue and inspection of it, the throat and larynx and subcutaneous examination of the skin. Those things were all done during the autopsy and strangulation was ruled out and all of the skin was examined and nothing was noted."

* * *

After the jury was dismissed for the day, the court handed out to both sides of counsel rough drafts of the jury instructions. Mr. Russell said that the State would not be calling any more witnesses.

The defense decided to turn down the arrest warrant sworn out for Dick Kidd because if he were arrested, it would make him less than cooperative. Millington later changed his mind and asked that the bench warrant not be quashed because Kidd still failed to appear when they wanted him to, in spite of a personal notice from Danny Miller and other notices given to whoever answered his telephone. "He willfully and contemptuously failed to obey the orders of this court." Hale let it remain pending.

The judge said that there would be six forms of a verdict of guilty or not guilty, and each charge offense was followed by instructions.

Millington requested to be allowed the "Willett's Instruction," which would provide them to argue with the State that by allowing

MURDER BY GRAVITY?

Joyce's body to be released by Tucson's medical examiner to be cremated it left them without a body for the defense's expert to determine the cause of death. It was an inspired Hail Mary on Millington's part, but the body had been in the Tucson's pathology lab for over a month before it was released. They had ample time to send an expert during that time. Not Millington, but Richard's attorney who was representing him at the time.

Russell argued that a full forensic autopsy was done and the defense was purely speculating. The Court determined there was no bad faith by the State and Judge Hale denied Willett's Instruction.

* * *

When the jury entered the courtroom, Millington stipulated the following:

That Phillip Seward Sr. was charged by the Yuma County Grand jury September 6, 1994 with committing the crime of sexual abuse on Joyce Handcock. The trial was set for January 13, 1995 and the charges against him were dismissed because Joyce was missing.

Closing remarks from both sides were eloquent. I was surprised when I heard what the prosecutor had to say about the scenario during which he thought Joyce had died that fateful day.

Mr. Russell told us that the evidence showed that Richard had attacked Joyce in the trailer after Nichole left for school, Joyce had told Richard about her plan to go to Tucson with him and they argued until Richard flew into a rage and hit her in the head three times with a blunt object that had left the chevron-shapes on her scalp. Then he took her unconscious body and rolled her up in the bloody sheets and egg crates from the bed and backed up his truck so he could carry her limp, but alive, body in it without drawing attention from the neighbors. Then he loaded other items from under the trailer to weigh her body down and drove to the Gila Gravity Canal, which took approximately forty-five minutes and was plenty of time for the legal definition of premeditation. While she was still unconscious, he tied her wrists and ankles intricately with thick strapping tape and wire and used the wire cutters that were in his truck then affixed the concrete blocks and milk crate with rocks and probably carried her into the canal where she drowned to death without regaining consciousness. Her body probably would not have been discovered that day had Richard made allowances for all the rain and the high water level in the Gravity Canal when he dumped her body that January day. He may have gotten away with murder if he had put her body deeper or shortened the strapping tape and wires that were connected to her. They were attached in such a way that he must have known that she might have become conscious again with the intricate wire going between the wrists and wrapping around them as well. She wasn't wrapped like somebody would just weigh a body down; it could have been done much easier if that had been the goal. But Richard was afraid she might regain consciousness and that was why the straps and wires on her wrists and ankles were so detailed.

In my mind, I was shouting, *is that what you think?* That wasn't what I was thinking after hearing all of the evidence. There was no blood to be found in that trailer. If she were hit three times, there would be cast-off blood on the low ceiling of the trailer, and on the walls and probably the floor. Richard would never be able to find all traces of it to clean it. For that reason, I was thinking that perhaps Richard had coaxed Joyce into getting into the truck with him. He could have told her that they were going to do something else first before going to Tucson; just made up another impromptu lie. Granted, the missing bedding was indeed suspicious. I think now Joyce may have been *hit with one object that left three marks,* as they were too precisely lined up straight. She could have fallen and struck her head on a piece of furniture that had corner molding; but no, they had built-in drawers in the trailer and only the bed in the room. It would be nearly impossible to strike somebody three separate times and have all three marks line up perfectly. None of the furniture in the trailer had decorative wood trim like that, I know, because we used to own an Avion several years beforehand and the design hasn't changed much. Though being assaulted at home could explain the lack of clothing and Richard burning the truck's bed. And Irma Stebbins, the neighbor who testified about seeing the convoluted rolled mattress, said that happened two days after Joyce disappeared; then later waffled on her time frame.

Bill Millington's closing remarks for the defense were inspired. He was more "there" than at any other time during the trial. His main argument was that Dr. Sperry said that the autopsy was incomplete and since the body had been cremated, there would never be any way to know for sure how Joyce died.

There wasn't sufficient evidence to prove that Joyce didn't overdose or commit suicide or that Phil Seward or Mike Deere or some other person or persons unknown could be the culprits as Richard, could account for where he was at the time, and Phil Seward wouldn't even take the stand but only plead the Fifth Amendment. The physical evidence could be seen and taken by anyone who went to their trailer and used it to drown Joyce. The prosecution's time of death was in no way exact. Joyce could have been in the gravity canal three days or nine days. The medical examiner couldn't tell us exactly because the cold water preserved the body to a great extent.

"This is all a circumstantial case. There are no eye witnesses. You have to have reasonable doubt. Richard did not kill Joyce."

At that point, I kept thinking why hadn't we heard from Mike Deere? I just assumed that we'd hear his testimony before this was over since he was a key figure in the events in Joyce's life. Also I wanted to hear from Danny Brooks, the new man in Joyce's life. The one that Mike introduced her to and that she left a love note for on the bulletin board at The Dark Place.

We were then told that the evidentiary portion of the trial was completed. The court read the very lengthy instructions that would actually control our deliberations; instructions that seemed wordy, almost counterproductive and confining. Each juror received a copy and followed along as Judge Hale read. We were told that our duty as jurors was to decide this case by applying these instructions and that *we must not guess, or be influenced by sympathy or prejudice. We were told that jurors are the sole judges of what happened.*

"You've heard closing arguments. What the attorneys say is not evidence. To stipulate means that both sides agree those facts do exist and are part of evidence. The State's proof must be more powerful than a reasonable doubt."

Judge Hale told us that the other alternant juror, Carol, the manager of the office supply store, was excused from duty. He said that her name had been drawn out of a hat, but we had all heard her say that she needed surgery and that she had spoken to the judge. I don't know why we were told the hat story. That's what the judge said at the beginning of the trial that they would do if the alternates weren't used during the trial; pick names out of a hat. I guess the judge liked to stick to the story like Richard did.

* * *

The judge continued instructions to the twelve of us remaining. *"There are very few things in this world that we know with absolute certainty in criminal cases. The law does not require proof that overcomes <u>every</u> doubt. In this case, the punishment is left up to the judge. You have heard that there are priors and you must not consider a prior conviction as evidence of guilt for which he is now on trial."*

"The State has charged the defendant with crimes of first-degree murder by premeditation, first-degree felony murder and kidnapping. Charges are not evidence. The defendant has pled not guilty. Each charge is a separate offense. The crime of first-degree murder consists of both first-degree murder by premeditation and first-degree felony murder. The crime of first-degree by premeditation requires proof of three things:

1. The defendant caused the death of another person
2. The defendant knew he would cause the death of another person
3. The defendant acted with premeditation

That means that the defendant had the intention or the knowledge existed before the killing *long enough to permit reflection. It may be as instantaneous as successive thoughts in mind and proven by circumstantial evidence."*

"Firs-degree felony murder and kidnapping requires proof of:

1. A definite committed or attempted to commit kidnapping and
2. The restriction was accomplished by
   a) Physical force and

MURDER BY GRAVITY?

        b) In a manner which interfered with a person's movements
        c) Moving a person from place to place
3.   The restriction was with intent to inflict death or injury.

After the lunch break, the judge read all of the six different variations of the verdicts we had to choose from and instructed us to deliberate in the courtroom for the afternoon because it would be laborious to move all the exhibits upstairs to the jury room. We were instructed not to examine any lawbooks in the room and to designate a jury foreman.

"All twelve of you must agree on a verdict and be sure you sign the verdict forms before returning." The bailiff stood outside our doors watchfully.

Finally, we were left alone in the courtroom instead of being sent out for a change. We sat in the gallery in a circle and elected Wayne, who sat next to me in the number six position as our foreman. Wayne was the elegant older Hispanic gentleman with snowy hair and a cane that I mentioned earlier, whose extended family were Grateful Dead groupies in California. He was also the only person among us who had served on a jury before and had experience. Everyone liked him, so it was a unanimous vote. We were off to a great start!

The first thing we did was take a straw vote. I thought for sure it would be a quick guilty verdict, and I was honestly shocked that it wasn't. The first go round we were six to six. I was one who was openly on the guilty side from the onset. So was the Baptist preacher, and I was relieved that we were on the same side, I must admit.

The preacher said, "I think he's guilty and I'm not going to change my vote, no matter what anybody says."

The housewife that had counted the holes in the ceiling tile said, "So, you expect us to change our votes then?"

"I'm saying *I'm not changing my vote.*" Of course that was what he was saying. Or we would be hung.

The foreman kept his vote secret until the end of deliberations. He stayed neutral and did a wonderful job.

We took a break late that afternoon outside and I happened to say to Karl, "Can you believe the names in this case, Hazel *Mess*, Mike *Deere*, The Bottoms Up. Who goes to a place called The Bottoms

Up?" I said thinking it was ridiculous. This was the first time we were able to discuss the case during breaks. We didn't know where each other stood on anything. It was so weird.

Karl looked at me as the sun was getting low and making everything pink and he grinned and said, "I go to The Bottoms Up Pub! It's just a neighborhood bar with pool tables in the shopping center on Fortuna." When he said that, I remembered that my stepdaughter used to go to a place in that shopping center to shoot pool with her boyfriend. Boy, did I feel dumb.

"Is that the English Pub by the chiropractor's office?" I asked.

"One and the same,"

"That's nicer than I pictured it to be all this time. I'm surprised. I haven't been inside, but it's a nice area." It was time to go back in as I finished pulling my foot out of my mouth.

We began deliberating again, "Did anybody change their mind yet?" The nervous laughter valve release opened fully. Karl, the former mortician, had such a hearty laugh. He got tears in his eyes.

Wayne said, "No, really!" He looked around and saw the faces were getting serious and no hands were going up, nobody spoke up. "Okay, somebody tell me why they think he's not guilty then."

One of the women said, "I just still have a reasonable doubt. I mean, he probably did it, but the police didn't get enough proof and the film was black, evidence lost. How can we convict him with that?"

CHAPTER 61

At five o'clock Judge Hale came in and asked if we had a verdict yet. We looked at each other and smiled. Wayne told him that we weren't even close! The judge went over our admonition again and told us not to discuss the proceedings outside the courtroom and instructed us to recess until the next day at nine o'clock, which was a Friday, December the 6th to resume deliberations.

That night, I just kept replaying the afternoon over and over again in my head. How could I convince my fellow jurors that there was no reasonable doubt? Doubt? Sure. *Reasonable*? Uh-uh, nada, none, zip. No sleep either. Well, I was *reasonably* sure I wasn't the only one.

The next morning Mrs. Handcock and Hazel Mess sat in the hallway outside the jury room. Talk about pressure! Every time one of us went to the restroom or on a break, they tried to read our faces. They were also quietly discouraging us and some of the jurors felt it strongly.

All morning we hacked at premeditation. Most people believed that Richard thought Joyce was already dead when he put her in the water. Twelve people, who had been nice and friendly to each other for over five weeks, suddenly weren't. Tension and beliefs ran deep to the core. It was finally decided by some to ask the judge some questions to further illuminate his instructions to the jury.

We returned to the court room and Wayne turned the questions into the bailiff. Judge Hale said, "We received your message containing three questions."

1. If the defendant wrongly assumed the body was dead before entering the water, is premeditation possible?
2. The same question about kidnapping.

We are not sure what you are asking for and we don't want to lead you in the wrong direction. Take a little time and be more specific in pinpointing your question."

Wayne said, "Your Honor, we are hung up on premeditation and need further definition!"

Not even addressing question number three, Judge Hale said, "I can't further define that for you at this time. While you rewrite the questions about one and three, advise the court more specifically how it can assist you."

We went back to the jury room disappointed and irked. At break time, Wayne told me, "You watch, one of them is going to say, 'I wish we had an eye witness.'" His voice was mockingly whiney.

"As if that would do much good; they're notoriously undependable," I said. I just figured out which side Wayne was on.

Sure enough when we got back inside, the hole-counting woman said, "I just wish we had an eye witness! That's the only way we can know for sure what happened to Joyce!" Wayne gave me an *'I told you' so* wink. By then our count was about ten to two for murder and kidnapping, but still hung much further apart on premeditation.

I'm the kind of person who tends to joke when things get too serious. I said, "Look, we know that Joyce was going to confront Richard that day and we also know that he had to get rid of the junk under his trailer. So he thinks, (as I hit the palm of my hand to my forehead like I just had an idea) *Why not just kill two birds with one stone? Get rid of Joyce and the junk at the same time!*" Karl laughed so hard, he laid his head on the table laughing for several minutes.

We all went to The Garden Patio Café for lunch and they hustled to get our food out fast under the circumstances.

"What is *reasonable doubt?*" Wayne asked us all.

"It means to reason, to think logically, uh, have common sense," somebody said.

"To base your conclusions on it."

"To analyze something."

"Within reasonable limits," Wayne put in.

"To quote Sherlock Holmes," I said, *"When you eliminate the impossible, whatever remains, however improbable, must be the truth."*

The hole-counting woman said pouting, "The police didn't give

MURDER BY GRAVITY?

us enough proof to go on!"

One at a time we chipped at her. "Remember the physical evidence puts Richard at the crime scene. Jeff Dupree had the defendant all wet and admitting that he'd just got out of the canal."

"Jeff Dupree could have an agenda of his own."

"What did everybody think about what Dr. Sperry said about Joyce's autopsy?" Wayne asked.

There wasn't a person there who believed anything he said. We believed that for a price he would travel and testify since he did it so much. That was a possibility, anyway; that and the fact that he never saw the body firsthand. It seemed odd that the defense had to go all the way to Atlanta to find a doctor who would say what they wanted. Also, Sperry's reasoning that Joyce died by overdose seemed ludicrous.

The women who sat in the front end of the jury, that would be seats one through four and eight through twelve complained that Richard gawked at them during the trial and they felt very uncomfortable about it. Some of the ladies were quite attractive and they felt like they'd forgotten to wear their blouses the way he watched; it turned their stomachs. Even the men sitting in those areas noticed that he did it.

We went back to the jury room and began squabbling over premeditation. We pulled out the evidence and looked at the pictures again. Especially the picture of Richard's truck backed in next to the trailer on the cement pad under the awning. It was easy to see that he could move a body from his back door to the bed of his truck without getting noticed even in the daylight.

The hole-counter said that the neighbor said that she saw Richard there at twelve o'clock to do his laundry.

"He didn't have a lot of spare time to do all of this!"

I pulled out my old-fashioned steno notes and re-read the testimony of Irma Stebbins. It read, "She said that she always eats lunch between twelve and one o'clock."

"Oh."

"Look at all of the stuff he did that an innocent man wouldn't do. I mean, where do you begin with all the lies he told her?" Pete said.

"If his attorney declared him insane or temporarily insane, I could buy that, not that it's a good excuse." I said. But I think that if it weren't for the drugs, this may not have happened. Perpetual methamphetamine drug use can cause psychosis. If his attorney had approached it from that angle . . . but I don't see Richard as an innocent by any means. I think he probably thought Joyce was dead after he hit her head and then hid the body in the Gravity Canal. Does that make his guilty of kidnapping? Heck, yeah! He should have taken her to the hospital. I think he struck her once while in a rage; not premeditatedly. He thought he was dumping a body. I don't know. I'm conflicted, too."

Larry was asked what he thought. Our Johnny Carson look-alike had been too quiet during deliberations. Finally he said, "I don't care if he did it or not; he probably did. But he's a habitual criminal and should be taken off the streets. I'll vote guilty."

I was floored. We were not supposed to base our conclusions on Richard's past behavior and I told him so. He didn't care, saying the world was better off with him in jail. I couldn't disagree with that.

At 6:00 PM the bailiff came in and told us to go home since we still didn't have a verdict and they wanted us back at 9:00 AM on Saturday. Damn, we weren't even getting the weekend off!

CHAPTER 62

We returned Saturday dressed more casually and met in the jury room; all of us looking like we hadn't slept in quite a while. While we realized the judge was going to fix the penalty in this case and we were glad to have that off our backs, we still knew that what we decided affected Richard's life very seriously and we did not make our decisions lightly.

I liked all of the people in the jury and had previously thought before deliberations that I should get all of their phone numbers and we'll have an anniversary party one year later. After deliberations, many people would never speak to each other again and nobody took phone numbers. I still see Walt at the paint department at Wal-Mart occasionally. I once ran into Detective Donna Graham in the grocery store during the trial and we both said hello. It was three minutes later before I realized where I knew her from and I'll bet it was the same with her. I've seen Karl and Wayne in restaurants since the trial and I saw Larry once. We catch up with each other's lives and ask if they know anything about any of the other jurors.

On Saturday with ten of us together asserting that those doubts that the last two jurors had were not *reasonable* and that we were told from the beginning that the case was circumstantial, but there was enough circumstantial evidence to go beyond a reasonable doubt. We were told during our instructions that we didn't have to go beyond *all doubt.*

Eventually, we were all twelve of one mind on felony murder and kidnapping, but we were hung on premeditation.

Wayne decided to ask one more time for the judge to give us further directions on this point and we all worded a note and gave it to the bailiff. The bailiff guided us back to the court room and all of the family members arrived the news cameras lined the back wall of the court room, it was packed.

I said to Wayne before the judge came in, "They think we have a verdict!"

All stood when Judge Hale came in. It was five o'clock and I thought when the judge found out that we didn't have a verdict yet, he would tell us to come back on Monday.

But no, that was not to be. The note that he assumed had a verdict asked again about premeditation; worded differently, as per his instructions earlier.

Judge Hale said, "I can't further define that for you at this time. We will simply allow you to resume deliberation here in the courtroom. Please notify the bailiff when you are ready to deal with those issues."

All the news people left; everyone filed out. And here we were with the world waiting outside. It was after the usual court hours, plus it was a Saturday. We were shot mentally as a group. Nerves were taut. Somebody said, "That seal on the crest behind the judge's chair has writing in Latin, does anybody know what it says?"

"Be just and fear not," I said.

Boy, were they impressed. Finally somebody said, "Really?"

And I said, "No, that's what it says on my family's coat of arms, but it sounded good."

Wayne said, "Okay we are all agreed now on first-degree felony murder and kidnapping, right?" Some faces looked a little unsure. "How about a show of hands?" *Everyone* raised their hands unanimously. "How many think that Richard is guilty of premeditation?" The count was eight for and four against. "Okay, let's fill out the paper work." Wayne started signing the appropriate pages.

The other housewife told me, "I hope they don't poll the jury! I don't think I could do it!"

And I said, "Why not?"

"I just, I don't know, I guess."

Just great, I thought.

Wayne got the papers ready and started to get the bailiff to notify her that we had a verdict and the hole-counter yells, "*Wait! How* do we know Richard did it?"

There were at least eight people groaning as Wayne made a U-

MURDER BY GRAVITY?

turn back in the court room. I just couldn't stand it any longer and I said, "We took a vote five minutes ago and you raised your hand that you believed he was guilty! For God's sake woman, be decisive!"

She got in a huff and said, "Okay, fine, he's guilty then!"

Wayne turned back and opened the door and let everyone inside.

* * *

When four or five television channels and their cameras and lights lit up the court room at six o'clock Saturday night, it was practically blinding. Everyone rose for Judge Hale as he stepped inside.

"Mr. Foreman, at this point in time, I understand that the jury has been unable to reach a verdict on count three. If you were given additional time, do you think that you could come to a verdict?"

Wayne said, "No, your honor." I disagreed on this point. If Richard was guilty of kidnapping, it would follow that he had to be guilty of premeditation. Doesn't it? Perhaps if the judge didn't make us work such long days, we may have been able to come to fruition.

"The defendant will stand and the clerk will read and record the verdicts."

"We the jury, upon our oaths, do find the defendant guilty of the crime of kidnapping."

"We the jury, upon our oaths, do find the defendant guilty of the crime of first degree felony murder." I watched Richard while the decisions were read. He just hung his head briefly. *Like, oh, nuts! I lost the Lotto!* Throughout the trial that was the closest he came to showing emotion.

Judge Hale asked, "Do either council wish the jury polled?" I held my breath.

Mr. Millington would like the jury polled.

I don't think I breathed much during the polling of the jury. Thank God they all agreed during the poll. I wasn't sure if there would be a couple of reneges or not.

Judge Hale thanked us for doing our duties. He said that the third count, the crime of first degree murder by premeditation was ordered and declared a mistrial as to that count at that time. He asked what our count was and Wayne told him eight to four.

CHERIE HUYETT ACHTEMEIER

Judge Hale told the jury, "I know it's been a lengthy trial. It's the longest trial that I've been involved in my fifteen years of criminal cases. Thank you for your attention that you have paid in this case particularly; it was a tough case. I think you did your level best to reach decisions and we all appreciate that."

"This case has been subject to media coverage. I want the jury to please let us know how you felt about it. You will receive a questionnaire in the mail. You may or may not put your name on it if you choose to return it. I will advise everyone present here, that I'm going to allow the jury to leave first. I require all to stay until the jury has had the opportunity to leave this courthouse, including the parking lot."

"I have also been advised through the bailiff that the jurors have requested that they not be approached by the media in an attempt to interview or question or obtain comments from jurors. I have no authority what media does beyond that. Counsel may wish to speak with you to see what some of your thoughts were. What issues were difficult and what was compelling. The trial is over and you are released from your admonition.

It's important to note that our sympathy for the victim's family did not enter into deliberations. I had the same sympathy for Richard's mother. When the jury filed out, number seven (that was me) always led the way. I had been wanting all during the trial to express my condolences to Mr. and Mrs. Perron and Joyce's two children who were standing next to them. They were on the end of the front row and I stopped and shook Lori Perron's hand and told her how sorry I was for her loss, then I shook Joyce's dad's hand and the kids' and then it very naturally became a procession line. Everyone behind me did the same.

We walked downstairs and said goodbye to fellow jurors we were still speaking to and we were all in a rush to get to our cars before the press was let out. I remember going out the double-glass front door and I looked back and saw Pete fifty feet away and he was headed toward the other exit. I waved and he waved back and we just stood there a few seconds like there was something to be said that would never be, because I turned and walked to my car before the press would be upon us.

In retrospect, I will never understand why the Perrons left town

MURDER BY GRAVITY?

that weekend when Joyce was missing, even though Mr. Perron had planned to go to a club function. And why didn't they put the flyers up when Richard failed to? I would have made even more flyers and had them all over town myself and I wouldn't have waited for Richard to report her missing, either. Some of their actions seemed odd to me. My husband has been through a quintuple bypass surgery and he wasn't coddled like Mr. Perron was. Maybe things have changed since then as far as recovery treatment goes. Maybe it depends on what you're going home to. Our lives weren't as altered as theirs.

Also in retrospect, I am amazed by Richard's mother, the other Joyce Handcock. She called the police before having all of Richard's junk thrown out! She had to have known that there might have been the slightest chance that they would find something incriminating.

The police never would have had a case if she hadn't called them. Hats off to Mrs. Handcock! She did the right thing and you don't see much of that in this world these days.

* * *

I was reading over the police reports again and I found a witness that *was not called to the stand*. On January 26, 1995, Detective St. Jons interviewed a neighbor of the Handcocks, who lived in space three, named Frank McLaughlan and they set up a deposition.

Frank said that the morning Joyce disappeared; he saw both Joyce and Richard in the truck, leaving together. McLaughlan said the Handcocks drive by his trailer whenever they come and go from the park.

"I'd say it was about a quarter to eight or five 'til. They left shortly before I did on Wednesday, the 11th of January. I was getting ready to leave and I saw them in the cab of Richard's truck as I looked out of my front window."

St. Jons asked, "Did you see anything strange or peculiar?"

"Nothing special caught my eye. It wasn't until later when I found out she was missing; and the flyers. I usually see her at the bar and everyone told me she was missing."

St. Jons asked, "You said that you saw the truck come back later in the morning . . . and he was alone?"

McLaughlan replied, "Yes, sir. That was somewhere between 9:30 and 10:00 o'clock. I was on a test drive for a vehicle and I went by my trailer to pick up some paperwork to take back to work."

The detective said, "I know I asked before, but I need you to tell it one more time on tape. How did you know it was *that day* as opposed to some other day?"

"Well, it was the last time I saw Joyce and the paperwork that had to be turned in *that day* for insurance."

"Can you pinpoint what car you were test driving?"

"Probably."

"That would be good. Do you go to The Dark Place every night?"

"No, but I belong to one of the dart teams. So I go on Monday nights and often."

"You saw Joyce the Tuesday night before?"

"Yeah, I saw her Tuesday night, then I saw them leave Wednesday morning, then I went to The Dark Wednesday night and she wasn't there and nobody else knew where she was," McLaughlan explained for the record.

"Did you see Richard in the park when you came home from work?"

"His truck was parked in front of the trailer. I didn't see him personally. I didn't see anybody moving around outside that night. I began to wonder if Joyce was all right or not."

St. Jons asked, "Why would you think that?"

"She and Richard weren't getting along."

It turned out that Joyce and Frank McLaughlan were pretty thick neighbors. He knew all about her problems and her history. He'd been invited over to their trailer for drinks and helped Richard work on his truck.

So why wasn't Frank McLaughlan called as a witness? I think it was because his information didn't fit into the County Attorney's preconceived idea that Joyce was murdered in the trailer. It also makes me think that my idea that Richard could have lied and talked Joyce into going somewhere else first with him that morning holds water. He didn't even have to lie; he could have started to go to Tucson with Joyce and head out Hwy. 95, and then turned off suddenly, by surprise.

EPILOGUE

In January of 1997, Richard was brought to court for sentencing. Judge Hale noted that the defendant was on parole at the time the two offenses for which he was on trial were committed.

"Are there any victims here today that wish to be heard?"

"Yes," Lori stood and walked to the judge. "We feel that he should get his natural life in prison, Your Honor."

"Anyone else?"

"Your Honor?" Millington stood, when nobody else did. "May I? Mr. Handcock still continues to maintain his innocence. He also maintains that previous violent activities against his wives he's had in the past were not true. We have other people that we could bring forward to show that there is no violence in him."

Excuse me, but they had that chance at trial. Millington objected to Richard's ex-wife taking the stand and testifying that he beat her almost to death. Could it be somebody made her an offer she couldn't refuse in the meantime?

"Mr. Handcock, do you have anything to say on your own behalf?"

Richard shook his head.

"Very well, I find aggravating circumstances existed as to count three kidnapping:

1. The defendant's previous record of felony convictions.
2. Kidnapping involved the transportation of the defendant's unconscious or semi-conscious wife out to a remote area where the defendant placed her bound and weighted body into the lagoon knowing it would cause death.
3. Aggravating is emotionally harmful to Joyce's immediate family and deprived Joyce's children from their mother."

"As punishment for these offenses, it is ordered that the defendant is sentenced to terms of *imprisonment and is committed to the Arizona Department of Corrections for life.*"

"In kidnapping, count 3, while on parole, he is also sentenced in the custody of the Arizona State Department of Corrections for a substantially aggravated *term of 12.5 years* to be *consecutively* served. The defendant gets zero for time served."

"I have been informed that Mr. Russell is not intending to re-try count one on pre-meditation, which would have to be recharged with a new indictment of premeditated without prejudice.

* * *

In defense of the Yuma Police Department and the Yuma County Sheriff's Office, I would also like to mention that during the same five weeks that the Handcock trial took place, the Jack Ray Hudson trial was of equal length and received national publicity about which I am currently writing. Jack was deep undercover for the Southwest Border Alliance who had named him Rookie of the Year just months before he became an addict and who late the night on July 4, 1995, broke into the evidence locker to steal money, electronics, weapons, and drugs. While there, his unarmed immediate superiors, Sgt. Crowe and Lt. Elkins, came to check-in after returning from vacation and caught him red-handed. Jack shot them both several times and continued as they tried to drag themselves away. Another officer was about to be executed when Jack's weapon jammed.

Judging from the treasures located in a search of Jack's house and cars Jack had been ordering for the department and stealing new equipment for a considerable time. He also had thousands of dollars stashed and enormous amounts of drugs of every type. To be fair, our sheriff and police could have used the fact that Jack Hudson had totally screwed around with the evidence in the Handcock case to make themselves look better.

Look for **Border Alliance Tragedy** to be published next year.

To bring you up to date, the old courthouse was declared structurally unsafe and engineers declared it could implode in February, 2006. The experts said, "The foundation was in such a state that nobody in their wildest imagination ever thought there could be this level of structural damage." The courthouse was built in the 1920's and had been renovated over the years. "The people who passed through it were in danger and didn't even know it!" The new courthouse that cost $27.2 million is now open.

The Yuma City Police Department is enjoying their modern, spacious station house that opened in 1999. Yuma now has people who have moved here permanently from Florida and Louisiana; hurricane escapee transplants. Yuma is presently the third fastest-growing city in the country. There is a two-year wait to have a house built now. The price of houses has doubled in the last ten years.

Many snowbirds, tired of driving back and forth, eventually sell their large homes in the Northern states. Yuma County now has a population of 189,480. The winter influx of snowbirds is over 100,000 in addition. That's twice as many people as those who attend the Olympics.

The County Sheriff's office moved out of their mobile home in the Foothills Substation, and in its place, just up the road now stands a brand new 3,200 square-foot Santa Fe-style office. The Foothills area has grown by leaps and bounds and is more than likely about to become incorporated into the City of Yuma, whether they like it or not; and many don't because their taxes will go up. There are now ninety recreational vehicle parks in the county and are full every winter.

Yuma Regional Medical Center has tripled in size in the last decade, and the staff in the emergency room complains about the growing problem of methamphetamine users testing positive. "It's very common, it's just so prevalent everywhere!" said one doctor to the *Yuma Daily Sun* in an article in January 2006

"Seventy-three percent of hospital officials report that emergency room presentations involving methamphetamine have increased over the last five years and 68% reported continuing increases over the last three years," said a survey among hospitals, quoted by a staff writer at the *Yuma Daily Sun.*

Yuma County law enforcement officials say methamphetamine is the number-one drug problem in the county and it's a highly addictive drug that is cheaper than cocaine, whose use has reached epidemic proportions in Yuma and other communities nationwide.

The "high" that the user gets from their first time using the substance can never be matched so users slip into a cycle, continually using meth in an attempt to replicate that first high, or so it is reported.

County Attorney Stephen Russell was voted in as a new judge. I wonder if he's still cracking jokes from his new position. I'll bet he is. I voted for him too. When he was sworn in he made the comment to the press, "I feel the responsibility. I want to use the authority fairly and wisely. I want people to remember how well-prepared I was for cases. It's not enough for me to go over there and fill a seat." Kudos to him!

Detective David St. Jons retired from the Yuma Police Department in 2000, and became a private investigator. I have since seen his name in the newspapers a few times for solving cold cases. One involved two murderers, whose crime went as far back as 1985.

Good news for Sheriff's Deputies in 2001. The County of Yuma decided that they should be paid for overtime! Their attorney argued that, "We perceive that purpose to be one discouraging government employers from routinely working their law enforcement officers for extended periods beyond a normal forty-hour work week," according to an article in the *Sun* in 2001. Perhaps now they'll get paid to take a photography class and catalog that illusive evidence, or at least get paid overtime for looking for evidence after dark.

In September of 2004, Judge Mancini took out a large section of a newspaper page thanking Yuma for their support after he'd been re-elected yet again, in spite of letting Richard go home to murder his wife while on an electronic monitor, when a simple doctor's examination would have told them that Richard was lying about having cancer. I hope he learned something from this experience. I did not vote for him.

On January 1, 1998, the Arizona Court of Appeals upheld the conviction of Richard's sentence of life. He will be eligible for parole in twenty-five years. He would be only sixty-five years old, and in this city, that's not old at all. In January 1999, Richard's attorney was getting more time to file his next appeal.

Judge Hale said, "Mr. Handcock isn't going anywhere." He said the appeals process needs to keep going and the victims need the case resolved. Handcock's new attorney in 1999 was planning to file a petition for post-conviction relief, which could have rendered a new trial.

On a personal note, I think the laws should allow all pertinent information into trial, whether or not it forms "prejudice." To me that could establish a possible pattern or history and the jury should have full disclosure and utilize their own discernment. Also, I think if anybody can be subpoenaed to testify, then certainly people in jail, like Mike Deere, Ben Handcock, and Danny Brooks should have been forced to testify even if there was a bounty on their heads from the Handcock brothers. They could have been moved to separate prisons. If a private citizen can be compelled to testify, then they should be too. Also, I would have liked to see Phil Seward's face when he took the Fifth Amendment on the stand. Just to get a feel about the guy.

I spoke with defense attorney Bill Millington after the trial and asked him why he put Richard on the stand and he said that was what Richard wanted to do. I asked if he had prepared him for trial questioning and he said he never does that with *any* of his clients. That seemed very curious to me.

Millington asked me, "Why didn't you believe Dr. Sperry's comments?" And I told him that none of us believed him and why. Did he expect us to believe that she overdosed and tied herself up? After I told him that his closing remarks were inspired he asked, "So why did you find my client guilty of murder?"

"It wasn't your fault you had a guilty client! Why, do *you* think he was innocent? You were there too!" I asked incredulous that Millington might think otherwise.

"After hearing all the testimony in court, I think he probably was guilty too. Richard never told us anything about what happened, so we weren't getting any help from him." So there you have it, his own attorney now believes him guilty.

So what do you think, dear reader? Was Richard Handcock guilty of murder by gravity? Do you have reasonable doubt? Do you agree with the jury? What about pre-meditation? Was Joyce bludgeoned three times or once? Where? By whom? Which pathologist made the most sense to you? Do you have reasonable doubt because of Phil

CHERIE HUYETT ACHTEMEIER

Seward's sexual harassment case? How would you have voted?

Richard is currently serving his life sentence in Buckeye, Arizona, so apparently the petition for post-conviction relief was denied. I just wish he were in the Phoenix prison where they make the prisoners live in tents in the desert!

I was told that after a long trial, they take you off the jury pool list for ten years and you don't have to serve unless you want to. I have a year and a half remaining to think of a really good excuse.